BF
724.6
.S 42
The seasons of a man's life

DATE DUE

| | | | |
|---|---|---|---|
| 1 | | | |
| | | | |
| | | | |
| | | | |
| | | | |
| | | | |
| | | | |
| | | | |
| | | | |
| | | | |
| | | | |
| GAYLORD 234 | | | PRINTED IN U. S. A. |

Laramie County Community College
Instructional Resources Center
Cheyenne, Wyoming 82001

THE AUTHORITARIAN PERSONALITY (1950)
with Theodor W. Adorno, Else Frenkel-Brunswik and R. Nevitt Sanford

THE PATIENT AND THE MENTAL HOSPITAL (1957)
co-edited with Milton Greenblatt and Richard H. Williams

PATIENTHOOD IN THE MENTAL HOSPITAL:
Role, Personality and Social Structure (1964)
with Eugene B. Gallagher

THE EXECUTIVE ROLE CONSTELLATION:
An Analysis of Personality and Role Relations in Management (1965)
with Richard C. Hodgson and Abraham Zaleznik

# THE SEASONS OF A MAN'S LIFE

# THE SEASONS OF A MAN'S LIFE

by
## Daniel J. Levinson
with
Charlotte N. Darrow
Edward B. Klein
Maria H. Levinson
Braxton McKee

Alfred A. Knopf   New York   1979

THIS IS A BORZOI BOOK
PUBLISHED BY ALFRED A. KNOPF, INC.

Library of Congress Cataloging in Publication Data
Main entry under title: The seasons of a man's life.
Includes bibliographical references and index.
1. Middle age—Psychological aspects. 2. Men—
Psychology. I. Levinson, Daniel J.
BF724.6.S42 1978 155.6'32 77–20978
ISBN 0–394–40694–x

An earlier version of some of the material in this book appeared in:
The May 1977 issue of Psychiatry.
Copyright © by The William Alanson White
Psychiatric Foundation, Inc. Used by permission.

We the People: American Character and Social Change
(Greenwood Press, 1977).

Life History Research in Psychopathology
(University of Minnesota Press, 1974).
Manufactured in the United States of America
Published March 21, 1978
Reprinted Six Times
Eighth Printing, February 1979
Since this page cannot legibly accommodate all permissions,
acknowledgments continue on page 353.

*To our families, whose generations*
*in their rich variety*
*have so enhanced our appreciation*
*of the seasons*

# Contents

# Preface

What does it mean to be an adult? What are the root issues of adult life—the essential problems and satisfactions, the sources of disappointment, grief and fulfillment? Is there an underlying order in the progression of our lives over the adult years, as there is in childhood and adolescence? Questions of this kind led me to undertake a program of research some ten years ago, and this book reports the progress my colleagues and I have made in answering them.

As our research progressed, it became increasingly clear that a developmental approach was needed in the study of adulthood, as of childhood. This was in itself hardly a new idea, yet despite its wide acceptance in the abstract it had remained curiously neglected in practice. When our work began, there was little theory and even less research evidence regarding adult phases in the life cycle and the nature of adult development.

Despite the increasing interest in adult development, there is still reluctance to study the course of adult life in some depth. The wish to learn more about the possibilities of personal growth is hampered by the fear that careful scrutiny will reveal only decline and restriction. Adults hope that life begins at 40—but the great anxiety is that it ends there. The result of this pervasive dread about middle age is almost complete silence about the experience of being adult. The concrete character of adult life is one of the best-kept secrets in our society, and probably in human history generally. People in the middle years generally find it difficult to discuss the course and meaning of their lives with their peers, younger co-workers or youthful offspring. Middle age has been one of the great taboo topics. In the last ten years there has been an increasing number of novels, plays and popular books (usually intended to be reassuring) on this topic. But our avoidance is still great and our knowledge limited.

The widespread fears about old age have been widely recognized. Long before old age is imminent, however, middle age activates our deepest anxieties about decline and dying. The most distressing fear in early adulthood is that there is no life after youth. Young adults often feel that to pass 30 is to be "over the hill," and they are given little beyond hollow clichés to provide a fuller sense of the actual problems and possibilities of adult life at different ages. The middle years, they imagine, will bring triviality and·meaningless comfort at best, stagnation and hopelessness at worst.

Middle age is usually regarded as a vague interim period, defined primarily in negative terms. One is no longer young and yet not quite old— but what is one in a more positive sense? The connotations of youth are vitality, growth, mastery, the heroic; whereas old age connotes vulnerability, withering, ending, the brink of nothingness. Our overly negative imagery of old age adds greatly to the burden of middle age. It is terrifying to go through middle age in the shadow of death, as though one were already very old; and it is a self-defeating illusion to live it in the shadow of youth, as though one were still simply young. Each phase in the life cycle has its own virtues and limitations. To realize its potential value, we must know and accept its terms and create our lives within it accordingly.

These personal and professional considerations shaped the definition of our research goals. The goals have been clarified and amplified over the years, but the basic idea is unchanged. Our primary aim is to create a *developmental perspective on adulthood in men.* We want to set forth a systematic conception of the entire life cycle, while paying primary attention to the major seasons of adulthood. Each season has its own intrinsic nature and value, though its character is molded by its place in the cycle. Our emphasis at first was on the "mid-life decade" from age 35 to 45; it was then extended to cover the span from the late teens to the late forties.

I began imagining and planning the study in 1966, before the recent activity in this field had started. In embarking upon this work, I seemed to be entering a lonely and uncharted territory. The study reflected in part my intellectual interest in the possibility of adult development. The choice of topic also reflected a personal concern: at 46, I wanted to study the transition into middle age in order to understand what I had been going through myself. Over the previous ten years my life had changed in crucial ways; I had "developed" in a sense I could not articulate. The study would cast light on my own experience and, I hoped, contribute to an understanding of adult development in general. Later it became evident that this decision reflected more than my personal feelings. There is a growing desire in our society to see adulthood as something more than a long, featureless stretch of years with childhood at one end and senility at the other.

During the academic year 1966–1967, having just come to Yale, I explored various theoretical issues within the broad domain of adult development and moved toward a specific research plan. In the fall of 1967, Charlotte N. Darrow, Douglas S. Derrer and Edward B. Klein joined me, and a research team was formed. Early in 1968, after conducting and analyzing some pilot interviews, we submitted a research proposal to the National Institute of Mental Health. The study was funded and had its formal inception in January 1969, although by this time the work was well under way. Our first subjects were interviewed in the fall of 1968, the last, early in 1970. Braxton McKee joined the project in 1968 and Maria H. Levinson in 1970, when Derrer left to take a position elsewhere. Ray C. Walker was a member of our group from 1968 to 1971. We owe him a special debt. He was the one Jungian in a group committed to other—chiefly Freudian—conceptions of the person. With great tact and persistence, he helped us to assimilate Jung's ideas without having to reject other viewpoints. All of us have become less sectarian as a result.

Our research funding ended early in 1973. By this time we had completed the initial and follow-up interviewing and much of the case analysis. In the process, we had moved from a study of the mid-life decade to a wider age span and a more general theory of adult development. The proper next step, we felt, was to develop further our concepts and findings, and to write a book about them. Unfortunately, in this field funds are ordinarily given to initiate research, not to write books. The writing of this book has thus been complicated by the lack of funds and the generally bleak economic situation of the universities.

Planning this book in the spring of 1973, we decided that I would write the chapters on the theory and findings, and each of the others would write a single biography. This division of labor has been followed. Charlotte Darrow wrote the biography of the novelist Paul Namson, whom she had interviewed. Edward Klein did the same for the executive James Tracy, and Braxton McKee for the worker William Paulsen. Maria Levinson joined the project after the interviewing had ended; she wrote the biography of the biologist John Barnes, whom I had interviewed. I completed the data analysis and the conceptualization, and wrote the remaining chapters. Braxton McKee was a great help to me in this work. He also made significant contributions to the revision of the manuscript.

Although I was the originator of the study and the primary author of the book, the research project was a cooperative one. As in all good collaborations, it is difficult to sort out the distinctive contributions of individual members. The five of us feel part of a collective process that yielded a common product.

From the start, our approach has been multidisciplinary. Our focus is on the individual and his development over the adult years, and this has traditionally been the territory of psychology and psychiatry. However, our interest in the evolving life course requires us to place the individual in society: we have to examine a man's engagement with his environment—his relationships, roles, involvements in the world as well as his fantasies, conflicts and abilities. This means, in turn, that we must draw upon the social sciences and humanities, upon disciplines such as sociology, anthropology, history and political science, along with psychology and psychiatry. We are then in the province of social psychology, which is a boundary discipline: it creates a structure of theory and knowledge linking the disciplines that deal primarily with the individual and the disciplines that deal primarily with society, culture and collective life. Our view of adult development is social-psychological in this sense.

This orientation is reflected in the composition of the research team. My intellectual roots are in psychology, psychiatry and sociology. The others' are primarily in psychology (Maria Levinson and Klein), sociology (Darrow) and psychiatry-psychoanalysis (McKee). Our intellectual history has brought each of us into all these disciplines, in a joint effort to create an enterprise at the boundaries.

In the spring of 1967, I invited several faculty colleagues at Yale to meet and review my embryonic research plan. A few meetings validated my commitment to the research and evoked the sustained interest of the others. That fall we began a faculty seminar on adult development; it continued with minor changes in membership over the next four years. In addition to the research team, the seminar members included: Kenneth Keniston, Gerald L. Klerman, Graham Little, Theodore M. Mills, John S. Montgomery, David F. Musto, Peter M. Newton and Daniel P. Schwartz.

The seminar was an essential part of our research method and helped shape the course of the project. We discussed theoretical approaches, research articles, literary essays, biographies, clinical case studies, the individuals in our pilot study and our primary research sample. We argued about the relative merits of various personality theories and the importance of societal influences in adult development. The seminar members had origins and evolving interests in various disciplines, and wanted to work at the disciplinary boundaries. Most of us were then between 35 and 45 and were personally struggling with the developmental issues of this decade. Those who were a bit older or younger were by no means free of these concerns. It soon became evident that, if we were to engage in incisive intellectual discussion of the lives of others, we had to discuss our own lives as well. Although the main function of the seminar was to facilitate the research enterprise, it contributed as well to our personal lives. I am deeply grateful to the individual members and to "the group" that in its own special way became a participant in the work.

As the manuscript took shape and the choice of a publisher had to be made, we were extremely fortunate in having the consultation of Jane Isay and Richard Grossman. Both of them read an early version of the manuscript and gave invaluable advice on the writing and on the issues of publication. With their help, we discovered Donald Cutler (of the Sterling Lord Agency), who became our agent and helped steer our course for the rest of the voyage. He has been a godsend. Charles A. Elliott, our editor at Knopf, has been a source of understanding, support and literary sensibility in completing the manuscript.

We are grateful also to Jack Shepherd, who, working closely with me for over a year, made a major contribution to the work of revision. If this book is substantial and serious, yet relatively free of the pedantry of so much scholarly writing, much of the credit goes to Shepherd and Elliott. Where it is not, the fault is our own.

Many individuals and institutions have been of great help over the past ten years. Frederick C. Redlich, then chairman of the Psychiatry Department at Yale University, provided the moral and material support that allowed me to begin the exploratory work before grant funds were available. Over a period of some 20 years, Gerald L. Klerman has been my student, colleague and friend; as Director of the Connecticut Mental Health Center from 1967 to 1969, he participated actively in the growth of this endeavor and in my professional development. Throughout my Yale years Boris M. Astrachan has been a valued collaborator and friend; this study has benefitted in manifold ways from his personal interest and administrative support. Peter M. Newton has spent countless hours with me in informal discussion, manuscript review and collaborative work on various projects. My relationships with Klerman, Astrachan and Newton give evidence that, in a good mentoring relationship, the mentor derives at least as much gain as his younger colleague. Esther Harding and Margit van Leight Frank contributed in powerful though indirect ways to the intellectual substance and psychological qualities of this work. Beyond her general influence on my life, my mother has made a very direct contribution to this book. Now 91, she has over the last several years been the primary source of my understanding of the possibilities for self-development in old age.

Barbara Kellerman and Wendy Stewart have written the first two doctoral dissertations utilizing our theory of adult development—Kellerman doing a biography of Willy Brandt, Stewart a study of the development of women from age 17 to 35. Kellerman also contributed to the revision of several chapters, especially the biography of James Tracy.

Our appreciation goes to the National Institute of Mental Health, which gave me a Research Scientist Award (Number MH-13032) as well as a research grant (Number MH-15982) for the present study. The operation of this project has been managed in succession by Katherine Cash, Judy Townsend and Sharon Canosa. Each, in her own way, has contributed beyond the call of duty to our collective work and individual well-being. In particular, Sharon Canosa has been secretary, administrator and stabilizing influence during the four long years this book has been a-borning. She is a full member of the enterprise.

We wish to thank the companies known pseudonymously as Ajax Industries and United Electronics for welcoming us and allowing us to be guests largely on our own terms. Our study was of no direct benefit to either company; we hope it had some indirect value for the companies and for the workers and managers who became our research collaborators.

Above all, our thanks to the forty men who took us so full-heartedly into their lives and allowed us to bring their experience to a wide audience. Since we cannot thank you by name, we express our gratitude to you anonymously for the help and insight you gave us. Finally, we are forever in the debt of the four men who agreed, after reading an early draft, to permit publication of their biographies. They support our fond hope that biographical research of this kind can be done on the basis of mutual respect and cooperative effort.

New Haven, May 1977                                        Daniel J. Levinson

# A View of
# Adult Development

# The Life Cycle
## and Its Seasons

Great masses of data have been accumulated about specific features of adult life. There are statistics on marriage and divorce, health and illness, life expectancy, occupation and income. There are studies of such stressful events as retirement and "the empty nest" syndrome. We have, in short, extensive information on adulthood—but a very limited understanding of its nature. The basic developmental principles of adult life remain an enigma.

We have a much better understanding of the pre-adult years, up to about age 20. We know that development occurs during this part of life and we are able to trace it through a series of periods: infancy, early childhood, middle childhood, pubescence, early and late adolescence. Our understanding of the pre-adult phase is more profound and systematic largely because we have examined it from a *developmental perspective*. We regard childhood and adolescence as a formative phase, a time of unique pleasures and conflicts, of growth and preparation for the adult life to come. The overall shape of the first twenty years emerges plainly: an incomplete, highly dependent child grows in complex biological, psychological and social ways to become, in greater or lesser degree, an independent, responsible adult.

A developmental approach to the pre-adult years means, too, that we can discern an underlying order in the child's movement through them. It is now generally accepted that all lives are governed by common developmental principles in childhood and adolescence and go through a common sequence of developmental periods. At the same time, each individual life has its own special character and follows its own special course.

A developmental approach is needed in the study of adulthood. In this book we present a conception of the life cycle as a whole, and a more detailed picture of development in early and middle adulthood. This is in itself hardly a novel idea, yet it has remained curiously neglected. The life cycle has rarely been studied in the social sciences, and there exists no theoretical framework to stimulate and guide a program of research in these disciplines. In academic psychology the situation was only a little better in the 1960s, although more interest has been generated in recent years.


## Conceptions of the Life Cycle

The most promising view of the life cycle, and of adult development, comes from the field know broadly as "depth psychology," founded by Sigmund Freud (1856–1939). Freud created a theory of personality encompassing its unconscious as well as conscious aspects, and showed how personality development in childhood profoundly influences one's life in adulthood. In the excitement of his discoveries about childhood development, however, Freud was inclined to regard adulthood primarily as a scene in which the early unconscious conflicts were re-enacted, rather than as a time of further development.

In our view, the person who can justly be considered the father of the modern study of adult development is Carl G. Jung (1875–1961). During most of his thirties, Jung was a disciple of Freud and a leading member of the newly forming psychoanalytic movement. In 1913 he split from Freud and gradually formed his own school, Analytical Psychology.

Of the many intellectual differences between Jung and Freud, two are of especial relevance here. First, Jung felt that Freud was too narrowly focused on childhood development and its influence on adult problems, conflicts and creativities. Jung forged a conception of the entire life cycle, giving particular attention to adult development in "the second half of life." Second, he believed that Freud's strongly clinical orientation had led to an overemphasis on psychopathology and internal ("intrapsychic") processes, to the neglect of social institutions, religion and mythology. Jung set out to develop a *social psychology*. He tried to understand individual development as a product of both internal psychological processes and exterior cultural forces. His theory is based on the clinical study of patients and the analysis of ethnography, mythology and symbolic creations from many cultures and historical periods.

Jung's main interest was the study of adult development. He understood that the young adult, as part of normal development, is still highly caught up in the emotional involvements and conflicts of childhood and is hard-pressed to cope with the demands of family, work and community. The personality cannot reach its full growth by age 20. He found that the next opportunity for fundamental change starts at about 40, "the noon of life."

Jung used the term "individuation" for the developmental process that begins then and may extend over the last half of the life cycle.

The next great figure in the study of adult development is Erik H. Erikson (born 1902). Although he is by training and allegiance a psycho-analyst, Erikson provides a historical and intellectual link between Freud and Jung. His modifications of psychoanalytic theory bring him closer to Jung, though he lacks some of the philosophical and mystical qualities that kept Jung at odds with the professional establishment. He was initially an artist and teacher. Seemingly by accident he became a Freudian psychoanalyst in Vienna at about age 30, shortly before moving to the United States.

Erikson's enormous influence in the humanities, psychology and the social sciences began in 1950 with the publication of his first book, *Childhood and Society*. Since then, he has devoted himself primarily to the study of adult development, using a biographical method and a combined historical-sociological-psychological mode of analysis. His work on childhood has been more widely understood and appreciated than his work on adulthood. Although he is on the boundary between the humanities and the social sciences, Erikson is primarily a humanist—a student of life more than an academic scientist. In this respect and others, he is closer to Jung than to Freud, whose thinking was deeply rooted in physiology and in nineteenth-century science.

On the psychological side, our thinking about adult development thus grows out of an intellectual tradition formed by Freud, Jung and Erikson. This tradition includes Rank, Adler, Reich and other socially oriented depth psychologists. In recent years, these sources have been used by Ernest Becker, Robert Lifton and others in creating a broader approach to adult life in society. The schisms that for so long have divided the various schools of depth psychology, and have restricted the scope of each viewpoint, are perhaps beginning to be outgrown. The absurdity of the old sectarian struggles is evident. The present study will, we hope, contribute to the emergence of a more integrative, nonsectarian approach.

In creating a deeper and more complex view of adulthood, one has to consider both the nature of the person and the nature of society. It is not enough merely to acknowledge that history, culture and social institutions influence the life of the individual adult. An adequate approach must be informed by concepts and ways of thinking from the social sciences. Our efforts to do this will be apparent throughout our book.

The literature of biology, psychology and the social sciences does not contain a systematic conception of the life cycle and its components. In the course of the study we discovered a good deal about the life cycle and arrived at a conception of our own. It will be presented in Chapters 2 and 3, and spelled out in later chapters. The starting point for our thinking was, however, not an articulated theory but an intuitively derived, metaphorical sense of what the life cycle is about.

Let us begin at the beginning, with concrete meanings and images. First, the term "life cycle." Other terms, such as "life span" and "life course," are often used as synonyms for it, but they have quite different meanings. "Life span" is simply a category referring to the interval from birth to death. It is a descriptively useful term, but it says nothing about how this interval is filled. "Life course" has more content. It refers to the flow of the individual life over time—the patterning of specific events, relationships, achievements, failures and aspirations that are the stuff of life. The life course is what we are trying to understand. A developmental theory provides one of several perspectives through which we try to analyze and understand the life course.

The term "life cycle" conveys another, more distinctive meaning. It suggests that the life course has a particular character and follows a basic sequence. According to the *American Heritage Dictionary*, the words "cycle" and "development" have the same root source: *kwel*. The Latin form of *kwel* is *colere*, the Greek *telos*. They are sources for contemporary English words such as circle, evolve, completion, wheel, inhabit, culture, cultivate. The term "life cycle" contains the basic meanings of such words, but they are rarely made explicit. I would like to articulate two of the key meanings.

First, there is the idea of a *process* or *journey* from a starting point (birth, origin) to a termination point (death, conclusion). To speak of a general, human life cycle is to propose that the journey from birth to old age follows an underlying, universal pattern on which there are endless cultural and individual variations. Many influences along the way shape the nature of the journey. They may produce alternate routes or detours along the way; they may speed up or slow down the timetable within certain limits; in extreme cases they may stop the developmental process altogether. But as long as the journey continues, it follows the basic sequence.

Second, there is the idea of *seasons*: a series of periods or stages within the life cycle. The process is not a simple, continuous, unchanging flow. There are qualitatively different seasons, each having its own distinctive character. Every season is different from those that precede and follow it, though it also has much in common with them. The imagery of seasons takes many forms. There are seasons in the year: spring is a time of blossoming, winter a time of death but also of rebirth and the start of a new cycle. There are seasons, too, within a single day—daybreak, noon, dusk, the quiet dark of night—each having its diurnal, atmospheric and psychological character. There are seasons in a love relationship, in war, politics, artistic creation and illness.

Metaphorically, everyone understands the connections between the seasons of the year and the seasons of the human life cycle. No one needs an explanation of the lyrics to "September Song." When the hero sings, "It's a long, long while from May to December/And the days grow short when you reach September," we all know that he is referring to the contrast between youth and middle age. When Dylan Thomas in his celebrated poem tells his aging father, "Do not go gentle into that good night," it is clear to all that the coming of night is experienced as the end of life.

To speak of seasons is to say that the life course has a certain shape, that it evolves through a series of definable forms. A season is a relatively stable segment of the total cycle. Summer has a character different from that of winter; twilight is different from sunrise. To say that a season is relatively stable, however, does not mean that it is stationary or static. Change goes on within each, and a transition is required for the shift from one season to the next. Every season has its own time; it is important in its own right and needs to be understood in its own terms. No season is better or more important than any other. Each has its necessary place and contributes its special character to the whole. It is an organic part of the total cycle, linking past and future and containing both within itself.

Before I present a more analytical view of the life cycle, a brief account of our study is in order.

## The Study of Adult Development

The character of this study was established during a two-year exploratory period. It grew out of my strong but vaguely defined interest in learning about the nature of adult development somewhere within the age span of 30 to 50. I felt intuitively that the years around age 40 have a special importance in a person's life. After some preliminary reading, interviewing and introspecting, I decided to focus on the decade from age 35 to 45. During this "mid-life decade," I reasoned, one made the shift from "youth" to "middle age." None of the above terms in quotes was precisely defined either in the research literature or in my own mind. My initial aims were to give a more factually grounded meaning to these terms and to examine the process of development—if any—in the mid-life decade.

Accordingly our research subjects were at the start in the age range between 35 and 45. Their ages varied fairly evenly across this decade. We considered having a more limited age range, say 43 to 45, so that all participants could review their lives over the decade. It seemed more important, however, to cover as wide a current age range as possible, within the limits of our aims. Since the sample was selected in 1969, the subjects were born between 1923 and 1934. They were at different ages when they experienced major social changes, such as the depression of the 1930s, World War II, the Korean War, the constricting conformist decade of the 1950s and the upheavals of the 1960s. The external phasing of their lives was not identical. The variation in age also enabled us to obtain a more vivid picture of the life in each part of the decade. We can review our recent experience with greater fullness and immediacy than we can reconstruct our remembrance of times past. The participants in their late thirties could not describe their lives in the forties, but they gave a richer account of the late thirties than could those of 44 or 45.

Many colleagues advised me to focus not upon a particular age span but upon a particular stage in the occupational or familial career. For example, I might have studied the "middle parenthood" stage when the children are of school age, the "empty nest" when the last child has left home, or the "mid-career" stage in the occupational sequence. Having already done several studies of occupational careers, I found this option too restricted. At this time in my own personal and intellectual development, I wanted to create an overarching conception of development that could encompass the diverse biological, psychological and social changes occurring in adult life. I made the risky bet that development in this sense does occur, and that the mid-life decade was a good place to look for it. The bet, as it turned out, was worth making.

The size of the sample was a major issue. Since each life would be studied intensively, the total number had to be limited. I clearly did not want to do a massive survey or to administer psychological tests to a large sample. Yet more than a few cases were required so that we could generate widely relevant theory and discover various forms of development under differing conditions. It would not be enough to do a single, richly textured biography. I decided, finally, on a sample of forty, the largest number our resources could handle. This small sample could not yield conclusive proof of any hypotheses, but then no investigation in this new field could be conclusive. Still, we might arrive at some significant ideas, tentative generalizations and useful research methods.

One of the most difficult decisions was that limiting the study to men. Ultimately, it is essential to study the adult development of both genders if we are to understand either. The challenge of development is at least as great for women as for men. They go through the same adult developmental periods as men, I believe, but in partially different ways that reflect the differences in biology and social circumstances. The periods themselves may be different in some respects for women. The approach presented here offers a basis for the study of women, without the assumption that the two genders develop in either identical or totally different ways. A first step in this direction has been made by Wendy Stewart. Studying a small sample of women in their mid-thirties, she found that all of them went through the same developmental periods as our men, though some of the specific issues were different. Additional studies are now under way.

Despite my strong desire to include women, I decided finally against it. A study of twenty men and twenty women would do justice to neither group. The differences between women and men are sufficiently great so that they would have to become a major focus of analysis. It was not simply a matter of testing another sample and letting the computer grind out the data. Given the intensive exploratory nature of the study, we would be examining each participant's life in detail. A sample of forty men containing several subgroups is more nearly adequate than twenty for studying male development under systematically different conditions. In retrospect, I believe that this was the right choice. We are now in a better position to learn about various other populations. In all candor, however, I must admit to a more personal reason for the choice: I chose men partly because I wanted so deeply to understand my own adult development.

Finally, I decided that the sample would be composed of four occupational subgroups, each containing ten men. A man's work is the primary base for his life in society. Through it he is "plugged into" an occupational structure and a cultural, class and social matrix. Work is also of great psychological importance; it is a vehicle for the fulfillment or negation of central aspects of the self.

Our task was to select a set of four occupations representing diverse sectors of society. They should differ widely in type of work, origins, and current social and psychological conditions of living. In the end, we chose: hourly workers in industry, business executives, university biologists and novelists. Other sets of occupations might equally well have been picked, but we found this choice to be very satisfactory. We have tried to discover features of adult development that are common to the sample as a whole, as well as differences among the various groupings.

Thus, our plan was to study forty men who were currently between 35 and 45 years old, equally distributed among four occupations. We then selected the men to be studied. The sampling procedure varied somewhat among the four occupations.

Two companies are the work places from which we drew both the workers and the executives. One we call the Industrial Firearms Division of the Ajax Corporation. (The names of all persons and institutions are pseudonyms.) This division manufactures a small number of products, including munitions and recreational equipment. Its products, technology and organizational structure have not changed radically over several decades, though recent changes in the corporate structure have led to a greater emphasis on modern management practices and product diversification. The second company, United Electronics, is an "infant," rapidly growing firm in the modern communication-information field. Its founders, who came from established corporations such as Xerox and IBM, have a dream that their infant will before long become a giant rivaling its forebears.

We selected these two companies after conducting a search within a radius of fifty miles of New Haven. In both companies, we selected samples of workers and executives. The men were told that the company endorsed our study but did not require anyone to take part in it. We emphasized that our interviews were confidential; the company would receive a copy of our published findings but would get no private report or evaluation of any individual. Confidentiality and other ethical issues were of great importance to us. We wanted to be sure that no one would suffer or gain unfairly because of his involvement in the study. Both companies honored our agreement to the full. We regret that the requirements of confidentiality keep us from stating publicly the names of the companies and individuals whose help we so greatly appreciate.

• The *hourly workers* were drawn equally from Ajax and United Electronics. In Ajax, where 60 percent of the hourly labor force (and none of the management) was Black, we chose three Black and two White workers. United Electronics had no Black workers and its employees were at somewhat higher levels of education and technical training. The ten workers varied in current age, occupation, labor grade, education and years with the company. All ten men accepted our invitation to participate. It became evident that some of them had initial doubts about our relation to management, and we had to work to establish our credibility. In this group, as in all the others, no one dropped out and several men continued for extra interviews as needed.

• Of the *executives*, six were from Ajax, four from United Electronics. From each company we obtained a table of organization for middle and top management, with each person's name, age and a few demographic characteristics. We then selected our sample so as to maximize diversity in age, rank in top and middle management, line and staff positions, and previous work in engineering, sales, finance and the like. We did not select for marital status, personality, ability and other such characteristics, but in the nature of our method we obtained great diversity in these respects. As with the hourly workers, all ten men we invited agreed to take part. It was helpful that the head of each company met our sampling criteria and accepted our invitation to be a subject. (Several executives had the feeling that the boss rather than the researchers had selected them; they wondered whether they were seen as budding stars or wilting failures. Again, we worked on this issue in the course of the interviews.)

• For the sample of *academic biologists*, we chose two excellent universities in the corridor between Boston and New York. In these institutions biology professors are generally "promising young men" or senior investigators of national reputation. Yet, as we knew from personal experience at Yale and elsewhere, the lives and professional careers of professors differ enormously. Biology is undergoing rapid change both as a scientific discipline and as a field of increasing social application (in areas such as medicine, population control, warfare and food production). Biologists are employed not only in the Biology Department but also in Biochemistry, Biophysics, Public Health, Forestry, even Urban Planning. We spent some time learning about the various departments and the ages, academic ranks and fields of specialization of their members. In each university we chose five men who differed widely in these respects. We got in touch with each man by letter and then by phone and personal interview. Eight of the ten agreed to participate. In all, we approached thirteen men before obtaining our full complement of ten. We thus have a small "volunteer bias," but it is far less than in most research. With the biologists we had neither the advantages nor the drawbacks of sponsorship by organizational authority.

• The sampling procedure was different again with the *novelists*. Here we operated entirely outside of any organizational framework. Once more, we used a quasi-anthropological method of studying what was for us a new culture. We began by trying to learn about the writer's world—a world that contains publishing houses, universities, mass media and many other institutions. We talked with a number of critics, teachers, editors and agents, and with some writers outside our chosen age group.

There is no accepted criterion for identifying a man as a novelist. Very few people can make the writing of novels a full-time occupation. Novelists often work also as critics, journalists, businessmen, teachers. We settled on two ground rules: that a man have published at least two novels, and that being a novelist is of major importance in his personal identity.

From various sources we compiled a list of over one hundred male novelists who seemed to meet these criteria and who lived somewhere between Boston and New York. In selecting ten names from this list, we tried to get variety in terms of quality and kind of writing. Some men chosen were highly gifted novelists whose work had been praised by serious writers and critics. Others, less well known, were regarded as promising or worthy of serious critical consideration. Still others were more popular and less "literary" novelists, who considered themselves craftsmen and worked hard at their writing. We wrote letters to each man on the initial list, followed this by a phone call and, if the man was interested, a personal interview. Seven of the first ten accepted our invitation. In all, we spoke to fourteen men before completing the group. The ten men selected differ greatly in social background, in literary style and aims, and in degree of critical and commercial success. Most of them do other writing—plays, films, poetry and nonfiction—and have occupations in addition to writing.

• *The sample* thus consists of forty men, distributed in age between 35 and 45. All are American born. There are ten in each of the four occupations selected for study. They currently live in the region between Boston and New York, though many of them were born in other parts of the country.

The sample is highly diverse in other respects. Let's quickly look at four characteristics: social class origins, racial-ethnic-religious origins, education and marital status.

The men come from varied *social class backgrounds*. Six of them (15 percent) are from poor urban or rural environments. These include four workers, an executive and a novelist. Forty-two percent are from stable working-class or lower-middle-class families, 32 percent from comfortable middle-class origins, and 10 percent from wealthy (upper-middle- or upper-class) backgrounds. The workers come entirely from poor or working-class families. Only two executives are from comfortable middle-class families; seven are from the working class or lower-middle class, and one grew up in poverty. Seven biologists and eight novelists are from families of moderate to high social position. They tilt the sample as a whole toward the higher end of the class structure in terms of social origins.

The sample is also diverse in terms of *racial-ethnic-religious origins*. There are five Black participants (12 percent)—three workers and two novelists. No Black biologists or executives between age 35 and 45 were employed by the organizations we studied. Twenty of the men are from Protestant families (50 percent), eight Catholic (20 percent), seven Jewish (18 percent) and another seven from families of mixed religious or ethnic parentage (usually Catholic-Protestant or mixed national origin).

Of the biologists, six are from Protestant families, one Jewish and three mixed Catholic-Protestant. The novelists include six from Protestant families (of which two are Black) and four from Jewish. The lack of Catholics among the biologists and novelists was not by design; it is a chance variation which may reflect the small number of Catholics in these occupations. The religious backgrounds of the executives are five Catholic (mainly of Polish, Italian or Irish extraction), two Protestant, one mixed Catholic-Protestant and two Jewish. The backgrounds of the workers: three Catholic, five Protestant and two mixed Catholic-Protestant.

With regard to *education*, 28 men (70 percent) completed college, and only six did not complete high school. This reflects the educational levels of the occupations represented. The workers were the least educated: five did not complete high school; three went through high school; and two had some college experience. All ten of the biologists finished college and then a Ph.D. degree in a biological science such as biochemistry, zoology or botany. Of the executives, nine completed college (including four at engineering schools) and two of these had some graduate education. The novelists too were highly educated. Nine of them completed college, six at elite schools such as Harvard, Dartmouth and Oberlin. A serious young novelist is likely to get his personal experience and the tools of his trade in an affluent pre-adult world and in an educational milieu that gives strong if ambivalent support to his literary aspirations at the start of early adulthood.

All of the men had been married at least once. Their current *marital status* varied as follows. Thirty-two of the forty men (80 percent) were in their first marriage. Of the eight who had been divorced, three had not remarried and five were in their second marriage. A few of the marriages were rather rocky, and we know of two divorces that occurred soon after the study ended. Roughly 80 percent of the men had children in their first or second marriage. There were no marked differences among the occupational groups.

Although our primary source of information about each man was the man himself, it is important to note that we had other sources as well. Most of the wives were interviewed once. Our main purpose here was to obtain an additional perspective on the husband, but we also learned something about the wife in her own right, as preparation for more intensive study of women. We also learned a good deal about the men's various occupations and work worlds. In the course of this, we in effect performed an informal organizational analysis of the two companies and the two universities in our study. We constructed a picture of the history, current structure, hiring and promotion policies, and problems of survival and growth of each organization, especially as these affected the men under study. Often, more than one man gave his personal version of a particular incident or individual; these contributed to our view of each work world. Our visits to a man's office, home and organizational space gave added dimensions and meaning to what he told us himself. The novelists, though they had no organizational affiliation, lived within a loosely organized occupational world, and from various sources we learned about this world and each novelist. We read some or all of each man's novels and other writings. We also read their reviews.

I emphasize these additional sources for two main reasons. First, because they gave us a richer and more valid picture than we could obtain solely from interviews with each subject. Second, because an understanding of a man's life requires that we know something about his external circumstances as well as his personal motives, aspirations and interpretation of events. We selected just a few occupations and work organizations partly so that we could study them and their part in each man's life. Our understanding of them was an essential ingredient in our analysis of individual life and development.

• The *interviewing* is the heart of our research method. During the interviewing phase of the study, we interviewed a man in his home or work place, or in our offices, according to his preference. The tape-recorded interviews usually lasted an hour or two and were held at weekly intervals. Occasionally, an interview would continue for an entire afternoon or evening; or several weeks would elapse between sessions. Flexibility was the keynote, within the basic requirement that we have enough privacy and time. In all, we saw each man five to ten times, for a total of ten to twenty hours, within a span of two or three months. In most cases, we had a follow-up interview about two years after the initial interviewing. The transcripts of the tapes averaged about three hundred pages per man. Each subject was interviewed by a single staff member.

As part of the interviewing, we showed every man a series of five pictures and asked him to tell a story about each of them. The pictures were selected from the Thematic Apperception Test devised by Henry A. Murray. This test is often used in personality diagnosis. We used the stories in an unconventional way, as an intrinsic part of the interviews. They often brought up personal experiences, interests and imaginings that might otherwise have been avoided or overlooked. An example of the usefulness of this method is given in the biography of John Barnes (Chapter 17).

The interviewing reflects what is most central in our theoretical approach. If I had to choose one term for this method, I would call it *biographical interviewing*. The primary task, as we informed our subjects at the start, was to construct the story of a man's life. Interviewer and interviewee joined collaboratively in this work.

We tried to cover the entire life sequence from childhood to the present: family of origin; marriage and family of procreation (in which the man is husband and father); important relationships with men and women; education; occupational choice and work history; leisure; involvement in ethnic, religious, political and other interests; illness, death and loss of loved ones; good times and bad times; turning points in the life course. At various key times we tried to pull together a picture of the man's life as a whole: how the various components of his life were interrelated at that time; how the life pattern at age 34, say, had emerged from the past and what were his hopes, fears, plans and imaginings for the future.

This was a lot of ground to cover, and there proved to be no single best way to do it. A man has a story to tell: incidents unfold in a particular sequence and he has strong feelings about the course and outcome of various chapters. The specifics of external situations are often important, as are the internal meanings, desires and conflicts with which he participates in them. The interviewer had to give the man a chance to tell his own story. He also had to intervene at times to get the story straight, to learn about specific situations, actions and feelings, and to explore the connections between different sectors of living and different times in the sequence.

A biographical interview combines aspects of a research interview, a clinical interview and a conversation between friends. It is like a structured research interview in that certain topics must be covered, and the main purpose is research. As in a clinical interview, the interviewer is sensitive to the feelings expressed, and follows the threads of meaning as they lead through diverse topics. Finally, as in a conversation between friends, the relationship is equal and the interviewer is free to respond in terms of his own experiences. Yet each party has a defined role in a sustained work task, which imposes its own constraints.

What is involved is not simply an interviewing technique or procedure, but a relationship of some intimacy, intensity and duration. Significant work is involved in forming, maintaining and terminating the relationship. The recruiting of participants, the negotiation of a research contract, and the course of the interviewing relationship are phases within a single, complex process. Understanding and managing this process is a crucial part of our research method. Managed with sensitivity and discretion, it is a valuable learning experience for the participant as well as the researcher. Although therapy was not a primary aim, the interviews may have had some therapeutic effects. Virtually all of the men, we believe, found this a worthwhile undertaking.

The basic aim of biography is to portray an individual life as it evolves over the years. It has different purposes for novelists, literary biographers, historians and psychologists. Biography may be used to show how a person was influenced by his times and how he helped to shape his times. It may provide a deeper understanding of a person's work—be it painting, military exploits or political leadership—by placing it within the context of his personal life and engagement in society. A poor biography depicts its protagonist as saint or villain, as merely a product of his times, a creature of his unconscious or a sequence of reactions without individuality.

Our essential method was to elicit the life stories of forty men, to construct biographies and to develop generalizations based upon these biographies. We do not have the data required for a book-length biography of each man, and there are important gaps in every story. Nonetheless, we have produced a systematic reconstruction of the forty lives. In each case, we began by immersing ourselves in the interview material and working toward an intuitive understanding of the man and his life. Gradually we tried more interpretive formulations and, going back and forth between the interviews and the analysis, came to a construction of the life course.

The preparation of biographies and the creation of a developmental theory thus went hand in hand. We did not start with a theory of developmental periods. The theory as it existed at a given time was used to obtain a more integrated view of the individual life; and each biography advanced the formation of specific concepts and ways of thinking. Some form of biographical method is essential, I believe, during the initial phase of research on adult development.

Because biography is so important here, the biographies of four men— a worker, an executive, a biologist and a novelist—will be presented. The men will be introduced in Chapter 4 and their lives described in subsequent chapters. Brief summaries or fragments of other lives will also be used to illustrate particular findings and concepts. One crucial test of a theory of adult development is the value it has for the writing of biographies and autobiographies.

In addition to the primary sample of forty men, we have created a secondary sample of men whose lives have been depicted in biography or imagined in fiction, poetry and theater. This sample has had an important part in the evolution of our thinking, and I shall occasionally draw upon it to provide more public examples of our ideas. It includes such men as Dante, Milton and Shakespeare; Abraham, Luther, Gandhi and Willy Brandt; Freud and Jung; Gauguin, Goya, Eugene O'Neill and Bertrand Russell; the fictional figures of Prospero, King Lear, Herzog, Willy Loman and George and Martha, the mutually destructive couple in Who's Afraid of Virginia Woolf?

Our aims expanded in the course of the study. Initially, our main focus was on the decade from age 35 to 45. Our goal was to determine what developmental process, if any, occurred within it. In reviewing our first cases, we reconstructed the life history prior to age 35 as a backdrop for studying the mid-life decade. We found ourselves full of ideas—stemming mainly from psychoanalytic theory—about the subject's development in childhood and adolescence. We could make many connections between these early periods and what happened at mid-life. It became increasingly clear, however, that we had no useful conception of early adult development from the end of adolescence to age 35. By regarding the mid-life struggles and adaptations as no more than a re-enactment of personality traits and conflicts formed in childhood, we were falling into the misleading simplicity we had set out to avoid. The emphasis on childhood development helped to illuminate adult life, but it kept us from examining what is new in adulthood.

It became evident, finally, that we had to deal seriously with the years between adolescence and the mid-life decade. So our major aim took shape: we had to create a theory of adult development, from the entry into adulthood until the late forties. This was a valuable but distressing insight, for it increased the scope, difficulty and length of our work. It made clear the actual nature of the choice implicitly made at the start: our subject was not solely the mid-life decade, but the entire developmental sequence during the adult years represented in our sample.

In Chapters 2 and 3 we describe our conception of the life cycle and the process of adult development. In Chaper 2 I present a view of the life cycle as a whole, moving from the metaphor of seasons to a conceptualization of eras. Chapter 3 introduces our theory of adult development as a sequence of periods in the evolution of the individual life structure. In subsequent chapters our theory and findings for each period are described in more detail.

# 2  Eras: The Anatomy of the Life Cycle

It is remarkable that we have no standard language for identifying the major seasons of the life cycle. Is there a valid and useful way to divide the total life cycle into several gross segments, each having its own distinctive character? We can probably agree without difficulty on an initial segment of some twenty years, a pre-adult phase embracing childhood and adolescence. There is also "old age," which starts at age 60 or 65. Gerontology has thus far provided considerable information, though little understanding, about this time of life. But what about the adult years between 20 and 65? Though everyday language provides terms such as "youth" and "middle age," there is little agreement regarding their definition and their place in the life cycle.

Our view of the life cycle is a product of our research. It is not an armchair speculation or assumption we made beforehand. We believe that the life cycle evolves through a sequence of eras each lasting roughly twenty-five years. The eras are partially overlapping, so that a new one is getting under way as the previous one is being terminated. The sequence goes as follows:

1. Childhood and adolescence: age 0–22
2. Early adulthood: age 17–45
3. Middle adulthood: age 40–65
4. Late adulthood: age 60–?

An era is a "time of life" in the broadest sense. Although important changes go on within it, each era has its own distinctive and unifying qualities, which have to do with the *character of living*. In studying the character of living, we take account of biological, psychological and social aspects, but do not focus on any one of these to the exclusion of the others. An era is thus not a stage in biological development, in personality development or in career development. It is much broader and more inclusive than a developmental stage or period. The sequence of eras constitutes the macro-structure of the life cycle. It provides a framework within which developmental periods and concrete processes of everyday living take place.

The eras are analogous to the acts of a play, the major divisions of a novel, or the gross segments into which a biographer divides the life of his subject. The developmental periods give a finer picture of the dramatic events and the details of living; the eras give an overview of the life cycle as a whole.

The main focus of our study, as I have mentioned, is on the years from the late teens to the late forties. On the basis of this study, we identify early and middle adulthood as separate eras in the life cycle. Early adulthood comes to an end in a man's forties, when the character of living once more undergoes a fundamental change and middle adulthood begins to emerge. One of the most important—and most controversial—contributions of this study is the demarcation between early and middle adulthood as clearly defined eras. I shall give the reasons for it shortly.

I have set forth a specific age at which each era begins, and another at which it ends. This is not to say, however, that a bell rings at precisely the same point for everyone, demarcating the eras as though they were rounds in a boxing match or classes in a highly regulated school. Life is never that standardized. There is an average or most frequent age for the onset and completion of every era. There is also a range of variation around the average. The variation is contained, however, within fairly narrow limits—probably not more than five or six years. The discovery of age-linked eras is another unexpected finding of our study. This finding goes against the conventional assumption that development does not occur in adulthood or, if it does, that its pace varies tremendously and has almost no connection to age. On the contrary, it seems to be closely age-linked.

The move from one era to the next is neither simple nor brief. It requires a basic change in the fabric of one's life, and this takes more than a day, a month or even a year. The transition between eras consistently takes four or five years—not less than three and rarely more than six. This transition is the work of a developmental period that links the eras and provides some continuity between them. A developmental transition creates a boundary zone in which a man terminates the outgoing era and initiates the incoming one.

Though pre-adulthood ends at roughly age 22, early adulthood begins several years earlier, usually at 17. The span from 17 to 22 is thus a "zone of overlap," a period in which the old era is being completed and the new one is starting. This period is the Early Adult Transition. It bridges the two eras and is part of both. Likewise, the Mid-life Transition extends from roughly 40 to 45. It serves to terminate early adulthood and to initiate middle adulthood. There is a subsequent transition in the early sixties, we believe, and perhaps another at about 80.

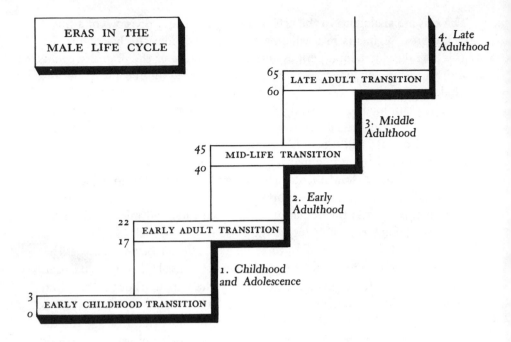

The eras and the cross-era transitions are pictured above. Let us now briefly review the eras in turn.


## Pre-adulthood

The pre-adult era includes childhood, adolescence and the Early Adult Transition. During this time one ordinarily lives within the family or an equivalent social unit. The family provides protection, socialization and support of growth during our pre-adult years. With adequate development, we can be relatively self-sufficient members of society as we enter adulthood. In pre-adulthood we are relatively (though decreasingly) dependent and vulnerable, growing in the most elemental sense of the term.

The "transition into childhood" starts sometime before birth and continues for the first two or three years of separate life. In this period the infant develops into a separate person. He learns to distinguish the "me" from the "not-me" and to form a primordial sense of self. During this time he also comes to realize that other persons have an enduring existence and character. Another transition at 5 or 6 leads from early to middle childhood. The child expands his social world from the immediate family to a larger sphere containing school, wider peer group and neighborhood. He begins to resolve his emotional struggles within the family and to become more disciplined, industrious and skilled. Puberty usually starts at 12 or 13 (plus or minus 2 years) and provides a transition from middle childhood to adolescence. It is touched off by the bodily changes leading to sexual maturity but it involves a variety of other changes leading toward full adulthood. Adolescence is the culmination of the pre-adult era.

The *Early Adult Transition* extends from roughly age 17 to 22. It provides a bridge from adolescence to early adulthood, and is part of both. Like all cross-era transitions, it is a crucial turning point in the life cycle. During this period the growing male is a boy-man; he is terminating his pre-adult self and his place in the pre-adult world, and at the same time starting to form his first adult self and to make the choices through which he establishes his initial membership in the adult world.

Childhood and adolescence together now make up roughly one-quarter of the expected life span. The pre-adult era is a time of extraordinary growth but it is only a prelude to adult living. Its result is an immature and still vulnerable individual making his entry into the adult world.

## Early Adulthood

Early adulthood is the second era of the life cycle. It ordinarily begins at 17 or 18 and ends at about 45. Ushered in by the Early Adult Transition, it is terminated by the Mid-life Transition, which links it to middle adulthood. Early adulthood may be the most dramatic of all eras. For men, the peak years of biological functioning are roughly from 20 to 40. The youth of 20 is at the height of his bodily vigor and is getting ready to take his place as a man in the society of adults. At the other end, as he passes 40, a new season starts to make itself felt; he begins to realize that the summer of his life is ending and autumn is fast approaching.

By 20, most of the mental and bodily characteristics that have been evolving in the pre-adult years are at or near their peak levels. The young man is close to his full height and his maximal level of strength, sexual capability, cardiac and respiratory capacity, and general biological vigor. He is also close to his peak in intelligence and in those qualities of intellect that have grown so measurably in pre-adulthood, such as memory, abstract thought, ability to learn specific skills and to solve well-defined problems.

These characteristics remain relatively stable and near their peak levels

until around 40. Biologists often use age 30 as a reference point for studying age changes in adulthood, because most biological functions remain
close to their highest levels until that age, and then decline gradually
through the remaining years. In the late thirties, a man is normally still
near his peak levels of biological and psychological capacity and within
the era of early adulthood.

Apart from impairments due to illness or accident, a man at 40 has
not fallen much below his maximal level of bodily functioning. The drop
is often great enough, however, to give him a distinct sense of bodily
decline at around this age. The visible "cosmetic" changes, such as bald-
ness, wrinkles and paunch, symbolize the loss of youth and the imminence
of "middle age," even though they involve little real decrease in bodily
health and capacity.

The span from 20 to 40 is the era of greatest biological abundance and
of greatest contradiction and stress. The man's instinctual drives are at
their height. He urgently seeks personal gratification of various kinds, but
he is burdened by the residues of childhood conflicts regarding such gratification. He is struggling to establish his place in society. This effort, too,
is both satisfying and stressful.

During his twenties, a young man ordinarily forms a preliminary adult
identity. He makes the first major choices, such as marriage, occupation,
residence and style of living, that define his place in the adult world. Early
adulthood is the time to pay his dues and make his essential contribution
to the survival of the species: begetting and raising children, maintaining
a marriage and family, giving his labor to the economy and welfare of the
"tribe"—that part of the species in which he is most fully involved. With
luck, he has the sense of doing something for himself as well as others,
of both satisfying his own needs and contributing to his society.

Within this era we find a basic sequence of change. Over its course
a man normally moves from being a "novice adult" through a series of
intermediate steps to the point where he can assume a more "senior" position in work, family and community. Going through the process of forming an occupation (often making more than one provisional choice), he
establishes himself first at a junior level and then advances along some
formal or informal ladder until, at around 40, he reaches the culmination
of his youthful strivings. He is now ending his early adulthood and beginning a new era.

In marriage and family, too, the young man begins as novice lover,
husband and father. Gradually, often painfully, he grows more understanding and responsible—better able to gain the satisfactions and bear the
burdens of being senior. The first several years in the growth of the family

tend to be especially stressful: small children add to the complexity of married life and increase the financial demands on the young man; but his earning power and capacity for meeting responsibilities are still rather limited.

If a man starts a family in his twenties, his offspring are in or near adolescence as he passes 40. His relationships with them are changing sharply. The nest is emptying and the nuclear family is dividing into separate households. The husband and wife together experience strong emotional losses and stresses. At the same time, the financial, social and emotional burdens of raising a family are greatly decreased.

A man's relationships with his parents and the members of his extended family also change over the course of early adulthood. At 20, he tries desperately to get them to regard him as an equal and a man, "not a kid." By 40, he is taking on parental responsibilities for parents, relatives and the generation of the elderly who look to him for care and leadership. And by 40 he is seen by the youth as senior, a full generation removed from them.

As compared with later eras, then, early adulthood is distinguished by its fullness of energy, capability and potential, as well as external pressure. In it, personal drives and societal requirements are powerfully intermeshed, at times reinforcing each other and at times in stark contradiction.

## Middle Adulthood

At around 40 a crucial developmental change occurs. Early adulthood is coming to an end and a new season begins to make itself felt. The Mid-life Transition, which lasts from about 40 to 45, is devoted to the termination of early adulthood and the initiation of middle adulthood. It is thus a part of both eras. Our discovery of the Mid-life Transition, and our conception of it as a link between two distinctive eras in the life cycle, are among the most controversial aspects of our work. We did not begin with the hypothesis of a highly defined transition at mid-life; it emerged in the course of our research. The evidence for it will be given in the following chapters. My main interest here is to present a brief account of middle adulthood as an era covering the span from roughly age 40 to 65.

The distinction between early and middle adulthood would have been discovered and accepted long ago, I believe, if there were a single event that occurred universally at around 40 and had great enough impact to shake the foundations of a man's life. A concrete, tangible event of this kind—a bodily change, a dramatic social event or a basic psychological change—provides a useful reference point for theory and research. Investigators can then determine whether the event is part of a fundamental developmental change. The prime example of such a reference point is puberty, which universally marks the shift from childhood to adolescence. It had been hoped that menopause would serve a similar function, but thus far it has not proven a useful guide in studying the adult development of women.

Investigators have as yet found no single event that universally heralds the end of early adulthood. There have been studies of various significant events such as divorce, depression, illness and the empty nest; but these occur at different ages and for different reasons. They do not provide the basis for a more general view of individual development. Likewise, bodily characteristics such as cardiac capacity or visual acuity decline gradually over the adult years. There is no age at which a set of biological or psychological characteristics shows a marked change that might reflect an underlying developmental process. The shift in eras will not be revealed by the study of concrete variables or events.

We get a different picture, however, when we examine the *lived life* as *it evolves*, rather than searching for a single, specific criterion. In the present study we have tried to examine the whole of a man's life as it evolves over time. Within this context, we then examine particular segments of life, such as work, family and bodily health. To identify the successive eras we must trace the individual life course over a span of years. When we take a more biographical approach, the eras come into clearer focus.

In the following pages I offer a schematic view of middle adulthood. I examine this era from three contrasting perspectives: (1) changes in biological and psychological functioning, (2) the sequence of generations and (3) the evolution of careers and enterprises. Each perspective offers a different vantage point from which to describe the changing character of living from one era to the next. They focus on different but interweaving elements in the individual's life, as I shall try to show. Many aspects of a man's personality and external circumstances are represented in each of these elements.

## Changes in Biological and Psychological Functioning

Although a man's bodily and mental powers are somewhat diminished after 40, they are ordinarily still ample for an active, full life throughout middle adulthood. A special illness, accident or defect may force him to restrict himself in certain respects; he may have to give up skiing or decrease his sexual activity or reduce the time and energy he devotes to work. But if he is not severely ill or impaired, and if his normal development has not been grossly hampered, he can maintain most of his earlier interests if he wishes.

The instinctual energies, too, pass their maximal level and are somewhat reduced in middle adulthood. A man is by no means lacking in the youthful drives—in lustful passions, in the capacity for anger and moral indignation, in self-assertiveness and ambition, in the wish to be cared for and supported. But he suffers less from the tyranny of these drives.

Moreover, the modest decline in the elemental drives may, with mid-life development, enable a man to enrich his life. He can be more free from the petty vanities, animosities, envies and moralisms of early adulthood. His normal sexual capacity in middle age is more than enough for a gratifying sex life. The quality of his love relationships may well improve as he develops a greater capacity for intimacy and integrates more fully the tender, "feminine" aspects of his self. He has the possibility of becoming a more responsive friend to men as well as women. He can be a more facilitating parent to his adolescent and young adult offspring as he recognizes that they are no longer children and that he is no longer the youthful controlling father. He can become a more caring son to his aging parents (for whom he increasingly assumes parental responsibilities), and a more compassionate authority and teacher to young adults.

Although biological decline ordinarily occurs gradually, several small changes often bring about a major, qualitative drop in body function by the early forties. This change may require considerable accommodation in the man's style of living and social roles, especially with regard to work. The effect is seen in many occupations that involve highly precise or strenuous labor; there is an upper age limit, usually in the thirties, after which a man must either leave his occupation altogether or shift within it to a managerial, consultative or physically less-demanding role.

The professional athlete who gives up playing ball at 30 has another ten years of early adulthood in which to establish himself in a new occupation or elsewhere in his sport. But the one who lingers on until, say, his late thirties, must go through a difficult occupational change even as he is entering the stressful period of the Mid-life Transition. Those who, for a variety of internal and external reasons, cannot alter their mode of work burn out or live a highly marginal existence.

Most men undergo a mid-life change in style of work and living. Early adulthood produces qualities of strength, quickness, endurance and output. Middle adulthood is a season when other qualities can ripen: wisdom, judiciousness, magnanimity, unsentimental compassion, breadth of perspective, the tragic sense. Great artists who continue their creative endeavors after 40 tend to produce more profound, more "sculpted" works than before, as Elliott Jaques has shown. In middle adulthood a man can make his most effective contribution to politics, diplomacy and philosophy. Although his most brilliant specific discoveries are often made in early adulthood, the creative scientist in middle adulthood tends to do more integrative theoretical work and to set new directions for the upcoming generation. At mid-life, many talented scientists turn increasingly to managerial, consultative and teaching activities. At their best, the new roles have great personal and social value; at their worst, they are a means of saving face and keeping busy, but contribute little to self or society and are a tragic waste of human life.

A man at mid-life is suffering some loss of his youthful vitality and, often, some insult to his youthful narcissistic pride. Although he is not literally close to death or undergoing severe bodily decline, he typically experiences these changes as a fundamental threat. It is as though he were on the threshold of senility and even death.

Jaques has identified the "middle crisis" as a normal development period starting in the late thirties and continuing for several years. He suggests that the experience of one's *mortality* is at the core of the mid-life crisis. Though we prefer the word "transition" in naming this period, our view of it owes much to his. The Mid-life Transition may be rather mild. When it involves considerable turmoil and disruption, we speak of a mid-life crisis.

Having a crisis at this time is not in itself pathological. Indeed, the person who goes through this period with minimal discomfort may be denying that his life must change, for better or worse. He is thus losing an opportunity for personal development. To experience the dangers and the possibilities of this period is, however, to open a Pandora's box of unconscious fantasies and anxieties. Dealing with his mortality means that a man must engage in mourning for the dying self of youth, so that the self can be made more whole. To do this, he must experience some degree of crisis and despair. This process begins in the Mid-life Transition but it extends through middle adulthood and takes a new form in the next era. It is never completed.

It is not at all certain, of course, that development will occur in middle adulthood. For large numbers of men, life in the middle years is a process of gradual or rapid stagnation, of alienation from the world and from the self. Severe decline and constriction are common enough so that they are often seen as part of normal middle age. In many populations, a good deal of decline is *statistically* normal in the sense that it occurs frequently. It is not, however, *developmentally* normal. Drastic decline occurs only when development has been impaired by adverse psychological, social and biological circumstances.

If conditions for development are reasonably favorable, and if impairments from the past are not too severe, middle adulthood can be an era of personal fulfillment and social contribution. This requires, however, that a man come to terms with the developmental tasks of the Mid-life Transition. (These are discussed in Chapters 13 to 16.)

## The Sequence of Generations

The shift from early to middle adulthood, and the character of living in the middle years, also involves a sequence of generations. Generational levels are features of individual and collective experience. They are marked by culturally defined age grades, by the phasing of familial, occupational and other careers, and by the historical rise and fall of successive generations. The meaning of the generations is shaped by biology, history, culture and social institutions. A man works out his own individual meanings as he struggles to make sense of his experience in the changing generations.

The concept of "generation" is of great importance—though still poorly understood and rarely used—in the study of the adult life course. Members of a given generation are at the same age level in contrast to younger and older generations. With the passing years, a young adult has the sense of moving from one generation to the next and of forming new relationships with the other generations in his world.

These age categories are, I believe, widely experienced during adulthood: other persons are roughly the same age as myself (age peers or coevals) if they are not more than 6 or 7 years older or younger. "My generation" thus covers a span of some 12–15 years. Where the age difference is somewhat greater, say 8 to 15 years in either direction, we tend to regard it as marking a half generation; the older one is in the position of an elder sibling, with an implicit claim to greater authority in the relationship. As the age difference increases to 20 and beyond, we are a full generation apart, and the older one seems to be more a parent than a sibling. When the age difference is 40 years, there is a distance of two generations, and the older one assumes the symbolic properties of grandparent.

Relationships between generational levels are important in all societies. While acknowledging the differences between generations, we can also learn to increase the interaction between them. At every age, all of us carry within ourselves aspects of every generation. Coming to know and use these aspects is a relevant task in every era. It is difficult in childhood, and even in early adulthood, to get more in touch with the "older" self and to have much empathy for persons who are more than ten years older than we are. A special task of middle adulthood is to become more aware of both the child and the elder in oneself and in others. Work on this task allows us to transcend in some measure the generational barriers and to relate in a more fully human way to persons of all ages.

A man of 30 to 35 is likely to be regarded as an older sibling (a half generation removed) by persons in their twenties. This may be his own preference, too. He still regards himself as "young" and very much part of the youthful generation. In his twenties he often fears that passing 30 means getting "old." He is relieved to discover in the early thirties that he still has his youthful powers, though he may find himself more naturally inclined to assume a variety of older sibling relationsips to those in full youth.

A new change in generational status ordinarily begins in the late thirties and is well established by the mid-forties. A man of 40 is usually regarded by people in their twenties as a full generation removed, as more established, as part of the establishment, in fact. He tends to be viewed more as a parent than an older sibling—as "Dad" rather than "buddy." This message, conveyed with increasing frequency and force, often comes as a surprise to the man entering mid-life. He may respond at first with feelings of puzzlement, irritation or depression. He wants to say: "This is ridiculous! I haven't really changed—I am still with you, not with them!" The "you" in this statement is the youthful generation in society and the youthful parts of the self. The "them" is less clearly defined and experienced. At a deeper level it refers to the "old," the generation that has lost its place in society and its capacity for youthful pursuits. More immediately, the statement expresses his growing realization that he is leaving the youthful generation and entering that vaguest and most disturbing of generations, "the middle-aged."

So it becomes important to identify the sequence of generations. There is no standard definition of generations in the individual life cycle. One useful starting point, however, is the Spanish philosopher José Ortega y Gasset's conception of generations in the history of society and in the life cycle. He identifies five generations:

1. Childhood: age 0–15
2. Youth: age 15–30
3. Initiation: age 30–45
4. Dominance: age 45–60
5. Old age: age 60+

The Youth and Initiation generations occupy the era of early adulthood. Youth (age 15–30) starts with the Early Adult Transition and extends through the "novice" phase of early adulthood. This generation is engaged in entering the adult world and making an initial place for itself there, as we shall see. The Initiation generation (age 30–45) includes the Mid-life Transition and the ending of early adulthood. It is intermediate between the Youth, who are not yet fully responsible participants in adult society, and the Dominant generation, which has the main burdens and satisfactions of senior leadership and authority.

The Dominant generation (45–60) makes its ideas and aims the governing ones in every sector of society (such as politics, business, religion, art and science) and devotes itself to implementing those aims. The upcoming Initiation generation receives the wisdom of its elders, begins to assert its own authority, and creates moderately or radically new ideas and goals. It will implement its own aims after taking the mantle of power in the forties and fifties.

At any given moment in history, says Ortega, the Initiation and Dominant generations are the two crucial ones, and the relations between them are fateful for the future of society. Even in a period when a youthful "protest" generation plays a dramatic part on the social scene (as it did in the 1960s), the immediate historic result of the protest is carried by the two older generations. The current Youth generation will have a more direct impact when it enters positions of increasing power and enacts its successive generational roles from age 30 to 60.

In his theory of the life cycle as a sequence of eight ego stages, Erik Erikson identifies a series of generations in adulthood. His first four stages cover early and middle childhood. The fifth, *Identity* vs. *Identity Confusion*, occupies adolescence and the Early Adult Transition. The sixth stage, *Intimacy* vs. *Isolation*, arises in the twenties, *Generativity* vs. *Stagnation* at about 40, and *Integrity* vs. *Despair* at 60. Erikson's last four ego stages thus unfold with the successive eras of early, middle and late adulthood.

Erikson's seventh stage, *Generativity* vs. *Stagnation*, is of special relevance here. Its onset coincides with the start of the Mid-life Transition, and it remains a predominant concern through middle adulthood. "Generativity" is often thought to mean the creation of a new generation of offspring. Being a father to young children is, however, a task of early adulthood. As a man passes 40, his task is to assume responsibility for new generations of adults—the generations of Youth and Initiation, in Ortega y Gasset's sense. He must become paternal in new ways to younger adults. He cannot treat them as if they were children under his benign control. He must find new ways to combine authority and mutuality—accepting his own responsibility and offering leadership, yet also taking them seriously as adults, inviting their participation and fostering their growth toward greater independence and authority. While he is becoming a senior member of the adult world, he must relate to persons in their thirties as junior but fully adult members who will soon succeed him, and to persons in their twenties as novices going through their initial formative period within the adult world.

In every stage, developing is a process in which opposite extremes are to some degree reconciled and integrated. Both generativity and its opposite pole, stagnation, are vital to a man's development. To become generative, a man must know how it feels to stagnate—to have the sense of not growing, of being static, stuck, drying up, bogged down in a life full of obligation and devoid of self-fulfillment. He must know the experience of dying, of living in the shadow of death.

The capacity to experience, endure and fight against stagnation is an intrinsic aspect of the struggle toward generativity in middle adulthood. Stagnation is not purely negative nor to be totally avoided. It plays a necessary and continuing part in mid-life development. The recognition of vulnerability in myself becomes a source of wisdom, empathy and compassion for others. I can truly understand the suffering of others only if I can identify with them through an awareness of my own weakness and destructiveness. Without this self-awareness, I am capable only of the kind of sympathy, pity and altruism that reduces the other's hardship but leaves him still a victim.

## Evolving Careers and Enterprises

The nature of each era is reflected in the evolution of a man's careers in work, family and other settings, his involvement in solitary and social enterprises, and his broader life plans and goals. The fabric of his life changes at around 40, with the start of middle adulthood. By 40, he has had a chance to build a life and to realize the fruits of his youthful labors. As he enters the Mid-life Transition, he is likely to review his progress and ask: "What have I done? Where am I now? Of what value is my life to society, to other persons, and especially to myself?" He must deal with the disparity between what he is and what he has dreamed of becoming.

These questions present themselves regardless of the outcome of his youthful efforts. If a man at 40 has failed to realize his most cherished dreams, he must begin to come to terms with the failure and arrive at a new set of choices around which to rebuild his life. If he has succeeded brilliantly, he must consider the meaning and value of his success. He may feel that his present life is satisfying and provides the basis for a good life in the future. Even in this fortunate but rare case, however, a turning point has been reached. His new life may stem directly from that of early adulthood, but it will nonetheless change in certain crucial respects. Often, a man who has accomplished his goals comes to feel trapped: his success is meaningless and he is now caught within a stultifying situation. Many men find their lives relatively satisfactory in some respects and disappointing or destructive in others. Whatever his life condition, every man in the early forties needs to sort things out, come to terms with the limitations and consider the next steps in the journey.

A man at around 40 has the experience of arriving at a culmination, a turning point. A specific event often serves as a marker indicating where he now stands and how far he can go. This *culminating event* represents some form of success or failure, of movement forward or backward on the life path. Several events of great significance may occur in the late thirties and early forties: promotions or failures at work, major difficulties or satisfactions in family life, personal illness, the illness or death of loved ones, recognitions or devaluations in his world. The one that operates as the culminating event has a special meaning: in his mind, it symbolizes the outcome of his youthful strivings; it represents the highest affirmation he will receive in this phase of his life, and he uses it to estimate his chances for realizing his aims in the future.

An example is given by the great philosopher Bertrand Russell (1872–1970). He begins Volume II of his autobiography as follows:

> The period from 1910 to 1914 was a time of transition. My life before 1910 and my life after 1914 were as sharply separated as Faust's life before and after he met Mephistopheles. I underwent a process of rejuvenation, inaugurated by Ottoline Morrell and continued by the War. It may seem curious that the War should rejuvenate anybody, but in fact it shook me out of my prejudices and made me think afresh on a number of fundamental questions. It also provided me with a new kind of activity, for which I did not feel the staleness that beset me whenever I tried to return to mathematical logic. I have therefore got into the habit of thinking of myself as a non-supernatural Faust for whom Mephistopheles was represented by the Great War.

His remarkable transition clearly went on for the first few years of World War I, so that its span is age 38–44. The culminating event of Russell's early adulthood was the completion of the *Principia Mathematica* at 38. This monumental work established his fame and brought him the Nobel Prize some years later. It was the product of a nine-year labor with his colleague and mentor, Alfred North Whitehead, who was eleven years his senior. During this entire period Russell had an emotionally cold, sexually celibate marriage that left him free to center his life around the passionate intellectual work with Whitehead. In the months after the book was completed, he realized that he was a great success as a philosopher and a failure as a human being. His life was devoid of most pleasures and human feelings; in fact, mathematics attracted him precisely "because it is not human."

At 39 Russell met Lady Ottoline Morrell, with whom he had an intense love affair. She opened a new world to him—a world of greater sexual freedom and, what was more important, of deeper feeling, esthetic sensibility and social concern. Three years later, the start of World War I provided new impetus for his growing pacifism and his interest in fame and power. His love for Ottoline Morrell and his hatred for the war played a basic part in this process. However, the change was not merely a reaction to these external events. The events were ingredients in a developmental process—the Mid-life Transition—through which he was rejuvenated and his life drastically altered. By his mid-forties the transformation was taking clear shape: he was struggling desperately to become less of a "logic machine" that gained its satisfaction from producing good ideas and from destroying bad ideas (and their advocates); and he was trying to live a fuller, more diverse life.

The struggle went on for the remainder of his 98-year lifetime. Russell changed his occupation from "pure" academic philosopher to a highly hyphenated hybrid: philosopher-politician-popular-writer-moralist-and-more. By word and example he became an advocate of sexual liberation. He never entirely outgrew some of the early tendencies—the splitting of intellect and emotion, the egocentric willfulness, the uneasy mixture of elitism and humanitarianism, the awareness of destructiveness in others more than in himself. Yet he showed a continuing evolution in his creative products and his personal life. This evolution, and not the attainment of any particular final state, is of the essence of human development.

A culminating event frequently plays an important part in instigating the Mid-life Transition. The same event, however, would have different meaning and consequences if it occurred at another time. A man at around 40 is not simply reacting to an external situation. He is reappraising his life. He makes an effort to reconsider the direction he has taken, the fate of his youthful dreams, the possibilities for a better (or worse) life in the future. He interprets the culminating event and others within this context. Our analysis, too, must take into account his initial adult aspirations and his involvements in work, family, politics, religion, leisure, friendship—all the segments of life that have significance for him, and their evolution over the years.

The idea of a Mid-life Transition was given its first modern formulation by C. G. Jung. He distinguished the first half from the second half of life, and placed the dividing period at around 40. Although he does not identify eras, the distinction between early and middle adulthood is evident in his thought. Jung observed that a resurgence of "individuation" may begin at around 40—the "noon of life" as he called it—and continue through the afternoon and evening of life.

As Jung conceived the term, and as it is commonly used by psychologists, individuation is a developmental process through which a person becomes more uniquely individual. Acquiring a clearer and fuller identity of his own, he becomes better able to utilize his inner resources and pursue his own aims. He generates new levels of awareness, meaning and understanding. Individuation is known to be a crucial aspect of development in childhood and adolescence. Jung was the first to recognize that individuation occurs, and is sorely needed, at mid-life and beyond.

Until the late thirties, says Jung, a man's life is of necessity rather one-sided and imbalanced. Many valuable aspects of the self have been neglected or suppressed. Of the four psychological functions—thought, feeling, intuition, sensation—that all personalities must exercise, only one or two are likely to have developed much. Although no one develops all four functions to an equal degree, it is possible in middle adulthood to strengthen the formerly weaker functions and lead a more balanced life.

Mid-life individuation enables us to reduce the tyranny of both the demands society places on us and the demands of our own repressed (instinctual) unconscious. We can begin giving more attention to what Jung calls the "archetypal unconscious," an inner source of self-definition and satisfaction. Archetypes are, so to speak, a treasury of seeds within the self. Most of them remain dormant in early adulthood. Through the process of individuation in middle adulthood, as a man nourishes the archetypal figures and gives them a more valued place in his life, they will evolve and enrich his life in ways hardly dreamed of in youth. Individuation is not without painful transitions and recurrent setbacks, but it holds the possibility of continuing self-renewal and creative involvement in one's own and others' lives. I shall return to this theme in the chapters on the Mid-life Transition.

## Late Adulthood

As I have mentioned, our study deals with the span of years from the late teens to the late forties. In developmental terms, we cover the period from the Early Adult Transition to full entry into middle adulthood. I am on more speculative ground in discussing the end of this era and the nature of the subsequent eras. Nonetheless, in order to complete this overview of the life cycle, I offer the following provisional view of late adulthood.

In the early sixties middle adulthood normally comes to an end and late adulthood begins. The character of living is altered in fundamental ways as a result of numerous biological, psychological and social changes. This era needs to be recognized as a distinctive and fulfilling season in life. It lasts, we believe, from about 60 to 85.

Middle and late adulthood, like the other eras, are not demarcated by a single universal event. Various marker events, such as illness or retirement, may highlight the end of middle adulthood and shape the transitional process. The Late Adult Transition lasts from about 60 to 65. It exists for the same kinds of reasons as the Mid-life Transition, though the specific content is different.

At around 60, there is again the reality and the experience of bodily decline. As I've mentioned, there is statistically a gradual decline starting at about 30 and continuing its inexorable course over the remaining years. A man does not suddenly become "old" at 50 or 60 or 80. In the fifties and sixties, however, many mental and physical changes intensify his experience of his own aging and mortality. They remind him that he is moving from "middle age" to a later generation for which our culture has only the terrifying term "old age." No one of these changes happens to all men. Yet every man is likely to experience several and to be greatly affected by them.

There is the increasing frequency of death and serious illness among his loved ones, friends and colleagues. Even if he is in good health and physically active, he has many reminders of his decreasing vigor and capacity. If nothing else, there are more frequent aches and pains. But he is also likely to have at least one major illness or impairment—be it heart disease, cancer, endocrine dysfunction, defective vision or hearing, depression or other emotional distress. He will receive medical warnings that he must follow certain precautions or run the risk of more serious, possibly fatal or crippling illness. The internal messages from his own body, too, tell him to make accommodations or major changes in his mode of living. Of course, men at around 60 differ widely. Some face a late adulthood of serious illness or impairment, while others lead active, energetic lives. However, every man in the Late Adult Transition must deal with the decline or loss of some of his middle adult powers.

In addition, there is a culturally defined change of generation ·in the sixties. If the term "middle-aged" is vague and frightening, what about our terminology (and imagery) for the subsequent years? The commonly used words such as "elderly," "golden age" and "senior citizen" acquire negative connotations reflecting our personal and cultural anxiety about aging. To a person in the twenties, it appears that passing 30 is getting "over the hill." In the thirties, turning 40 is a powerful threat. At every point in life, the passing of the next age threshold is anticipated as a total loss of youth, of vitality and of life itself.

What can it mean, then, to approach 60 and to feel that all forms of youth—even those seemingly last vestiges remaining in middle age—are about to disappear, so that only "old age" remains? The developmental task is to overcome the splitting of youth and age, and find in each season an appropriate balance of the two. In late adulthood the archetypal figure of age dominates, but it can take various forms of the creative, wise elder as long as a man retains his connection to youthful vitality, to the forces of growth in self and world. During the Late Adult Transition, a man fears that the youth within him is dying and that only the old man—an empty, dry structure devoid of energy, interests or inner resources—will survive for a brief and foolish old age. His task is to sustain his youthfulness in a new form appropriate to late adulthood. He must terminate and modify the earlier life structure.

Once again the ending of an era brings the culmination of the strivings that were important within it. In late adulthood a man can no longer occupy the center stage of his world. He is called upon, and increasingly calls upon himself, to reduce the heavy responsibilities of middle adulthood and to live in a changed relationship with society and himself. Moving out of center stage can be traumatic. A man receives less recognition and has less authority and power. His generation is no longer the dominant one. As part of the "grandparent" generation within the family, he can at best be modestly helpful to his grown offspring and a source of indulgence and moral support to his grandchildren. But it is time for his offspring, as they approach and enter middle adulthood, to assume the major responsibility and authority in the family. If he does not give up his authority, he is likely to become a tyrannical ruler—despotic, unwise, unloved and unloving—and his adult offspring may become puerile adults unable to love him or themselves.

In his work life, too, there will be serious difficulties if a man holds a position of formal authority beyond age 65 or 70. If he does so, he is "out of phase" with his own generation and he is in conflict with the generation in middle adulthood who need to assume greater responsibilities. It sometimes happens that a man in his seventies or older retains a pre-eminent position in government, religion, business or other institutions. Names come quickly to mind: Mao Tse-tung, Chou En-lai, Churchill, Ben Gurion,

Gandhi, de Gaulle and John D. Rockefeller. But, even when a man has a high level of energy and skill, he is ill-advised to retain power well into late adulthood. He tends to be an isolated leader, in poor touch with his followers and overly idealized or hated by them. The continuity of the generations is disrupted. The generation in middle adulthood suffers from powerlessness and conformism, while the generation in early adulthood suffers from the lack of innovation, moral support and tutelage they need from their immediate seniors.

Some men can retire with dignity and security as early as 50, others as late as 70. Within this range, the age at which a man retires from formal employment, and especially from a position of direct authority over others, should reflect his own needs, capabilities and life circumstances. After "retirement" in this specific sense, he can engage in valued work, but it now stems more from his own creative energies than from external pressure and financial need. Having paid his dues to society, he has earned the right to be and do what is most important to himself. He is beyond the distinction between work and play. He can devote himself in a serious-playful way to the interests that flow most directly from the depths of the self. Using the youthfulness still within him, he can enjoy the creative possibilities of this season. Financial and social security are the external conditions for this freedom of choice. We are just beginning to learn how to create facilitating environments for development in early and middle adulthood so that more men will have the internal resources for meaningful work-play in their later years.

A primary developmental task of late adulthood is to find a new balance of involvement with society and with the self. A man in this era is experiencing more fully the process of dying and he should have the possibility of choosing more freely his mode of living. Without losing his love of humanity, of his own tribe and of his self, he can form a broader perspective and recognize more profoundly our human contradictions, creativity and destructiveness. Greater wisdom regarding the external world can be gained only through a stronger centering in the self. This does not mean that a man becomes more selfish or vain. Just the opposite. It means that he becomes less interested in obtaining the rewards offered by society, and more interested in utilizing his own inner resources. The voices within the self become, as it were, more audible and more worthy of his attention. He continues to be actively engaged with the voices and realities of the external world, but he seeks a new balance in which the self has greater primacy. (For a discussion of this issue in middle adulthood, see Chapter 15.)

If a man creates a new form of self-in-world, late adulthood can be a season as full and rich as the others. Some of the greatest intellectual and artistic works have been produced by men in their sixties, seventies and even eighties. Examples abound: Picasso, Yeats, Verdi, Frank Lloyd Wright, Freud, Jung, Sophocles, Michelangelo, Tolstoy. Countless other men have contributed their wisdom as elders in a variety of counseling, educative and supporting roles in family and community.

In Sigmund Freud's late adulthood, passionate vitality was in constant struggle with morbid pessimism. Ernest Jones, in his great biography, divides Freud's life into three segments that correspond to the eras presented here. Volume 1, *The Formative Years and the Great Discoveries: 1856–1900*, carries Freud through his Mid-life Transition and his shift from neurology to psychoanalysis. Volume 2, *Years of Maturity: 1901–1919*, covers the years of middle adulthood from age 44 to 63. During this time Freud sought to establish psychoanalysis as a clinical specialty, a scientific theory and a movement that would strongly influence the academic and psychiatric world. He was totally engaged in this struggle.

Volume 3, *The Last Phase: 1919–1939*, describes his late adulthood. During this era Freud's creativity took new forms. He turned 60 in 1916, and World War I was an intrinsic part of his Late Adult Transition. Again we see a convergence of societal history and individual development: as Freud was leaving the peak years of his middle adulthood, the Western world was starting its transition out of an age (dominated by the imagery of reason, science, gradual and continuing progress toward the good society) that had existed for over two hundred years. He had to deal with his own decline as well as the decline of the culture to which he was so ambivalently committed. His previous scientific and clinical interests continued, but they were overshadowed by his growing concern with philosophical-religious issues and with the origins and fate of human civilization.

Late adulthood is an era of decline as well as opportunity for development. Erikson's final ego stage occurs in this era. It begins at about 60, and its key polarity is Integrity vs. Despair. As a man enters late adulthood he feels that he has completed the major part—perhaps all—of his life work. His contribution to society and to his own immortality is largely completed. He must arrive at some appraisal of his life. The developmental task is to gain a sense of the integrity of his life—not simply of his virtue or achievement, but of his life as a whole. If he succeeds in this, he can live without bitterness or despair during late adulthood. Finding meaning and value in his life, however imperfect, he can come to terms with death.

To gain a genuine sense of integrity, a man must confront the lack of integrity in his life. During the Late Adult Transition, everyone at times has a sense of utter despair. This always has some basis in actuality as well as in irrational self-accusation. He feels that his life has been of no value to himself or others, that its good qualities are far outweighed by the recurrent destructiveness, stupidity and betrayal of the values he holds most dear. Worst of all, the damage is done: there is no further opportunity to right the balance.

Whatever our values, we cannot live up to them fully. In the end, we must effect a reconciliation with the sources of the flaws and corruptions in our lives. The sources are multiple: they are in ourselves, in our enemies and loved ones, in the imperfect world where each of us tries to build a life of integrity. Making peace with all the enemies in self and world is an important part of this task. To make peace in this inner sense does not keep a man from fighting for his convictions; but it does enable him to fight with less rancor, with fewer illusions and with broader perspective.

## Late Late Adulthood

More people are now living into the eighties and beyond, but very little is known about development in those years. It is obviously an oversimplification to regard the entire span of years after age 60 or 65 as a single era. Given the lack of research data, we can only speculate about this concluding segment of the life cycle. The following hypothesis is offered mainly as a point of departure to stimulate further work on this issue. We suggest that a new era, late late adulthood, begins at around 80.

Most men who survive to enter their eighties are suffering from various infirmities and at least one chronic illness. The process of aging is much more evident than the process of growth. The life structure usually contains only a small territory, a few significant relationships and a preoccupation with immediate bodily needs and personal comforts. Under conditions of severe personal decline and social deprivation, life in this era may lose all meaning. Under more favorable conditions, however, there is psychosocial development as well as senescence.

What does development mean at the very end of the life cycle? It means that a man is coming to terms with the process of dying and preparing for his own death. At the end of all previous eras, part of the developmental work was to start a new era, to create a new basis for living. A man in his eighties knows that his death is imminent. It may come in a few months, or in twenty years. But he lives in its shadow, and at its call. To be able to involve himself in living he must make his peace with dying. If he believes in the immortality of the soul, he must prepare himself for some kind of afterlife. If not, he may yet be concerned with the fate of humanity and with his own immortality as part of human evolution. Development is occurring to the extent that he is giving new meaning to life and death in general, and to his own life and death in particular. If he maintains his vitality, he may continue to be engaged in social life. He may provide others an example of wisdom and personal nobility.

Above all, he is reaching his ultimate involvement with the self. What matters most now is his final sense of what life is about, his "view from the bridge" at the end of the life cycle. In the end he has only the self and the crucial internal figures it has brought into being. He must come finally to terms with the self—knowing it and loving it reasonably well, and being ready to give it up.

# Developmental Periods: The Evolution of the Individual Life Structure

The sequence of eras, described in the previous chapter, forms the gross scaffolding of the life cycle. Within this framework we can pursue the fundamental question of this inquiry: Is there a normal process of individual development in early and middle adulthood? As our study progressed, our findings led us from the idea of a steady, continuous process of development to the idea of qualitatively different *periods* in development. We began to identify a sequence of periods, from the end of adolescence to the middle forties, through which all of our subjects passed.

Some clues as to the nature of the periods have been noted in the discussion of the eras. As I have said, the shift from one era to the next is a major developmental change. It does not occur easily or quickly. Rather, there is a cross-era transition, a developmental period that normally lasts four or five years. In the Early Adult Transition (age 17 to 22) we conclude pre-adulthood and begin our entry into early adulthood. The Midlife Transition (age 40 to 45) enables a man to terminate early adulthood and to initiate middle adulthood. The discovery of these periods led us to ask whether there are not additional developmental periods in each era.

We found too that the eras are distinguished by changes in the overall character of living. The eras do not necessarily show themselves when one focuses on a single aspect of living, as most investigators have. To grasp the nature of adult development, we had to begin with the individual life in its patterning at a given time, and trace its evolution over the years. When we looked at each man's life from this vantage point, we first observed in broad outline the eras and cross-era transitions. Then, examining the life course more closely, we found within each era a series of developmental periods, similar in their basic nature to the cross-era transitions.

Many concepts and techniques are available for studying specific aspects of living. But how do we study the character of a man's life and its evolution over a span of years? Many will say that this is too difficult a task, that it includes "too many variables" and takes us beyond the limits of a single discipline. My answer: yes, the study of an individual life is beyond the scope of any single discipline, and it is very difficult to do well—but it can be done! In the present study we have, I believe, made a significant start, though it is only a start and there is a great deal left to do.

The concept we have created for this purpose—and it is the pivotal concept in our entire work—is the individual life structure. By "life structure" we mean the underlying pattern or design of a person's life at a given time. Here we are studying the lives of men. A man's life has many components: his occupation, his love relationships, his marriage and family, his relation to himself, his use of solitude, his roles in various social contexts—all the relationships with individuals, groups and institutions that have significance for him. His personality influences and is influenced by his involvement in each of them. We must start, however, with the overall life structure. Once the character of the individual's life has been identified, we can study in more detail the changes occurring in personality, in the marital and occupational careers, and in other components of life.

We have found that, over the years, the life structure evolves through a standard sequence of periods. The developmental periods I shall soon describe are thus periods in the evolution of the life structure. I want to emphasize and re-emphasize this point, as it is frequently misunderstood. I am *not* talking about stages in ego development or occupational development or development in any single aspect of living. I am talking about *periods in the evolution of the individual life structure.* The periods, and the eras of which they are a part, constitute a basic source of order in the life cycle. The order exists at an underlying level. At the more immediate day-to-day level of concrete action, events and experience, our lives are often rapidly changing and fragmented.

We are now prepared to maintain that everyone lives through the same developmental periods in adulthood, just as in childhood, though people go through them in radically different ways. Each individual life has its own unique character. A valid theory of development is not a mold or blueprint specifying a single, "normal" course that everyone must follow. Its function, instead, is to indicate the developmental tasks that everyone must work on in successive periods, and the infinitely varied forms that such work can take in different individuals living under different conditions. Such a theory increases our sense of human potentialities and of the variousness of individual lives; it does not impose a template for conformity.

# The Individual Life Structure

The concept of life structure—the basic pattern or design of a person's life at a given time—gives us a way of looking at the engagement of the individual in society. It requires us to consider both self and world, and the relationships between them. Our study has shown that the life structure goes through a process of development in adulthood. It is the primary focus of our analysis. When I speak of adult development, I mean the evolution of the life structure during the adult years.

The concept of life structure provides a tool for analyzing what is sometimes called "the fabric of one's life." Through it we may examine the interrelations of self and world—to see how the self is in the world, and how the world is in the self. When an external event has a decisive impact, we consider how processes in the self may have helped to bring it about and to mediate its effects. When an inner conflict leads to dramatic action, we consider how external influences may have touched off the conflict and decided how it would be played out. We try to determine how various aspects of self and world influence the formation of a life structure and shape its change over time.

The life structure may be considered in terms of three perspectives:

a. The individual's *sociocultural world* as it impinges upon him has meaning and consequences for him. To understand a man's life, therefore, we must take into account the society in which he lives. We must place him within various social contexts—class, religion, ethnicity, family, political system, occupational structure—and understand their relevance for him. His life is modified by changes in the surrounding culture, in social movements and institutions, in the economy and the political climate. He is affected by massive events such as war and depression, and by more particular conditions in his own work, family and community life.

b. Some *aspects of his self* are lived out; other aspects are inhibited or neglected. The self includes a complex patterning of wishes, conflicts, anxieties and ways of resolving or controlling them. It includes fantasies, moral values and ideals, talents and skills, character traits, modes of feeling, thought and action. Part of the self is conscious; much is unconscious; and we must consider both parts. Important aspects of the self, initially formed in the pre-adult era, continue to influence a man's life in adulthood. We have to see how the person draws upon the self, or ignores it, in his everyday life. The self is an intrinsic element of the life structure and not a separate entity.

c. We need to examine the man's *participation in the world*. The external world provides a landscape, a cast of characters, a variety of resources and constraints out of which a man fashions his own life. A man selectively uses and is used by his world, through his evolving relationships and roles as citizen, lover, worker, boss, friend, husband, father, member of diverse groups and enterprises. Participation involves transactions between self and world. The transactions take obvious forms, but subtle meanings and feelings play an important part in them.

When studying the evolution of life structure, we are being biographical in the most fundamental sense: we start with the concrete life course as it evolves over time. The task of the biographer is to present a full picture of his subject's life. He tries to arrive at an interpretive construction that is factually accurate and that "makes sense" of the nature and sequence of this life. He places his subject in his social and historical context, and at the same time probes into the self, attempting to grasp the most private aspirations, qualities of character, torments and fulfillments. He tries to show how the person is both a reflection of his society and a creative agent making his unique contribution, large or small, to the continuity and change of his world. The term "biography" thus refers to a complex enterprise including a task, a method of work, a theoretical conception and a product. The biographer is, as it were, a hybrid: he is a historian-psychologist-sociologist-man-of-letters. While bringing together various theoretical approaches and sources of information, he must maintain his fidelity to the unique, idiosyncratic life of his subject. We are engaged here in one form of biography.

How shall we go about describing and analyzing the life structure? The most useful starting point, I believe, is to consider the *choices* a person makes and how he deals with their consequences. The important choices in adult life have to do with work, family, friendships and love relationships of various kinds, where to live, leisure, involvement in religious, political and community life, immediate and long-term goals.

Making a significant life choice is a complex matter. Choosing to enter an occupation is not like choosing a dessert or a brand of soap (though many models of decision-making treat them as if they were the same). The decision to marry grows out of a premarital relationship and is the starting point for an evolving marital relationship. A man's self and world are heavily involved in the character of the initial relationship, in the decision to marry, and in the further vicissitudes of the marriage.

So in describing the important choices in a man's life at a given time it is not enough to deal with the "choice" in isolation. It is not enough, in other words, simply to say that he is married to a particular woman, that he is a member of occupation X and employed at work place Y, or that he belongs to religion A, political party B and fraternal order C. It is necessary to go beyond a mere listing of items. We have to consider the meanings and functions of each choice within the individual life structure. As a component of the life structure, every choice is saturated by both self and world. To choose something means to have a *relationship* with it. The relationship becomes a vehicle for living out certain aspects of the self and for engaging in certain modes of participation in the world.

The primary components of the life structure are choices, in the sense I have just described. The components are not features of the self, such as motives and abilities, nor are they features of the world, such as institutions, groups and objects. In characterizing each choice, however, it is necessary to understand the nature of the man's relationship with it, to place it within the life structure, and to see how it is connected to both self and world.

The components of the life structure are not a random set of items, like pebbles washed up at the seashore. Rather, like threads in a tapestry, they are woven into an encompassing design. Recurring themes in various sectors help to unify the overall pattern of the tapestry. Lives differ widely in the nature and patterning of the components.

One or two components (rarely as many as three) have a central place in the structure. Others, though important, are more peripheral, and still others are quite marginal or detached from the center. The central components have the greatest significance for the self and for the evolving life course. They receive the largest share of one's time and energy, and they strongly influence the choices made in other aspects of life. The peripheral components are easier to detach and change; they involve less investment of the self and are less crucial to the fabric of one's life.

The life structure may change in various ways. A component may shift from center to periphery or vice versa, as when a man who has been totally committed to work starts detaching himself from it and involves himself more in family life. A formerly important component may be eliminated altogether. The character of a man's relationships within a given component may change moderately or drastically. For example, a man may remain in the existing marriage but enrich and deepen the marital relationship; he may modify the nature and meaning of his work, without changing occupations; or he may make a new choice of wife or occupation that leads to a qualitative change in the character of his life.

The components most likely to be central in a man's life are occupation, marriage-family, friendship and peer relationships, ethnicity and religion. Leisure may also have a central place, when it serves important functions for the self and is more than a casual activity. Playing sports after work, or watching sports on TV, is a serious matter for many men.

We found that occupation and marriage-family are usually the most central components, though there are significant variations in their relative weight and in the importance of other components. Work and family are universal features of human life. Let's consider these components more closely.

• OCCUPATION. In all societies, work is a major part of individual life and of the social structure. Every man is required to contribute his labor in some form of work deemed useful for the tribe. A man's occupation is one of the primary factors determining his income, his prestige and his place in society. Universally, work is organized into a number of socially defined occupations that are taught, accorded differential value and reward, and integrated into simple or complex economic structures.

Over a span of years, a man chooses and forms an occupation. All men make one or more changes, some of them quite marked, within the original occupation or from one occupation to another. A man's occupation places him within a particular socioeconomic level and work world. It exerts a powerful influence upon the options available to him, the choices he makes among them, and his possibilities for advancement and satisfaction. His work world also influences the choices he makes in other spheres of life.

Occupation has important sources within the self and important consequences for the self. It is often the primary medium in which a young man's dreams for the future are defined, and the vehicle he uses to pursue those dreams. At best, his occupation permits the fulfillment of basic values and life goals. At worst, a man's work life over the years is oppressive and corrupting, and contributes to a growing alienation from self, work and society. In studying a man's life, we need to understand the meaning of work and the multiple ways in which it may serve to fulfill, to barely sustain or to destroy the self.

• MARRIAGE AND FAMILY. In all societies, a man is expected to marry and to take certain responsibilities within a familial system. There is, of course, great variation in the culturally defined roles of husband and father and in the structure of the family. A man usually wants to marry and to make his family a central component in his life structure.

Marriage ordinarily creates a new home base for the young man. It is a center on which he establishes his place in the community and his changing relationships with friends, parents and extended family. It provides a vehicle for traveling a particular path in early adulthood. His marital choice reflects some of his emerging values but violates others. It links him to certain social contexts while separating him from others.

If he marries "the girl next door," the marriage may make for stability and continuity in his life. In this case, he is more likely to live in the same neighborhood, to have an occupation and life style consistent with parental values, and to integrate his life within the ethnic and religious patterns of his forebears. On the other hand, marriage to a woman of different background and aspirations is likely to be part of a major shift in his life. Many of the meanings and functions of a marriage are implicit or even unconscious: they play themselves out over time in changing and often unanticipated ways.

A man's family life usually has a major effect on his ongoing life as a whole. His immediate family connects him to various other components of life, such as his original family, ethnicity and occupation. It places him within a larger world and provides a vehicle that is well designed for certain life journeys and poorly designed for others. It enables him to live out certain parts of the self and to leave others dormant or repressed.

The various professions and scientific disciplines often focus on one component of life to the relative exclusion of the others. For example, a good deal of research and counseling has been devoted to occupational careers. Investigators acknowledge that a man's work career is influenced by other factors, such as personality, family life and ethnic context. In general, however, they tend to ignore the non-occupational components or to consider them in only a cursory fashion. They have had no theoretical framework within which to interrelate the various components. Likewise, a good deal of research and counseling has been devoted to marriage and family. However, family and occupation have rarely been brought together in our understanding of adult life.

In the fields of personality research and clinical practice, the primary focus is usually on the self, to the neglect of the actualities of work, marriage, ethnicity and class in a man's life. Personality theory and psychotherapy will be strengthened when they take more account of the adult self as it is engaged with social institutions and with the fragmentation, destructiveness and creative possibilities which are the stuff of adult life in society.

# The Self Is in the World, The World Is in the Self

In the scientific study of humanity, there has been a powerful tendency in each discipline to focus on a few aspects of human life and to neglect the others. One of the primary divisions is that between individual and society. Psychology and psychiatry focus chiefly upon the individual. Social sciences, such as sociology, social anthropology and political science, focus primarily upon society and collective life. They tend to ignore the individual altogether or to regard him as a simple product of the shaping forces in society. Although the study of the individual life cycle is generally considered an appropriate field of inquiry in the social sciences, nevertheless it remains virtually untouched.

It is necessary to take a broader approach. We need to encompass both self and society, without making one primary and the other secondary or derivative. We need to take seriously the idea of adult development—that there is some underlying order in the life cycle—and the idea of adult socialization—that the self exists within a world and its evolution is intimately bound together with that world. The concept of life structure provides a starting point for this approach.

The individual life structure is a patterning of self and world. However, self and world are not two separate entities. They are not like billiard balls that, colliding, affect each other's course but not each other's nature. An essential feature of human life is the *interpenetration* of self and world. Each is inside the other. Our thinking about one must take account of the other.

The interpenetration of self and world has been beautifully portrayed by Arthur Miller in his plays and essays. His social-psychological view of drama parallels closely our view of adult development:

> . . . society is inside of man and man is inside society, and you cannot even create a truthfully drawn psychological entity on the stage until you understand his social relations and their power to make him what he is and to prevent him from being what he is not. The fish is in the water and the water is in the fish.

Miller criticizes the "social realism" that prevailed in the American theater during the 1930s. Plays of this period depict the conflicts and contradictions in society but their characters are lacking in individuality. He also criticizes many plays of the 1950s, which depict the subjective experience of adolescents but have little to say about the adult self dealing with the responsibilities and potentialities of living in a complex society. Miller writes:

> In my opinion, if our stage does not come to pierce through affects to an evaluation of the world it will contract to a lesser psychiatry and an inexpert one at that. We shall be confined to writing an "Oedipus" without the pestilence, an "Oedipus" whose catastrophe is private and unrelated to the survival of his people, an "Oedipus" who cannot tear out his eyes because there will be no standard by which he can judge himself; an "Oedipus," in a word, who on learning of his incestuous marriage, instead of

tearing out his eyes, will merely wipe away his tears thus to declare his loneliness.

If we are to have a more truly adult theater, says Miller—and a more adequate basis for studying adult development, say I—we must recognize this interpenetration of self and world. The self is an intrinsic part of the external world. We cannot adequately grasp the nature of a man's world without seeing how it is colored and shaped by his self and the selves of others. And the external world is an intrinsic part of the self. We cannot grasp the full nature of the self without seeing how diverse aspects of the world are reflected and contained within it.

The structure of society is reflected in the self and the life structure. Every man's life gives evidence of his society's wisdom and integration as well as its conflicts, oppression and destructiveness. Society makes available to each of its members a limited range of individuals, groups, material resources, occupations and possibilities for social involvement and self-fulfillment. It influences his choices among these options, making some more attractive or more highly rewarded than others. Through its own structure, society brings about a patterning in the choices a man makes. A particular choice moves a man into a given world, or strengthens his position in that world; and at the same time it moves him away from other worlds he has been considering.

The external world also contributes to the substance of a man's changing attachments, aspirations, anxieties, identifications, creative productions. Every organization and social world has a culture, social structure and material conditions which affect the character of the relationships among the members. A man's particular external world presents significant meanings, feelings, identities and myths which he selectively uses and internalizes. It provides invitations to heroism, martyrdom, empty conformity, bitter or zestful struggle. It encourages the development of certain parts of the self, while hindering the development of others.

Although every man's life structure reflects the structure of society, it is also in some respects unique—a reflection of his specific self and circumstances. Out of the possibilities and constraints given in his environment, he makes his own choices and builds his own world. The self is a crucial factor in the formation and transformation of each individual's world.

To be truly engaged with his world, a man must invest important parts of his self in it and, equally, he must take the world into his self and be enriched, depleted and corrupted by it. In countless ways he puts himself into the world and takes the world into himself. Adult development is the story of the evolving process of mutual interpenetration. If we are to understand it we must learn how, in Miller's vivid imagery, the fish is in the water and the water is in the fish.

# Tasks and Periods
# in the Evolution of the Life Structure

When we used the concept of life structure in writing the biographies of our 40 men, we made a remarkable discovery: *the life structure evolves through a relatively orderly sequence during the adult years.* The essential character of the sequence is the same for *all* the men in our study and for the other men whose biographies we examined. It consists of a series of alternating stable (structure-building) periods and transitional (structure-changing) periods. These periods shape the course of adult psychosocial development.

The primary task of every stable period is to build a life structure: a man must make certain key choices, form a structure around them, and pursue his goals and values within this structure. To say that a period is stable in this sense is not necessarily to say that it is tranquil and without difficulty. The task of making major life choices and building a structure is often stressful indeed, and may involve many kinds of change.

Each stable period has additional tasks of its own which reflect its place in the life cycle and distinguish it from the other stable periods. No two periods in the life cycle are identical. They may have some common elements but they also differ in essential ways. Old age is not "merely" a second childhood, though it resembles childhood in certain aspects, and the Mid-life Transition is not "merely" a second adolescence, though developmental issues of adolescence (and other periods) are reactivated within it. A stable period ordinarily lasts six or seven years, ten at the most. For various reasons, internal and external, the life structure that has formed the basis for stability comes into question and must be modified.

A transitional period, as we have seen, terminates the existing life structure and creates the possibility for a new one. The primary tasks of every transitional period are to question and reappraise the existing structure, to explore various possibilities for change in self and world, and to move toward commitment to the crucial choices that form the basis for a new life structure in the ensuing stable period. Each transitional period has other, distinctive tasks reflecting its place in the life cycle. These periods ordinarily last four to five years.

Since the transitional periods play such a vital part in development, let me articulate their nature more fully. A transition is a bridge, or a boundary zone, between two states of greater stability. It involves a process of change, a shift from one structure to another.

The Mid-life Transition, for example, is a boundary zone between two great eras in the life cycle. As it starts, the person is primarily in the era of early adulthood. When it ends, middle adulthood is fully under way. During the Mid-life Transition itself, however, the person is truly "on the boundary": he is both in early adulthood and in middle adulthood. This transition separates the two eras, enabling one to end so that the next can begin. It serves also to connect them, bringing about interchange so that the past can be drawn upon and used selectively in building for the future. It is an intrinsic part of both eras and can be understood only from the conjoint perspective of both. Similarly, the Age Thirty Transition is a means of terminating the first adult life structure and of initiating a new structure for completing early adulthood, as we shall see.

A termination is an ending, a process of separation or loss. In some cases the separation is complete: I terminate a casual relationship, job, membership in a group or community, ownership of a house or book—and they pass entirely out of my life. I have no further contact with them, I rarely think about them, and only the most limited residue of their existence remains within me.

When the relationship with an object (person, group, setting, thing, symbol) has great meaning for me, however, termination does not mean a complete ending of the relationship. The relationship continues but in a changed and changing form. The most clear-cut and dramatic separations of this kind involve total loss of a significant object: someone I love dies; a quarrel leads to permanent parting from a friend or mentor; I move to a new locale and leave a world behind. I experience a profound loss and must come to terms with painful feelings of abandonment, grief and rage. Over time the lost object is more fully internalized and the relationship continues to evolve within my self and my life. Important aspects of the relationship are ended, but other aspects continue and new ones are created. I have lost the external object but I maintain the relationship with the now-internal object.

The separation is often partial rather than total. I continue to have some contact with the person or group, but a major change occurs in the nature of the relationship: a romantic love relationship becomes a modest friendship; an intense mentoring relationship becomes a more casual association in work; a marriage ends in divorce and the relationship goes on in new forms, such as friendly co-parenting or continuing hostility and recrimination. The relationship comes to a turning point and must be modified or transformed if it is to continue. A transitional period is required to terminate the past and start the future.

A good example is the young adult in the process of separating from parents. His developmental task is not to end the relationship altogether. Rather, he has to reject certain aspects (for instance, those in which he is the submissive or defiant child relating to all-controlling parents), to sustain other aspects, and to build in new qualities such as mutual respect between distinctive individuals who have separate as well as shared interests. Neither the young adult nor his parents find this an easy task.

As students of childhood development have shown, the processes of *separation* and *individuation* are closely linked. Drastic change and loss may be damaging, but under reasonably supportive conditions the process of separation leads to enrichment, differentiation and development of the self. This is as true of adulthood as of childhood.

The task of a developmental transition is to terminate a time in one's life: to accept the losses the termination entails; to review and evaluate the past; to decide which aspects of the past to keep and which to reject; and to consider one's wishes and possibilities for the future. One is suspended between past and future, and struggling to overcome the gap that separates them. Much from the past must be given up—separated from, cut out of one's life, rejected in anger, renounced in sadness or grief. And there is much that can be used as a basis for the future. Changes must be attempted in both self and world.

These tasks produce features common to all transitions. They are frequently times of crisis—of profound inner conflict, of feeling "in a state of suspended animation" as one of our men put it. After hearing a talk on the Mid-life Transition, a young man asked me, "How is it that I, at age 31, am having many of the experiences you ascribe to age 41—am I in a precocious Mid-life Transition?" The answer is, of course, no: he is going through a different transition appropriate to his place in the life cycle, but it is one that has many qualities in common with the other transitions such as those at mid-life and at puberty.

Along with the common features, certain developmental tasks and life issues are specific to each period and give it its distinctive character. The Age Thirty Transition, for example, is strongly colored by the imminence of Settling Down and the need to form a life structure through which one's youthful dreams and values can be realized. The Mid-life Transition brings new concerns with the loss of youth, the assumption of a more senior position in one's world, and the reworking of inner polarities. Some preoccupation with death—fearing it, being drawn to it, seeking to transcend it—is not uncommon in all transitions, since the process of termination-initiation evokes the imagery of death and rebirth. But the meanings of death and the kinds of developmental work to be done differ greatly from one transition to another.

As a transition comes to an end, it is time to make crucial choices, to give these choices meaning and commitment, and to start building a life structure around them. The choices mark the beginning of the next period. They are, in a sense, the major product of the transition. When all the efforts of the past several years are done—all the struggles to improve one's work or marriage, to explore alternative possibilities of living, to come more to terms with the self—a man must make his choices and place his bets. He must decide, "This I will settle for," and start creating a life structure that will serve as a vehicle for the next step in the journey.

A man may choose to reaffirm the commitment to an existing part of his life. He decides to remain in the marriage with the intention of making it work better. He gives up a serious extramarital relationship—or he embarks upon such a relationship in the hope that this will enrich his life while allowing the marriage and family to continue. Likewise, he may choose to remain in his present job rather than make a more drastic change entailing greater risks and discontinuity. If this is an active reaffirmation, he will make significant improvements in the character of the work even if the job title remains the same.

The decision to stay put is not always based on a reaffirmed commitment. It may stem more from resignation, inertia, passive acquiescence or controlled despair—a self-restriction in the context of severe external constraints. This kind of surface stability marks the beginning of a long-term decline unless new factors intervene (perhaps in the next transitional period) and enable him to form a more satisfactory life structure.

The choices made in a transitional period usually lead to moderate or drastic change in life structure. A man may divorce, remarry, change his job or occupation, make a geographical move, start new avocational pursuits that modify and enrich his life. A choice is often marked by an event that takes only a few days or weeks. The event is, however, embedded within a process of change that ordinarily extends over a span of several years. Thus, a divorce or a job change is the most conspicuous event within a complex transition that contains many other changes. In making the transition a man must de-structure his existing life pattern, work on a number of basic developmental tasks, and restructure a new life.

A transitional period comes to an end not when a particular event occurs or when a sequence is completed in one aspect of life. It ends when the tasks of questioning and exploring have lost their urgency, when a man makes his crucial commitments and is ready to start on the tasks of building, living within and enhancing a new life structure.

We did not begin this study with preformed hypotheses about developmental periods unfolding in an age-linked sequence. We were as surprised as everyone else by these discoveries. The findings with regard to age may be summarized briefly as follows. There is a single, most frequent age at which each period begins. There is a range of variation, usually about two years above and below the average. Thus, the Age Thirty Transition most often starts at age 28, the range being 26 to 29. The next period, Settling Down, usually starts at 33—and never before 30 or after 34, in our sample. The four occupational groups in our study showed only minor differences in the age at which every period began and ended. More specific data on age will be presented in the chapters on the successive periods.

The *developmental tasks* are crucial to the evolution of the periods. The specific character of a period derives from the nature of its tasks. A period begins when its major tasks become predominant in a man's life. A period ends when its tasks lose their primacy and new tasks emerge to initiate a new period. The orderly progression of periods stems from the recurrent change in tasks. The most fundamental tasks of a stable period are to make firm choices, rebuild the life structure and enhance one's life within it. Those of a transitional period are to question and reappraise the existing structure, to search for new possibilities in self and world, and to modify the present structure enough so that a new one can be formed.

Implicit in the concept of task is the idea that it may be carried out well or poorly. When a task is rather specific and concrete, it is usually not difficult to evaluate how well it has been performed. Evaluation of work on the developmental tasks is much more difficult. In some cases it seems clear that the tasks of a period have been met very poorly or very well, but in most cases the picture is mixed. The assessment cannot be based on a few criteria. It is important to understand the developmental tasks and processes in their full complexity, and to avoid making premature and oversimplified evaluations as to how well the tasks have been handled.

We have made a small start, however, toward dealing with the problem of evaluation. Since the developmental tasks have so much to do with building, modifying and rebuilding the life structure, it becomes important to define and evaluate the "satisfactoriness" of a structure. During a stable period, a man tries to build a structure that will in some sense be satisfactory for him. During a transitional period, he tries to reappraise (evaluate) the current structure and to move toward a new and more satisfactory one. What meanings does "satisfactory" have for him, and how shall we use this term for our own purposes?

Broadly speaking, a life structure is satisfactory to the extent that it is *viable in society* and *suitable for the self*. The perspectives of both society and self are needed here. A structure is viable to the extent that it works in the world. Within it, a man is able to adapt, to maintain his various roles and to receive sufficient rewards. A structure may be externally viable and yet not internally suitable if it does not allow him to live out crucially important aspects of his self. On the other hand, a structure may be suitable in terms of his inner dreams and values, and yet not be workable in the world. Often, a man's life structure is "fairly satisfactory": it works pretty well in the world, though it does not bring all the rewards the man had hoped for, and is moderately suitable for the self, though it does not permit him to live out some important wishes and values.

Every life structure provides diverse gains and costs for the man himself, for others and for society. The elements that constitute its great strengths are also sources of weakness and take their toll. A structure is never all of a piece. It contains some mixture of order and disorder, unity and diversity, integration and fragmentation. It is always flawed in some respects. It contains contradictions and gaps which can be modified only by basic changes in the structure itself. The contradictions often have painful consequences, but they may also enrich the process of living and provide an intrinsic basis for change and development.

No matter how satisfactory a structure is, in time its utility declines and its flaws generate conflict that leads to modification or transformation of the structure. It is as Marx said: every system contains within itself the seeds of its own destruction. The once-stable structure passes into a new transitional period. The seasons change. Developmental tasks are undertaken anew, and the lessons of growth are gathered and stockpiled against the new period coming. The pattern of adult development continues.

A period is defined in terms of its developmental tasks. It is *not* defined in terms of concrete events such as marriage or retirement. Many investigators have searched for significant events that might serve as signposts for developmental periods. This search has not been fruitful in generating a developmental theory, though it has contributed to the study of problems in adult life. It is more fruitful, I believe, to conceive of development in terms of tasks and periods in the evolution of life structure. We can then use this developmental perspective in understanding the significance of particular events.

Our lives are punctuated by events such as marriage, divorce, illness, the birth or death of loved ones, unexpected trauma or good fortune, advancement or failure in work, retirement, war, flourishing times and "rock bottom" times. We use the term *marker event* to identify an occasion of this kind, which has a notable impact upon a person's life. Marker events are usually considered in terms of the *adaptation* they require. They change a man's life situation and he must cope with them in some way. The further changes in his relationships, roles and personality are then understood as part of his adaptation to the new situation.

Yet, we also need to regard marker events from the viewpoint of *development*. They can occur at various ages and do not in themselves cause the start or end of a period. However, the age at which an event occurs is important. The significance of a marker event for an individual depends partly upon its place in the sequence of developmental periods.

Getting married, for example, is a marker event in a man's life, whatever his age and circumstances. It makes a great difference, however, just where in the evolution of the periods it occurs. If a man marries at the start of the Early Adult Transition, say at age 18 or 19, the decision to marry and the character of the marital relationship will be highly colored by his current developmental tasks. He is engaged in the process of separating from parents and forming an initial adult identity. He wants to be more independent and "adult," but he also feels unprepared for adult life and tends to seek a dependent relationship with a protective-caring-controlling figure other than a parent. The hazard of marrying at this point in his development is that the marital relationship may perpetuate the struggles with his parents. The result, often, is that he retains the childish qualities he had consciously rejected and fails to attain a more genuinely adult identity. There are similar hazards for the woman at this time, and each partner is implicated in the other's developmental struggles.

Likewise, a marital relationship that takes shape early in the period of Entering the Adult World, say at age 23 or 24, will reflect the developmental tasks of that time: to explore the possibilities of the adult world and to form a provisional life structure. The choice of a mate influences, and is influenced by, the overall character of that structure. One man tries to build a structure in which he can pursue his special dream or vision; he marries a woman who shares that dream and wants to join him on the journey toward its realization. Another man betrays his dream: seeking to build a structure that is more acceptable to parents or is "safer" in some inner sense, he marries a woman who will value and support this conservatism. At some later time he may blame her, with much or little justification, for her part in leading him away from his dream. The meaning and further vicissitudes of the marital relationship will be markedly different in the two cases. The variations are endless.

If the marriage occurs at the start of a period, when the developmental process is just getting under way, the early character of the marital relationship will be intimately bound up with the struggles of entering a new period. In contrast, a marriage occurring toward the end of a period is likely to be a culmination or outcome of the developmental efforts of that period and an indication that a new period is emerging.

In many cases, the marker event is not the result of a man's voluntary effort or choice, but is a result of circumstances beyond his control (such as war, economic depression and the illness or death of others). His current developmental period does not influence the timing of this event, but it does shape his adaptation to it and the influence it has on his subsequent life.

# Preview of the Periods in Adult Development

The sequence of periods begins with the Early Adult Transition (age 17 to 22), which links adolescence and early adulthood. It is followed by a structure-building period, Entering the Adult World, which lasts from about 22 to 28; the primary task of this period is to create a first adult life structure. This structure is modified in the Age Thirty Transition. During the Settling Down period (33 to 40), a man builds a second structure and reaches the culmination of early adulthood. The Mid-life Transition, from about 40 to 45, links early and middle adulthood. It is followed by a more stable period, during the middle and late forties, when a man builds a first life structure for middle adulthood.

The sequence of periods is pictured on page 57. In later chapters each period will be explored in detail. Here we shall briefly preview the periods and give an initial picture of their tasks and developmental sequence.

## The Early Adult Transition: Moving from Pre- to Early Adulthood

The Early Adult Transition begins at age 17 and ends at 22, give or take two years. Its twin tasks are to terminate pre-adulthood and to begin early adulthood. The first task is to start moving out of the pre-adult world: to question the nature of that world and one's place in it; to modify or terminate existing relationships with important persons, groups and institutions; to reappraise and modify the self that formed in it. Various kinds of separation, ending and transformation must be made as one completes an entire season of life.

The second task is to make a preliminary step into the adult world: to explore its possibilities, to imagine oneself as a participant in it, to consolidate an initial adult identity, to make and test some preliminary

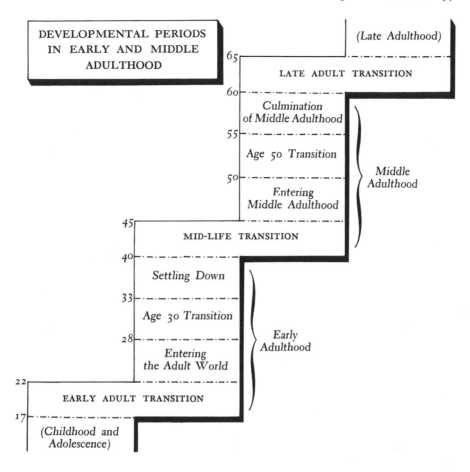

DEVELOPMENTAL PERIODS
IN EARLY AND MIDDLE
ADULTHOOD

(Late Adulthood)

65

LATE ADULT TRANSITION

60

Culmination
of Middle Adulthood

55

Age 50 Transition

50

Entering
Middle Adulthood

Middle
Adulthood

45

MID-LIFE TRANSITION

40

Settling Down

33

Age 30 Transition

28

Entering
the Adult World

Early
Adulthood

22

EARLY ADULT TRANSITION

17

(Childhood and
Adolescence)

choices for adult living. In this period a young man is on the boundary between adolescence and adulthood. The transition ends when he gets beyond the boundary and begins to create a life within the adult world.

## The First Adult Life Structure: Entering the Adult World

This period extends from about 22 to 28. Its chief task is to fashion a provisional structure that provides a workable link between the valued self and the adult society. A young man must shift the center of gravity of his life; no longer a child in his family of origin, he must become a novice adult with a home base of his own. He makes and tests a variety of initial choices regarding occupation, love relationships (usually including marriage and family), peer relationships, values and life style.

The young man has two primary yet antithetical tasks: (a) He needs to *explore* the possibilities for adult living: to keep his options open, avoid strong commitments and maximize the alternatives. This task is reflected in a sense of adventure and wonderment, a wish to seek out all the treasures of the new world he is entering. (b) The contrasting task is to *create a stable life structure*: become more responsible and "make something of my life." Each task has sources and supports in the external world and in the self.

Finding a balance between these tasks is not an easy matter. If the first predominates, life has an extremely transient, rootless quality. If the second predominates, there is the danger of committing oneself prematurely to a structure, without sufficient exploration of alternatives. It is an exciting yet often confusing and painful process to explore the new adult world and, at the same time, to try building a stable life within it. There is usually moderate or great discontinuity between the pre-adult world in which a man grew up and the adult world in which he forms his first life structure.

## The Age Thirty Transition: Changing the First Life Structure

This transition, which extends from roughly 28 to 33, provides an opportunity to work on the flaws and limitations of the first adult life structure, and to create the basis for a more satisfactory structure with which to complete the era of early adulthood. At about 28 the provisional quality of the twenties is ending and life is becoming more serious, more "for real." A voice within the self says: "If I am to change my life—if there are things in it I want to modify or exclude, or things missing I want to add—I must now make a start, for soon it will be too late."

Men differ in the kinds of changes they make, but the life structure is always different at the end of the Age Thirty Transition than it was at the beginning. Some men have a rather smooth transition, without overt disruption or sense of crisis. They modify their lives in certain respects, but they build directly upon the past and do not make fundamental changes. It is a time of reform, not revolution.

But for most men, our study reveals, this transition takes a more stressful form, the *age thirty crisis*. A developmental crisis occurs when a man has great difficulty with the developmental tasks of a period; he finds his present life structure intolerable, yet seems unable to form a better one. In a severe crisis he experiences a threat to life itself, the danger of chaos and dissolution, the loss of hope for the future. A moderate or severe crisis is very common during this period.

These first three periods—the Early Adult Transition, Entering the

Adult World and the Age Thirty Transition—generally last about fifteen years, from age 17 or 18 until 32 or 33. Together, they constitute the preparatory, "novice" phase of early adulthood.

The shift from the end of the Age Thirty Transition to the start of the next period is one of the crucial steps in adult development. At this time a man may make important new choices, or he may reaffirm old choices. If these choices are congruent with his dreams, talents and external possibilities, they provide the basis for a relatively satisfactory life structure. If the choices are poorly made and the new structure seriously flawed, he will pay a heavy price in the next period. Even the best structure has its contradictions and must in time be changed.

## The Second Adult Life Structure: Settling Down

The second life structure takes shape at the end of the Age Thirty Transition and persists until about age 40. This structure is the vehicle for the culmination of early adulthood. A man seeks to invest himself in the major components of the structure (work, family, friendships, leisure, community—whatever is most central to him), and to realize his youthful aspirations and goals.

In this period a man has two major tasks: (a) He tries to establish a niche in society: to anchor his life more firmly, develop competence in a chosen craft, become a valued member of a valued world. (b) He works at making it: striving to advance, to progress on a timetable. I use the term "making it" broadly to include all efforts to build a better life for oneself and to be affirmed by the tribe.

Until the early thirties, the young man has been a "novice" adult. He has been forming an adult life and working toward a more established place in adult society. His task in the Settling Down period is to become a full-fledged adult within his own world. He defines a personal enterprise, a direction in which to strive, a sense of the future, a "project" as Jean-Paul Sartre has termed it. The enterprise may be precisely defined from the start or it may take shape only gradually over the course of this period.

The imagery of the ladder is central to the Settling Down enterprise. It reflects the interest in advancement and affirmation so central to this period. By "ladder" we refer to all dimensions of advancement—increases in social rank, income, power, fame, creativity, quality of family life, social contribution—as these are important for the man and his world. The ladder has both objective and subjective aspects: it reflects the realities of the external social world, but it is defined by the person in terms of his own meanings and strivings.

At the start of this period, a man is on the bottom rung of his ladder and is entering a world in which he is a *junior member*. His aims are to advance in the enterprise, to climb the ladder and become a *senior member* in that world. His sense of well-being during this period depends strongly on his own and others' evaluation of his progress toward these goals.

At the end of the Settling Down period, from about age 36 to 40, there is a distinctive phase that we call *Becoming One's Own Man*. The major developmental tasks of this phase are to accomplish the goals of the Settling Down enterprise, to become a senior member in one's world, to speak more strongly with one's own voice, and to have a greater measure of authority.

This is a fateful time in a man's life. Attaining seniority and approaching the top rung of his ladder are signs to him that he is becoming a man (not just a person, but a male adult). Although his progress brings new rewards, it also carries the burden of greater responsibilities and pressures. It means that he must give up even more of the little boy within himself— an internal figure who is never completely outgrown, and certainly not in early adulthood.

## The Mid-life Transition: Moving from Early to Middle Adulthood

The late thirties mark the culmination of early adulthood. The Mid-life Transition, which lasts from roughly age 40 to 45, provides a bridge from early to middle adulthood. It brings a new set of developmental tasks. The life structure again comes into question. It becomes important to ask: "What have I done with my life? What do I really get from and give to my wife, children, friends, work, community—and self? What is it I truly want for myself and others?" A man yearns for a life in which his actual desires, values, talents and aspirations can be expressed.

Some men do very little questioning or searching during the Mid-life Transition. They are apparently untroubled by difficult questions regarding the meaning, value and direction of their lives. Other men realize that the character of their lives is changing, but the process is not a painful one. They are in a manageable transition, one without crisis. But for the great majority of men this is a period of great struggle within the self and with the external world. Their Mid-life Transition is a time of moderate or severe crisis. They question nearly every aspect of their lives and feel that they cannot go on as before. They will need several years to form a new path or to modify the old one.

We need developmental transitions in adulthood partly because no life structure can permit the living out of all aspects of the self. To create a life structure I must make choices and set priorities. Every choice I make involves the rejection of many other possibilities. Committing myself to a structure, I try over a span of time to enhance my life within it, to realize its potential, to bear the responsibilities and tolerate the costs it entails. During a transition period—and especially in the Mid-life Transition—the neglected parts of the self more urgently seek expression and stimulate the modification of the existing structure.

## Entering Middle Adulthood: Building a New Life Structure

The tasks of the Mid-life Transition must be given up by about age 45. A man has had his allotted time for reappraising, exploring, testing choices and creating the basis for a new life. The opportunity to question and search is present throughout middle adulthood and beyond, but at this point new tasks predominate. Now he must make his choices and begin forming a new life structure.

The end of the Mid-life Transition, like all shifts from one period to the next, is marked by a series of changes rather than one dramatic event. It may be evident only as a man looks back a few years later that he was in fact committing himself to the choices around which a new life structure took shape.

In some lives the shift is signaled by a crucial marker event—a drastic change in job or occupation, a divorce or love affair, a serious illness, the death of a loved one, a move to a new locale. Other lives show no conspicuous change: life at 45 seems to be just as it was at 39. If we look more closely, however, we discover seemingly minor changes that make a considerable difference. A man may still be married to the same woman, but the character of his familial relationships has changed appreciably for better or worse. Or the nature of his work life has altered: he is quietly marking time until retirement; his work has become oppressive and humiliating; or seemingly small changes in his mode of work have made his work life more satisfying and creative. A man's life structure, we have found, necessarily changes in certain crucial respects during the course of his Mid-life Transition.

The life structure that emerges in the middle forties varies greatly in its satisfactoriness, that is, its suitability for the self and its workability in the world. Some men have suffered such irreparable defeats in childhood or early adulthood, and have been so little able to work on the tasks of their Mid-life Transition, that they lack the inner and outer resources for creating a minimally adequate structure. They face a middle adulthood of constriction and decline. Other men form a life structure that is reasonably viable in the world but poorly connected to the self. Although they do their bit for themselves and others, their lives are lacking in inner excitement and meaning. Still other men have started a middle adulthood that will have its own special satisfactions and fulfillments. For these men, middle adulthood is often the fullest and most creative season in the life cycle. They are less tyrannized by the ambitions, passions and illusions of youth. They can be more deeply attached to others and yet more separate, more centered in the self. For them, the season passes in its best and most satisfying rhythm.

## The Subsequent Periods in Middle Adulthood

By his late forties, a man has formed an initial life structure for middle adulthood. Where does he go from here? Although we did not study men beyond this age, there is evidence that the sequence of stable and transitional periods continues over the entire life cycle. The developmental process of growth, decline and change continues. Here is a tentative view of the subsequent periods in middle adulthood.

There is an *Age Fifty Transition*, which normally lasts from about age 50 to 55. The functions of this period in middle adulthood are similar to those of the Age Thirty Transition in early adulthood. In it, a man can work further on the tasks of the Mid-life Transition and can modify the life structure formed in the mid-forties. It may be a time of crisis for men who changed too little in their Mid-life Transition and then built an unsatisfactory life structure. In our opinion, it is not possible to get through middle adulthood without having at least a moderate crisis in either the Mid-life Transition or the Age Fifty Transition.

From roughly age 55 to 60, a stable period is devoted to *building a second middle adult structure*, which provides a vehicle for completing middle adulthood. For men who are able to rejuvenate their selves and enrich their lives, the decade of the fifties can be a time of great fulfillment. This period is analogous to Settling Down in early adulthood. Finally, from about 60 to 65, the *Late Adult Transition* terminates middle adulthood and creates a basis for starting late adulthood. The tasks of this transition are to conclude the efforts of middle adulthood and to prepare oneself for the era to come. It is a period of significant development and represents a major turning point in the life cycle.

In every cross-era transition a new season is born and takes its initial shape. These transitions have a great effect on the future, but they never tell the whole story. Each new period makes its essential contribution to the life course. In every period we suffer because of the undone developmental work of previous periods—for ultimately these chickens do come home to roost—but we also have an opportunity to do further developmental work and to create a life more suitable to the self.

# 4 Four Men

As immediately observed and experienced, every life is idiosyncratic, disorderly and variegated. The differences are far more marked than the similarities. Yet the basic thesis of this book is that even the most disparate lives are governed by the same underlying order—a sequence of eras and developmental periods. This order is often not immediately evident. It must be inferred from a truly staggering array of biographical data. But if our developmental theory of adulthood has any validity—and I am convinced that it does—it will enable us to find shape and meaning in any individual life course. And it will do this without reducing the raw material—the wonderfully various details of each single human's existence— to a simple set of categories or prescriptions for normality.

This study is biographical in its theoretical approach, its method and its subject matter. We are concerned above all with the individual life as it is lived over the years. Thus it is appropriate that we should make use of actual biographies in reporting our findings. The biographies illustrate the kind of material from which we derived our ideas and the extraordinary applicability of these ideas over a wide range of personalities and social conditions. In passing, we will refer to many of our forty subjects. But the lives of four men will be dealt with in some detail. Their biographies fall somewhere between a long vignette and a short book.

In these biographies, as in the book generally, we focus primarily on the adult portion of the life course. We try to say enough about a man's internal psychological processes, and about his external circumstances and social world, to show how all these are interwoven in the fabric of his evolving life. We certainly do not claim that the biographical sketches are complete portraits of our subjects. In fact, they point to the need both for more extended biographies and for methods of writing brief biographies that will be useful in studying particular facets of adult development.

The four men represent each of the four occupational groups—executives, workers, biologists and novelists—in our study. I want to emphasize, even though this may sound contradictory, that we do not regard them as "representative" of their occupations in any specific sense. No one man can fully exemplify the abundant variety in the lives of others, even those who share the same kind of work with him. Each of these four men is "special" in certain respects, but then every one of the forty men had his own form of specialness.

In deciding which four men would be reported in detail here, we used several criteria. First, a man had to be over 42 at the time of interviewing, so that his reported life would extend across most of the span covered by the study. Second, we wanted four men who had been interviewed by four different members of our research team currently active on the project (some staff members had moved elsewhere). These two criteria narrowed the pool to about a dozen men. In selecting four men from this pool— given the requirement of one executive, one worker, one biologist and one novelist—we tried to maximize the diversity of the group in terms of social origins and life course. We did *not* choose one man over another because he was interesting or dull, neurotic or well-adjusted, a success or a failure, talkative or reticent. The men varied in these respects to just about the same degree as did the sample as a whole.

The four men who emerged from this selection process are remarkably different from one another. Considering them separately, it is at first difficult to see any common developmental pattern in their life histories. They differed widely in personality, in current state of mind and external circumstances, and in the sequence of events in their lives. We introduce them to you now, in the order of their appearance.

Our first man is Jim Tracy (the name, like those of all the others in our study, is a pseudonym), a business executive. He was interviewed for a total of about 12 hours by Edward Klein during the fall of 1968 and the spring of 1969, with a follow-up interview in 1971. In 1969 Tracy was 44, a vice president and general manager of the Firearms Division of the Ajax Corporation, with authority over several thousand employees in Hartford and two Midwestern plants.

A strong, trim man with a full head of salt-and-pepper hair cut close, Tracy presented himself to the interviewer as a man who had achieved much in the world, and was proud of it. For most of his life, he sustained a central self-image: Jim Tracy the responsible leader of men, the model hero in the military-industrial world. He was strongly work-oriented, an extremely active man who could look back with satisfaction on his career as a navy officer and then an executive. Yet at the time of the interviews Tracy was going through a major, and difficult, reappraisal. His business career seemed to have peaked. A few years earlier he had ended a long but unhappy first marriage; his second marriage, after a very happy beginning, was looking problematical.

In subsequent chapters we will examine Tracy's whole life step by step, showing how the developmental forces—the sequence of eras and periods—helped to shape it. Chapter 7 will take him through the first three periods of early adulthood, until age 34 and the end of his Age Thirty Transition. Chapter 11 will cover his life in the Settling Down period, from age 34 to 41, while Chapter 19 concentrates on Tracy's Mid-life Transition and his entry into middle adulthood—the troubled time he was living through when we talked with him.

William Paulsen was 44 and an hourly worker at United Electronics when Braxton McKee interviewed him in 1969. McKee spent about eight hours with him in that year, plus a separate interview with Paulsen's wife, Ruth. Two years later McKee and Paulsen met again for a single interview, and they talked briefly a few years after that.

Born and raised in a working-class family in Brooklyn, Paulsen in his forties was a lean, wiry man, quick in his movements, neat in his dress, careful in his manner. His hair was crew-cut and his face deeply lined, mobile and expressive. He often smiled wryly, reflecting, in McKee's opinion, a certain cockiness. But this was belied by his eyes, which were sad, and by the stories he told about his life. These stories frequently struck McKee as an attempt to impress the other person and to bolster Paulsen's somewhat shaky self-esteem. One theme stood out particularly strongly. In order to feel better about himself he consistently deluded himself about the real nature of a given situation and his place in it. Again and again throughout his adult life he had taken on more than he could manage.

In the preceding five years Paulsen had changed jobs several times, going through a series of failures and fresh starts. Each new job had kindled his hopes of being promoted, at last, into middle management. Now, at 43 and 44, he had begun to confront his illusions and to acknowledge his limitations for what they were. He was reconciling himself to the prospect of a job that offered security and modest income, but little in the way of satisfaction and room for advancement. It seemed possible that Paulsen would not attain even this limited goal. Yet it was also clear, from the study of his entire biography, that certain flaws and failures at specific developmental stages—difficulties having their sources in him and in his external circumstances—had contributed to his present plight. Contending with his plight was again a matter of understanding and dealing with developmental problems.

In Chapter 8 we will examine Paulsen's life in detail to age 32—the end of the Age Thirty Transition and the novice phase of early adulthood. Chapter 18 will complete his history, to the late forties.

Writing has been a central dream for Paul Namson, yet one that regularly fell into conflict with other occupational choices and social demands. In this sense he was like most novelists in our sample. But in some other respects he was not. A successful financier in his twenties, actually a millionaire in his thirties, Namson had a complex, exciting and troubling life, full of satisfactions and disappointments.

Interviewed by Charlotte Darrow in 1969, Namson had then, at 43, been out of the family brokerage firm for six years, was trying to realize his dream of being a novelist and was going through a mid-life crisis. In spite of his modest critical success as a novelist, he was having difficulty moving forward. A follow-up interview, fifteen months later, when he was 44, found him resolving the divisions of his life and forming new commitments as a writer, husband and father. His wife, Sarah, was also interviewed at this time.

Namson was an intense, gentle man, tall and slight, with an introspective manner and evident intelligence. Perhaps because of his own experience in trying to analyze feelings and motives in fictional terms, he tended to speak analytically when he described his life. We shall tell of Namson's first 40 years, with the main emphasis on the last 12 years of that span (the Age Thirty Transition, Settling Down and Becoming One's Own Man), in Chapter 12. His life in the forties will be described in Chapter 18.

Our fourth man, John Barnes, was a professor of biology at Columbia University and had an international reputation. He was known as a forceful, articulate man, an effective teacher and administrator. When I first interviewed him, he was just turning 44. I also talked with his wife, Ann. Follow-up interviews took place when he was 46, and again when he was 50. The analysis of his life was done by Maria Levinson.

Barnes was a calm man with clean-cut features and the build of an athlete. His manner conveyed a sense of strength, controlled energy and eagerness to get things done. His speech could be pedantic, but it was also plain and blunt. Barnes had the poise and pride, the self-control and care for personal privacy, and the elitist attitude of social responsibility befitting his aristocratic Yankee background. One could imagine him cutting trees or doing carpentry with the heavy deliberation of a New England farmer. At his best when engaged in rational analysis of concrete issues, he had more difficulty in dealing with emotion and personal relationships.

Yet, during a severe mid-life crisis, he conveyed his personal experience with great poignancy and richness.

At the time of our first interview, Barnes had reached a serious impasse in his life, in spite of his considerable achievements and public success. No longer a "promising young man," he was faced with the need to accept a wholly new vision of himself. He hoped to discover a significant occupational role to which he could devote the rest of his working life. But he was profoundly uncertain about what this might be.

The signposts that mark off the stages of John Barnes's life—first marriage and family, scientific achievements, divorce and remarriage, promotions upward through the academic hierarchy—may be viewed as purely exterior phenomena. But their meaning and timing are enormously significant and can be seen to characterize a deeper pattern. In Chapter 17 we will examine his life in some detail, paying particular attention to its most dramatic portion, the period we call the Mid-life Transition.

In the following chapters we shall traverse the sequence of developmental periods. First, the Early Adult Transition, Entering the Adult World and the Age Thirty Transition, which comprise the novice phase of early adulthood (Chapters 5 to 8). Second, the period of Settling Down and Becoming One's Own Man, in which a man reaches the culmination of early adulthood (Chapters 9 to 12). Finally, the Mid-life Transition and Entering Middle Adulthood, when he makes the shift from youth to middle age (Chapters 13 to 19).

# The Novice Phase
# of Early Adulthood

# The Novice Phase: The Early Adult Transition, Entering the Adult World and the Age Thirty Transition

The process of entering into adulthood is more lengthy and complex than has usually been imagined. It begins at around age 17 and continues until 33 (plus or minus two years at either end). A young man needs about fifteen years to emerge from adolescence, find his place in adult society and commit himself to a more stable life. This time is an intrinsic part of adulthood. It is not, even in its most chaotic or immature form, a "delayed adolescence." Unresolved adolescent problems may make it more difficult, but the primary developmental tasks to be met are those of adulthood.

So important is this developmental sequence that we have given it a special name: the novice phase. It is composed of three distinct periods: the Early Adult Transition, Entering the Adult World, and the Age Thirty Transition. Each of these periods has its own tasks. Together they form a single phase that serves a crucial developmental function: *the process of entry into adulthood*.

The novice phase begins with the Early Adult Transition (roughly age 17 to 22). A young man is now on the boundary between pre-adulthood and early adulthood. He is creating a basis for adult life without being fully within it. The second period, Entering the Adult World, lasts from about 22 to 28. His tasks now are to explore the possibilities of this world, to test some initial choices, and to build a first, provisional life structure. The third period, the Age Thirty Transition, provides an opportunity for revising the initial structure and moving toward a second structure.

The Age Thirty Transition frequently begins with a vague uneasiness, a feeling that something is missing or wrong in one's life and that some change is needed if the future is to be worthwhile. Initially the main questions deal with the life one has created: What parts must I give up or appreciably change? What is missing from it? Toward the end of the Age Thirty Transition the man's orientation is more toward the future— finding a new life direction and making new choices or strengthening his commitment to choices already made.

As the Age Thirty Transition ends (at about 33), the preparatory phase must also be terminated. A man is now a full-fledged adult, committing himself to a new life structure through which he will reach the culmination of early adulthood. The new structure is built in the next period, Settling Down, but it has to be seen as the outcome and chief product of the novice phase. This structure provides a groundwork for the effort to attain his youthful aspirations during the thirties.

The novice phase thus extends from the onset of the Early Adult Transition to the conclusion of the Age Thirty Transition. For our sample as a whole, the average age of onset is 17.4, the average age of completion 32.7. The average duration of the novice phase is 15.3 years, with a range of 13 to 18. There was again a modest variation among the occupational groups. On the average, the Age Thirty Transition ended at age 32.1 for the workers, followed by the executives at 32.4, the novelists at 32.8 and the biologists, 33.6.

The primary, overriding task of the novice phase is to make a place for oneself in the adult world and to create a life structure that will be viable in the world and suitable for the self. A man often assumes he is doing this in the early twenties when he forms an initial adult structure. But the first structure inevitably has serious flaws and limitations. The Age Thirty Transition gives him an opportunity to reconsider the early choices and to make changes, large or small, in his situation and his self. At the end of the Age Thirty Transition a man must begin the second structure and form a niche in the world, especially with regard to occupation and marriage-family. This structure ordinarily remains stable for the rest of the thirties, although important changes occur within it. Some men attempt in their late thirties to modify a faulty Settling Down structure, but this is always a painful, long-term process, as we shall see in the cases of Jim Tracy and Paul Namson. The structure that starts to emerge at the end of the novice phase has tremendous consequences for future living and development.

With this overview of the novice phase as a whole, let's now look at its three component periods: the Early Adult Transition, Entering the Adult World and the Age Thirty Transition. Each period has its own specific tasks, course and outcome, as well as features common to the entire novice phase.

## The Early Adult Transition

The Early Adult Transition is a developmental bridge between the eras of pre-adulthood and early adulthood. An early adult self is taking shape, containing and to some extent transforming the child and adolescent selves.

The boy-man is on the boundary between the childhood era, which was centered in the family of origin, and the early adult era with its new responsibilities, roles and life choices. He is half in and half out of both worlds. He is still very much in adolescence, yet he is also stretching toward the enticing—and forbidding—adult world ahead.

In our sample, the Early Adult Transition typically began at age 17 or 18, lasted five years, and ended at 22 or 23. In no case did it start earlier than sixteen or later than eighteen, and it never lasted less than four or more than seven years. This period started at roughly the same age in all four occupational groups. On the average, it lasted 5.2 years for the novelists, 5.0 years for the biologists, and 4.7 years for the workers and executives.

The Early Adult Transition presents two major tasks. One task is to terminate the adolescent life structure and *leave the pre-adult world*. A young man has to question the nature of that world and his place in it. It is necessary to modify existing relationships with important persons and institutions, and to modify the self that formed in pre-adulthood. Numerous separations, losses and transformations are required. The second task is to *make a preliminary step into the adult world*: to explore its possibilities, to imagine oneself as a participant in it, to make and test some tentative choices before fully entering it. The first task involves a process of termination, the second a process of initiation. Both are essential in a transitional period.

• LEAVING THE PRE-ADULT WORLD. A major component of this task is to separate from the family of origin. The process of separation proceeds along many lines. Its external aspects may involve moving out of the familial home, becoming financially less dependent, entering new roles and living arrangements in which one is more autonomous and responsible. Its internal aspects involve an increasing differentiation between self and parents, greater psychological distance from the family, and reduced emotional dependency on parental support and authority.

A man's family circumstances may differ widely in the teens. At one extreme, a young person may leave the parental home in childhood or early adolescence, through death or abandonment, running away, going to reformatory or private school. His new life setting may provide a quasi-home, where he functions in part as a child in relation to parent surrogates, so that he has the opportunity to wait until the start of his Early Adult Transition to work on the tasks of terminating his pre-adult life. Otherwise, this boy may be forced prematurely (say at age 12 or 14) to give up his status as child and his relationships to parents. This is very early to do the developmental work of the Early Adult Transition. Having separated far too early in an external sense, he remains internally tied to the family as an adult. He may become a pseudo-adult whose yearnings for parental caring and grief for the lost family, continue to interfere with the emergence of a valued adult self.

On the other hand, a person may continue living in the parental home until the early twenties or later. Under these external circumstances, he may still be able to work at the developmental tasks of the Early Adult Transition by becoming internally more differentiated from parents and externally more self-sufficient in ways other than those related to place of residence. The crucial thing is to separate enough to form a basis for living more genuinely as an adult in the next period.

The forty men in our sample differed widely in their relationships with parents during the novice phase. Only seven men (18 percent) stayed close to their parents, personally and geographically, in the twenties. This group contained three workers, three executives and a biologist. At the other extreme, eight men (20 percent) had a major conflict with their parents—most often with the father—that went on for several years and in a few cases permanently. Six of these men were novelists, two were workers.

Between these extremes, there were twenty-five men (62 percent) who, without bitter conflict, and in some cases to avoid conflict, moved a considerable distance geographically or socially from the parental world. Some of these men retained close ties with parents and built a life structure that "made sense" to the parents. For most of them, however, the ties to parents eroded steadily during their twenties. The erosion had a strong emotional aspect—an increasing indifference or alienation. But the total erosion process was *psychosocial*: the young man was entering a world that his parents found alien, mystifying and beyond their ken. If we combine the two groups, those who experienced "major conflict" and those who "moved away," we have 82 percent of the total sample!

The process of separation from parents continues over the entire life course. It is never completed. It is thus more accurate to speak not of separation but of changes in the degree and kind of attachment in various key periods. During the first two or three years of life, the child establishes the distinction between self and non-self. This brings about an initial separation from the mother, though the attachment remains very strong and she provides an external centering for his life. At age five or six, with the shift from early to middle childhood, the bounds of the child's life expand beyond the household to include new relationships and institutions. An adolescent's world is more complex, but it is still primarily a pre-adult world, centered in the family and in peer groups. Adults figure as authorities, teachers, helpers and enemies but not as peers. The boy may at times enter their world but he is not of it.

During the Early Adult Transition, he has to separate from the family in a new way. He must remove the family from the center of his life and begin a process of change that will lead to a new *home base* for living as a young adult in an adult world. This does not mean, of course, that the ambivalent attachment to family has ended. A person is a son or daughter, brother or sister, throughout the life course. It is only the character of the relationship that changes.

The process of separation during the Early Adult Transition involves more than the family of origin. A young man must modify or give up relationships with other important persons and groups, with pre-adult components of the self, with adolescence as an age grade in society—with the entire pre-adult world. All terminations bring a sense of loss, a grief for that which must be given up, a fear that one's future life as a whole will not provide satisfactions equal to those of the past—as well as hope and anticipation of a future brighter than the past. In the Early Adult Transition one must start to give up certain aspects of the pre-adult self and world while internalizing other aspects as a groundwork for adult development.

• INITIATING EARLY ADULTHOOD. The second major task of the Early Adult Transition is to form a basis for living in the adult world before becoming fully a part of it. As this period begins, a young man's knowledge, values and aspirations for a particular kind of adult life are rather ambiguous and colored by private fantasies. He needs to obtain further training and learn more about himself and the world. Gradually he articulates his earlier fantasies and hopes into more clearly defined options for adult living. As the transition ends he will make firmer choices, define more specific goals and gain a higher measure of self-definition as an adult.

Most of the men in our sample had experience in the armed forces in World War II or the Korean War, which had a formative effect on the separation from pre-adulthood and the entry into early adulthood. During their Early Adult Transitions, 26 men (65 percent) were in military service: two spent this period entirely in the military, five divided it between military and work, and nineteen between military and college.

College is another institutional setting in which many young men begin the separation from family and do the developmental work of the Early Adult Transition. Twenty-eight of our men (70 percent) completed college, including all ten biologists as well as nine novelists and nine executives. Two of the workers had some college experience. The impact of college often resulted in an expansion and redirection of the young man's outlook. Those from more modest backgrounds often raised their sights toward higher-status business and professional careers. And many from more affluent business and professional families moved away from the establishment toward occupations and life styles they considered more fulfilling or socially valuable. One of our biologists, the son of a corporation lawyer, was amazed to discover in college that his long-standing interest in nature and animal life could be transformed into the occupation of biologist—and could free him from the destiny of becoming a lawyer.

Between the military, college and other changes, most men moved out of their parental homes in the Early Adult Transition. Still, it should be noted that seventeen men (42 percent) made their primary residence in the home of parents or close relatives during a considerable part of the Early Adult Transition. This was true of seven workers and six executives (most of whom were of working-class origins). Young men in the working class enter the labor force sooner than the more affluent and educated population, but they also maintain direct ties with their families longer.

• CONTINUITY AND DISCONTINUITY IN THE SHIFT FROM PRE-ADULTHOOD TO EARLY ADULTHOOD. There are wide differences in the degree of continuity of the life course as one moves from the pre-adult to the early adult world. In a relatively stable, undifferentiated society a young man's choices are highly constrained. His adult roles and circumstances are prefigured by his pre-adult world. In a technologically advanced, fragmented and changing society such as the United States, he has the advantages and the burdens of greater choice. More options are available in his environment. He is encouraged to seek his own way rather than to follow literally in his father's footsteps. As a result, his early adult world is likely to differ in important respects from his pre-adult world. The differences between traditional and modern societies are, however, far from absolute. In the most stable societies there are possibilities for choice and change over the individual life course; and in the most fluid societies there are massive shaping forces that limit the scope of individual choice.

We examined the ways in which our men retained ties to the world of their origins, and the ways in which they changed. The overall finding can be stated simply: *the great majority of the forty men formed a life in early adulthood quite different from that of their parents.* The shift usually started in the Early Adult Transition and was extended steadily or in recurrent jumps throughout adulthood. Only a small percentage of the men around age 40 lived in a world that had much in common with their childhood world.

Most executives and some workers have advanced beyond the class-income level of their parents. Most of the biologists and novelists came from affluent families in the business-professional world, and have moved into an academic or artistic world very different from that of their origins. They do not differ markedly from their parents in income or class level. The big difference is in values and life style, and in most cases the discontinuity is enormous.

Few of the men strongly reject their origins, but the great majority have only tenuous ties to the familial ethnic and religious traditions. Many have changed their religion or have married a woman of a different religion. Thus, 18 of the 40 men (45 percent) married women of other religions or ethnicities. Two of the workers intermarried, as did 5 or 6 men in each of the other occupations. In 16 cases (40 percent) the marital choice formed part of a broader pattern of upward mobility: the wife was chosen not solely for her money or social background, but as part of a process by which the man left his pre-adult world and moved toward another world more consonant with his ambitions, values and interests. By contrast, the marriages of 14 men (35 percent) actively sustained their link to the pre-adult world.

All but one of the men married during the novice phase: 20 men (50 percent) married in the Early Adult Transition, 11 (28 percent) in Entering the Adult World, 8 (20 percent) in the Age Thirty Transition and 1 in Settling Down. The average age at first marriage was 24.6, the range 17 to 35. The average age at marriage for workers (22.9) was similar to that for executives (23.2) and novelists (24.3). In each of these groups, 60 percent married during the Early Adult Transition. The biologists were distinctly slow to the altar: their average age at marriage was 28.1, and only one married in the Early Adult Transition. They were the most restrained of the four occupational groups in their sexuality and their relations with women generally.

Half of our sample got married in the Early Adult Transition. This early marriage was part of the process of separation from parents and pre-adult life. It was highly colored by the young man's struggles to terminate, and at the same time to maintain, the relationships with parents and the pre-adult aspects of the self. It often stemmed from a conscious effort to leave the family and become more adult, but it also served unconscious needs to perpetuate his dependency and remain fixed in an immature child-mother relationship. (For further discussion of early vs. later marriage, see Chapter 6.)

Beginning with the Early Adult Transition, and throughout the novice phase, a young man is making choices and establishing relationships that will define the character of his life in early adulthood. In some cases his early adult life is consistent with that of his parents and his pre-adult world: he may live in roughly the same kind of community, have the same ethnic and religious ties, enter an occupation and a marriage appropriate to this world, and become the kind of person his parents and childhood friends expected him to be. Specific features of his adult life may differ from those of his parents, but his basic way of living and place in society are much the same as theirs. In such cases there is high *continuity* between the pre-adult and early adult eras.

Conversely, there is *discontinuity* when a marked change in trajectory occurs—when a man's life in the late twenties is sharply different from the life he seemed about to enter in his teens. Discontinuity may take many forms: a change in ethnic attachments and life style; a change in religious affiliation or identity; marriage to a woman of different social background (although the differences may be modulated in the kind of family life they develop); movement into a class or subculture very different in values and outlook from that of the parents.

In order to get a rough picture of these changes, we did a rating of the "degree of discontinuity between pre-adult and early adult world" for each of our 40 men. In making this rating, we compared the character of a man's life in the late teens and the late twenties. The discontinuity was rated "high" for 40 percent of the sample, "medium" for 42 percent and "low" for 18 percent. Among the occupational groups, the novelists showed the greatest discontinuity, with the biologists a close second. The workers and executives had somewhat less discontinuity, but a rating of "low" was received by only four workers and two executives.

Whatever the degree of discontinuity in a young man's life, the Early Adult Transition is a time of profound change in self and world. He is still adolescent in many respects, yet he is also a novice adult. He is still modifying or ending his relationships with parents and other family members, with the settings and institutions of adolescence, and with his peer groups and friends. He is trying to make the choices that will form the groundwork for his first adult life structure.

## Entering the Adult World: Building a First Life Structure

The Early Adult Transition, like all developmental transitions, is followed by a more stable period in which a new life structure must be built. We call this new period Entering the Adult World. It involves a number of basic processes: exploration of self and world, making and testing provisional choices (cautiously, or with a great enthusiasm which masks their provisional quality), searching for alternatives, increasing one's commitments and constructing a more integrated life structure.

This period usually begins at age 22, give or take two years. It lasts about six years—never, in our sample, more than eight or less than four—and ends at 28 or 29. There were only negligible differences among the four occupational groups in the age at which this period began. Its duration was slightly greater for the biologists and novelists than for the workers and executives: just over six years for the former, just under six for the latter. We thus find a common sequence and timing for the various occupations, as well as a range of individual variation around the typical (modal) ages.

In Entering the Adult World, a young man has to fashion and test out an initial life structure that provides a viable link between the valued self and the adult society. He must now shift the center of gravity of his life from the position of child in the family of origin to the position of novice adult with a new home base that is more truly his own. It is time for full entry into the adult world. This requires multiple efforts: to explore the available possibilities, to arrive at a crystallized (though by no means final) definition of himself as an adult, and to make and live with his initial choices regarding occupation, love relationships, life style and values. He faces two major tasks:

• EXPLORATION. A young man has to discover and generate alternative options. The exploratory stance requires him to "hang loose," keeping his options open and avoiding strong commitments. This task has sources in the world and in the self. To varying degrees, the external world provides multiple possibilities and invites the young man to try different choices before making more firm commitments. Also, his own youthful vitality generates a sense of adventure and wonder, a wish to seek out and discover all the treasures of the new world he is entering. Even when he makes relatively binding initial choices regarding marriage and occupation, they still have a provisional quality: if they don't work out, change is still possible.

• CREATING A STABLE STRUCTURE. In every period, the several developmental tasks are contrasting or antithetical. Just as the Early Adult Transition requires a young man both to terminate one era and to initiate the next, Entering the Adult World requires him both to explore freely and to make firm choices. He must take on adult responsibilities and "make something of his life." This task, too, has sources in the external environment and in the self. Externally, there are pressures to "grow up," get married, enter an occupation, define his goals and lead a more organized life.

In the self there are desires for stability and order, for roots, membership in the tribe, lasting ties, fulfillment of core values.

The distinctive character of this developmental period lies in the co-existence of its two tasks: to explore, to expand one's horizons and put off making firmer commitments until the options are clearer; and to create an initial adult life structure, to have roots, stability and continuity. Work on one task may dominate, but the other is never totally absent. The balance of emphasis on the two tasks varies tremendously.

At one extreme are men who devote themselves primarily to the task of exploration. They go through the entire period on a highly provisional basis with no lasting commitments or goals. Some of these men lead a transient life, frequently changing jobs, residences and personal relation-ships. They create a loose structure characterized by flux and easy move-ment. They don't invest much of the self in the world or take much of the world into the self. Other men live in a more stable way but they too are very tentative in their choices and make only limited attachments. Toward the late twenties, however, as the period of Entering the Adult World comes to an end, the limitations of this provisional life structure become evident. The men experience increasing internal need and external pres-sure to work at the other task and to get more order, purpose and attach-ment into their lives.

At the other extreme are men who early in this period make strong commitments and start building what they hope will be a stable, enduring life structure. These men usually make their key choices, especially of spouse and occupation, in the Early Adult Transition and try to maintain great continuity with the pre-adult world. They tend not to explore alterna-tive possibilities or to question the life structure they have built. Even these men, however, regard the initial life structure as provisional and not a final unalterable choice. It is a vehicle for entering the adult world but not necessarily a permanent one. As this period nears its end, even these men have questions: Did I commit myself prematurely? Were my horizons too narrow? Do I want to maintain this way of life forever, or are there more fulfilling possibilities I should strive for?

Most men fall between these extremes. There are many ways of trying to balance exploration and stable structure. A young man may opt for stability in one part of his life and transiency in another: he may form a stable marriage but remain occupationally nomadic; or he may devote him-self passionately to an enduring occupational dream while his relationships with women take the form of intense but troubled love affairs, casual promiscuity or avoidance of all closeness. Again, he may lead a nomadic life with minimal commitments until perhaps 25 or 26, and only then begin to form a more stable structure.

Regardless of his life course during the twenties, a man is likely to experience at least a moderate crisis in the Early Adult Transition and/or Entering the Adult World, somewhere between the late teens and the late twenties. We found that 70 percent of our men experienced a moderate or severe crisis during this time. In only five of the forty cases was it clear that life had gone quite smoothly. (In seven cases we could not make a firm judgment regarding the severity of the problems.) The incidence of crisis varied among the four occupations. It occurred in the lives of nine novelists, eight workers and seven biologists. Only four executives gave clear evidence of crisis, though another four were ambiguous.

For the *novelists*, as one might expect, the problems of making writing an occupation were enormous. They could not earn a living from their fiction, but holding a regular job gave them little time to write. In most cases, moreover, their parents actively disapproved of novel writing as an occupation. To pursue their literary dreams, they had to make a sharp break with parents and the pre-adult world. Not surprisingly, the novelists more than the other men had intense, intimate and stormy relationships with women; the love-marriage-family aspect of their lives was often problematic.

Entering the Adult World had its problems for the *hourly* workers as well. It is commonly assumed that young men of the working class are firmly situated in a rather stable if restricted life by their mid-twenties. In fact, eight of our ten workers had difficulties of crisis proportions during their twenties. For five of them this was a "rock bottom" time of life. Many workers went through at least one period in which it seemed unlikely that they would ever get married and have a stable family or that they would find steady employment with reasonable prospects for interesting work and promotion.

Over half of our *executives* did not enter the managerial ranks until they were over age 30. Before that they were engineers, accountants, salesmen, military officers, technicians. Many of them, as I noted earlier, came from working-class or lower-middle-class backgrounds. Much or all of their twenties was taken up not only with occupational mobility but also with a change in class level, educational-cultural (and often religious) milieu, family life, residential community and life style. The challenge and excitement of "moving up" generally outweighed the stress, but the stress was usually great and at times almost unmanageable.

The situation is superficially different for the *biologists*. They usually spend the period of Entering the Adult World in graduate school getting a Ph.D. and perhaps having an additional year or two as a postdoctoral fellow or a very junior faculty member. Occupationally, they are part of a prestigious system that demands hard work but also promises great rewards to those who perform well. But this group too has its stresses: getting the doctoral degree, dealing with the highly competitive struggles of the academic system (which is no less competitive than industry), establishing oneself as a "promising young scientist," and getting a faculty position in a strong university that will facilitate one's research and career progress. In addition, as I've mentioned, the biologists are usually rather inhibited in their relationships with women. They tend to marry late and to have difficulty in establishing a marriage and family life.

These findings cast doubt on the widely held view that young men normally conclude their "adolescent" uncertainty and exploration by the early twenties, after which they choose a path and move along it in a relatively steady, stable way. Very few young men build that first adult life structure without considerable difficulty and occasional crisis. Moreover, having a smooth time in Entering the Adult World is no guarantee that one is building a very satisfactory life structure.

A man's difficulties during this period are often accentuated by specific aspects of his situation—economic recession, discrimination, the rivalries of a highly competitive world—and by his own emotional problems of committing himself to an occupation, relating to women and separating from parents. In addition to these specific obstacles, there is a more elemental, underlying problem: the developmental tasks of Entering the Adult World are intrinsically difficult and contradictory. No one can fulfill them to anything like an optimal degree. It is not possible to form an ideally satisfactory life structure the first time around. The tasks of this period are in their nature antithetical, and we are too young, inexperienced and torn regarding our own wishes to be able to resolve the contradictions. We do well to have only a moderate crisis, to create a fairly satisfactory structure, and to form a basis on which a fuller, more balanced life can be made in subsequent periods.

Toward the end of the twenties, Entering the Adult World comes to a close. A man has until roughly age 28 or 29 to explore the possibilities of adult life and to fashion a first, provisional life structure. This structure has multiple facets: a pattern of relationships with women, usually leading to marriage and family; an involvement in work which leads to forming an occupation; a home base as bachelor or married person, in a particular kind of dwelling, neighborhood and larger community; a pattern of relationships with parents and family of origin; an involvement, great or small, in religious, political, recreational and other groups. Various parts of the self are lived out to different degrees in these facets of the life structure. However, some important parts of the self must remain neglected or allowed only partial expression.

This first life structure may be a relatively integrated whole with a few components at the center and others built around them in mutually supportive ways. Occupation and marriage-family are the components most likely to be given central importance. One task is to choose and follow an occupational direction that permits him to live out important parts of the self. A related task is to form a marital relationship with a wife who supports his aspirations and is ready and able to join him on his journey. If both of these choices have been wisely made and can coexist compatibly at the center of his life, they provide the basis for a satisfactory, well-integrated structure.

Yet no one can succeed fully in these tasks. For most men, the life structure of the late twenties is incomplete or fragmented. Major choices remain to be made, and the direction of life is uncertain or unsatisfactory. To get a more precise picture of this, we did a rating of the "satisfactoriness of the life structure" at the end of Entering the Adult World. We found that 57 percent of the sample experienced their lives as incomplete, oppressive, not going anywhere or heading in the wrong direction. The life structure was unsatisfactory in important respects for eight novelists, six workers, five executives and four biologists.

The difficulty can take many forms. Some men achieve a relatively stable, organized life, and yet important parts of the self have no place in it. In this case, a man feels that his life is a sham, an unwanted compliance with the dictates of parents or society, and a betrayal of what he holds most dear. He may have several strong interests leading in different occupational directions, and be plagued by choices and contradictions. He may be married to a woman he cares for and yet have doubts about whether he loves her, about her feelings for him, about the durability of the relationship or the possibility of integrating marriage-family and work.

For most men, the life structure of the late twenties is unstable, incomplete and fragmented. A man may have had a series of jobs and yet have no occupation or clear occupational direction. Although a transient existence without heavy responsibilities may have suited him well for a while, the insecurity and rootlessness of this life begin to weigh on him. If he has not yet married, the question of marriage becomes more urgent and he begins to examine more closely his usual form of relationship with women, such as shy avoidance of real contact, sexual promiscuity, enduring but nonsexual friendships, or intense but abortive affairs. The lacks and limitations in his life structure become intolerable. It is more distressing now if he does not have a wife or an occupation or a home base of his own. He becomes more aware that his life has no center, that it is fragmented into parts he cannot integrate. Or he realizes that he made the major choices with minimal commitment and investment of the self. He feels the need for a change.

No matter how satisfactory his life has been, no matter how integrated or fragmented the present structure, new developmental tasks are pushing to the fore in the late twenties. The period of Entering the Adult World is coming to an end, and a new period is getting under way.

## The Age Thirty Transition

The Age Thirty Transition is a remarkable gift and burden. It provides an opportunity to work on the flaws in the life structure formed during the previous period, and to create the basis for a more satisfactory structure that will be built in the following period.

As we have seen, the main tasks of Entering the Adult World were to explore the adult world and to fashion a first, provisional life structure. This work is ordinarily done by age 28 or 29. If adult life were more static, the next step would be simply to settle into this structure and pursue further goals within it. If adult life typically evolved in a simple, continuous course, the first life structure would be relatively stable; it would change gradually and in small steps over many years. We find, however, that the life structure evolves through a series of qualitatively distinct periods. The Settling Down period ordinarily begins at age 32 or 33. At that point life becomes less provisional. A man must make stronger commitments, form deeper roots and (with whatever mixture of joy, apathy or resignation) settle for a new life structure that will shape his life for the rest of early adulthood.

Connecting the two structure-building periods—Entering the Adult World in the twenties and Settling Down in the thirties—is the Age Thirty Transition. Like all transitional periods, it serves to terminate one structure and to initiate another. A man has a span of several years in which to reappraise the past and consider the future. He asks: What have I done with my life? What do I want to make of it? What new directions shall I choose?

For our sample as a whole, the Age Thirty Transition typically began at age 28, with a range of 26 to 29. It ended between 31 and 34, most often at 33. The duration was usually five years. Only minor differences were found among the four occupational groups. The average age at onset of the Age Thirty Transition was 27.6 for the workers and 28.2 to 28.4 for the others. This period had the longest duration for the biologists (5.1 years), the shortest for the executives (4.1 years). Again, the variability in the timing of this period is small enough to indicate a common timetable, yet large enough to stimulate our interest in individual and group differences.

During the Age Thirty Transition, the provisional, exploratory quality of the twenties is ending and a man has a sense of greater urgency. Life is becoming more serious, more restrictive, more "for real." He has the feeling: "If I want to change my life—if there are things in it that I don't like, or things missing that I would like to have—this is the time to make a start, for soon it will be too late." The Age Thirty Transition provides a "second chance" to create a more satisfactory life structure within early adulthood.

All men make some changes during this period, so that the life structure at its end is necessarily different, for better or worse, from that at the start. As with all transitions, there are exquisite individual variations in the onset, course and outcome of this period. We have found it useful to distinguish a few broad sequences.

• SMOOTH PROCESS OF CHANGE. For some men the Age Thirty Transition proceeds in a smooth, continuous fashion, without overt disruption or sense of crisis. As they approach 30, they find their lives reasonably complete and satisfactory. They have satisfactory relationships with family and friends. They are moving along an occupational path that suits them well and provides the desired rewards. They are progressing in accordance with their own timetable. The provisional life structure formed in the twenties provides a groundwork on which the second structure can be built.

Under these conditions, a man uses the Age Thirty Transition to modify and enrich his life. The transition may be so smooth as to be hardly noticeable, but a transition does occur and its outcome is a life structure based directly on the previous one but significantly different from it. An easy transition, without drastic change or turmoil, may occur primarily because a man's life is going well and needs only minor adjustments. Or the life structure may be seriously flawed, but he is unable (for various internal and external reasons) to acknowledge the flaws and work at changing them. The illusions and unacknowledged difficulties often surface at a later time, when they exact a heavier cost.

The Age Thirty Transition went rather smoothly for an executive, Leo Heinz. On finishing college at 23, he married and went to work as an accountant for a large corporation. He and his wife had the same aspirations: a large, close-knit family and a middle-class life based on religious values and church affiliation. He wanted to get ahead in his work but was not markedly ambitious or dedicated to a particular occupation. The couple moved into his wife's community, became part of her extended family and religio-ethnic network, and had the first of their six children.

At 27 Heinz had a relatively integrated life structure. Its central elements were the family, the religio-ethnic community and a secure but limited job in an accounting office. He then took a job in middle management in the business office of a major corporation. This marked the start of his Age Thirty Transition. Five years later, at 32, he had established himself as a promising young middle manager. During this five-year transitional period, his life changed markedly: he moved from city to suburbs, from stable lower-middle-class to upwardly mobile middle class, from religio-ethnic enclave to diverse secularized community, from extended family network to isolated nuclear family. In short, from a modest, secure and orderly world to one that was affluent, competitive, demanding and turbulent. He gave occupational ambition, and all that goes with it, a more central part in his life. Heinz's new life structure emerged out of the old and yet was qualitatively different from it. It would take him another ten years to understand what he had gained—and what he had lost—through the change.

• PAINFUL TRANSITION: THE AGE THIRTY CRISIS. For most men, the Age Thirty Transition takes a more severe and stressful form. We speak then of the age thirty crisis. A man encounters great difficulty in working on the developmental tasks of the period. The difficulty may be so great that at times he feels he cannot go on. It is as though he had no basis for further living.

One suggestive metaphor for a developmental crisis is a man alone on a body of water trying to get from Island Past to Island Future. He fears that he will not reach Future. He feels that he can move neither forward nor backward, that he is on the verge of drowning. A man may experience himself as swimming alone, as rowing in a leaky boat, or as captain of a luxurious but defective ship caught in a storm. There are wide variations in the nature of the vehicle, the sources of threat and the nature of Past and Future. The critical thing is that the integrity of the enterprise is in serious doubt: he experiences the imminent danger of chaos, dissolution, the loss of the future.

Developmental crises have certain common characteristics whether they occur in adolescence, at age 30, at 40 or whenever. However, the character of every crisis is shaped by the developmental issues of the current period. Thus, a time of special difficulty occurring around age 30 must be seen in the context of the Age Thirty Transition. An age thirty crisis is not "merely" a delayed adolescent crisis, though unresolved conflicts of adolescence will be reactivated and perhaps more fully resolved in it. Nor is it a "precocious" mid-life crisis, though it has much in common with the transitional problems of persons who, at about 40, feel caught in a life structure that has become intolerable.

A stressful Age Thirty Transition was more the rule than the exception in our study. Twenty-five of the men (62 percent) went through a moderate or severe crisis. Only seven men (18 percent) had a fairly smooth transition, and for eight men (20 percent) the picture was mixed or ambiguous. Crises were experienced by nine of the novelists and eight of the workers. There was clear evidence of crisis in five of the biologists; in another four the picture was mixed, and only one had a clear absence of crisis. Among the executives, three went through a major crisis, three had a relatively smooth transition, and four were unclear.

There is no firm basis for saying whether the age thirty crisis is more frequent in this generation, born between 1924 and 1934, than in others. The Age Thirty Transition is also difficult for the generation born between 1940 and 1949, which entered adulthood during the "protest" decade of the 1960s and turned 30 during the 1970s. Many young adults of every generation, as they pass 30, have serious doubts about the value and the viability of our society and about the possibility of forming a life structure worth having. Perhaps every generation feels that its life problems are unique in character and severity—and each of them may be right. We shall not know until we learn how to study the adult life course in some depth, and with full appreciation of its complexity.

Of the four occupations, the novelists had the hardest time in the Age Thirty Transition and used it most actively to improve their lives. Nine of the ten novelists had age thirty crises and five of these obtained psychotherapy or psychoanalysis during this time. (In comparison, while four biologists had psychotherapy, no workers or executives did, though many of the latter had crises.)

The novelists' crises reflected, in part, the neurotic problems typical of creative and self-demanding persons. To understand them, however, we must look at the broader framework of their lives during the novice phase. These men spent many years trying to become novelists and to put this occupation in the center of a life structure, under the most difficult circumstances. Most of them came from a pre-adult world in which novel writing was regarded with indifference, if not contempt. They became distant or actively alienated from parents and from other important parts of the pre-adult world. During their twenties they struggled to enter an adult world and create a life sharply discontinuous with that of childhood.

Only one of the ten novelists, Allen Perry, was in a position to work full time at writing in his early twenties, first through a small allowance and much scrounging, and then with the income from a successful first novel at 26. Still, he had difficulties that led to a flawed first life structure in the twenties. After an age thirty crisis characterized by inner turmoil and writing block, he was able to build a more satisfactory life structure, with writing and marriage at the center, in his early thirties.

Most of our writers earned their livelihood by other means during their twenties: they became journalists, teachers or businessmen as well as novelists. It was not clear for many years (often well into their thirties or even forties) whether novel writing could become their primary occupation or survive at all in their lives. At the end of Entering the Adult World, in the late twenties, they had not been able to make writing their primary occupation and to build a life structure that could contain it. Many used the Age Thirty Transition to make major changes. By age 33 or 34, they were stabilizing a life in which writing had a significant, though rarely unproblematic, place.

Richard Taylor was one of two Black novelists in our study. Following a long military service in World War II, he started college at 21, married a year later, and immediately started a family. His wife continued her work as a secretary to supplement his income from the GI Bill. Her aspiration was to have a secure life within the middle-class Black community. But he was already writing poetry and fiction, and his cultural interests pulled him to a world she could not share. His dreams were alien to her, and he could not provide the stability so essential to the life she wanted. For three years after college, he tried to maintain a steady job that would pay the bills and leave room for writing, but it didn't work.

At 28, he realized that he could not build a life containing both his aspirations and hers. The life they had was unsuitable for them and their children. He gave up the struggle, divorced and dismantled the fragile structure. Breaking up the family—and re-enacting the corrosive theme of the Black father abandoning his wife and children—caused him inner wounds that took years to heal. After the breakup, he worked harder at fatherhood than do most fathers in intact families.

Taylor's Age Thirty Transition, from age 28 to 34, was spent in a kind of limbo: moving around, often living from hand to mouth, working at transient jobs, hitting "rock bottom," nearly succeeding in killing himself, getting psychotherapy, starting a serious love relationship—and through it all finding time to write his novels. At about 34 his life took on some order and stability, and a new structure emerged. The central elements of this structure were writing novels and an enduring love relationship. The structure was made economically feasible by a hyphenated occupation: he earned money chiefly as journalist and writer on public affairs. Thus, the outcome of his Age Thirty Transition was a life structure that could contain the novel writing, but just barely. It took several years longer to make this structure secure and move his writing into the center of it.

Taylor's crisis in the Age Thirty Transition was similar in magnitude to that of many White writers, but the racial aspects gave it special bitterness and poignancy. The struggle to remain true to his dream is never easy for a Black man in this society. And a Black man with heroic aspirations—literary, political, scientific or whatever—draws upon himself with increasing intensity all the destructive forces of individual and institutional racism. These forces must be part of our understanding of the adult development of Black men.

# 6  Major Tasks of the Novice Phase

We have examined the sequence of developmental periods in the novice phase. The periods begin with the Early Adult Transition, that boundary period when the young man terminates his pre-adulthood and forms the basis for full entry into early adulthood; they continue with Entering the Adult World, whose primary tasks are to explore the possibilities of this world and to build a first, provisional life structure; and they conclude with the Age Thirty Transition, which offers an opportunity to reappraise the first adult life structure, to consider how suitable it is for the self, and to seek ways of reforming or drastically restructuring it.

Each period of the novice phase has its own particular tasks, which have to do with building or modifying the life structure. In addition, the three periods have common tasks which are essential to the process of entry into adulthood. These common tasks characterize the novice phase as a whole. The work done on them changes from one period to the next, but the tasks themselves are of primary importance over the entire phase. Work on a task is not steady and gradual, but proceeds unevenly, with recurrent ups and downs. None of the tasks can be completed before the end of this phase. In fact, it is a developmental accomplishment to have made even moderate progress with all of them by the early thirties.

Four major tasks of the novice phase are:

1. Forming a Dream and giving it a place in the life structure
2. Forming mentor relationships
3. Forming an occupation
4. Forming love relationships, marriage and family

There are other common tasks, such as relating to authorities and gaining greater authority oneself; forming peer relationships with men and women; relating as an adult to people at different age levels; forming an adult outlook and values with regard to religion, politics, ethnicity, community. These issues were discussed in our interviews. In reviewing the lives of our men, however, we found that the four tasks listed above were the most prominent and merited special attention. These tasks give the novice phase its shape and substance. They involve the formation of vitally important aspects of the life structure.

# Forming and Living Out the Dream

During the novice phase of early adulthood a man is exploring the adult world, developing adult interests and values, making important choices with regard to work, marriage and family, and forming an adult identity. The process of exploration and choice is strongly shaped by the influences of family, class, subculture and social institutions. It is affected by his own active striving, competence and rational consideration of alternatives. It is both facilitated and hindered by various aspects of his personality: motives, values, talents, anxieties and life goals. In the course of our study, we have discovered another factor that plays a powerful and pervasive role in early adulthood. This factor, often portrayed in mythology and literature, is rarely considered in academic research. We call it "the Dream." (We use the initial capital to identify and emphasize our specific use of the word.)

In everyday language, we say that someone "succeeded beyond his wildest dreams," or that he "dreamed of a world he could never have." These are neither night dreams nor casual daydreams. A "dream" of this kind is more formed than a pure fantasy, yet less articulated than a fully thought-out plan. It is the central issue in Martin Luther King's historic "I have a dream" speech. It is the meaning Delmore Schwartz intended with the title of his story "In Dreams Begin Responsibilities." Many young men have a Dream of the kind of life they want to lead as adults. The vicissitudes and fate of the Dream have fundamental consequences for adult development.

In its primordial form, the Dream is a vague sense of self-in-adult-world. It has the quality of a vision, an imagined possibility that generates excitement and vitality. At the start it is poorly articulated and only tenuously connected to reality, although it may contain concrete images such as winning the Nobel Prize or making the all-star team. It may take a dramatic form as in the myth of the hero: the great artist, business tycoon, athletic or intellectual superstar performing magnificent feats and receiving special honors. It may take mundane forms that are yet inspiring and sustaining: the excellent craftsman, the husband-father in a certain kind of family, the highly respected member of one's community.

Whatever the nature of his Dream, a young man has the developmental task of giving it greater definition and finding ways to live it out. It makes a great difference in his growth whether his initial life structure is consonant with and infused by the Dream, or opposed to it. If the Dream remains unconnected to his life it may simply die, and with it his sense of aliveness and purpose.

Many young men develop a conflict between a life direction expressing the Dream and another that is quite different. A man may be pushed in the latter direction by his parents, by various external constraints, such as lack of money or opportunity, and by various aspects of his personality, such as guilt, passivity, competitiveness and special talents. He may thus succeed in an occupation that holds no interest for him. The conflict may extend over many years, evolving through various forms. Those who betray the Dream in their twenties will have to deal later with the consequences. Those who build a life structure around the Dream in early adulthood have a better chance for personal fulfillment, though years of struggle may be required to maintain the commitment and work toward its realization. During the Mid-life Transition they will have to reappraise the magical aspects of the Dream and modify its place in their middle adult lives.

Our conception of transitions in adult development, and especially of the Dream in early adulthood, have been strongly influenced by Donald W. Winnicott's views regarding "transitional phenomena" in early childhood. In a transitional period, says Winnicott, the child imagines various possibilities of his self and world in the future. He enacts these imaginings in daydreams, play and other "make-believe" explorations. Does the child believe that he is truly the person he has created in his play? Winnicott's answer: Yes and no; and the ambiguity is the nub of it. The child's play occurs on the boundary between reality and illusion, between the clearly "me" and the "not-me," between what "is" and what "might be." The play world is a boundary region between the concretely objective external reality and the entirely subjective internal image or hope. In play the child can transform imaginings of what might be into illusions of what now is, in preparation for the hard work of making the illusions more real in the external world. He can create, experiment with, and slowly actualize a new self-in-world that is just starting to take shape.

A crucial aspect of mothering, according to Winnicott, is to provide a supportive context for the child's play. Winnicott offers a conception of the "good enough" mother—not a tyrannizing ideal, yet adequate for the complex purposes of mothering. The "good enough" mother helps to generate a space between herself and the child where he can play creatively— can play, that is, without having to worry about the distinction between reality and illusion. We can thus speak of a *boundary region between child and mother*, in which he feels safe from external and internal dangers. In this space he can gradually define and test out a newly emerging self, and he can gain the mother's blessing for what he is trying to become. The "good enough" mother allows the child his playful-serious productions without requiring him to identify them as either "me" or "not-me." She does not question or disparage his playful illusions.

This relationship is produced and sustained by both mother and child. Through it, and the play that can occur within it, the child gains the "I am" feeling, the sense that "I exist in the world." This feeling underlies his often difficult efforts to explore the world and make a place for himself there. It provides a source of hope, self-esteem and personal integrity. The transitional phenomena serve developmentally as forerunners of later, more realistic and adaptive efforts in the social world. Winnicott draws parallels between the "good enough" mother and the "good enough" therapist, who helps generate a space in which the patient can work-play creatively. He points to truly artistic and religious experiences as transitional (and transformational) phenomena of adult life.

Similarly, a Dream of adult life arises as a transitional phenomenon in the Early Adult Transition and Entering the Adult World. As a boy-man begins his entry into adulthood, he imagines exciting possibilities for his adult life and struggles to attain the "I am" feeling in this dreamed-of self and world. His Dream of adulthood is initially as fragile as that of the small child. Though it has origins in childhood and adolescence, the Dream is a distinctively adult phenomenon: it takes shape in the Early Adult Transition and is gradually integrated within (or, in many cases, is excluded from) an adult life structure over the course of early adulthood. The novice phase is the crucial time for establishing the Dream in one's life.

As the novice adult tries to separate from his family and pre-adult world, and to enter an adult world, he must form significant relationships with other adults who will facilitate his work on the Dream. Two of the most important figures in this drama are the "mentor" and the "special woman." I shall discuss them shortly.

First, however, I want to examine ways in which the Dream was formed or neglected by the several occupational groups in our sample during the novice phase.

## Biologists

For about half of the biologists, entry into this occupation was the realization of a powerful, exciting Dream. Their interests in nature and science began in childhood. They thought seriously about biology as an occupation in high school and made the decision in college. They devoted themselves to their work with tremendous commitment and energy throughout the novice phase.

Yet, even when the choice of academic biology reflected the Dream, there were often inner conflicts and external difficulties. In some cases the father strongly wanted his son to enter another occupation, such as business or law. The father sensed, usually with intuitive accuracy, that the son's occupational choice was based in part upon a rejection of his own values and personal qualities. The son, who also loved his father and was vulnerable to such criticisms, got caught up in the conflict and could not devote himself wholeheartedly to his work. One of these men became much more creative and free in his research only in his early thirties, after his father's death.

For several biologists the Dream was ambiguous or poorly formed. At the end of college, after considering various occupational options, they decided on biology because it interested them and their professors were encouraging, but not with a sense of its special rightness for them. Their lack of excitement about biological research and their limited investment of self in work led to continuing career problems.

## Novelists

Several novelists had a youthful Dream of becoming a writer, and for them too the Dream had various fates. Four novelists began writing in high school or earlier, decided in college to make writing their vocation, and spent the novice phase becoming accomplished writers. During their novice phase all of them went through a bitter struggle to learn their crafts, to avoid the detours and pitfalls that constantly awaited them, and to remain true to the muse. By the start of the Settling Down period, three had established themselves as serious, promising young novelists. The fourth, having written several novels and some documentary nonfiction, decided at this point to give up novels. He cast his lot with the writing of nonfiction, which was better suited to his talents and character. In making this choice he turned partially away from the original Dream and first occupation of being a novelist, but he continued to use his creativity in becoming a first-rate nonfiction author.

For the other six novelists there were much larger obstacles, in themselves and in their life circumstances, that complicated the effort to live out the Dream. In some cases, the Dream of novel writing was in conflict with other desires and with powerful external influences. Paul Namson, for example, was drawn into the family brokerage business by a persuasive uncle and by the part of himself that wanted to become a sucessful businessman (see Chapter 12). Although he did some writing during his twenties, he had to go through a major crisis in the Age Thirty Transition before he could give writing a modest place in his life.

In some novelists, the Dream remains stunted. Carl Berg formed some literary interests in college but assumed that he would take over his father's business. The conflict with his father was so severe, however, that he soon left and determined to become a writer. During his twenties he published two novels but was very divided in his commitment to writing. He was tremendously involved in the conflictful relationship with his father, to whom the idea of novel writing as an occupation was simply absurd. His mother could not understand the meaning of writing for him and was emotionally quite distant. There was a chasm between his anti-intellectual pre-adult world and the writers' world he was trying to enter. Under these conditions the Dream of writing could not grow. It was not until his early thirties, when he had made some progress in resolving the inner conflicts and had married a loving woman, that he could devote himself more single-mindedly to writing. By this time, however, it was late to develop his talents. The initial Dream of becoming a respected novelist seemed very far from realization. Perhaps the wonder is that the Dream survived at all, that the undernourished seedling became even a small tree.

## Executives

The early Dream played an important part in the choice of occupation for many biologists and novelists. Only a few of the ten executives, however, were impelled by a youthful Dream. An example is Frank Radovich. During his college years he formed the Dream of leaving his lower-middle-class origins and becoming the head of a major corporation. By age 32, he had become vice president in the corporate structure of a great company and had amassed a personal fortune of over a million dollars. But this was merely the end of his novice phase: he was now preparing to make his mark in a new world. As the Age Thirty Transition ended, he founded his own small corporation. He looked forward to making his firm the giant of its industry and to becoming himself a leading figure on the international scene.

Four executives made a strong commitment to work, but they did not have a special occupational Dream. Their Dream involved a certain kind of family-community life. They sought advancement as a reward for good work, but they were not prepared to sacrifice family and community ties to the claims of ambition. All of them spent the novice phase in their original occupation (such as engineering or accounting) and entered middle management in their early thirties. They were of lower-middle-class origins and retained strong ties to their pre-adult ethnic worlds. Three of them, in their forties, were living in or near the towns where they were born and had turned down opportunities to move elsewhere. The fourth had made two major geographical moves, but in his forties he was restricting his occupational ambitions in favor of a stable family-community life. All of them worked hard to reconcile the conflicting demands of occupational advancement and family-community stability. The struggle was never easy and in most cases exacted a considerable cost.

Most of the executives entered the managerial ranks in their Age Thirty Transition, without a solid basis for long-term achievement and satisfaction as executives. Their primary interests, skills and aspirations were not in the executive functions, but in their original work (such as engineering or accounting) and in non-occupational activities involving family, nature or community. Many of them became managers chiefly because the company needed large numbers of middle managers. The company stimulated their hopes and illusions about further promotion. By their late thirties or early forties, however, most managers have reached the ceiling of their upward rise. The position they hold is often beyond their competence and satisfaction. They are left with neither their original occupational preferences nor a managerial role through which they can live out important aspects of the self.

## Workers

The evolution of the Dream during the novice phase is difficult, too, for the workers. None of them formed and lived out an occupational Dream comparable to those mentioned above. Only one worker, Ralph Ochs, went through a relatively simple sequence of forming a stable occupation, getting married and starting a family during the novice phase. At the end of high school he became an apprentice plumber under his father in a manufacturing firm. Over the next fifteen years he became a master plumber, started a family, moved out from under his father, and took an active part in establishing a union. By his early thirties he was firmly settled in his occupation, work place, family and community. He took pride in his work, but the good life lay in the total patterning of work, family and community. His adult world had great continuity with the pre-adult world of his origins, but within this world he built a life reflecting his particular wishes, aspirations and values.

All of the other workers went through a more complex sequence, with recurrent difficulties, during the novice phase. Most of them had a Dream relating to occupation, but they could not live it out. In two cases the Dream was to be a star professional athlete. Alby Russell was a star athlete in high school and wanted to play professional ball. After high school, he joined the military service and remained in it for almost twenty years. At 19 he got married and soon started a family. In the service he devoted himself mainly to starring on the football, baseball and basketball teams. It was only in the Age Thirty Transition that he gave up the fantasy of becoming—and perhaps the illusion of actually being—a major-league athlete. In his early thirties he got seriously involved in his family life. He became a Little League coach and a teacher-mentor to young soldiers. In his abundant leisure time he followed the fortunes of teams in several sports, watching them on TV, reading avidly about them, and in imagination functioning as owner, manager and recruiter for each of them. His erudition in this field was amazing. He thus continued to live out the Dream in a special way, as a virtually full-time avocation, but he could not make a true occupation of it.

Most workers had various jobs but no evolving occupation throughout the novice phase. Five of them formed their first stable occupation at the end of the Age Thirty Transition, after a rather transient work history. Two others still had marginal work skills and no defined occupation. Very few workers go through the entire process of forming an occupational Dream—defining it, getting the needed support and training, and putting it into their lives—during the novice phase. For some, the vision of the good life involves a mixture of work, family and community involvements. For others, the Dream remains inchoate. Still others, perhaps the largest number, begin the Early Adult Transition with fantasies about exciting kinds of work and accomplishment, but the incipient Dream cannot be articulated or explored. It is gradually covered over by the more immediate problems of survival.

## The Mentor Relationship

The mentor relationship is one of the most complex, and developmentally important, a man can have in early adulthood. The mentor is ordinarily several years older, a person of greater experience and seniority in the world the young man is entering. No word currently in use is adequate to convey the nature of the relationship we have in mind here. Words such as "counselor" or "guru" suggest the more subtle meanings, but they have other connotations that would be misleading. The term "mentor" is generally used in a much narrower sense, to mean teacher, adviser or sponsor. As we use the term, it means all these things, and more.

The mentoring relationship is often situated in a work setting, and the mentoring functions are taken by a teacher, boss, editor or senior colleague. It may also evolve informally, when the mentor is a friend, neighbor or relative. Mentoring is defined not in terms of formal roles but in terms of the character of the relationship and the functions it serves. A student may receive very little mentoring from his teacher-adviser, and very important mentoring from an older friend or relative. We have to examine a relationship closely to discover the amount and kind of mentoring it provides.

I shall speak of mentors in the male gender. This reflects the current reality: the men in our study had almost exclusively male mentors. Indeed, they rarely had women friends at all. This is further evidence of the gap between the genders in our society. In principle, a mentor may be either the same gender or cross-gender. A relationship with a female mentor can be an enormously valuable experience for a young man, as I know from my own experience. The increased entry of women into currently male-dominated occupations will have a salutary effect on the development of men as well as women.

There is some evidence that women have even less mentoring, male or female, than men. One of the great problems of women is that female mentors are scarce, especially in the world of work. The few women who might serve as mentors are often too beset by the stresses of survival in a work world dominated by men to provide good mentoring for younger women. Some young women have male teachers or bosses who function as mentors. This cross-gender mentoring can be of great value. Its actual value is often limited by the tendency, frequently operating in both of them, to make her less than she is: to regard her as attractive but not gifted, as a gifted woman whose sexual attractiveness interferes with work and friendship, as an intelligent but impersonal pseudo-male or as a charming little girl who cannot be taken seriously.

What are the various functions of the mentor? He may act as a *teacher* to enhance the young man's skills and intellectual development. Serving as *sponsor*, he may use his influence to facilitate the young man's entry and advancement. He may be a *host and guide*, welcoming the initiate into a new occupational and social world and acquainting him with its values, customs, resources and cast of characters. Through his own virtues, achievements and way of living, the mentor may be an *exemplar* that the protégé can admire and seek to emulate. He may provide *counsel* and moral support in time of stress.

The mentor has another function, and this is developmentally the most crucial one: to support and facilitate the *realization of the Dream*. The true mentor, in the meaning intended here, serves as an analogue in adulthood of the "good enough" parent for the child. He fosters the young adult's development by believing in him, sharing the youthful Dream and giving it his blessing, helping to define the newly emerging self in its newly discovered world, and creating a space in which the young man can work on a reasonably satisfactory life structure that contains the Dream.

The mentor is *not* a parent or crypto-parent. His primary function is to be a transitional figure. In early adulthood, a young man must shift from being a child in relation to parental adults to being an adult in a peer relation with other adults. The mentor represents a mixture of parent and peer; he must be both and not purely either one. If he is entirely a peer, he cannot represent the advanced level toward which the younger man is striving. If he is very parental, it is difficult for both of them to overcome the generational difference and move toward the peer relationship that is the ultimate (though never fully realized) goal of the relationship. The actual parents can serve certain mentoring functions, but they are too closely tied to their offspring's pre-adult development (in both his mind and theirs) to be primary mentor figures.

The mentor who serves these transitional functions is usually older than his protégé by a half-generation, roughly 8 to 15 years. He is experienced as a responsible, admirable older sibling. Age differences much greater or less than this are not common, and they pose special hazards. When the mentor is a full generation older—say twenty years or more—there is a greater risk that the relationship will be symbolized by both in parent-child terms. This tends to activate powerful feelings, such as excessive maternalism or paternalism in the elder, and dependency or Oedipal conflicts in the younger, that interfere with the mentoring function. When the age difference is less than 6 to 8 years, the two are likely to experience each other as peers. They may then be intimate friends or collaborative co-workers, but the mentoring aspects tend to be minimal.

Still, a person twenty or even fifty years older may, if he is in good touch with his own and the other's youthful Dreams, function as a significant mentor figure. And a person the same age or even younger may have important mentoring qualities if he has unusual expertise and understanding, and if both have the maturity to make good use of the mentor's virtues.

In the usual course, a young man initially experiences himself as a novice or apprentice to a more advanced, expert and authoritative adult. As the relationship evolves, he gains a fuller sense of his own authority and his capability for autonomous, responsible action. The balance of giving/receiving becomes more equal. The younger man increasingly has the experience of "I am" as an adult, and their relationship becomes more mutual. This shift serves a crucial developmental function for the young man: it is part of the process by which he transcends the father-son, man-boy division of his childhood. Although he is officially defined as an adult at 18 or 21, and desperately wants to be one, it takes many years to overcome the sense of being a son or a boy in relation to "real" adults. The process extends over the entire novice phase of early adulthood and becomes problematic again in the late thirties (see Chapter 9). Mentors can thus play a significant role throughout early adulthood.

I have described the mentoring relationship in its most developed and constructive form. Of course, relationships vary tremendously in the degree and form of mentoring involved. Mentoring is not a simple, all-or-none matter. A relationship may be remarkably beneficial to the younger person and yet be seriously flawed. For example, a teacher or boss cares for and sponsors a protégé, but is so afraid of being eclipsed that he behaves destructively at crucial moments. A relationship may be very limited and yet have great value in certain respects. Some men have a purely symbolic mentor whom they never meet. Thus, an aspiring young novelist may admire an older writer, devour his books, learn a great deal about his life, and create an idealized internal figure with whom he has a complex relationship.

In a "good enough" mentoring relationship, the young man feels admiration, respect, appreciation, gratitude and love for the mentor. These outweigh but cannot entirely prevent the opposite feelings: resentment, inferiority, envy, intimidation. There is a resonance between them. The elder has qualities of character, expertise and understanding that the younger admires and wants to make parts of himself. The young man is excited and spurred on by the shared sense of his promise. Yet he is also full of self-doubt: Can he ever become all that both of them want him to be? At different times—or even at the same moment—he experiences himself as the inept novice, the fraudulent impostor, the equal colleague and the rising star who will someday soar to heights far beyond those of the mentor.

Mentoring is best understood as a form of love relationship. It is difficult to terminate in a reasonable, civil manner. In this respect, as in others, it is like the intense relationship between parents and grown offspring, or between sexual lovers or spouses.

The mentoring relationship lasts perhaps two or three years on the average, eight to ten years at most. It may end when one man moves, changes jobs or dies. Sometimes it comes to a natural end and, after a cooling-off period, the pair form a warm but modest friendship. It may end totally, with a gradual loss of involvement. Most often, however, an intense mentor relationship ends with strong conflict and bad feelings on both sides. The young man may have powerful feelings of bitterness, rancor, grief, abandonment, liberation and rejuvenation. The sense of resonance is lost. The mentor he formerly loved and admired is now experienced as destructively critical and demanding, or as seeking to make one over in his own image rather than fostering one's individuality and independence. The mentor who only yesterday was regarded as an enabling teacher and friend has become a tyrannical father or smothering mother. The mentor, for his part, finds the young man inexplicably touchy, unreceptive to even the best counsel, irrationally rebellious and ungrateful. By the time they are through, there is generally some validity in each one's criticism of the other.

And so it ends. Much of its value may be realized—as with love relationships generally—after the termination. The conclusion of the main phase does not put an end to the meaning of the relationship. Following the separation, the younger man may take the admired qualities of the mentor more fully into himself. He may become better able to learn from himself, to listen to the voices from within. His personality is enriched as he makes the mentor a more intrinsic part of himself. The internalization of significant figures is a major source of development in adulthood.

# Forming an Occupation

It is often assumed that by his early twenties a man normally ought to have a firm occupational choice and be launched in a well-defined line of work. This assumption is erroneous. It reflects the prevailing view that development is normally complete by the end of adolescence.

We have found that the sequence is longer and more difficult than the above version suggests. The imagery of *deciding* on an occupation is too narrow and superficial. It is far more useful to speak of *forming* an occupation, a complex, social-psychological process that extends over the entire novice phase and often beyond.

An initial serious choice is usually made during the Early Adult Transition or Entering the Adult World, sometime between 17 and 29. Even when the first choice seems to be very definite, it usually turns out to represent a preliminary definition of interests and values. The transformation of *interests* into *occupation* is rarely a simple or direct process. A young man may struggle for several years to sort out his multiple interests, to discover what occupations, if any, might serve as a vehicle for living out his interests, and to commit himself to a particular line of work. Often, he seriously considers two or more occupational directions. A vivid example is given by our novelist, Paul Namson (see Chapter 12).

Young men who make a strong occupational commitment in the early twenties, without sufficient exploration of external options and inner preferences, often come to regret it later. On the other hand, those who don't make a commitment until the thirties, or who never make one, are deprived of the satisfaction of engaging in enduring work that is suitable for the self and valuable for society. One of the great paradoxes of human development is that we are required to make crucial choices before we have the knowledge, judgment and self-understanding to choose wisely. Yet, if we put off these choices until we feel truly ready, the delay may produce other and greater costs. This is especially true of the two great choices of early adulthood: occupation and marriage.

Once his initial choice of occupation is made, a man must acquire skills, values and credentials. He must develop a more differentiated occupational identity and establish himself within the occupational world. Along the way, a man may fail or drop out, to begin again on a new path. He may stay narrowly within a single track or try several directions before settling more firmly on one.

The sequence lasts several years. A scientist or professional (such as an academic biologist) spends many years as a student in the university. A novelist must discipline himself to the solitary work of writing out of his own imagination. Executives usually spend their twenties in engineering, sales and lower-level management. Hourly workers in industry need several years to explore the work world, acquire some training and experience, get acquainted with a particular industry and union, move beyond the apprentice status and find a more stable occupational niche. The sequence varies, but for all occupations it extends over the course of the novice phase. Not until the end of the Age Thirty Transition does a man complete his occupational novitiate and assume a fully adult status in the work world.

The level of attainment a man reaches by age 33 or 34 also varies. A biologist may be an associate professor with a national reputation or an assistant professor just starting to do independent research. A novelist may be a celebrated "promising young writer" or an unknown. An executive may be on the first rung of management or near the top. A worker may be a highly skilled machinist and shop steward or an unskilled laborer without job security.

The sequence of forming an occupation is in some cases relatively direct and monotonic, progressing in a straight line without gross conflicts or shifts in direction. A man sets himself a course and maintains his momentum on it until he is fully "in the occupation" and ready to settle down. This sequence is well exemplified by several (though by no means all) biologists in our study. In college they make the decision to become academic biologists. This choice is consistent with intense earlier interests, such as the outdoors, hiking, reproductive phenomena, a basement chemistry lab, tinkering with the hands. They may consider other occupational choices, such as medicine or engineering, but by the end of college they set aside the alternative options, perhaps to take them out again in a later period. After four or five years in graduate school, they often take a year or two of postdoctoral study, and then a university position as assistant professor. Some men complete the Age Thirty Transition at this time, others after they have been faculty members for a few years. Only at the end of the Age Thirty Transition, however, does a man complete the preparatory phase of his occupational development. Our biographee John Barnes is an example of this sequence, as we shall see in Chapter 17.

It is commonly assumed that men normally form an occupation in this steady, single-track manner. However, this sequence was not the norm in any of our occupational groups. It is not necessarily more "normal" or healthy than others. Even among the biologists, for whom the university training system exerts a powerful socializing influence, there are other sequences of equal or greater frequency.

For example, one of the most creative biologists in our study, Barry Morgan, quit high school at 16 against his parents' wishes. He spent three years in military service, then returned home and completed college at 24. Not yet ready to go out on his own, he remained for two years of graduate study and did excellent independent research. He could then make the shift to graduate work in a first-rank biology department, where he completed his doctoral degree at 31.

Morgan's choice of biology was made in college, during the Early Adult Transition. It was consonant with his early interests and his Dream of adult life. Still, he had recurrent doubts about this choice, and went through a three-year "crisis of commitment" before finishing the Ph.D. degree. It was only at 33, after a postdoctoral fellowship and a year's teaching in an elite university, that he completed the novice phase and embarked upon a more responsible, autonomous career. About this time he was also able, at last, to get married.

The novelists went through other complications during this formative phase. They generally had strong pre-adult interests in writing. By the Early Adult Transition, in most cases, a budding novelist was actively engaged in writing and had formed the Dream of becoming a writer. The vicissitudes of that Dream over the next fifteen years differed widely from one writer to another. In no case was the course simple or monotonic. One of our writers, Kevin Tyrone, got married and completed his first novel just before finishing college at age 23. He spent the next four years in a highly encapsulated life structure containing primarily his marriage and his writing. Work and marriage were organically linked by his wife's role in sustaining his Dream and supporting his literary efforts. Her work, and his own part-time job, provided an income at low emotional cost. By age 28, he had published three books and established a reputation as a creative (but not commercially successful) novelist. Now he could begin to believe that he might become a genuine writer.

At 28 Tyrone was a hard and serious worker, but his writing work did not constitute a money-earning occupation. The straight line had to zigzag. He became a part-time instructor in writing at an excellent university, with the blessing and the sponsorship of his devoted mentor. During the next four years, in the course of his Age Thirty Transition, he became an English professor at another university, continuing his writing and giving up the mentoring relationship that had served so well for about ten years.

Like many other men, and virtually all novelists, Tyrone had formed a hyphenated occupation. His version of this was writer-professor. In the period of Entering the Adult World, he established the groundwork for an identity and career as a novelist; and he learned that he could not count on earning a living by writing novels. He then used the Age Thirty Transition to form a new, academic occupation. In his early thirties, he started the Settling Down period with a life structure built around his two-sided occupation and his family.

It is often assumed that the life courses of working-class men in early adulthood are simple and static: they complete all or most of high school, get jobs, marry and start families, and by the mid-twenties are on paths that will continue with minimal change—barring surprises of fortune or misfortune—for many years. Our findings contradict this view. Working-class men go through the same underlying developmental periods as those in other classes and occupations, though they have their own class-related problems of entering the adult world and establishing a place for themselves within it. Eight of the ten workers in our sample experienced great difficulty forming a satisfactory occupation in Entering the Adult World and had a moderate or severe crisis in the Age Thirty Transition.

An example is Floyd Thomas, one of the three Black workers in our sample. In childhood Thomas was known as the "bad" son, "just like his father" (who had abandoned the family), in contrast to the "good" brother who was more studious and industrious, like the mother's side of the family. Thomas quit high school in the eleventh grade, worked in a foundry and at 18 enlisted in the army during the Korean War. While in basic training he married a woman who had been to college and led a more stable, middle-class life. He performed well in Korea as a demolition technician and was promoted to sergeant; but he then went AWOL and was discharged.

A civilian at 22, Thomas rejoined his wife in her home town. After a few months of holding a menial job and living a conventional life with his wife and her family, he deserted her and returned to his own home town. For the next four years he lived a rather disorganized life "on the street." He worked mostly in gambling and numbers, occasionally holding a more standard job until it became too oppressive. His Dream during this time was to become a boxing champion. It was not possible to make boxing his primary occupation, but he had a manager (a partial but important mentor) and established a local reputation. He had two or three brief reunions with his wife, who helped him become more independent of his mother. By age 26 he was becoming increasingly distressed with his chaotic life and aware that he would never realize his boxing Dream.

Thomas's Age Thirty Transition (age 27 to 31) was a time of struggle and recurrent crisis. He used it to terminate the fragmented life structure and to create the basis for a new life. With the help of his manager and his wife, he gave up the abortive boxing career and instead taught boxing to boys at the community center. He limited his extramarital sexual relationships and strengthened his commitment to the marriage. He rejoined the church at 28 and maintained a modest tie to it. Finding a job as machine operator in a local factory, he became a skilled worker and received several promotions.

By 31 Thomas had established the structure of his new life. Since both he and his wife worked, they could afford two cars, regular vacations and an increasingly middle-class life style. The tensions within the marriage were less severe but recurrently acute. His social life was mainly "with the boys": playing golf and engaging in milder versions of the earlier gambling, drinking and sexual promiscuity. His world and his wife's remained largely separate. His commitment to her was still conflicted: he found her moralistic, sexually forbidding and intolerant of his carefree, sensual side; but she provided a stable center that he needed and could find no other way of obtaining. At the end of his novice phase he was forming a life structure that could contain and give expression to these contradictory parts of himself, but they coexisted in an uneasy truce, not fully integrated. It would be the work of subsequent developmental periods to integrate, modify or drastically change this structure.

For all the occupations, our general finding is this: the process of forming an occupation extends over the novice phase of early adulthood. The process goes on for those who make an early, intense commitment to an occupation, for those who remain undecided, and for those who make major occupational shifts during their twenties. At the end of the Age Thirty Transition, the more open, formative phase is concluded. A man must now make more enduring choices and build on the groundwork established by that point. The formative process continues throughout early adulthood, but usually within the pattern established by the early thirties.

## Forming a Marriage and Family

While the wedding and the birth of the first child are important marker events in the history of the family, the process of forming a marriage and family starts well before the marker events and continues long afterward. As with a man's occupation, his marriage and family life go through a highly formative process throughout the novice phase and often much longer.

The process starts in a man's Early Adult Transition and continues in the succeeding periods. His first developmental task is to form the capability of having *adult peer relationships with women*. These relationships may have many components in many combinations: affection, sexuality, emotional intimacy, dependency, nurturing, romantic love, friendship, collaboration, respect, admiration, enduring commitment. It takes time for a young man to learn about his inner resources and vulnerabilities in relation to women, and about what they offer, demand and withhold from him. He has a lot to learn about the characteristics of women that attract him, and what it is about him that women find appealing. His pre-adult development prepares him, partially but never sufficiently, to undertake this developmental work. But it also leaves him with a legacy of guilt, anxiety and mystification. This legacy complicates his efforts to know women, to take them seriously, and to join with one woman in the long-term enterprise of building a marriage and family. In the light of these difficulties, it is small wonder that a man remains a novice at this task until the early thirties, and that relating to the feminine in others and in himself should be a lifelong developmental task.

And yet, ready or not, young men in all cultures, for countless generations, have been marrying and starting families in the novice phase. There has probably never been a society in which the average age at first marriage for the total population was greater than 25 years. (China may become a modern exception, through rigorous government policy, but this remains to be seen.) There are, of course, individuals and subgroups who marry later or not at all. Powerful forces impelling us toward some form of marriage and family seem to be given in the biological and psychological makeup of the individual and in the nature of human society. The question is not *whether* to have the family as a social institution, but *what form* of family institution is best suited to foster the development of children and parents under particular societal conditions.

A man in early adulthood needs to form relatively enduring relationships with women as well as men. He also needs to accept the responsibilities and pleasures of parenthood and to live out in some measure both the "masculine" and the "feminine" aspects of the self. Under reasonably favorable conditions, being a husband and father contributes to his development. It is in part a developmental failure when a young man is unable to function adequately in the family. When this occurs on a large scale it also reflects a failure of society and has destructive consequences for society.

How well these developmental tasks involving man-woman relationships, marriage and family are met is crucial for the well-being of individual, society and species. Given the fundamental importance of these tasks, it is astonishing that nature's timing is so bad: we must choose a partner and start a family before we quite know what we are doing or how to do it well. This is another of the bootstrap operations so common in human development, and another aspect of human complexity, growth and irrationality.

In deciding to marry, a young man vows to maintain a long-term relationship and, ordinarily, to create and raise a family. The fact that he undertakes this obligation does not necessarily mean, however, that he is prepared for it. Most men in their twenties are not ready to make an enduring inner commitment to wife and family, and they are not capable of a highly loving, sexually free and emotionally intimate relationship.

If a man marries during his Early Adult Transition (age 17 to 22), as about half of our sample did, he has had little experience in forming peer relationships with adult women. Courtship and marital choice are likely to be heavily bound up with the tasks of the Early Adult Transition, and especially with his efforts to separate from parents. He wants both to be very grownup and to maintain his pre-adult ties to parents and others. He is hardly a step beyond adolescence, where sex is so often a frightening mystery or an exploitive act. In the Early Adult Transition, a young man's efforts to establish an intimate marital relationship are complicated by his continuing sense of himself as a little boy in relation to a powerful maternal figure. He is engaged in a struggle both to express and to control his various fantasies of this figure as devouring witch, feeding breast, sexual seducer, humiliating rejecter, willing servant and demanding master. His wife attracts him in part because she seems to lack the qualities he fears and resents in his inner maternal figure. Yet their relationship may actually contain these and other aspects of the mother-son interaction (such as her indulging or admiring him), which in time are likely to become more problematic.

About 30 percent of the men in our study got married during the period of Entering the Adult World (roughly age 22 to 28). These marriages are colored by the tasks of this period and enriched by the developmental work done in the Early Adult Transition. Now, a man has more fully carried out the termination of pre-adulthood and is actively building his first adult life structure. He seeks a woman who will appreciate his emerging aspirations and want to share his planned life with him. Marriage during this period usually arises within, and is consonant with, the adult world he is entering and the life goals he is setting.

Still, there are many sources of difficulty for these marriages as well. Often the couple who marry in this period have known each other since the Early Adult Transition or before. However, the relationship formed earlier is less suitable for subsequent periods. This is one reason why romances formed in the teens usually break up after several years of seeming inseparability. If the couple do marry, it is frequently with serious misgivings in one or both partners—misgivings that are suppressed out of a sense of obligation to the partner or to the family and social network.

If a man is still a bachelor in his late twenties, he is likely to "get more serious" about marrying during his Age Thirty Transition. He is encouraged or pressed to marry by parents, friends and occupational network, and by voices within himself. His bachelorhood may earlier have been a delight: an opportunity to explore, to be sexually promiscuous, to have a few serious (but flawed) love affairs, or even to remain emotionally distant from women without worrying too much about having a "problem." During his Age Thirty Transition, however, being unmarried is usually experienced as a gap in his life, a lacuna in the life structure. The man who begins married life during this period, as 20 percent of our sample did, has the possible advantage of knowing more about himself and his relationships with women, and of having resolved more fully some of the conflicts from the past. He also has the possible disadvantage of marrying under pressure. Feeling that this is his last chance, he may make the choice in an effort to "normalize" his life more than to fulfill a deep love relationship.

Whatever the period in which marriage occurs, all marital relationships begin with some combination of strengths and problems. A couple is never fully prepared for marriage, no matter how long and how well the partners have known each other. Couples who settle early for a very limited relationship may find this sufficient for a while, but in time the discontents will erupt in gross conflict or will lead to a stagnant marriage. Continuing developmental work is required of individuals and couples in successive periods of the life course, if the marriage is to evolve in mutually satisfactory ways. The stability of marriage as an institution has traditionally been sustained by the binding forces of culture, religion, extended family and

law—and, frequently, by the tacit acceptance of discreet extramarital relationships. In contemporary society, as the legitimacy of authority and the
bonds of social integration are weakened, marital stability receives less institutional support and depends much more on the efforts of the spouses.

A man's love relationships with women can take many forms and serve
many functions. I want to describe one type of relationship, in which he
experiences her as the *special (loved and loving) woman.* (She too may experience him as the special man.) This is a unique relationship that ordinarily includes loving, romantic, tender and sexual feelings, but it goes
beyond this. The special woman is like the true mentor: her special quality
lies in her connection to the young man's Dream. She helps to animate the
part of the self that contains the Dream. She facilitates his entry into the
adult world and his pursuit of the Dream. She does this partly through her
own actual efforts as teacher, guide, host, critic, sponsor. At a deeper psychological level she enables him to project onto her his own internal feminine figure—the "anima," as Jung has depicted it—who generates and supports his heroic strivings. The special woman helps him to shape and live
out the Dream: she shares it, believes in him as its hero, gives it her blessing, joins him on the journey and creates a "boundary space" within which
his aspirations can be imagined and his hopes nourished.

Like the mentor, the special woman is a transitional figure. During early
adulthood, a man is struggling to outgrow the little boy in himself and to
become a more autonomous adult. The special woman can foster his adult
aspirations while accepting his dependency, his incompleteness and his
need to make her into something more than (and less than) she actually is.
Later, in the Mid-life Transition, he will have to become a more individual
person. With further development, he will be more complete in himself
and will have less need of the actual and the illusory contributions of the
special woman.

A couple can form a lasting relationship that furthers his development
only if it also furthers hers. If his sense of her as the special woman stems
mainly from his wishful projections and hardly at all from her own desires and efforts, sooner or later the bubble will burst and both will feel
cheated. If in supporting his Dream she loses her own, then her development will suffer and both will later pay the price. Disparities of this kind
often surface in transitional periods such as the Age Thirty Transition or
the Mid-life Transition.

A man's wife may be his special woman in the sense I have just described. Alternatively, they may have a relationship that is loving and supporting but has little connection to his Dream. Indeed, his wife may in
certain crucial respects be antithetical to his Dream. What she loves in

him, and what she wants to build into their life, may hinder or preclude the pursuit of the Dream. Choosing to marry her was, in effect, choosing to follow a direction away from the Dream. If her Dream is different from his, or antagonistic to it, their marriage starts with a contradiction that will have to be dealt with in time. A disparity of this kind may emerge only after years of marriage, often to produce bitter discontent and conflict.

This is an aspect of the current controversy between the various "traditional" and "liberated" versions of the woman's life. For the more traditional woman, primarily involved in her roles as wife and mother, the Dream is to have a certain kind of family and community life. Her identity is largely fashioned on and appended to the husband's. She helps him to realize his Dream, unless it preoccupies him too much and pulls him too far from marriage and family. His Dream thus serves as a vehicle for defining and pursuing her interests. The big challenge for her comes in the thirties and forties: her husband and children need her less and offer her less, and she must then form a more distinctive identity of her own.

The more liberated woman tries to form her own specific Dream. If she gets seriously involved in an occupation, she and her husband must make tremendous efforts at mutual accommodation and individual development. Acknowledging and managing the disparities between their Dreams is a crucial problem in the relationship between lovers and spouses. It is hard enough to form a life structure around one person's Dream. Building a structure that can contain the Dreams of both partners is a heroic task indeed, and one for which evolution and history have ill prepared us.

I have discussed this matter chiefly from the vantage point of the man. Ultimately, of course, it must be examined from the multiple perspectives of the man, the woman, the marriage, family and society.

## The End of the Novice Phase

How satisfactory were the life structures of our men as the Age Thirty Transition drew to a close? To answer this question, we divided the sample into three groups: (a) life structure predominantly positive; (b) mixed positive and negative, or ambiguous; (c) predominantly negative. There were fifteen men in category a, twenty in b and five in c. The "predominantly positive" category included three workers and four from each of the other groups. The five men in the "predominantly negative" category included three biologists, one executive and one novelist.

While some life structures are more satisfactory than others, no structure is without flaws and contradictions. Even the best structure has its limitations and must in time be changed. Every stable period is used to build, live within and enhance a particular structure. It is followed by a transitional period devoted to modifying or destroying that structure and creating the basis for a new but never permanent stability.

To get a sense of the developmental changes that occur during the novice phase, it is instructive to compare a man's life at 17 and 33. The contrast is remarkable. A qualitatively new structure is emerging. It always contains some elements from the past, but their meaning has changed within the context of a new life. In the Early Adult Transition a man's life is still strongly rooted in the family of origin and the pre-adult world; the process of separation is just getting under way. He has a Dream, inchoate or differentiated, and diverse hopes, fears, fantasies, plans for the future.

Fifteen years later, in the early thirties, his adolescence seems part of the distant past, far removed from the current world. Even if a man has continued to live in the same community and social context, changing times have brought changes in the fabric of his life. Most often, however, he lives in a new geographical locale and a new sociocultural world. By this time he almost certainly has a wife and family—perhaps is even divorced and remarried—and his sense of what it means to be a husband and father has altered dramatically. So too has the meaning of being a son: one or both parents may have died or, if they are alive, the balance is shifting toward his becoming a parent to them or losing contact with them. The character of his occupational life is taking a new shape. Even if his present occupation is the one he had hoped for, it contains possibilities and limitations he did not imagine in the Early Adult Transition. In most cases, the occupation is different in crucial ways from his earlier expectations.

As the Age Thirty Transition ends, a man moves toward major new choices or recommits himself to existing choices. A great deal hinges on these choices. If they are well made—from the viewpoint of the individual's Dream, values, talents, possibilities—they provide the center for a relatively satisfactory life structure. If the preparatory work has been poorly done and the new structure is flawed, life in Settling Down will become increasingly painful and attempts to create a more satisfactory structure will be more difficult and costly.

# 7 The Life of James Tracy, Executive (I)

James Bradford Tracy was born in 1924 in Exeter, New Hampshire, when both his parents were about 27 years old. In 1929 they moved to Haverstraw, a small New York town, and Jim's only sibling, George, was born that same year. The family revolved around Jim's mother.

> She and I fought like cats and dogs. We both had tempers, and I was continually losing my temper at her or she at me. She ground it into me that I wasn't supposed to lose my temper. She was a very strong person, very intelligent, a strong ruler and clearly ran the whole show.

His mother had graduated, Phi Beta Kappa, from Sweet Briar College in Virginia. She was ambitious, willful, bright and domineering:

> Our personalities are quite a bit alike. She ruled the roost, there's no question about that, and still does. She's always been very active in town. She was president of the garden club, head of the local welfare society, a big wheel in the town. My mother and father got along quite well, I'd say, and still do. They have been married almost 50 years; they're about 75. My growing up was reasonably normal, if there's any such thing. I had friends, played baseball and football. I was always very interested in athletics.

Jim's recollections of his early life focused on his mother. He had less to say about his father:

> My father came from a very poor family in Maine. His father died when he was three years old and he was brought up by his mother and worked from childhood on. He was the youngest of seven children in a tiny town. He got a scholarship out of high school to the University of Maine, went there three years, got the war fever and went into World War I. He became a pilot and never graduated from college. There was no GI Bill, or that kind of thing.
>
> My father's bright, I'm not saying he has better than average intelligence, but he's a smart guy and had a very good job at Owens-Corning. He was head industrial engineer, which is a very responsible job. While we were not well off during the depression, we certainly had food and clothing and

were a hell of a lot better off than a lot of people. I never wanted for anything.

His mother's side of the family was clearly superior in terms of class, creativity and accomplishment. A well-educated, genteel young lady from a well-to-do Protestant family, she married a lower-class, upwardly mobile Catholic New England college dropout. Although her husband was a stable man and good provider, the marriage might well have been a rebellious act against her father, Robert Bradford, who was far more powerful and charismatic than her husband. The Bradfords had come over on the Mayflower and had settled in Boston. To young Jim, his maternal grandfather was a heroic figure:

> My grandfather went to Rensselaer Polytechnical Institute. He took a four-year course in electrical engineering in three years and had the highest grades ever recorded. He ended up as an inventor in the electrical field. My grandfather was a great big tall man, about six feet four, with a violent temper—a huge man. A lot of people were afraid of him but he and I got along very well, for some reason or other, and I was just a little kid. Anyhow, Kettering, the inventor of the electric starter for cars, came in one day and tried to hire him and take him to Detroit. My grandfather was always very proud of the fact that he threw Kettering bodily out of his shop. He didn't want to be one of his goddamn flunkies. He had I don't know how many basic patents, which he sold to General Electric.
>
> When he was 34 years old, he accidentally lost the sight of one eye and weakened the other. He had to quit inventing because he couldn't see, and he lived for the rest of his life on his royalties. He lived very well. He had a Cadillac and a big house in Darien, Connecticut. He had about four acres of land right smack in the middle of Darien—woods, gardens and orchards. I used to have to do my chores, work in his garden every morning, and then I would be able to play in the afternoon.
>
> He started writing history books about the Pilgrims. There's a fabulous book collection about the Pilgrims which he gave me in his will. He was a cantankerous old bastard in his later years, but a very bright guy. I think I was closer than most anyone to him, which was strange, because my cousin lived with him. But I got the Pilgrim books, which were his prize possession.
>
> He gave the world things which I think are quite important. He was the first to make printing presses run by electricity as opposed to steam, and he did the same thing for other industries.

Jim's mother carried the flavor and power of this man. She had his temper, and so did Jim. She had his ambition, intelligence and will. She made Jim feel special, the favorite. She guided and sometimes pushed him.

While Grandfather was the model, Mother was the one who nourished and sustained Jim's dream of himself as a leader of men:

> I have the same drive my mother had. I'm reasonably intelligent and I think I'm more like her in that respect. My mind is more like hers. I have a quicker mind than my father, who has a slower, more methodical mind. My mother is very quick.

Father paled by comparison. "He's always been sort of a shadow," Jim said. "He hasn't had very much influence on me at all. He's been there, and I like him, but he just hasn't really had much influence on me." Father remained in the background, overshadowed by the driving mother and genius grandfather. Mother and grandfather stood for individual initiative, accomplishment and success; father represented stability, but a stability that was mundane.

His younger brother, George, was more like their father—a shadowy, passive, retiring figure. George was the devalued one, who did not stand out academically or in sports. He was large, good-looking and more outgoing, but he couldn't keep up with his older brother.

Jim Tracy was shy and introverted. He learned, via messages from his mother, to exercise self-control and to commit himself only in situations from which he would emerge looking good. "I had a feeling about not wanting to look *foolish*," he said at 44, when he was interviewed. "I've outgrown a good part of it, but I still hate to look foolish, just as my son does. I hate to enter into something where I'm not going to do well. I just hate to do something where somebody is thinking that I'm compromising myself or just looking silly."

In Haverstraw, a neighbor and retired naval captain who had "only daughters," began, with Mother's encouragement, to treat Jim as a son. When Jim was ten he began going with the neighbor to football games at Annapolis. Soon it was assumed that he would eventually attend the naval academy.

Jim enjoyed athletics as a boy. With his competitiveness and determination, he compensated for his average ability and was able to excel. He went to a YMCA summer camp which gave an award to the outstanding camper. "Whoever won that award automatically became a counselor the next year. Well, I won the damn thing! It was the first time I'd ever won. I was very pleased, needless to say. So I went back for two more years as a counselor. That's how I spent my summers." Winning that competition at twelve was a symbolic event. He had competed against his peers, and won. His victory, free of parental influence and taking place hundreds of miles from home, was an achievement of his own.

Feeling that the local high school was inadequate for her son, his mother decided to send him to a first-rate prep school. His father thought this was risky: Jim might have to repeat a year of high school. Father struggled but, as usual, Mother won. Through the influence of her old family friends, she got her son into the elite, all-male Exeter Academy. He entered at 17 as a "half sophomore/half junior. I had to take extra courses that year and go to summer school. I lost only one year instead of two. It took me five years to get through high school."

Socially, Exeter meant a marked change from the more casual Haverstraw public school:

> During my last couple of years in high school, I went with one girl for a long time. Then at the prep school I broke up with her. The guys I ran around with in high school were interested in athletics. We spent most of our time playing seasonal sports. I went out for track, and concentrated on being a distance runner. We played sports during the day and had movie dates on Friday and Saturday nights.
>
> Exeter was pretty liberal as far as prep schools go. They used to give us one weekend a month, where, if your grades were up, you could go to Boston and raise holy hell. We used to make out with local girls. Funny coincidence, a woman that my mother roomed with in college ran a local girls' school, which I thought was going to be a big "in" in terms of going out with girls. I tried it once, but she gave me the biggest dog in the school and I never went back. Exeter was a very tough school academically. I had to study like hell. I didn't have time for anything else other than studying and athletics.

As graduation approached, the naval captain neighbor arranged for his congressman to recommend Jim for Annapolis. He took a competitive exam that summer and placed second.

> You talk about blind luck. The two courses I had to take in the summer at Exeter were algebra and geometry. Then I took a seven-hour exam for the academy and it was on algebra and geometry. I came in second of 200. Then my friend Captain Anderson really got into action. He went to the local congressman, who traded a West Point for an Annapolis; sent two guys to Annapolis rather than one to each.

Jim was being groomed by his mother to be the kind of man she most respected. It was she who did the educational planning and who made everything happen through the interventions of her Exeter friends, Captain Anderson and the New York congressman. Mother's dream that her son would become a leader was now his Dream as well. Her family had landed at Plymouth Rock. This heritage was carried by Grandfather, who symbolized the heroic aspects of American creativity and industrial know-how. He transferred this legacy to Jim, favoring him with a gift of cherished books. Mother communicated similar themes of high achievement and leadership to her first-born son. Father did not reject this orientation, but he did not represent or communicate it in the way that Mother and her family did.

## The Early Adult Transition

Jim started at Annapolis in 1943, at age 19. He was starting a transitional period that carried him into early adulthood. Because of the war, the academy had shortened its length of study to three years. During his first year, Jim did extremely well and ranked near the top of his class. He watched himself carefully, keeping tight control over his friendships and his academics.

> It was extremely rigid. I have tried to remember my first three weeks there and it's an absolute blank. I did very well my first year, mainly because I wanted to stay out of trouble. . . . Exeter is a very fine school academically, and really set me up. I had good grades. During the war they crammed four years into three and forgot all the "nonessential" subjects. I never had a lot of courses that I would have liked to have taken, like philosophy. We had a lot of history, math, sciences, tactics, just wham wham wham.

Jim's Dream found a supportive environment at the naval academy with its emphasis upon authority, leadership and team effort. The traditional values of his family were given expression in his life at the academy. He taught at the Annapolis Sunday school. His grades began to drop during his second year, and he eventually graduated in the middle of his class. He then volunteered for the U.S. Marines.

At the naval academy, Jim had shown a lack of initiative in his relationships with women. Talking excitedly about his Annapolis roommate, an athletic hero, he told several stories which centered on the theme of the devouring woman:

> He was my roommate for six months, until he flunked out. He was a very nice guy. He married a Hollywood star, or she married him. She nailed him. A fabulous athlete . . . but he was just totally innocent, and people would constantly take advantage of him, because he was absolutely naïve. And boy, she did! He really got taken to the cleaners.

Jim was not to be similarly consumed. In fact, he did not date seriously until he met Victoria in his last year. She was a Catholic, the only child of an admiral who had died in combat during World War II. Jim met her one weekend when another midshipman brought her to Annapolis for a dance. They began a one-year courtship, conducted primarily through the mail: "She was very popular with a lot of different midshipmen. She was relatively highly thought of by various people. I dated her a lot, and we got along very well. She was a good dancer."

Although Victoria was a virgin, Jim had had some prior sexual experience. Like his other relationships with women, the long-distance relationship with Victoria lacked depth and maturity.

During the Early Adult Transition, which Jim was completing at this time, a man has to make preliminary choices out of which a new life structure can be formed in the next period. Jim Tracy graduated from the naval academy with hopes of a distinguished career as a Marine officer. He single-mindedly followed this traditional path laid out by his mother and others. But he spent little time or energy on personal relationships, especially with women. His Early Adult Transition was focused on career to the detriment of his personal life. These choices had consequences for Jim's subsequent development.

## Entering the Adult World

After graduating at 22, Jim Tracy was assigned to a marine base in Virginia. He felt isolated. Two months later, he proposed to Victoria and they were married. "I went down to Virginia after I graduated. I was lonely as hell," he said. "Some of the guys were married and they looked like they were having a ball. I thought it would be a great idea. . . . I had been penned up for three years. It was a stupid move, but I did it."

Victoria, the "Navy brat," seemed a logical choice for someone hoping to rise in the military ranks. But there were problems from the start. For one thing, Victoria's religion:

> I got fed up with Catholicism. They made me read a 1500-page instructional book. The head priest, a very fine guy, gave it to me, and I read it from cover to cover. The more I studied, the more I realized that I would never become a Catholic. I just couldn't believe it. And then I married Victoria. She went to a Catholic church. I went with her for a while and then just quit. I never went back to church, which made me feel guilty every once in a while.

Victoria was quite frivolous: she spent most of her time at golf, bowling and tennis with the other officers' wives. She was "kind of cold, semifrigid, a slob and a poor housekeeper." Yet this time was "the best of my marriage":

> She didn't respond very well sexually. She didn't like the physical act itself. She would be very interested in foreplay. I don't think the physical act repulsed her, she just sure as hell didn't get much out of it. . . . We were pretty happy. She was still lousy in bed, but I would say it was a pretty good marriage for the first year and a half, or at least the time we were down there. We had a lot of fun. She was a good companion.

Their first child, Linda, who was not planned, was born two years after their marriage. Soon after, the Tracys went to England, where Jim began a round of affairs with anonymous women, some married, some single, and all but one younger than he. While he was having an intense affair with an Irish woman, Victoria became pregnant again. A son, Robert, was born after they returned to the States. Tracy was 27. The two unplanned children were their major ties. Linda became "the apple of my eye. . . . I poured my love out to Linda because I had no desire to pour it out to Victoria. That's the way I've always looked at it. I'm not making any excuses for myself."

His connection to Robert was minimal.

> He was treated equally with Linda. I think he must have sensed that I didn't have the same affection for him that I had for Linda. It wasn't any obvious thing. It's not that I didn't like him and I did like her. It's just that I loved her more, if it's possible to love someone more.

His feeling for his children contrasted sharply with his cold, distant, impersonal relationships with women. The women did not have names; they were literally sexual objects:

> The first affair that was really other than totally casual was an infatuation. I can't say I loved her; I don't think it was that strong, but I felt a great desire for her. I liked going to bed with her, and it was an all-consuming desire. The women were a mixture of some totally spur-of-the-moment casual types and others that weren't. It wasn't a pattern other than they were pebbles on the beach.

Jim's idealistic but unexamined hopes for a good marriage had been shattered. His relationships with other women made him feel a failure as a husband and father.

> I didn't have any feelings of guilt as far as Victoria was concerned. I had a feeling of guilt as far as the family situation was concerned, because by that time I had a sense of loyalty to Linda, whom I was really very fond of. I think the real thing that kept me in my family was my daughter.

As a marine, Jim Tracy did well during these six years. There were promotions and the glimmer of a bright future. Older men were always in positions of authority over him. A marine general in England was impressed by Jim, and asked him to become his aide. Jim served for a year in that post, and during that time accompanied his general to the war college. "I met all kinds of people, heard all sorts of things and was exposed to a lot of high-ranking people in the Navy. Most of them are now admirals or retired."

These powerful men provided numerous opportunities and responsibilities. Tracy thrived, rose from company officer to battalion G-3, a planner for large numbers of men. He attended several military schools, volunteered for the paratroops, learned to fly, and became a general's aide. In this position, as a captain, he became an instructor of well-known admirals.

From roughly age 24 to 27, Jim Tracy knew many women. Only one of them had an identity for him—like Victoria, she was an admiral's daughter. They met while Jim was stationed at the war college.

> The one that I really flipped over was an admiral's daughter. I was working for the admiral and it would have been kind of a political scandal since she was engaged to another officer. We were getting hot and heavy the last few months, and then she got married. I was an usher at the wedding, so it was amusing. I'll never forget it as long as I live. I wasn't laughing too much at the time! Then she went off with this guy. We corresponded for four or five months and then sort of broke it off . . . sounds pretty sordid. I guess it was.

By having an affair with the admiral's daughter, Tracy was taking a risk. "Looking back on it, I can laugh, but you know, a marine post is a small community. I would never take some of those chances again."

There was a frantic "prowling" quality about his sexual life.

> I felt very badly about it. I thought about it quite a bit, what a son of a bitch I was, running around with all of those people's wives. It was a hell of a way to be. But I did it. I had a great sexual attraction to those girls. I sort of had an insatiable desire, something kept pushing me. I was constantly on the prowl, and I mean constantly.

Behind the prowling, there was a vague longing:

> I felt a sense of failure. I just had a great, strong urge to be chasing after people. It wasn't a guilt feeling against Victoria, but a guilt feeling against the principle. There was something wrong with me. I always felt that what I really wanted was to love somebody and be completely faithful to them. That was a real ambition that I had. This was after I married Victoria, and I was probably rationalizing all over the place. I

really wanted to be faithful to somebody all the time I was running around
like a madman.

What kept me at it, as much as anything else, was not feeling that
strongly about anybody. I'd be madly in love with somebody, but when it
came right down to should I really get divorced and break up the family
and leave my kids, I'd back off.

In his early twenties, Tracy's life structure had two primary elements:
his budding career as a military officer, and his new marriage. He married
a woman he hardly knew. She lacked many of the qualities required in this
occupational world. She could not support his heroic Dream. Soon the
marriage began to disintegrate, and instead of working on it, he withdrew.

By 28, there were three elements in his life structure: work, family
and the "other woman." Work was central, although Jim was having serious
doubts about his suitability for military life. The family was important, but
the relationship with Victoria was becoming progressively more destructive
for both of them. He was not indifferent to the changing relationship with
Victoria. He wanted more, but as things got worse, he gave less and tried
less to improve the marriage.

The "other woman" played an important role: she allowed Jim to deal
with tensions by having two different women as foils. Casual affairs with a
series of women culminated in the intense relationship with the admiral's
daughter when he was 27. For the first time he experienced rejection by a
woman.

## The Age Thirty Transition

By 1952, at age 28, Jim Tracy had had six years of marriage and the marines.
At this point, he started asking himself: Is there anything more to life
than the lock-pace of the marines, a cold marriage, and sexually exciting
but empty encounters with women? The rewards doled out by older men
proved inadequate compensation for his lack of rapid advancement and
his personal defeats. He did not have a special woman or a mentor who
might have helped him sustain the Dream and give it expression. On his
own, awkwardly, he sought a new way.

Although he could not leave his family, he began to think seriously
about leaving the marines. He had earned several promotions, but he knew
that his chances for becoming a general were nil. More than that, his
desire for the military life was equally low. After stewing for several months,
Tracy volunteered for combat duty in Korea: "I had never been shot at and

I had a peculiar philosophy. Maybe it sounds corny, but I really meant it. I felt the country educated me, and I owed them something. Having missed World War II, I volunteered for combat in Korea."

Volunteering for combat was a critical event. It marked the decision to end his military career. By going through the ordeal of combat, he could repay society, family and military, and leave the service with a sense of dignity. The volunteering also reflected the desire to explore new ways of living. Finally, it represented a turning away from his mother and her aspirations for him toward an unknown future of his own making.

In 1953, about a year after signing up for combat, Tracy got to Korea. It was a remarkable experience:

> The guy who was the corps commander said, "I am assigning you not only the worst company in the division, but the worst company in Korea. Your mission is to straighten it out." That was my interview. I said, "Yes, sir," got in the jeep and arrived at this company. I had never felt lower in my life. This company was something, just unbelievable. They had a patrol going out that night led by a sergeant. I asked the acting company commander, "Where do you suggest I go while this patrol is out?" He said, "You can sit in the observation post and listen on the radio." The patrol supposedly set up an ambush, but *they* got ambushed. One guy was killed and four wounded before midnight. We hauled one guy up to the battalion hospital. He had his balls shot off. That was always a great fear of mine; being in combat and having my balls shot off. I went back to the company about three in the morning. That was a pretty full day.
>
> I found out that they had been on patrols every single night doing the work of the infantry battalions that were up manning the front line. They were taking casualties and getting no recognition, which was totally demoralizing. The next morning, I went to the G-3 and said, "Colonel, I would like my company pulled off all combat duty. Give me a week to get them straightened out, and then we will be ready to go again." He said okay. I went back to the company, told everybody what the drill was and that started it. We ended up with a pretty good company.

The men responded positively to the change. Jim began to feel that it was his company, and with that came a sense of great accomplishment. Still, he felt that "lady luck" was in evidence throughout.

> You know, luck is a strange damn thing. On the third day there, we were roaring down the road in wintertime and I had my .45 underneath my parka. Suddenly I saw two Korean pheasants. I told the driver to stop and I started to jump out of the jeep. By this time, the first pheasant took off and I was trying to get the flap off my holster. About the time I got the pistol out, the second pheasant took off. I pumped a round into the chamber of the gun and it went boom, like a cannon, and there were all

kinds of pheasants running around. We paced off the distance. It was 48 paces from where I shot to, which would be a long shot for a shotgun. I mean it was just absolutely a lucky shot. We went out and picked up the pheasant, and brought it back to the company area. The jeep driver went around and told everybody that the old man was a crack shot with a .45. Anywhere I went, all I could hear about was my .45. Little things like that can be so goddamn important, just a blind-ass lucky shot. I don't know why I shot at it; I will never know.

His stories had a modest tone but made his success clear. There was the persistent implication that he just happened to be in the right place at the right time. He was always the modest, unassuming hero, but let there be no mistake, he remained possessed of heroic qualities.

Jim proved himself again to those in authority by turning the unit into "the best one in the command." After five months of combat, the general helicoptered into Tracy's area and told him, "Now that you have gotten your nose bloody, I want you in command headquarters." For the first time in his military life, he had nothing to do with women and was given jurisdiction over younger men. He experienced a great sense of achievement: he had paid his debt to society and his leadership skills had been affirmed.

After a brief tour of duty back in the states, in 1954, Jim reassessed his life. The war was ending and he was a 30-year-old captain with 8 years of service. He knew that "only 3 out of 800 men from Annapolis can make admiral or marine general." It was time to decide: "Am I going to stay in the marines, or am I going to do something else?" He made plans to leave.

It was just a feeling of wanting to get ahead at my own speed and then seeing if I could, as opposed to getting ahead at the speed of the marines. There were a whole bunch of little things that contributed to it, but I think that was the overriding thing. I wanted very much to be a general.

He was questioning not just the service, but his whole life structure. Although both his marriage and his military career were untenable, he decided to maintain the family stability in order to cope with the instability of leaving the marines.

Tracy began looking for a job in industry. His father suggested Ajax Industries, an arms manufacturer. For the first time, his father offered to help and Jim allowed him to do so. Objectively, his father was well able to play this role, as he was an engineer and company manager who was knowledgeable about industry. Jim's ability to accept his father's help may also represent an effort to redress the old parental imbalance. To an extent, he now rejected the aggressive mother and her dream of him as military hero, in favor of the helpful father and his own wish to be an industrial leader. It foreshadowed a new life, although the specific shape was still ill-defined.

While stationed at Brooklyn Navy Yard, he put on a civilian suit and crossed the East River for an interview. The initial interview was dull until "a huge man with rolled-up shirtsleeves started to talk to me." They spent an hour in excited discussion.

> I went out to the receptionist and said, "What does he do?" She said, "He's the vice president for operations and four divisions report to him." His name was Albert Hugo. I went home and got hold of a *Fortune* article on Ajax. Instantly I said, "Boy, here is one smart man." He called me at ten o'clock the next morning and made me an offer. It was exactly the same amount of money I was making as a captain in the marines, $6,000 a year. I accepted it. This was about the middle of June, and I said to him, "Well, what do I do now?" He said, "When can you report to work?" I said, "The 23rd of August," which was my brother's birthday. He said, "Fine." I never got a piece of paper or anything. I got out of the marines and put on my civilian suit and got on the train. I started the 23rd of August and worked for him until April. He was the most fantastic guy I've ever met. He was a Woodrow Wilson scholar, doctor of physics, Massachusetts Doubles Tennis Champion, and about six feet five. He had everything going for him. He was a hell of a nice guy and brilliant. There's very few of them. I loved him.

Six months after starting with Ajax in New York, Jim was told by Al Hugo that Hercules, an Ajax subdivision in Chicago, was having difficulty. Tracy was to work temporarily at Hercules. Within six months, he turned the company around and became a top manager.

Tracy admired Al Hugo's philosophy about work.

> Al told me that there are very few people who really want to accept responsibility. He said that's what he saw in me, not only wanting but having a real desire to accept responsibility. He said that most people instinctively don't, whereas I was just eager to. I wanted to stick my neck out at that stage in my life, just wanted to prove that I could do things.

Once again, Tracy had found an older man in authority who nurtured and helped guide him. He was closer to Al Hugo than he had been to the admirals and generals, but there was the same quality of hero worship, a quality first articulated in his attitude toward another large and bright man: his grandfather. Al recognized Jim's need to be a responsible leader, and helped him bridge the gap between the military and civilian side of management.

The key question for Jim Tracy at 33 was whether he could adapt to the role of managing a civilian enterprise. After succeeding in Chicago, he was promoted to a management position in Hartford. He moved from a subsystem with a few hundred workers to the "main action," the Firearms Division of Ajax Industries. The next level was the corporate structure in New York City! The Firearms Division was doing well, but its management was in a transitional stage. These changes increased the challenge and the anxiety for him.

During his first month in Hartford, Jim was assigned a secretary, Joan, who was married and ten years his junior. They soon started an affair, seemingly just another of his many conquests. But something had changed. After a few months, by mutual agreement, he got her a job in the Chamber of Commerce and they continued their relationship. Jim found himself investing more in Joan than he had in other women. Obtaining a job for her symbolized his wish—and initial commitment—that their relationship might become more intimate and lasting. Later, he described her as follows:

> I consider her my equal. She's very intelligent, personable, has all the
> social graces, and speaks very good English. Joan, somehow, has taught her-
> self all these. She's bright as hell, but not very well read, and is therefore
> worried about how she comes off. . . . She's always been a loner. I think
> I'm the first person she ever opened up to. She just kept everything within
> herself all her life. She comes from a poor, large family. She's totally differ-
> ent from the rest of her family. I think they don't understand her. . . .
> With regard to her marriage, she was seriously considering divorce before
> she met me, but put it off. I guess after she got married, she discovered
> that she had never gotten along with her husband. Suddenly being face to
> face with him alone in the house really shook her up and she didn't want
> any part of him.

The relationship with Joan matured, and he stopped seeing other women. The driven, aggressive voice within Jim was subdued; he became more concerned and loving. He remained with his family and kept Joan at the periphery, but for the first time he had a serious relationship with a woman.

Jim was thus modifying both his Dream and his love life. The experience in Korea enabled him to act on his earlier desire to leave the service. Instead of becoming a general, he would become a corporate leader. The move to civilian life involved an awakened respect for his previously devalued father. With the shift in occupation, he slowly started to change his personal life. His slowness in taking direct action related to his difficulty in forming an intimate relationship with an adult woman. It may have been necessary for Jim to get his mother and her Dream for him out of his life before he could establish a more mature relationship with another woman.

The responsibility for the deteriorating marriage was shared. Jim's overly negative view of Victoria suggests that he was not ready, in this season of his life, to address his own role as failed husband. To do so would have required a more balanced view of the relationship, and an ability to look within for his own part in it. This would mean a dramatic turn from his characteristic goal-oriented attitude, a questioning of his past and a readiness to explore new ways of living. He was not yet ready for this.

At 28, Tracy had started to question his first adult life structure and to ask what else life might have in store for him. At 34, he answered this question. He made three critical choices which provided the basis for a new life structure. They marked the end of his Age Thirty Transition and the start of the Settling Down period.

First, he decided to continue with Victoria and the children. Fatherhood remained important to him. He was being true to his traditional upbringing, although it was painful to go on living with his family.

Second, he confirmed his earlier, tentative decision to become an executive. Tracy made a place for himself within the Ajax organization, and held high aspirations for advancement to the top of the corporate structure.

Third, he decided to have a more intimate, enduring relationship with a woman. The question of marriage had not emerged, but he was beginning to hope that she would become special for him.

In Chapter 11, we shall discover what kind of life structure he built around these choices, and how his life evolved during the Settling Down period.

# The Life of William Paulsen, Worker

William Paulsen was born in 1925 and raised in a Scandinavian and Irish community in the Bay Ridge section of Brooklyn. His grandmother, a central figure in his early years, had come to this country as a child from Norway. The family revolved around her. There was continual friction between the dominating grandmother and her daughter, reflected in Bill's belief that if you put two women under the same roof you're asking for trouble.

Each summer, Bill's grandmother left Brooklyn for upstate New York, where she ran a 28-room boardinghouse. With his mother and sister, Bill accompanied her for the summer. He was responsible for many of the chores around the boardinghouse and farm: taking care of the chickens, milking the cows, bringing in the hay. It was "a hard life but a good one." He worked from 5:30 A.M. to 7 at night, and called himself the "farmer from Brooklyn."

Bill learned early that his grandmother ruled his family. She was a "shrewd businesswoman, a penny-pinching Scandinavian," and Bill admired her toughness. She worked hard, ran the whole show with great skill, and saw to it that everything was done her way. "She knew what she wanted," Bill said, "and if she didn't get it, everybody look out." She provided the structure and discipline in Bill's life.

Bill's mother was very different. She lived in her mother's shadow. She was a troubled woman, high-strung and nervous, who found it hard to manage on her own. She was very dependent on her own mother and yet resentful of her control. This was evident in her work as a waitress in her mother's boardinghouse. His mother was quite protective and indulgent of Bill: if he wanted something, she would give it to him, even if that meant depriving others in the family. By indulging Bill, she encouraged him to lean on her, to let her do for him rather than to fend for himself. She seems to have been a helpless person who implicitly invited Bill to be like her.

Bill's father was a good man without great ambition, content to settle for a modest place in life. For 38 years he held the same clerical job with a stock-brokerage firm on Wall Street. He never got more than a $10-a-week raise—which bothered Bill—but he felt lucky to be working at all during the depression years. He had a lot of common sense and was generous with his attention and advice. When there was trouble, he and Bill would sit down and talk. He was "more a buddy than a father." Implicit in Bill's description was the view of his father as a kind man who had failed to achieve the things Bill wanted. At the same time, he was Bill's "best friend."

Bill's family offered limited resources and models for his later development. He admired his grandmother's ambition, hard work, toughness and concern with fairness. Like her, Bill was to work to make a better life for himself. From his parents came other attributes. Like his mother, Bill would have a continuing struggle against the wish to be given what he wanted when he wanted it, and the wish to give up and be looked after. Like his father Bill would strive to make his peace with the world and to settle for a modest place in it. Like him, he would come to love his pastimes and see them as a major source of pleasure and satisfaction in his adult life.

These diverse aspects of Bill's pre-adulthood created the tensions that ran through the core of his adult life: the tension between striving and giving up; between going after and being given to; between ambition and settling for a modest life. Few people served as models for an adult life he could find inspiring. He admired his grandmother's way of living, but did not aspire to do what she did. He was very critical of his mother and tried to reject her way of living. He loved and admired his father, but was also critical of his settling for so little. There was no admired teacher, relative or friend whose life Bill wanted to emulate. All in all, his world offered him little in the way of models or opportunities. The importance of this was apparent in Bill's description of himself at 18: ". . . just a green kid, had never been away from home, always ran back to Mother and Dad for any of my problems or what not, never had to take care of my own clothes or anything." He came to the end of adolescence feeling that he had no particular capabilities or interests. He didn't know what he wanted to do with his life.

## The Early Adult Transition

At 18, there was nothing the "green kid" wanted to do, and nothing he felt he could do. But it was 1943, and the realities of World War II swept him up: he was drafted shortly after his eighteenth birthday. The event marked the beginning of a transitional period in Bill's life.

He trained as a forward observer in the field artillery and went to Europe three days after D-Day. He was in combat for a year and a half in a dangerous and exciting job. It was up to him to establish forward observation posts locating enemy fire. Bill, a member of General George Patton's Third Army, was involved in the dash across France into Germany. Though often terrified, he found the experience valuable: "It made men out of us instead of little boys."

The military experience helped Paulsen learn to take responsibility for himself and for his place in a larger enterprise. He found that he could manage his own life and could work effectively. But this was achieved in a structured organization where he generally knew what was expected of him. While he might fend for himself, he was never required to determine his own goals or make his own way. Upon leaving the service, Bill needed to return to earlier, unfinished developmental work. He had to form a clearer sense of himself, a fuller personal identity. He needed a guiding vision of himself in the adult world, a Dream that would give direction in his attempts to build a life.

Bill left the army in 1945. Re-entry into civilian life was hard for him. He didn't know what he wanted and was unable to make the critical choices so important in determining his life course. There was a sense of aimlessness, of starting adult life and work late. He made basic decisions almost haphazardly.

Just like every other veteran that came back, we wallowed around and whooped it up and, of course, had no direction in life that we wanted to go to. I wasn't married, not going with any particular gal at that time, and this went on for about 3 to 4 months. I didn't even go to work. Didn't know what I wanted to do. Didn't have any capabilities at the time. So, my best friend and his brother, we sat down one afternoon and I turned and looked at Ed and said, "Hey, why don't we go to college for a couple of years?" So Ed and I decided, let's go to technical school. We found this N.Y. State Agricultural College that was starting up a technical division. We were fortunate to get in as the first technical class. Then the decision, what are we going to take up? He looks at me and says, "You know, you and me we've been fooling around with transformers and lights, and wiring our cellars for ourselves, and we sort of enjoy it. Why don't we take up electrical work?" So we did. . . . When we graduated I was in the top 20 or 25. We had excellent grades, which surprised him and me and our parents because they figured that, ah—we were known as the three holy terrors of Brooklyn, and we'd never amount to anything. But I guess we sort of proved them wrong.

Paulsen acquired a skill that could provide a job and a living. But the work did not involve the realization of a plan, nor did it have much meaning in terms of major values, goals or aspects of the self.

In his last year of college, Bill met Ruth, who was two years older. He felt they had much in common and enjoyed being with her. But Bill's mother opposed the choice. According to Bill, she felt that Ruth was taking him away from her and she wanted to hold on to him. It seems likely that his mother also had a feeling that both Bill and Ruth talked about: that he was not "mature" enough for marriage.

The issue was joined not around the question of Bill's "maturity" but around the problem of Ruth's religion. Bill was a Protestant, Ruth a Catholic. She wanted him to convert. His mother opposed the conversion and the marriage. Bill defied her. He received instructions in the Catholic Church, was converted, and married Ruth in early 1949, when he was 23.

It was important for Bill to leave Brooklyn and live with Ruth in a place removed from his family. They bought "a regular house, a Cape Cod type" on Long Island, sixty-five miles from his parents. For the first time, Bill was demonstrating a readiness to separate from his family and a willingness to fight for what he wanted in the face of his mother's protest.

When he married, Bill was working for IBM and commuting into New York City. He left home at six in the morning and got back for supper at eight or nine at night. He felt that his job was too demanding and didn't allow enough time to be with his wife. Although he liked IBM, he quit after a year. At age 23, he took a job with the Long Island Lighting Company, and worked there for six years. In making this decision, Bill gave no thought to what either company offered him in terms of future job advancement and satisfaction. He was primarily concerned about the quality of his life at the time, not the long-term consequences of his choice.

The Early Adult Transition lasted from age 18 to 23. During this period he moved from a life structure characteristic of late adolescence to one characteristic of early adulthood. At 18 he was a "green kid," closely tied to his family, not knowing what he wanted to make of his life, and feeling that he was "without capabilities." His life was built around his relationships with his family and friends in Bay Ridge. Over the next five years he effected a radical transformation in this structure: he started earning his own way in the work world, got married, and lived in his own home away from parents. He lived in a community very different from that in which he had grown up. He had severed his ties to the ethnic community, which had been so vital a part of his early life, and had changed his religious and political affiliation. These changes reflected his work on the developmental tasks of this period.

The new structure was flawed, however, by Paulsen's failure to do other important developmental work. He still lacked a clear sense of himself as a person. Nor did he develop a Dream. In these respects he failed to do the developmental work of the Early Adult Transition. He made the central choices of this period primarily in terms of his wish to get away from the past. He was oriented to the present and had little sense of the future. Both Bill and Ruth commented on this. Bill spoke of his immaturity. Ruth told of her feeling that he wasn't ready to marry:

> Before we were married he used to say, "We're going to the movies at least three times a week." And I said, "We'll go to the movies if we have the money but if we don't have the money we won't go." He had been used to doing things when he wanted to do them.

## Entering the Adult World

The life structure begun at 23, with his marriage and new job, remained relatively stable over the next six years. Paulsen's work for the Long Island Lighting Company was in the Emergency Service Department. He started as a "glorified telephone operator," taking emergency calls through the switchboard and directing repair men in the field. He worked up to being "a special service operator" in charge of one of the work shifts. Of this Bill said: "I didn't get any satisfaction from the type of work I was fooling around with. I didn't know what I wanted to do, didn't have any capabilities."

The job offered security, paid well and met his immediate needs. But, as he knew, it led nowhere. The job did not draw on his education in electronics or his training at IBM, nor did it prepare him for other positions at Long Island Lighting. There was little with which to build a career.

This didn't concern Paulsen at the time. He had a secure job that paid a living wage, and Ruth worked as a bookkeeper. Between them they had the kind of life they wanted at that time. They bought furniture for their home, Bill set up a woodworking shop (like his father's) in the basement, and they started "a nice little bank account." He enjoyed drinking beer with old friends, playing tennis with his father, and doing woodwork in the basement.

Neither Bill nor Ruth found it easy to discuss personal issues beyond the practical concerns of day-to-day living. This, together with the tendency of both to withdraw in stubborn anger from any serious disagreement, made it difficult to work out their differences.

They both wanted children, but "the good Lord didn't see fit to give us one just then." The doctors were unable to find any physical explanation for this. It was a source of concern and disappointment; they worried that something was wrong with one or both of them. This tension continued for the first ten years of their marriage, with almost no discussion of it.

It meant a great deal to Bill that his wife's mother lived with them during this period. She was a wonderful person, "more my mother than her daughter's mother." He was very fond of his mother-in-law; it was like having a new, doting mother.

> Mom stuck up for me more than she did her own daughter. I could do no wrong in that house. I could talk to Mom anytime I wanted to. If I had any sort of problem with my work, or whether we should do this or whether we should do that, Mom would give her advice.

Bill also remained close to his father, relying on his counsel in a variety of decisions. He felt he was a young kid "without a pot to piddle in." Whenever he felt uncertain—as when buying his home—he would call his father, who was always happy to give advice.

Paulsen began the period of Entering the Adult World in what appeared to be a reasonably solid position, but his first life structure was built on a weak foundation. The weakness stemmed from three main sources. First, there was his failure late in adolescence to establish a secure personal identity. It was hard for him to become adult when he so strongly wanted to remain a boy who would be helped by others through all of life's difficulties. Second, there was the continuing lack of a Dream, a vision of the kind of life he wanted to create for himself and his family. Third, he did not find a mentor who could facilitate his entry into adulthood and help him establish a place there.

The job at Long Island Lighting proved to be an occupational backwater in which Paulsen wallowed for over six years—narrowing his interests, acquiring few new skills, and learning little about capabilities which might enable him to develop a career. He drifted through his twenties, enjoying himself where possible, not thinking about the future and making little effort to explore the possibilities in the adult world. With some help from his mother-in-law, father and wife, he stayed in this backwater.

At 29, Bill Paulsen presented himself to the world as a responsible adult, while continuing to act in many ways like a boy tied to his family. With his considerable talent for self-deception, he told himself that he was an adult, ready and able to manage his life. In fact he was not. This was brought home to him in a most painful way during the next few years.

## The Age Thirty Transition

When Paulsen was 29, a series of events confronted him with losses and responsibilities he couldn't manage. This precipitated the breakup of the life structure he had maintained during the previous six years.

His father died at age 53, after an illness of six to eight months. The death, Bill said, "hit me hard. I was very down in the dumps after his death . . . down in the dumps. You'd call me a nervous wreck at that time for a year or two."

Paulsen's mother had depended on his father almost entirely. After Grandmother's death, when he was 23, his mother had become incapable of looking after herself. When his father died, she turned to Bill. The entire family expected that he would take her in and look after her as his father had.

> The responsibility that hit me all of a sudden . . . I just couldn't cope with it at the time. I don't know . . . I just couldn't make all those major decisions for my mother. I don't think I was prepared for it. Maybe I wasn't mature enough. This is possible . . . more probable than possible.

Bill took her in, but the situation quickly soured. Ruth was nearing the end of her first pregnancy after six years of marriage. She was anxious about the pregnancy and uneasy about living with Bill's mother. They had never gotten along well together, and having her with them soon proved unbearable. His mother was quite unable to look after herself and demanded a great deal of care—much more than Bill or Ruth could provide. Bill proposed that she live in a nursing home. She opposed this, and the rest of the family were angry with Bill for suggesting it. She remained with them, and the situation deteriorated: "It got to a point where my wife was becoming a nervous wreck. My mother would crawl into a shell of sorts and wouldn't talk at all. I just about blew my cork."

Ruth got so upset, she said, that "I tried to commit suicide then because I couldn't face it." In the ninth month of her pregnancy, Ruth's child was stillborn. In their distress and fury, Bill and Ruth insisted that his mother live with his sister. But she wouldn't go. A battle developed. "She said that I didn't love her, that I just wanted to get rid of her. That's what got me to be very nervous. I became irritable and did a little over-imbibing."

Three months after she had come to live with them, Bill's mother did go to live with his sister. Things then settled down somewhat in the Paulsen household. But he felt that he had failed in his responsibilities as his father's successor. These feelings of shame and guilt were exacerbated by other members of the family:

> Being the older son and the man of the family, I thought at the time it was up to me. But I just couldn't do it. I turned out to be the black sheep of the family. They wouldn't listen to me. That was the worst thing in the world. Nobody would talk to me for almost ten years. They thought it was up to me as the man in the family . . . that Mother would come and live with me for the rest of her days.

During this period of turmoil, the Paulsens faced yet another disaster. While Bill's mother was living with them, Ruth's mother became ill. She developed "lung trouble and hardening of the arteries," was bedridden for a year, and died. Like his father, she had been a great favorite of Bill's and he felt her loss sharply.

In the course of a single year, from age 29 to 30, Bill lost both his father and his mother-in-law, who had been crucial sources of comfort and support to him during his twenties. He became a "nervous wreck" and began to drink heavily, which in turn affected his work. He worried about losing his job. "It was like being in the middle of the ocean with no life preserver," he said. "I didn't know which way I was going to go."

Ruth's brother was helpful to Bill during this time. He had come to Long Island from Oregon when his mother was ill. He then lived with the Paulsens for several months while he separated from his wife. He re-married, moved to Florida, and found a job that he liked. Once settled, he encouraged Bill and Ruth to join him. They decided to make the move.

At 31, Bill was ready for a change. Full of the feeling that life had not worked for him in Long Island, he wanted to go somewhere else and start again. Florida seemed as good a place as any. Things couldn't be any worse there. Once again, however, Paulsen had little sense of where he was going. He didn't know what he would be getting into, what sort of people he would encounter, what jobs would be available. The only important thing was to get away. He felt a great urgency and responded directly to it.

Bill and Ruth had a difficult time starting all over again in Florida.

During the first six months, Bill worked for a Frigidaire dealer as a serviceman, earning $62 a week. Then he worked eight months for a building company, but was still getting "slave wages." Their little nest egg disappeared.

After over a year in Florida Bill felt dispirited. He wasn't getting anywhere "working for ditchdigger wages." With a new surge of effort, he determined to find a better way. Bowles & White, a computer company, had just opened a new plant in Fort Lauderdale, and he applied for a position. His electronics and IBM training helped. They hired him and sent him to Boston, where he learned to operate their new computers. When he returned, he was the first IBM computer operator at the Bowles & White Florida Research and Development Center. His starting salary was $75 a week, and he felt encouraged.

At 32, Paulsen began to make a place for himself in Florida. He had a position in which he could use his training and skills, within an organization that offered opportunities for advancement. He was looking ahead and planning for his future. He had a satisfying occupation that would provide a better livelihood for his family in the long run. The new job marked the end of three years of crisis and chaos in his life.

In the transitional period from age 29 to 32, his first life structure was dismantled, a period of turmoil ensued, and a new structure began to take shape. Major changes in his family initiated this developmental work. The death of his father made him the family head, and the death of his mother-in-law deprived him of a "Mom." These deaths both forced and enabled him to become more adult, to assume more responsibility for his own life. He and Ruth could finally establish their own family. No longer were Ruth's mother and Bill's father there to guide, support and influence them in this undertaking. It was hard to build a life on their own, but for the first time they were free to try, free to assume responsibility for themselves.

Paulsen was preoccupied with this personal work when he moved to Florida. His first jobs there provided some degree of financial security that permitted him to work on the developmental tasks. After he established himself more securely as the man in the family, he was able to work on the occupational issues. For the first time, he sought a position that would draw on his talent and training. His decision to seek work at Bowles & White signaled a very important change. No longer willing to work for "ditchdigger wages," he was determined to find a position that offered him opportunities for advancement.

These changes represented a substantial advance in his development. Paulsen came to act less like a carefree boy and more like a man who wants to make his place in the world and is ready to take responsibility for doing this. He had not yet formed a Dream, however, nor had he found a mentor who could help him get established in the adult world.

In Chapter 18 we shall conclude the story of Paulsen's life, following him through the remaining periods of early adulthood and the entry into middle adulthood.

# The Settling Down Period

# Settling Down: Building a Second Adult Life Structure

The end of the Age Thirty Transition is the end of the preparatory phase in early adulthood. A man has completed the allotted time for exploring and getting established in the adult world. It is time to enter the Settling Down period, which marks the culmination of early adulthood and produces the final fruits and thorns of this era. The shift from the Age Thirty Transition to Settling Down is one of the crucial steps in adult development.

The underlying task is to "settle for" a few key choices, to create a broader structure around them, to invest oneself as fully as possible in the various components of this structure (such as work, family, community, solitary interests, friendships) and to pursue long-range plans and goals within it. A man has a stronger sense of urgency to "get serious," to be responsible, to decide what is truly important and shape his life accordingly.

As I mentioned in Chapter 5, the Settling Down period ordinarily begins at age 32 or 33. In our sample, it usually ended at 40 or 41—not earlier than 39 or later than 42. Its duration was usually between six and nine years (7.8 on the average). It lasted the longest among the workers and executives (8.3 and 8.4 years, respectively), as compared with 7.7 years for the novelists and only 6.8 for the biologists. The differences result mainly from the fact that Settling Down started later for the biologists and novelists than for the others. There were negligible differences among the occupations in the age at which Settling Down ended and the Mid-Life Transition began.

The Settling Down life structure gives certain relationships, aspirations, and aspects of the self a prominent place in one's life while requiring that others be made secondary or put aside altogether. It may permit the expression of many or few aspects of the self. A relatively integrated structure has a few central elements which serve as focal points for the structure as a whole, and other, peripheral elements which enrich and expand the structure. However, even a rather broad, complex structure cannot enable one to live out all aspects of the self. The aspects which have been excluded often return to demand their due in later periods, as we shall see. To the extent that the initial Settling Down structure is viable in the world and suitable for the self, it helps make possible a relatively stable and satisfying life. It is not likely to change until the next period, the Mid-life Transition, ushers in new developmental tasks. If the initial structure is seriously flawed, it will produce strains and pressures toward change. Our study showed, however, that it is very difficult to change the life structure during this period.

The Settling Down period presents two major tasks. Individual men differ considerably in the relative emphasis they give to these tasks and in their ways of working on them.

TASK 1. TO ESTABLISH ONE'S NICHE IN SOCIETY. To dig in, build a nest and pursue one's interests within a defined pattern. This is the initial step in Settling Down. A man needs a sufficiently ordered, stable life. It is time to deepen his roots, to anchor his life more firmly in family, occupation and community. He takes a greater sense of pride in knowing who he is, having his own home base, developing competence in a chosen craft, belonging, being a valued member of a valued collective entity.

TASK 2. TO WORK AT ADVANCEMENT. Planning, striving to succeed, moving onward and upward, progressing along a timetable. Whereas the first task contributes to the stability and order of a defined structure, the second involves progression within the structure. I use the term "advancement" in the broadest sense: building a better life, improving and using one's skills, becoming more creative, contributing to society and being affirmed by it, according to one's values. The goals may be wealth, power, prestige, recognition, scientific or esthetic achievement, particular forms of family and community life. The Settling Down period is the time for a man to fulfill his Dream, pursue his ambitions and become the hero in the scenario of early adulthood. At the start, he has the sense of being on the low rung of a ladder, preparing to make his way to the top. Imagery of the ladder is an important part of life in this period.

Tasks 1 and 2 are to some degree antithetical. Generally speaking, family and local community are the main forces making for stability, occupation the main force for movement and change. To the extent that a man wants order and roots, he must be ready to moderate the upward striving that might rock the boat and threaten the stability of his life. Conversely, a man who wants desperately to make his mark, to attain great heights of power, virtue or achievement—Caesar, the Shakespearean kings, Abraham, Faust and Gauguin come to mind—cannot afford to make strong commitments to particular persons or place great value on stability. While one of these tasks may predominate, the other is always present and creates difficulty if it is overly neglected. The second task tends to assume special strength in the late thirties, as early adulthood reaches the climactic phase of Becoming One's Own Man.

Both tasks reflect the primary character of Settling Down. It is time for a man to join the tribe as a full adult on terms he can accept: time to find his niche, get plugged into society with greater commitment and responsibility, raise a family and exercise an occupation and do his bit for the survival and well-being of the tribe. In modern complex society the meaning of "tribe" varies widely. It may include his local community, religio-ethnic group, profession or nation or humanity at large—whatever part of the species has the most significance for him. But everyone during Settling Down is strongly connected to a segment of his society, responsive to its demands and seeking the affirmation and rewards it offers.

We have found two distinct phases within the Settling Down period, each lasting three or four years. The first we call "Early Settling Down" and the second, which ordinarily starts at age 36 or 37, "Becoming One's Own Man."

# Early Settling Down

During his twenties, a man is a "novice" or "apprentice" adult. The task at the start of the Settling Down period is to go beyond the apprenticeship and become a full-fledged adult. The initial life structure of this period provides a base on which one can plan for the future and identify long-term goals. I shall use the term "personal enterprise" to include the central features of a man's life structure and what he wants to accomplish through them—the direction of his life, the broad aspirations and specific goals—with whatever clarity or ambiguity they are defined. A man's Settling Down enterprise is the main vehicle for his realizing youthful ambitions and goals.

This enterprise contains in some form the imagery of the *ladder*. A man has devoted himself until the early thirties to creating a foundation on which the ladder can be built. The more he has accomplished, the higher the level on which he starts the enterprise. One man begins this period in middle management and hopes to reach the top of his division of a corporation. Another, already at the top of a division, begins Settling

Down by forming his own small corporation, with the aim of becoming the giant in his field. The place at which both men start Settling Down represents the bottom rung of a ladder. The top rung may be clear or vague in their minds, but both have a strong sense of being at a starting point and of aspiring to move up. If a man soon discovers that advancement toward his goals is impossible, or that it gives him little satisfaction, he will have a more difficult time in the last phase of Settling Down.

Novelists too are on a ladder, though it is not expressed in terms of an organizational hierarchy. At 33, one novelist has written three novels and is regarded as "a promising young writer," but he has yet to prove that he can produce a body of work of the caliber he wants most. Another has written a single novel that sold well but received poor reviews; he is now ready to commit himself to writing as his primary occupation, but his possibilities are still untested. A third, who has written several unpublished novels, decides to make business his primary occupation and to give novel writing a peripheral place in his Settling Down structure, with the hope that he can subsequently get out of the business world and make writing central. (This case is exemplified by Paul Namson, whose life we shall present in Chapter 12.)

Other men define their plans for advancement not in occupational terms, but in terms of their family or community, or in other non-work contexts. But nearly all men, regardless of specific life circumstances, start the Settling Down period with some hopes of advancement.

The ladder may have many rungs or few. The ambitions may be vast and burning, or modestly realistic. The ladder may lead toward realization of the Dream or in another direction. It has both external and internal aspects, and a man's course along it is shaped by both external and internal forces. Externally, it may involve such things as status in an organizational hierarchy (labor grade, managerial or academic rank) and reputation in the community or occupation. The occupation usually provides a rough timetable for reaching various levels of advancement. If a man falls behind the timetable, he is afraid that further advancement is unlikely and the entire enterprise may be in trouble. Internally, the meaning of the ladder is colored by a man's concerns with fame, creative achievement, power, human welfare, the superiority or inferiority of his class or ethnic or regional origins, and parental injunctions and rejections from the distant past. These and many other internal forces help to define the ladder and to shape the meanings of success and failure.

In early Settling Down, then, a man starts a new personal enterprise on the bottom rung of his own psychosocial ladder. Entering a world in which he is a *junior member*, he seeks to advance in the enterprise, to climb the ladder and become a *senior member* of that world. Over the next several years, his sense of well-being as a person will depend upon his evaluation of how far and how fast he is moving toward these goals. Becoming "senior" is crucial in the second phase of Settling Down.

The start of Settling Down also changes a man's involvement in marriage and family. If he is not married, he is likely to feel great pressure to get married or to commit himself formally to some type of bachelor existence. The decision to marry comes not only from affection or love, but also from the need for a more stable, balanced life in which marriage-family is a central element.

Most men have families by the late twenties. As I have noted, the marriage may be questioned and reappraised by both partners during the Age Thirty Transition. This may strengthen the marriage ties and give greater richness and mutuality to the relationship as the Settling Down period begins. If the couple has a satisfactory love relationship, if she values and to some degree participates in his Settling Down enterprise, and if he can do the same with hers, their overall life structure is strengthened at the center. (Later on, of course, he may come to feel that this structure was all wrong for him, and he may blame her for getting him into it or keeping him in it.)

As he enters the Settling Down period, a man has a great need to maintain a stable structure. He prefers to deal with problems by making accommodations within the existing framework rather than attempting major structural changes. He may decide to remain in his marriage even though there are serious problems in the marital relationship, the family life, or the wider life structure in which the family is an essential element. The decision to stay in a questionable marriage reflects not only his feelings of love or obligation toward his wife but also his commitment to the family and the life structure that contains it. He may form a relationship with another woman, intending to make this a limited element of the structure and not a threat to the marriage—though it may well not work out this way in the long run, as Jim Tracy discovered (see Chapter 11). Our four biographees provide four contrasting pictures of marriage and family life in the Age Thirty Transition and Settling Down.

In any case, the early Settling Down phase is devoted to building a life around the initial choices. It is a time for making one's niche in society, defining an enterprise, getting on with the work, "taking care of business." After three or four years a new phase begins. This phase is also part of the Settling Down period. It contains the outcome of the enterprise started earlier, but has a qualitatively distinct character.

## Late Settling Down:
## Becoming One's Own Man

The effort to be more fully one's own person—to be more independent and self-sufficient, and less subject to the control of others—is found at many ages. Its form at each age reflects the character of the current developmental period. We see it, for example, in the two-year-old stubbornly insisting on his rights and trying to maintain his own initiative in a world that seems forever to be constraining him. In the Early Adult Transition, the adolescent-becoming-adult has a special concern for his own independence as he struggles to pull away more completely from parents and from the pre-adult self that is still so strongly tied to them.

This issue takes a new form, and a central place, in the end phase of Settling Down. This phase is so distinctive that we have given it a name: Becoming One's Own Man. It ordinarily extends from about 36 or 37 to 40 or 41. It represents the culmination of Settling Down and, more broadly, the peaking of early adulthood and the first stirrings of what lies beyond.

A man's primary developmental tasks in Becoming One's Own Man are to accomplish the goals of Settling Down, to advance sufficiently on his ladder, to become a senior member of his enterprise, to speak more clearly with his own voice, to have a greater measure of authority, and to become less dependent (internally as well as externally) on other individuals and institutions in his life.

There is a built-in dilemma here. On the one hand, a man wants to be more *independent*, more true to himself and less vulnerable to pressures and blandishments from others. On the other hand, he seeks *affirmation* in society. Speaking with his own voice is important, even if no one listens—but he especially wants to be heard and respected and given the rewards that are his due. The wish for independence leads him to do what he alone considers most essential, regardless of consequences; the wish for affirmation makes him sensitive to the response of others and susceptible to their influence.

It is not clear why a developmental phase having these tasks should occur at this time. It was not something we expected to find when we began this study. Rather, we discovered it in the course of our work. As with the other periods, its onset is not linked to a single dramatic event or condition. It does not have a single, specific source in the individual's biological, psychological or sociocultural evolution. The basic sources lie in all of these, and many specific factors operate variously in different individuals and societies. In the late thirties a man is becoming a full generation older than those just entering adulthood. He must become more senior, more established. He is at or near the peak of his advancement in early adulthood, and the possibilities for his future life are heavily influenced by what happens now. For many men, the sense of bodily decline is a goad to greater striving. The concern with decline and death will become even stronger and take on additional meanings in the next period.

The developmental tasks of Becoming One's Own Man—carrying through the Settling Down enterprise, becoming more senior and expert, and getting affirmed by society—assume primary importance during the late thirties. A man is likely to be rather sensitive, even touchy, about anything in the environment or in himself that interferes with these aims. Since the successful outcome of this period is not assured, he often feels that he has not accomplished enough and that he is not sufficiently his own man. He may have a sense of being held back—of being oppressed by others and restrained by his own conflicts and inhibitions.

These concerns reflect external realities and internal processes, and we must take account of both in our efforts to understand this phase. External circumstances during these years are frequently restrictive and damaging to self-esteem. Organizations often operate so rigidly or corruptly that an individual places his career in jeopardy if he is very forthright or eager to take the ball and run. It is generally safer to avoid controversy and be a loyal member of the "team"—and not speak too loudly with one's own voice. As a man advances, he comes in closer contact with senior men who have their territories to maintain and protect. Their interest in him often contains a subtle mixture of support and intimidation. He receives a double message: "Be a good boy and you'll go far," together with "Make trouble and you're dead."

The difficulties of this period have important internal sources as well. The wish for affirmation and advancement makes him especially vulnerable to social pressure. A man who has prided himself on his ability to act autonomously realizes now that he is not as independent as he had thought. In crucial situations he has been too eager to please, too sensitive to criticism, too conforming to speak and act on the basis of his own convictions. He wants to be his own man, but he also wants desperately to be understood and appreciated, to have his talents affirmed, to succeed in his enterprise.

But the difficulty goes deeper than this. Becoming One's Own Man represents a peaking in the aspirations of early adulthood. A man wants to become a "senior" adult, to realize the fruits of the labors of the past fifteen or twenty years, to accomplish goals that in turn will provide a base for his life in the years to come. He wants, in short, to become manly in a fuller sense than ever before. The urgency of the desires for manhood, however, bring about a resurgence of the *little boy* in the adult.

It is not necessarily a sign of pathology or impaired development in early adulthood that many boyish qualities operate with great force. The self that takes shape in the twenties is but a small step beyond adolescence and normally contains many aspects of the child and adolescent self. The boy continues to exist, providing many of the strengths as well as the vulnerabilities of the young man. With luck, a man will sustain his child-like qualities and his youthfulness, in changing forms, throughout the life cycle.

The activation of the boyish self during the late thirties is part of normal psychosocial development. The effort involved in Becoming One's Own Man activates the unresolved pre-adult conflicts, including the boy-ish wishes and anxieties. Indeed, the intensification of the boy-man conflict is a step forward. It creates the possibility of resolving the conflict at a higher level.

During this period, however, the intensified conflict becomes an inner source of difficulty. The adult self desires to fulfill certain values, to be a productive member of society, and to bear as best he can the responsibilities that this demands. The boyish self contributes to this effort in many ways with his imagination, energy and idealism, his sense of adventure and wonderment. However, the boyish self is also a source of opposition and discontent. He wants to attain great heights through magical omnipotence rather than the sweat of his brow. He wants things to go effortlessly his way, without having to consider the conflicting needs or requirements of others. When sufficient recognition is not forthcoming, the little boy feels totally deprived and humiliated. When a boss or other authority is restrictive or imposing, it is the little boy who feels utterly helpless and intimidated. The boyish self becomes the ingratiating syco-phant, the ever-agreeable "nice guy" or the impulsive, self-defeating rebel —but not the persevering worker or the leader who uses his authority for constructive, humane ends. It is the little boy inside the man who trans-forms the ordinary mortals with whom he is involved—bosses, wives, men-tors, colleagues—into tyrants, corrupters, villainous rivals, seducers and witches.

There is always some mixture of reality and distortion in these experi-ences. To some degree the persons and institutions in a man's life are tyrannical, corrupting and exploitive. He often finds it hard to sort things out. During this time he frequently vacillates between the extremes of depressive self-blame (when he feels absolutely inept, impotent and lacking in inner resources) and paranoid rage (when he blames an evil or uncaring world for suppressing or ignoring his enormous talents and virtues). When these internal conflicts and external stresses are at their height, it is difficult indeed to maintain one's good judgment and initiative.

During the period of Becoming One's Own Man, *mentor relationships* are likely to be especially stormy and vulnerable. The termination of a close tie with a mentor just now is often a mutually painful, tortuous process. A man in his late thirties is not only giving up his current mentor, he is outgrowing the readiness to be the protégé of any older person. He must reject the mentoring relationship not because it is intrinsically harmful but because it has served its purpose. It has helped him to make a basic developmental advance.

Whereas in pre-adulthood he was a boy-son in relation to a father, in early adulthood he has become a young-man-apprentice in relation to an admired mentor. The mentor in turn has regarded him as a full-fledged but young (junior) adult. In the late thirties a new task arises: a man must move toward becoming a senior adult and full peer of his former mentors, teachers and bosses. He himself must become a mentor, constructive authority, father, and friend of other adults. This developmental achievement is of the essence of adulthood. If a man is to assume responsibility for others and for himself during middle adulthood, he must attain his "seniority." The formative steps in this process are taken during the time of Becoming One's Own Man and the Mid-life Transition.

A man's struggles with his mentor and his hardships in being a protégé are intensified during Becoming One's Own Man by the renewed struggle with the little boy in himself. The little boy desperately wants the mentor to be a good father in the most childish sense—a father who will make him special, will endow him with magical powers and will not require him to compete or prove himself in relation to would-be rivals. It is also the little boy who anxiously makes the mentor into a bad father—a depriving, dictatorial authority who has no real love and merely uses one for his own needs. The relationship is made untenable by the yearning for the good father, the anxiety over the bad father, and the projection of both of these internal figures onto the mentor, who is then caught in a bind.

Central features of the pre-adult self—involving the boy's elemental struggles with dependency, sexuality, authority and the like—often come to the fore with special strength during the phase of Becoming One's

Own Man. When severe conflicts and difficulties occur at this time, they must be seen both as a renewal of pre-adult problems and as a reflection of the developmental work of becoming more fully adult. The overthrow of the mentor is not just an irrational re-enactment of boyish Oedipal revolt. Even more, it is part of the developmental process by which a young man becomes an adult and mentor. This process cannot evolve along purely rational lines. Many persons in early adulthood have the skill to be excellent teachers and advisers. But the developmental work of Becoming One's Own Man is essential in moving further and acquiring the maturity to be a wise mentor.

One of our novelists, Allen Perry, presented us with a vivid example of a significant mentor relationship. At 44, he recalls the story as if it had happened yesterday. In his early twenties, after college and military service, Perry went to New York with the single aim of becoming a writer. He took an extension course taught by Calvin Randall, who was then an editor at a leading publishing house. They immediately formed a close bond:

> Randall gave me tremendous support and encouragement. I was very close to this man—enormously, deeply committed to him in fact. He had a wonderful quality, but I later realized that this quality was good only if you were very young, and once you became a man yourself it almost became a matter of competition. I had to break, and it was too bad because there was a lack of insight on his part, I think.

But the break occurred some years later. The relationship flowered in Perry's mid-twenties, during the writing and publication of his first novel. The book was a commercial and critical success and established him as a writer of promise. For the next several years he traveled a good deal and wrote a few minor pieces, but was not able to complete the novel he had in mind. Although the relationship with Randall continued, they were not in close contact.

The next chapter began when Perry was 35. He had just completed the second novel and taken it to his mentor. By this time Randall was editor-in-chief and a nationally known figure, "due partly to his connection with my work." It took him two weeks to get around to the manuscript. And, when they finally met, it was a great disappointment:

> I realized that he wasn't interested in my work so much as his own career. If there was ever a person who demonstrated the sad effects of the sin of hubris, it's him. He really lost touch with his protégés, myself included. I'd come to discuss a manuscript and he'd spend two or three hours describing his great publishing plans. When he moved to another

firm, he asked me to shift with him. If the relationship had remained as it was, I wouldn't have hesitated. Instead, I decided to give him up. I still remember distinctly the letter I wrote him almost ten years ago. These are close to the actual words: "To go with you now, even including the fact that I admire you so much, would be an admission that you are absolutely essential to my development, when in fact you must be aware that this is not true. It's no insult to you, your credentials or your talent, but it would have been demeaning to my integrity as a writer."

I learned later from someone who was there that he burst into tears when he read the letter. He was hurt for a long time and felt that I had betrayed him. For me, however, it was an act of liberation. It's nice to have a sympa-thetic person to ricochet things off, but there comes a point when we're no longer dependent on those figures. I realize now that 35 is really a very vulnerable period. I can remember when I was in my twenties thinking that when I was 35 I'd be the jauntiest, most debonair, free individual on earth, but in reality I wasn't at all. Breaking with Calvin Randall was just the beginning of some liberating process.

Allen Perry's bitterness did not destroy his attachment to Randall. His son, born at the time of the break, was named after the mentor. The relationship is now amicable but reserved—perhaps as good as it can be.

I'm very thankful at this moment that we've patched it all up. I'm a grown man, you know, and not his boy. I have an excellent editor now. We are friendly, but it's not the kind of passionate relationship I had with Randall. I don't think I'll ever have that again, or want it. Now it's my turn to give that help to others, though I'll never have Calvin's inter-est or skill at it.

Men rarely have mentors after about 40. A man may have valued re-lationships with family, friends, counselors and co-workers, but the men-tor relationship in its developed form is rare. It is surrendered, with other things, as part of Becoming One's Own Man. One result is a greater ability and interest in being a mentor to others.

# 10 Five Sequences Through the Settling Down Period

The Settling Down period is the culmination of early adulthood, the time for a man to realize the hopes of his youth. What are the various ways of going through this period, and what are its outcomes? We have found it useful to distinguish five ways of establishing a second adult life structure and Becoming One's Own Man. There is nothing absolute about these five categories; they are simply a convenient means of describing variations. But all of our forty men—and others whose lives we have studied—went through one or another of these sequences:

A. Advancement within a stable life structure
B. Serious failure or decline within a stable life structure
C. Breaking out: trying for a new life structure
D. Advancement which itself produces a change in life structure
E. Unstable life structure

In Sequence A, life goes at least moderately well and a man advances toward his major goals. In B he experiences considerable failure or decline. The life structure in both cases is relatively stable.

In Sequences C and D the man forms a stable structure at the start of the period, but various internal and external forces lead to change. In Sequence C the structure established in the early Settling Down phase (age 33 to 36) proves to be intolerable. During the phase of Becoming One's Own Man (36 to 40), the man attempts to break out, to dismantle his existing life and create a new one. In Sequence D, advancement in income and status during his late thirties propels him, often unexpectedly, into a new world.

Sequence E differs from the others in that a stable structure is not formed at all. Instead, the Settling Down period begins with very tenuous choices that cannot be followed up, and the life structure remains in flux over the entire Settling Down period.

## Sequence A. Advancement Within a Stable Life Structure

Here, life proceeds more or less according to expectations. During the early Settling Down phase a man makes his primary commitments, defines an enterprise and gradually enriches and elaborates the initial life structure. In the phase of Becoming One's Own Man, his ambition heightens from within and an emphasis on advancement is intensified from without. He defines more precisely the last few rungs of his Settling Down ladder and magnifies his efforts to reach the top. To a large extent, he succeeds. He may experience a good deal of hardship and suffering, but the stresses are manageable and the satisfactions outweigh the difficulties.

In our study, 55 percent of the men followed predominantly the pattern of Sequence A, and several others showed significant aspects of this pattern (see table, page 152). The remaining 45 percent had major difficulties during this period, and its outcome was less satisfactory for them. More novelists and biologists experienced the advancement of Sequence A than workers and executives, but the differences were not dramatic. Since our sample is more middle class and probably more stable in occupation and marriage-family than the population as a whole, these findings may underestimate the degree of difficulty experienced by men during their thirties.

The final goal of advancement in Sequence A is often defined concretely in terms of a key event which in the man's mind symbolizes true success. This event carries the ultimate message of his affirmation by society. The young writer does not want to write just another book. He wants to make a quantum leap in his writing. He hopes above all to be identified as an established writer of a certain kind and quality. The academic biologist aspires to become a full professor, to achieve seniority in his university and discipline, to make a major breakthrough in his research or, if truth be told, to win the Nobel Prize. The executive knows by 35 that he must reach a certain level by 40. Otherwise, he will be unable to advance further. He will be trapped in one position, given a "lateral promotion" that represents failure, or demoted to make room for the younger men now moving up. The worker too seeks a higher job grade or a supervisory position. He may obtain a union position such as shop steward, which carries another form of seniority. Or he may define his goals less in terms of occupation and more in terms of family, leisure or community.

Whatever their goals, the men in Sequence A form a life structure early in the Settling Down period and maintain it throughout. Impor-

| Sequence | EXECUTIVES | WORKERS | NOVELISTS | BIOLOGISTS | Number in total sample |
|---|---|---|---|---|---|
| **A. Advancement in a stable structure** | | | | | |
| 1. Mainly positive outcome | F. Radovich* M. Kowalski | N. D'Amico R. Ochs | B. Loeb* K. Tyrone D. McLean* | B. Edwards B. Morgan* | 9 |
| 2. Mixed outcome | R. Wise* D. Jaffe | V. Minelli L. Strode F. Thomas* | L. Newman C. Berg* A. Perry R. Taylor | J. Barnes G. Marabian W. Mead E. Northrop | 13 |
| **B. Decline-failure** | O. Angstrom M. Gallagher L. Heinz | W. Paulsen L. Doby | none | S. Brenner* N. Kromer* | 7 |
| **C. Change via breaking out** | P. Maloney J. Tracy | A. Russell P. Abbott* | P. Namson | none | 5 |
| **D. Change via advancement** | R. Mohn | none | H. Parker | A. Treloar* | 3 |
| **E. Unstable structure** | none | H. McCloud* | D. Osborn* | C. Ruger* | 3 |

* Not yet to end of Settling Down, but the basic sequence is clear.

tant changes may occur—in place and kind of residence, job, income, life style, family pattern—but these represent advancements, enrichments or difficulties within the existing framework and not a change in the basic structure. There may be great hardship along with the progress: times when advancement is in serious question, problems of marriage and family life, serious illness or death of loved ones, frequent moves and stressful living conditions of various kinds. The hardships are tolerable, however, and the overall sequence during Settling Down is primarily one of advancement within a relatively stable enterprise.

Around 40, these men reach the top rung of their Settling Down ladder and attain goals that represent the culmination of years of striving. Reaching this level is not the end of the story. There are new heights to be climbed—but the next step is not simply another rung on the same ladder. The top of the first ladder turns out to be the bottom rung on a new ladder. The successes of this period bring a man into a new and different world. He is now a newcomer, entering a "senior" world. In the process of establishing himself he has joined an establishment. It bears the responsibility for many people—whether in industry, the university, writing-publishing, trade union, or extended family. He starts afresh in this world and, if he remains in it, his life structure will evolve in unanticipated ways over the course of middle adulthood. He does not move directly from the life structure of the Settling Down period to the creation of a new structure. There is an intervening developmental period—the Mid-life Transition—in which crucial changes may occur. These changes have a strong influence on the shape of his subsequent life.

Given their considerable progress in the Settling Down period, it is not surprising that the men in Sequence A generally have a strong sense of self-esteem, of proving themselves and getting what they really want. There is always some mixture of reality and illusion in this. A man's sense of satisfaction and well-being is genuine to the extent that his Settling Down enterprise is consonant with his Dream, that it enables him to live out important aspects of the self, and that his sense of achievement and contribution is consistent with the actual values of his performance. Clearly, this is a matter of degree.

The experience of advancement and success is always based to some degree on illusion. Even when a man is doing well in an external sense, he may be gaining rewards that will turn out to have little meaning or value for him. His life may provide genuine satisfactions but at great inner costs. In order to devote himself to certain goals, he may have to neglect or repress important parts of the self. Finally, a man's strivings for advancement are often stimulated by a fantasy that has the magical qualities of a fairy tale: "If I get to the top of my ladder, I will have everything I really wanted and live happily ever after." This omnipotent fantasy is rarely conscious during the Becoming One's Own Man phase, though it is often evident to others. The man himself may become aware of it during the Mid-life Transition, when he attempts to reappraise his life and penetrate his illusions. The biologist John Barnes exemplifies this sequence, as we shall see in Chapter 17.

People are inclined either to idealize or devalue the men in Sequence A. Those who take an uncritically favorable view may, impressed by the evidence of steady progress or of meteoric success, assume that life must be good for anyone who is receiving such recognition and reward. Others, taking a more debunking attitude, may emphasize the limitations of success and the great costs involved in pursuing it. Neither attitude allows one to arrive at a balanced evaluation of a person's life. The question is much more complicated. Any individual life is a mass of costs and gains.

Sequence A is one way of going through the Settling Down period. In this pattern, a man's advancement is in accord with his own timetable, the stresses are manageable, the gains outweigh the costs of the struggle, and his inner sense of success exceeds his sense of failure. In the next developmental period, starting at around 40, he will have the task of reappraising the course and outcome of his life in the thirties. He may then find it absolutely necessary to re-evaluate his goals and seek new directions.

## Sequence B. Serious Failure or Decline Within a Stable Life Structure

About 20 percent of our men exemplify this sequence. Some of them fail in gross and obvious ways during the course of Settling Down. Others achieve a good deal of external success but fail in certain crucial respects which make the entire enterprise pointless in their own eyes. We found this pattern in two workers, three executives and two biologists (see page 152).

None of the hourly workers found it possible to make a significant advance in job level during their late thirties. A few were reconciled to this and found other ways—through their unions, families or community life—to gain a sense of progress and seniority. Two of the ten workers, however, were trapped in a constricting, oppressive life that held little promise for the future.

Luke Doby, a Black man, had been steadily employed as a construction worker. At 39, however, he was forced by a series of illnesses and operations to give up heavy work. He became a janitor, which he found degrading. When his income fell below the poverty level, it was supplemented by welfare payments. This in turn undermined his position in the family, which until then had been relatively well integrated and stable. His life held less and less value for his family, society and himself. The process of decline had become quite marked when we saw him at 43: he was mentally and physically dying. (His life after 39 is described in Chapter 18.)

An example of more moderate failure is the worker William Paulsen, whose life through the novice phase was presented in Chapter 8. We shall continue his story in Chapter 18.

Equivalent kinds of failure in Settling Down were found in three of our ten executives. All three had with great effort achieved a position in middle management by their mid-thirties. They started the phase of Becoming One's Own Man with great hopes for advancement, and failure came to them as a bitter disappointment. Mike Gallagher was an engineer from Carnegie Tech. He became head of an important unit in his company at 34 and was regarded as a real comer. At 37, however, he received a "lateral promotion" which meant exile within the company, and his career was in ruins. When we saw him at 39 he was in a state of quiet desperation, not able to advance and not ready to move elsewhere.

Other middle managers received occasional promotions and were able to remain in the company without too much humiliation. By the late thirties, however, they had reached their ceilings: not only would they fail in their goals, but their sense of direction and their possibilities for the future were undermined. The structure of management in industry is pyramidal, with only one position in top management for every 15 or 20 in middle management. Since the culture of management places a great value on upward mobility, most middle managers are doomed to personal failure, ranging in degree from moderate to devastating.

A similar pyramid exists—although with different characteristics—in our universities. The outcome of that competition can be as devastating as in industry. Two of our ten biologists went through Sequence B, and the experience of failure figured strongly in the lives of several others at this time. Some of them, faculty members at an elite university, were told in their late thirties that they would not be promoted to tenured professorships and would have to leave the following year. This is more the rule than the exception in such universities: the majority of younger faculty members—like middle managers in industry—do not gain senior positions. Most of them go to other universities, at various academic levels and salaries. In each case the change represents both advancement and a kind of demotion. It is accompanied by the most contradictory self-evaluations and feelings.

Norman Kromer, a biologist who was let go at 39, had strong feelings of failure about himself as a scientist and a person. He felt that he had not been able to speak with his own voice, and therefore could not gain recognition as an eminent biologist. In planning his next move, he could not begin by asking, "Where can I get a job?" He had to start with more fundamental questions: "Have I anything important to contribute as a scientist? Shall I maintain my primary commitment to theory and research, despite my limited success? Or shall I settle for a position involving mainly teaching and administration, though I (and my discipline) value these less? Or perhaps I should get out of the university altogether and pursue other interests that I have neglected for years."

Another biologist, Steven Brenner, was in a very different situation. At 37 he had a national reputation and became a tenured associate professor. The promotion was given in reward for his past accomplishments and, even more, in anticipation of his future contribution. In accepting the promotion he was, in effect, giving a promissory note for products to be delivered shortly. He was then starting a research partnership with a colleague working at another university. By the time Brenner had reached 39, the project was completed and received great acclaim. His collaborator's laboratory, however, had done the bulk of the work and was given the primary credit. Although Brenner received recognition as a major contributor to the work, the other man was seen as the creative source of a real breakthrough. It was not clear how much Brenner colluded in his own defeat, and to what extent an injustice was done. Despite his considerable success, at 39 he regarded himself and his life as essentially a failure.

## Sequence C. Breaking Out: Trying for a New Life Structure

In Sequence C, a man in his late thirties experiences with new awareness and greater urgency the flaws of the life structure established at the start of the Settling Down period. He previously had some dissatisfaction with this structure, but now, at age 36 or 37, his life becomes intolerable. He may focus upon one area, such as work or marriage, or he may feel profoundly alienated from his entire world. He feels suffocated, constrained and without space in which to be himself and to do what matters most. He cannot go on as he has.

Life experiences of this sort can occur at any age. They are by no means specific to a given period. What is distinctive here is the overall pattern of self-in-world and the developmental context in which it occurs. Just a few years before, the man had committed himself to certain choices and started building a life structure that would, he hoped, serve him and his family for some time. In most of these cases, the Settling Down structure involved a reaffirmation of choices (especially in marriage and work) made during the twenties. The paradox is that now, after he and his family have invested so much time and effort in it, he finds this structure increasingly oppressive and feels compelled to break out.

Sequence C is perhaps the most dramatic example of the late thirties as a time of crisis. Just when he is most eager to become his own man and to fulfill his adult aspirations, he feels that there is something fundamentally wrong. Having made his bed (marital, occupational or whatever), he cannot continue to lie in it. Yet to change is to tear the fabric of his life, to destroy much that he has built over the last ten or fifteen years. As he struggles to make the fateful decision—to break out or to stay put—he is likely to be moody, uncommunicative, alternately resentful of others and blaming of himself.

The difficulty lies partly in the actuality of his life. This man's life structure is indeed flawed. It does not permit him to live out crucially important aspects of the self, and it requires him to be someone he can no longer accept. But the flaws have existed, and have been tolerated, for some time. They become intolerable now because the tasks of Becoming One's Own Man are so urgent: it is essential to pursue the Dream, to be a person of independence and integrity, to be more fully a man, to be less enslaved by the little boy in himself who desperately needs to be cared for and who is victimized by his inner ties to powerful, exploitive adults.

The process of "breaking out" may go on in *marriage* and other relationships with women. As a man struggles with the little boy in himself, he struggles as well with the maternal figures in himself and his wife. He experiences his wife largely in maternal terms: at best, a good mother benignly nurturing her flock and managing the family life; at worst, a destructive witch or selfish bitch, using both her strength and her weakness to keep him in line and prevent him from becoming what he truly wants to be.

As he sees it, his wife cannot hear what he is trying to tell her, nor can she appreciate his need for a greater measure of autonomy and intimate sharing. From her point of view, he is unaccountably upset, full of strong but inchoate grievances, suddenly critical of her and of the life they have labored so long to achieve, yet unable to tell her what he now wants. It is difficult to sort out the various elements in this situation: what she is actually like; what he projects onto her; how they both participate in creating and maintaining a relationship hurtful to both; to what extent each of them is ready to form a more mutual, adult relationship with a new balance of attachment and separateness. Both, I must emphasize, have been involved in creating the relationship, and both will have a part in determining its outcome.

The result may be separation and divorce, but there are other outcomes as well. A period of open warfare or silent conflict may end in a kind of "cold war" truce in which a poor marraige is endured because of various external and internal constraints. In some cases the couple are able to change themselves and their lives, and make their marriage more satisfactory than before.

Five of our forty men (13 percent) were predominantly in Sequence C (see page 152). These included two workers, two executives and a novelist. In several other cases, including some biologists, "breaking out" occurred in another pattern or in a subsequent developmental period. Sequence C is probably more common in the general population than in our sample, since men who are executives, novelists and biologists at age 40 to 45 are likely to have pursued this occupation for some years, without breaking out.

This sequence highlights the difficulties and potential costs of forming a badly flawed life structure at the start of the Settling Down period. As a man starts the phase of Becoming One's Own Man, the flaws become less tolerable and he is faced with a terrible dilemma. If he remains in this structure there is the danger that he will be unable to become his own man. On the other hand, he has already made major commitments within the early Settling Down structure and changing them may be hurtful to family, co-workers and others who depend on him. Breaking out of this structure is a tough undertaking indeed.

If a man tries to terminate his occupation or his marriage, it will take several years to carry through the process of separation. The first occupation and marriage-family will continue to occupy a significant place in his life, though they will have new meanings and a new place in the structure. The breaking out may be dramatized by a single decisive act, a marker event such as moving out of the home or quitting a job or going to another part of the country. But the process of breaking away began earlier and will go on for much longer than is usually recognized. The process of breaking in —making new choices and building a new life—is also time consuming. A man may remarry soon after leaving his first wife, but it will take several years to establish a new marriage (and, often, a new family). If he makes a change in occupation, he will go through a period of transition as he leaves one occupational world and gradually enters the next.

Finally, and this is the hardest blow of all: before a man who breaks out at 37 can create a new life structure in which to realize his early adult aspirations, he enters the Mid-life Transition at 40 or 41. Now all of his aspirations and illusions come into question. We found that every man who attempted a major life change in the late thirties, as part of Becoming One's Own Man, went through a period of considerable instability and flux lasting eight to ten years. It is not possible to establish a new structure until the Mid-life Transition ends and a new stable period, Entering Middle Adulthood, begins in the mid-forties (see Chapter 18).

Are the costs of Sequence C greater or less than the gains? Should a highly flawed Settling Down structure be dismantled, or should a man stay put and try to repair or endure it? There are no simple answers here. The problem is that the key choices a man makes in forming his life structure at the start of Settling Down are very hard to modify. A highly flawed structure will be extremely costly in any case, whether he stays put or breaks out. Part of the difficulty is that a man in this predicament cannot predict the costs and gains of any course of action. Small wonder, then, if he feels overwhelmed by the negative prospects of either choice: staying put may lead to a kind of living death (or suicide); breaking out may be destructive to his loved ones and not bring the better life he craves.

Of course, there are intermediate options between remaining passively stuck within the existing structure and making drastic changes that entail great sacrifice by the man and his family. More modest accommodations in the life structure might be the more judicious, "reasonable" course. However, because of the high stakes and the intense passion involved in a developmental crisis, moderate change is often not feasible. Before a realistic choice can be made, it is essential to place the problem in wider perspective. A problem of marital conflict or job dissatisfaction during the late thirties frequently reflects a deep fault in the life structure. Efforts at improvement must be based on an understanding of this structure and its roots in self and world.

Various discussions of "mid-life crisis" refer to times of great difficulty in "the middle years," which may cover any part of the span from 35 to 65. Crises occurring at different ages within this span have many features in common. The nature, sources and consequences of the crisis will differ, however, in different developmental periods. A crisis occurring in the late thirties will be shaped by the developmental context of Becoming One's Own Man. Likewise, a crisis occurring in the early forties will reflect the developmental issues of the Mid-life Transition. We prefer to use the term "mid-life crisis" only for one that occurs within the Mid-life Transition, and to identify others by the name of the period in which they happen. For example, Jaques showed that many artists have crises in their late thirties (the peak age being 37). In our view these are crises of Becoming One's Own Man, although they usually extend into the Mid-life Transition.

Two of our four biographees exemplify the pattern of breaking out in the Settling Down period. In Chapter 11 we shall describe the Settling Down period of James Tracy, the executive, who broke out of his first marriage; in Chapter 12, the Settling Down period of Paul Namson, the novelist, who broke out of his first occupation.

As a briefer example, let us consider Philip Abbott, a technician in the electronics industry. He dropped out of college after one year, married at 19 and obtained some engineering training in the army before returning to his home town. Over the next ten years he took occasional college courses, read widely in the technical as well as humanistic-psychological literature, and held increasingly good jobs in "research and development" or as a production supervisor. In his early thirties he became a manager in a small plant and could have remained at this level. But he soon quit. He concluded that a manager had to compete mercilessly with other managers and put company profits ahead of more humane values, and he was not ready to do this.

At 34, Abbott took a supervisory position as an hourly worker in another company. He now found himself suspended between workers and management. With his managerial perspective he understood how poor management was causing problems of production and of human relationships. Yet as a worker he was not in a position to do anything about this. It was painful to be part of a hurtful system and do nothing to change it. Although he tried to detach himself emotionally from the work situation, he continued to experience alienation and helpless rage. At 37 he and his wife began to talk about alternative possibilities. She too was expanding her horizons and wanted a better life for both of them. At 38 they moved to a Western state with the idea of living more in nature (an old love) and developing an occupation outside of the industrial firm. The move occurred in the context of Becoming One's Own Man. We do not know how it worked out.

## Sequence D. Advancement Which Itself Produces a Change in Life Structure

In Sequence A, as we have seen, a man advances within a stable life structure. There may be changes in job, income, family, social network and life style. But the basic character of the life structure remains relatively unchanged. In Sequence D, however, advancement brings with it a significant change in life structure.

The basic pattern is as follows: A man receives a promotion or a drastic increase in income. At first glance the increase seems to be a great boon, an opportunity to live better and do things that he has long wanted to do. But this gain propels him into a new world in which he has new roles and relationships. It activates new aspects of the self, while providing little room for the expression of other, formerly important aspects. In short, it leads to a change in his life structure. The advancement is a mixed blessing, and it may turn out to be a curse.

Three of our forty men—a biologist, an executive and a novelist—exemplify Sequence D (see page 152). Another three cases were "mixed types": they went through a change in life structure in the late thirties, partly as a result of advancement, but other factors (such as breaking out) played a more significant part.

This sequence is well represented by an executive, Roger Mohn. After getting his engineering degree, he returned to his home town and took a job in a large manufacturing firm, where he has worked ever since. At 24, he got married and began a life that had great stability until his mid-thirties. During this time he worked in a shop that made special products. He found the work interesting, and he had little desire for advancement. By his early thirties Mohn was the head of the shop, and traveled around the country developing and testing new products. He and his wife bought a home in a modest middle-class neighborhood. Their two children were born at his age 31 and 35. This time—the early Settling Down period—was the high point of his adult life. He loved his work and devoted long hours to it. He had what was for him an optimal level of responsibility: "I was the Jesus Christ of the metals shop." He was building a family and doing well in the community of his origins.

When Mohn was 37 the company rewarded him with a middle-management position as purchasing manager. Unable to refuse this advancement, he entered a new occupation and a new world. The promotion was a first step in changing his life structure. He gave up the leadership of the small, production-centered world he loved, and took on managerial functions in an impersonal, competitive world that lay beyond his earlier ken. Although he enjoyed it less, he was excited by the challenge and did well. As he turned 40, he was offered a senior position as manager of manufacturing, with responsibility for 400 people.

From 37 to 40 Roger Mohn succeeded occupationally beyond his most extravagant dreams. But the advancement changed the character of his life. It eliminated what had been the central element of his earlier life structure—the metal shop and his distinctive role within it. It introduced a major new element: an executive position for which he lacked experience and motivation, and for which he was given minimal training. The new job tripled his income and placed him among colleagues at work whose class level was markedly above his, It enabled him—or forced him—to move out of the lower middle class in which he had been firmly rooted by his family of origin and his own commitments. In brief, Roger Mohn's promotions during the phase of Becoming One's Own Man, from age 37 to 40, took him off the ladder he had earlier chosen. The new ladder permitted much greater external success but was beyond his primary aspirations and alien to his primary cultural world. He overreached himself. The years from 41 to 44 were the low point of his life (see Chapters 13 and 18).

The biologist Arthur Treloar offers a different example of change through advancement in Settling Down. Trained in biochemistry, he began his academic career at 32 as an assistant professor and "promising young researcher" in a prestigious university. During the next few years he realized that he greatly enjoyed teaching. He also realized that his talent for research was small and his interest even smaller. As he told us, "I'll never win the Nobel Prize." At 38 he was promoted to a tenured position, and with this came the freedom to leave. The next year he accepted a position as professor in an innovative but less prestigious university in the West. His major function in the new department, and the thing that most attracted him, was to develop new courses of his own and to plan a new curriculum for the undergraduate major. His research productivity was not essential here.

The change in job represented both an advancement (Sequence D) and a breaking out (Sequence C). The advancement was in academic rank and authority. From the point of view of the scientific community, this gain was more than offset by the drop in the prestige of the university and in his reputation as a researcher. From Treloar's own point of view, the advancement was great, but it was to a new ladder. In the early Settling Down period, research and teaching coexisted uneasily as central elements in his life structure. Now, although he was still an academic biologist, he had made a major career change: from scientist to educator.

It was not until the phase of Becoming One's Own Man that Treloar could make the change, and the differences were crucial. Research was a peripheral element of the new life structure, and teaching was central. He was becoming an educational administrator. In time he would advance further to be department chairman or university administrator.

The move west thus represented a change from the initial career built around the research ladder symbolized by the Nobel Prize. It involved a change in other respects as well. He dreamed of starting a new life in a new world. The new university would be more benign and devoted to humane educational ideals. He would devote more time to his family and his leisure interests—skiing, mountain climbing, the enjoyment of natural beauty.

Treloar made this change at the height of Becoming One's Own Man, in an effort to live with greater autonomy and fulfillment. Much self-analysis, planning and exploration went into the choice of a new life setting. There were sound reasons for pulling up his fragile roots and taking this new direction. At the same time, he was making a big bet: the new world might not be up to his expectations, and he might not have the talent or character needed to succeed in the new enterprise. His anticipations of the future were cautiously hopeful—and extravagantly optimistic. His plans were realistic—and filled with illusions.

Our story ends at this point. We leave Arthur Treloar at age 40, embarking upon a new life. He is about to enter the Mid-life Transition, when the existing structure comes into question, when illusions are confronted, when new aspects of the self demand expression and new paths must be formed. The character of his life will change, in part because the new situation will bring new opportunities and demands, and even more, because he is in a process of inner growth that will lead him in unexpected directions.

## Sequence E.  Unstable Life Structure

In all the previous sequences, a relatively stable life structure is formed early in the Settling Down period. In Sequences A and B this structure is maintained to the end of Settling Down, whereas in C and D there is a major change in the phase of Becoming One's Own Man.

In Sequence E, the life structure remains relatively unstable and in flux throughout the entire Settling Down period. None of the men in this sequence actively sought or welcomed the recurrent change and transiency of his life. All of them made an effort to work on the tasks of Settling Down. In each case, a variety of external circumstances and internal difficulties conspired to prevent the man from achieving his aims. No one whose life structure went through frequent change during his thirties experienced this decade as a time of personal fulfillment or of reasonably happy, free choice. There may be men who live happily in this way during these years, but we believe they are rare. The psychological and social costs of following Sequence E in the thirties are likely to be grave in the years that follow.

This sequence was found in three of our forty men: a worker, a biologist and a novelist (see page 152). In three other cases, a biologist and two executives, the life structure was rather precarious but stable enough to be included in one of the other sequences. Our mode of sampling probably gave us an overrepresentation of more stable lives.

A worker, Hank McCloud, went through Sequence E. He had grown up in the poverty and isolation of the West Virginia mountain country. At 17 he volunteered for the army and spent two years as a loner, with minimal education and job skills. He then had the luck—good or bad?—to be wounded, and he spent three years in a military hospital. This was a high point in his life. For the first time he had the leisure, social supports and resources to lead an interesting life. Without formal schooling he became a radio operator, established a hospital radio station, recruited and managed a staff, and formed a Dream of becoming a radio or television personality.

At 22, Hank McCloud left the army "like an eagle on its first flight from the nest." Unfortunately, the army hospital had nourished his hopes of flying but had given him very little in the way of education, occupational skills or preparation for civilian life. After getting training as a radio announcer he held a series of jobs around the country. He was an attractive, articulate young man, "very big with the teenagers." He had many casual relationships with women but no strong attachments or commitments. In time he experienced more acutely the emotional emptiness and purposelessness of this life. Periodically he returned to his father in West Virginia, clinging to the hope of securing their relationship and starting a life there —and learning again and again that the relationship was impossible and the situation intolerable.

The time from 27 to 29 was a low point for McCloud. He began to hate his nomadic life and then to seek a more stable, purposeful life in the East. At 29 he had a flare-up of his army illness and spent several months in a convalescent home. During this time his old interest in nature returned and he started painting landscapes. Over the next few years he worked as a salesman, purchasing agent and counselor in a boys' reformatory, but he could not establish a clear occupational direction or a stable work history.

At 33, he married a woman nine years younger than he. She was a gentle but strong person who shared his love of nature. In his mind, she was almost too good to be true—the special woman. He was still the lost country boy trying to make it in the genteel, urban world. She was of that world, the only child in a stable, lower-middle-class family, the apple of her parents' eye. He looked to her to be a center for the life he so desperately wanted to build. The marriage helped him to begin the process of Settling Down, but his hopes of establishing a more secure occupational base did not materialize. In the next four years he held office jobs in three different firms, and in each case he quit or was fired after getting into conflict with his boss. Just after our interviewing started, at 37, he was given notice on the current job.

At 37, then, McCloud's life presented a very mixed picture. He had been married for four years, owned a small home and had a first child. His family was the central focus of his life and a strong support. Otherwise, however, he was still in total flux. During his twenties he had lost all connection with his pre-adult world in West Virginia, but at 37 he was just beginning to put down fragile roots in his wife's New England world. He would have to decide soon whether to keep trying to form an occupation in the business world, or to do work that stemmed more directly from his early identity and skills, even though it was less middle class.

Hank McCloud knew it was late to be working on these choices—late in the timetable of the occupational world, late in terms of his own goals and family requirements. It was also late in terms of his developmental work on the tasks of Settling Down and Becoming One's Own Man. In talking about his prospects after the current job failure, he said, "If it comes to it, I can always do carpentry or pump gas." He was trying to accept this possibility, with full awareness of the grim implications. It meant that he had to curtail his aspirations for a more affluent life just at the time when advancement was so important. His wife might have to work again as a nurse and have her parents care for the baby. And that meant that her parents would let them both understand that their predictions about him were coming true. He had to face the fact that he was not yet master of his own ship, and the ship was in stormy seas.

These are the possibilities—and the tragedies—of the Settling Down period. The basic character of this period is the same for all men. It stems from the major developmental tasks and issues confronting us all. At the same time, men work on these tasks in myriad ways and there are infinite variations in the individual life course. Whatever its course and outcome, this period comes to an end at around 40 as new developmental tasks gain primacy and a new period begins.

# The Life
# of James Tracy (II)

In Chapter 7 we followed the life of James Tracy through the Age Thirty Transition. When we left him at age 34, he had just completed the shift from military to civilian life. He was establishing a new life built around three main components: his new executive position in Hartford with the Ajax Corporation; his continuing family life with his wife and children; and his fragile but growing love relationship with Joan. This life structure had its contradictions and tensions, but it was the best basis he could create for starting to Settle Down.

Just as things were getting stabilized, Tracy's mentor, Al Hugo, left Ajax.

> I had tremendous respect for Al. I literally loved him. He was the guy that hired me and sent me out on my first assignment. Then he got in a fight with the president of Ajax. They got at cross purposes and Al resigned. Whether he got fired or not I will never know. I doubt it. Nobody would fire him. The president was kind of a knucklehead, so he might have. I have seen Al off and on since. He is now working as an executive vice president for a smaller company.

Tracy too thought of leaving Ajax. His descriptions of the corporation at this time are filled with criticisms of its cliques and the social pressures. He felt vulnerable because he wouldn't conform. To participate in the clique at work, he would have had to include his wife. But he knew that their relationship was shattered, that he and Victoria could not join in a social network.

When Al Hugo left, work had little meaning for Jim. Without a mentor, he had only a job. He filed his aspirations away, ready to take them out again if conditions improved. With Ajax in transition, and Hugo gone, could he maintain his job? For the sake of fatherhood, could he improve his marriage? If he wanted more intimacy with a woman, could he sustain the necessary effort?

From age 34 to 37, these questions and tensions grew. Jim Tracy's position became progressively more difficult and absurd. He wanted Joan more in the center of his life, and Victoria out of it. He thought constantly of Joan and their possible future together. He wanted to break out of his current situation and construct a new life. Joan offered that opportunity, but he was unable to make up his mind. It was hard to acknowledge the total defeat of his marriage and take a chance with another woman who seemed to offer love. He had always prided himself on being a dutiful father; he now faced the conflict between responsibility to his children and to himself.

The worldly accomplishments that had seemed so important in adolescence and early adulthood no longer represented the whole dream. The three major elements—work, marriage and the "other woman"—conflicted more than ever; he had to modify them and integrate the fractured life structure.

## Becoming One's Own Man

It took Jim Tracy until age 37 to be able to take a decisive step. At this point he realized how unfair he had been to himself and to Joan: "I just kept stringing her along, saying that when the children are older, we'll get together." Joan was bitterly unhappy in her own marriage and eager to marry Jim. He understood the duplicity in the relationship and finally had to act.

> Since I didn't want to leave the children, it had to be something pretty strong to pull me away from them. Finally, Joan was strong enough, or I felt strongly enough about her to make it seem worthwhile. . . . I just remember the incident. I happened to be in a hotel room in Los Angeles, and I was thinking about it, and finally said, you know, I am being a goddamn fool. I called her and said, "I have had it. I have just made up my mind." The minute I got home I was going to talk to Victoria, and I did.

Jim and Joan agreed on a complicated arrangement that would enable them both to get out of their respective marriages. Jim told Victoria that he could not live with her, and moved out.

> I had not loved her for years and she was getting under my skin. I just told her that I had had it. She tried very hard to keep it from happening. Finally, she agreed that I should go live by myself for a while. Her hope was that I would get straightened out and come back. She kept the thing dragging for over a year and then finally consented to divorce me with a

very liberal settlement. She cried hysterically for a couple of days, off and on, and I just steeled myself against it.

By this time Jim had little inclination for sympathy toward Victoria. He was impatient to get on with the task of building a new life. To show much feeling for her would be a threat to his decision. There was no place for self-doubt, no turning or looking back.

Over a fourteen-month period, Jim and Joan obtained their divorces and were married. He was 38, and she 28, with a 3-year-old son. Jim recalled this period of separation and remarriage with enthusiasm, excitement and a sense of accomplishment, not unlike his experiences in combat:

> I was really taken to the cleaners when I was divorced. My bank account was down to $75.60. I had a 1957 Ford convertible and the clothes on my back. I had the salary check and then the big alimony, but we started with nothing. Joan didn't have any money. I paid all the bills at once. We rented a house in Glastonbury for the first year, and then Joan went around and finally found this place. It was very nice, but small, a four-room house with a big living room. We bought it and added to it twice, and bought some additional property. It's got a nice river down from the back yard and it was in terrible disrepair as far as landscape went. I was so damned happy to be out from under that I didn't realize how tough it was going to be for a little while. But it worked out.

Jim's enthusiasm helped him deny the problems emanating from the divorce and remarriage. He minimized the emotional and financial costs they entailed. While supporting Victoria and their two children, he and Joan and her son were living in a small rented house.

For an action-oriented man, the introduction of uncertainties was upsetting. He suppressed the doubts and fears, and pursued an objective course of action. His plans and strategies masked the chaos within him. Tracy defended himself strongly against all inner doubts. Underneath, there may have been a fear of retribution for his violation of a traditional pattern of behavior.

Tracy began making his new family more central to him: he spent time with them, bought land, developed a new home. True, there were economic and emotional stresses. But he had brought about change, and it held exciting possibilities for the future. He had broken out of the old pattern, and he could hope that the new one would give him more stability, intimacy and love.

Shortly after Jim left Victoria, there was a major reorganization at Ajax. Donald Bond and Walter Johnson came in from Chicago "to turn Ajax around." Bond, eight years older than Tracy, was a hard-driving man.

In the general housecleaning he instigated, Tracy was the only local executive who survived. It was a very exciting time. Tracy had great respect for Bond, who took him into his confidence, gave him a deeper understanding of the company, and most importantly, revealed the personalities of the highest company executives.

> Don was a very tough-minded businessman who literally turned Ajax around. After losing millions in the gun plant, we now were making a 10 percent return on investment. He was one of these guys who knew what he was doing and had great will. Working for Bond was like going to school every day of the week. I just lapped it up. I watched every move he made. I had a close business relationship with him. We just sort of got along together. It was the greatest thing that ever happened to me, working for this guy directly for three years. . . . He was a fine manager and had tremendous insight into people. He did an awful lot of things for me, let me grow, and taught me things. Don would tell me things that, Christ, he'd never tell anyone else in the world, not even his wife, about his relationships with people in New York that I had no business to know. He'd ask me questions about it, he'd bounce things off—sort of a sounding board,

Don Bond, close in age to Tracy, emerged as a clear mentor figure. He was much more intimately involved in Tracy's life—even attending the wedding to Joan—than any of the other powerful older men who had previously helped his career. And Tracy was considerably more receptive to this kind of intense relationship than he had been earlier.

During his late thirties, Tracy was outstandingly successful at work. The previously powerful aspects of his mother's influence had diminished; the more positive parts of his father were being integrated. He was moving closer to both men and women. The new commitment to Joan had opened him up and made it possible to have a more intimate relationship with a man as well. Don's arrival on the scene and the developing mentor relationship facilitated his growth and sense of worth. This period, from age 38 to 40, was marked by excitement, accomplishment and future potential. He was becoming his own man.

The Tracys bought a plot of land in Glastonbury and began designing their "dream home." Initially this was a small four-bedroom structure, but it was gradually extended. Architect's plans were constantly revised to make it "just right." When Jim was 40, their son Tommy was born. He saw Joan as a "helpmate" who would facilitate the development of a new life to replace the previous restless, frantic searching. She was a special woman who would help him pull his life together, enrich it and give expression to his hopes and dreams.

Then, suddenly, Don Bond left Ajax to become chief executive of a smaller company. Walter Johnson was promoted into Bond's position and became the number one executive in Hartford. Tracy was number two, the general manager of the Firearms Division, but on a probationary basis. He still had to prove himself at this level. At 40, Tracy felt that his mentor had abandoned him and left him exposed to the machinations of the organization. He began looking "in a half-assed way" for another job. He experienced the year between 40 and 41 as a time of testing.

In addition, Tracy was now concerned about his own aging.

> When I hit 40, it was a really traumatic experience. As long as I was in my thirties, I visualized myself as a kid. When I hit 40, I really felt that. I'd always viewed myself as a young guy who is doing pretty well, a young guy on his way up, and all of a sudden, I am not a young guy anymore. I cannot do things I once did. It's kind of scary.

At 41, Jim received a firm promotion to general manager and vice president of the Firearms Division, one of the largest and most profitable divisions of the corporation. He now had authority over thousands of employees in Hartford and two Midwestern plants. This was the "culminating event" of his early adulthood. He had reached the top rung of his Settling Down ladder. The full meaning of this turning point became evident only in the next few years. It launched him into a new world—and into his Mid-life Transition. We shall continue the story in Chapter 19.

# 12 The Life of Paul Namson, Novelist

Paul Namson was born in the summer of 1926. Two years later his only sibling, Joel, was born. The setting was West End Avenue in Manhattan—an ordered, comfortable Jewish world. It was a business family. Both grandfathers had been successful businessmen in New York City in the early 1900s. His father's father had been in the cosmetics business in Budapest and come to the United States in the 1880s. Paul's father also made a reasonable success of the cosmetics business. Though attractive and appealing, he was nonetheless a "bullshit artist," often dishonest with himself and his children.

His mother, on the other hand, was "absolutely straight." A shy woman, she read popular books and enjoyed going to concerts and the theater with old friends from her childhood and finishing-school years. She took little pleasure in the social life her husband loved—at the clubs, playing cards. It was her family, the Asches, who dominated the Namson household as Paul grew up. The two men whom Paul respected most were Cyril Asch, his mother's brother (and Paul's godfather), and her favorite cousin, Noah Handler. Cyril came to play a central role in Paul's life. A brilliant and dynamic businessman, he was a millionaire several times over by the time he was thirty, a cultured Manhattan executive, a model to be emulated. Noah, who became a famous poet, was admired for his excellence in the world of the arts, though also regarded with some disdain by the men in the family because of his homosexuality, artistic qualities and rejection of the business world.

For Paul his mother was "very shadowy." "Early in my life my mother disappeared; she never seemed to be there." He related this absence to his brother's birth, when he was "farmed out to an aunt" to make it easier for his brother. Paul felt that he lost his close relationship to his mother at the start and never regained it. He was much more emotionally involved with his father. His brother, on the other hand, was close to his mother, who "pampered" him.

Paul's brother, Joel, knew very early in his life that he wanted to be in the arts. He would be an actor, a writer and a director of plays. "By the time he was eight or nine Joel knew exactly what he wanted and never strayed for a minute from that." From his close relationship to his mother, Joel could move more comfortably into the arts and also, later, into a homosexual life.

For Paul, more tied to his father, the arts were not an acceptable option—not part of a man's world. But where was he to go? When he was quite young Paul decided he didn't want to follow his father into the cosmetics business. Father was popular and could sell anybody anything but he was a card-playing con man looked down on by his wife's family. Paul did not admire these qualities of his father's. He would have to look elsewhere for a man to emulate.

Although his father was relatively uneducated, a "simple man," he was also socially ambitious and took good care of his family. Despite the depression, he moved up in the world through his own efforts. In the depression years, there was a drop in the barriers that had kept Hungarian Jews out of the upper-middle-class German-Jewish world he aspired to. When they moved to a new home in 1937 Paul was able to leave public school and enter a private school for boys. He was accepted by his schoolmates and their friends, many of whom were the children of upper-class German Jews. His years at this school were happy ones; his account of them is full of names and scenes and people he felt connected with.

In the private school he began to develop a sense of what he might do as an adult.

> Although I was very confused about what I wanted to do, I had a vague idea I wanted to be a psychiatrist. I'd done a lot of reading in psychiatric literature, and done very well in the sciences in high school. I was in love with a girl whose father was a doctor. So it seemed to me medicine would be a good career.

When he graduated, just before turning 16, the yearbook described him as "a member of the Swank Set."

He chose to attend Brown University largely because he wanted to get away from New York City and from his family. Paul now carried the Dream of his parents. He was making a place for himself in the German-Jewish milieu, and gave promise of realizing his father's hopes that he would move to the top in this world. Paul's next steps were to graduate from a good college, go into a business or profession, and marry into this world.

At 16 Paul felt tied to his father—one of the "beautiful Namsons"— and yet he rejected much of what his father stood for. He was similarly torn in relation to his mother. He was drawn to her qualities of character and the business and artistic values of her family. At the same time he struggled under the burden of her family's attitude toward the arts. He should be interested in them, but should understand that a man does not become an artist. These inner struggles, deriving from his early years in the family, played a continuing role in Paul's adult life. He might wish to be a businessman like Cyril, but not a "bullshit artist" like his father. He might wish to be an artist like Noah. But to be an artist was to enter a feminine, homosexual world. It was no place for a man.

## Early Adult Transition

Paul was still very much in his parents' world when he arrived on campus that fall. It seemed natural, therefore, to join a "very tony" Jewish fraternity that was "almost monolithically German Jewish." But, in contrast to his account of his high school years with the fullness of named friends and close intimacies, the story of his college years contained a relatively anonymous group of young men, "all headed for family businesses."

Three events stand out in Namson's account of the first two years of college: joining the fraternity; deciding not to go to medical school; and "my discovery of literature." His interests quickly shifted from psychiatry and science to literature. He read a great deal and began to write in secret. He began to feel a new sense of animation.

In June 1944, just as he was finishing his third semester at Brown, the Allies invaded Europe and he volunteered for the navy. "It was the most broadening experience of my life." He had never experienced anti-Semitism; now he was assigned to an LST with a group of white Southerners—"the only Jewish boy" on the ship. "It was made clear to me pretty fast. I was aware of it all the time I was on that ship." The navy was an experience in learning to fight back. It was also an experience that "shook up all my values." He realized that he had been raised in an "arrogant self-satisfied atmosphere." "The Navy threw me harshly into the big world, but it made me a more compassionate person."

He got out of the navy in the summer of 1946, just after turning 20. He stayed in New York only briefly and returned to Brown. Now certain that he did not want to be a doctor, he switched his major from pre-med to English, with a minor in economics. He took writing courses and wrote for the college humor magazine. He also wrote, semi-secretly, serious fiction about his navy experiences and about the conflicts between his family's values and those he had encountered in that "big world." He began to receive support for this work. An older man invited him into the writing world: "I took a lot of creative writing courses. Several of them were with Austin Garrison. He started a literary magazine and published a story I wrote in my senior year."

At the same time he developed an interest in business. During one summer he worked in the new underwriting firm of Asch and Company, which Cyril Asch had just started. Paul was interested in seeing for himself what his hero's business world was like.

During this time, too, he became seriously involved with two women of contrasting dispositions and values. Nora belonged to his writing world. She appreciated his writing and wanted to become a writer herself. To Paul she was "like Rebecca at the well, large, mature, serious." She was the person to whom he showed his serious fiction. After reading a story, "She came and found me and kissed me very shyly and said, 'You really have done it, Paul.' "

The other woman in Paul's life at this time was Sarah, whom he had met at a dance. "She had such a sensuous face." Sarah and Nora appealed to two different sides of Paul. Nora was serious, intellectual, a writer. Sarah was spirited, independent, "one of the best social dancers of my generation," a perfect helpmate for a rising young businessman. It was Sarah he fell in love with and decided to marry. When Nora discovered this, she told him in tears, "I hope you will be very happy with that social butterfly."

He married Sarah at age 21, just before graduating from college. Years later, he started telling us his life story with these words: "It all began eloping with my wife when we were in college over twenty years ago." He married a woman who represented the familial, Jewish, business world and supported his connection to it. At the same time the marriage was in part an act of rebellion and a crucial event in his separation from his parents.

The couple married suddenly and secretly. After the ceremony they returned to New York and told their families. Paul's father had a raging tantrum. The gist of his tirade was that Paul had married beneath his level. "Look what I had done with all the chances he and my mother had given me. He meant I could have married a more socially acceptable girl." Namson went on:

> I got married as a way of not returning home. I was almost 22 and had been away from home since 16. The thing that frightened me most at graduation was the idea of having to return home. I came up with a brilliant irrational solution to the whole problem. I would elope and get away. I didn't think what would happen after that.

Paul didn't have a plan for the future. He and Sarah had thought of going to Mexico "and I would write." They would live on the income from a $20,000 legacy he had received. Their marriage produced so much turmoil and distress in Paul's family, however, that they didn't do it. In his guilt he decided to remain in New York. After some part-time summer work, the fall found him without a job.

Paul had used the years from 16 to 22 to begin the difficult work of separating from his family. He had also begun giving shape to a Dream: a vision of himself as a creative writer. He was helped in this work by Austin Garrison and by Nora, who affirmed him in this view of himself. At the same time, just as he had minored in economics, so he held a minor Dream—a view of himself as a cultured businessman like Cyril. In his work with Cyril, he made a tentative approach to the business world. In marrying Sarah, he moved another step toward this world and its values. He was thus heading in two directions at once, toward writing and toward business. The tension between writing and business was to dominate his life throughout early adulthood.

# Entering the Adult World

In the fall of 1948, when Namson was 22, Cyril Asch came up with a plan that combined business and writing. He persuaded Paul that his chances of his becoming a successful writer were much less than of becoming a successful businessman. At the very least, Paul should give business a try. He could write on the side. Cyril had just bought an apartment house. He proposed that Paul manage the building and oversee the modernizing of the kitchens. He offered Paul $50 a week and an apartment in the building.

Paul accepted the offer and tentatively became a businessman-writer:

> I expected to stay just long enough to write a best-seller and leave. My basic idea, at least initially, was to write evenings and weekends. Initially I did have a lot of spare time and I sat in this office and wrote. I was attracted to short forms—stories, poetry, prose poems, brief essays—because it was very hard to sustain the writing. Somebody would always have a leaky faucet or a john that didn't work.

He wrote a lot that first year, but "the rejection slips came back so fast it was shocking." It was a discouraging experience. The work in the apartment house, however, went well. At the end of the first year, Cyril suggested that he apprentice out to another brokerage house as a salesman of stocks and bonds. Paul again accepted his offer.

He went to work for an established firm and got involved in the world of high finance. He was able to make some substantial deals and earned

large commissions, the first money he had made on his own. As a freelance
salesman he had a great deal of free time. He became intensely interested
in painting and the art world. "I began to drift into a lot of art galleries; the
paintings seemed to me a very real and meaningful world." The art galleries helped relieve the strain of "mechanically turning on the charm and
sincerity" to sell stocks.

At the end of this year, when Paul was 24, Cyril asked him to join
Asch and Company. As usual, Cyril was being proved right: Namson was
failing as a writer and succeeding as a businessman. He was attracted by
the opportunities of the business world. For the third time he took Cyril's
advice, and joined the family business.

In their middle twenties, then, Paul and Sarah Namson became young
Manhattanites, a handsome couple about town.

> Going ga-ga over these town houses and wanting that, beginning to get
> more and more involved in high living. We wanted to get to the chic
> parties and the interesting lofts. We were both interested in that. And I
> think some of our relationship was a little bit like Scott and Zelda Fitz-
> gerald. I don't mean to suggest I have his talent or will ever have his
> success.

The work with Cyril Asch provided the base for his entry into "the
high life." The investment house was small but flourishing, and he and
Asch were becoming important to each other.

> I was Cyril's right-hand man or something. He was a very stimulating
> example, I guess, in terms of emulation, for a considerable period of time.
> The deeper I got into the investment business the more responsibilities
> I had. I got interested in the dynamics of money making and found it
> increasingly fascinating. I did a very good job.

While becoming a businessman, Paul managed to continue with his
writing. He wrote five novels during his twenties. They did not seem
good books to him and he was unable to get them published. These disappointments were "a lot to stomach," and they influenced his decision
to write criticism for the art magazines of the 1950s.

> I began, at first, almost as a self-education for myself. I would go to a
> gallery opening on Saturday morning and take my notes. On Sunday I would
> write into the night to have it ready. I found it much easier to publish
> these art pieces than I did to publish my fiction.

By 28, Namson was writing in art journals and was buying important
abstract expressionist paintings. The early 1950s were exciting years in
this world. He grew with it and was developing as an appreciator, collec-

tor, and critic of the visual arts. The collecting was probably the major outlet for his creative needs at this time. The art criticism seemed mere "advertising copy," promoting his friends' work. This writing was more a part of his life as a businessman than of his work as a serious writer.

The paintings, though, were important in their own right and involved him in a complicated and interesting world. Business gave him the financial means to participate in this world. But business also involved him in a world of action and power, and Namson enjoyed this. Moreover, it was what his family wanted for him. Once they could see him established in business, his peripheral interest in the arts was not upsetting. By his late twenties, his early Dream of writing fiction was relatively dormant. He was barely connected, through his art criticism, to a writer's world. His view of himself as a creative writer was truncated, a backdrop to the rest of his life.

In creating a first adult life structure during his twenties, Paul moved toward Cyril and his world. He and Sarah were drawn to the Manhattan "high life," a romantic world like that of Scott and Zelda Fitzgerald. Art became an appendage to that glorious life. His creative writing withered. The side of Paul that was like his father, and that aspired to be like Cyril, was in the ascendancy. He was moving toward the life of the cultured businessman and, in this way, becoming the man his family wanted him to be. This was the life Sarah wanted and could support. They were closer during this time than they were to be in the years ahead.

# The Age Thirty Transition

At 28 Namson's relationships in the art world led him to an intense mentor relationship with Sheridan Fisher, a sculptor and a central figure in that world. Fisher came to represent the primacy of writing and the rejection of the business world. Through their relationship, the tension between these two sides of Namson re-emerged as the central issue in his life.

In the autumn of 1954, just after Namson turned 28, he bought a Sheridan Fisher sculpture. He also wrote a critical piece on Fisher's work, and was drawn into the small circle of people interested in him. Very few of Fisher's pieces had then been bought by collectors, so a mutual friend brought Fisher around to meet Namson. Their friendship started with the first meeting. Namson was drawn to Fisher and felt that Fisher was drawn to him as well. That spring they found themselves having dinner together as often as twice a week. Fisher was in psychoanalysis and would drive into New York from his country home. He would stay in the city for two or three days and spend some of his evenings with Namson. The friendship became more intimate.

Basically I was attracted to the idea of a man who had gone all the way in art and had somehow survived. I can only guess about what his feelings were toward me. Maybe I'd be safer talking about how I felt about him. I mean he did represent to me something like a heroic figure in the sense of the art hero. Art is a trackless waste; there are no rules and there are no signs for the kind of artist Fisher is. He also represented a fantasy of a wilder and more American background than I thought mine was. There was certainly on my part a romantic identification with him.

He was extremely direct. He was rather inarticulate, but he insisted that one talk about one's own feelings. When I tended to digress into art theory, or to be much more intellectual than I am today, he would keep pulling me back. He'd say, "But what does it mean to you, Paul? Why does it interest you? What's your commitment? What's your involvement?" I mean those were his favorite words, "commitment," "involvement" and so forth. "How are you involved?"

Fisher saw through Namson's compromises and pressed him with troubling questions. How could he possibly be committed to two things at once? How could he lead a "schizophrenic life"? Paul had to face in himself the conflict "between the excitement of the New York financial scene and a growing desire to write as a full-time occupation." With the discovery of a mentor whom he wanted to join as a creative artist, the desire to commit himself to his writing took root again.

He was fourteen years older than I, and my feeling toward him was something like toward a dream father or older brother, that kind of thing. Certainly the word "hero" is not an overstatement. For me he was a hero, a romantic figure, heroic figure. Typically, we didn't talk about art. We drank together, we'd walk along the beach together, we'd swim together. I remember croquet games. A certain kind of roughhousing, trading punches, that kind of playfulness and male camaraderie. But there was a side that was very loving and tender. It was one of the freest relationships I ever remember having with another man. And without wanting to make it sound queer, this punching and bear hugging, great admiration, great affection, I guess there was something like love.

The following summer, two weeks after Paul's thirtieth birthday, Fisher died suddenly of a heart attack. It was a "terrible shock" for Paul. The funeral intensified his awareness of how important Fisher had been to him.

I remember the shock of feeling how good it was to cry. It was just an amazing experience for me. I hadn't really cried since I was a child. My whole life up to that point went before my eyes. So maybe the word "love" isn't too strong. There was an intense attraction both to the man and what he stood for.

After Fisher died, Namson began to recast radically a novel he had written about the art world. It was entitled *The Dealer*. An aging art dealer, a man of elegance and taste who is slowly destroying himself because the world he once belonged to has all but disappeared, comes into conflict with an exuberant, arrogant young painter. Between them is a beautiful young woman, who is mistress to the art dealer and half in love with the painter. At the end she leaves both of them and the art world they represent, and tries to find a center for her own life.

Namson recognized that all of these characters represented parts of himself, parts he was trying to sort out. The woman has relationships with the art dealer and the painter, but she has no occupational identity of her own. Her story is very much Paul's and reflects his own search. Like her, Paul felt after his experience with Sheridan that he was alive and growing again. With this feeling came a sense of wonder and happiness—and an uncertainty as to where it would lead.

During those two years Fisher's entry into their "high life" disrupted the "romantic relationship" Paul and Sarah had maintained through their twenties. At the same time, Sarah tried in another way to change that life. She had been wanting to have children, and Paul had not. He felt that the business and writing were as much as he could manage; adding children to his life would swamp him. As they approached 30, Sarah's need became so great that he agreed to have a child. When conception did not occur, he again acceded to her wishes and they decided to adopt a child.

At 32, when he was rewriting the novel, they adopted an infant son and named him Sheridan Namson. "When Sheridan arrived, we pretty much made up our minds that we would have at least one more child, and space seemed a necessity." They bought an elegant twelve-room brownstone looking out on a garden and the East River. They set about making it into a family dwelling. Sarah had a housekeeper-cook and an au pair girl to help with Sheridan. Paul had a writing room where he could isolate himself, "a solitary character in an unfurnished room."

During the Age Thirty Transition, two developments substantially altered the provisional life structure Namson had created during the previous period. The relationship with his mentor, Sheridan Fisher, led him to move creative writing more to the fore in his life. He was determined to commit himself to that solitary work in his "unfurnished room." Adopting little Sheridan and buying a new home gave Sarah a new focus for her life. These two changes, each critically important to Paul and Sarah, tended to separate them. It was as if Paul isolated himself in his writing room while Sarah busied herself with the new child and home.

The foundation of this life was the role of the cultured businessman, living on the boundary between the business and art worlds. Namson was a businessman by day and a writer at night and on weekends. The conflicting demands of these pursuits were exhausting. Devoting himself to these two parts of his life, he had little to give Sarah and their new child. What time and energy he had left went to their "high life." The tension in this structure was enormous: "It was my fate always to have my stomach tied in knots." Nevertheless this was the life structure with which he began the Settling Down period.

# Settling Down

By 1959 Cyril Asch was living part of the year in Florida, and Paul, at 33, was a vice-president and director of the company.

> I was involved profoundly and increasingly in business at increasingly higher levels. With Cyril away part of the year I was almost running the company. The choice of investments and the envisaging of their proper development was as much my responsibility as anyone's.

In 1959 Asch and Company was still a family-held company, but they were planning to form a publicly held corporation. It was an exciting time. "The chips were getting larger and larger." In roughly ten years the firm had grown from 7 or 8 people to 140, and from a net worth of $200,000 to $100 million. As one of the main officers, Paul was offered stock participations and he began an intense effort to buy as many shares of stock as were offered to him.

> It seemed like lunacy. I was borrowing money to take these participations. I had been working for about eleven years now, and I had about $600,000 in debts and about $1,000 in the bank. But this tremendous potential . . . At 33, I was very anxious to cash in some of these chips, but I was still a few steps from becoming a millionaire and still very much caught up in the excitement of big-time Wall Street.

During this same time his involvement in the visual arts reached a new peak: he became chairman of the building committee for a major new museum of modern art. He was taking his place among the New

Yorkers so admired by his family: he was a man of excellence in business with a commitment to the cultural life of New York City.

The social life Paul and Sarah built around the arts helped hold their life structure together during these years. They had a "vast social network" of art openings and parties, dancing until dawn and developing friendships with artists and others. This network enlarged in summers to include Southampton and an international scene in Paris and London. Their "high life" was expanding.

In the midst of all this activity Paul tried to maintain his writing world, encapsulated in the small room off their bedroom. Here he worked at giving form to his "distilled fantasies." He did this by removing himself, more than in the past, from Sarah. The romantic marriage of "the first ten years" gave way:

> It seemed we were drifting apart. My situation in business was taking more and more of my time. And my interest in writing was becoming more and more serious. I was not only not seeing her during the day, I was probably a bit impatient at night. I wanted time to read and write.

At 34, he wrote "the first part of *Currents,* the most lyrical opening section." He worked on this novel for the next several years. From time to time portions of it were published. A kind of diary, it wound like a bright thread through the fabric of his life between 34 and 42. In contrast to other major writing he did during this period, the *Currents* diary contained his joyous, celebratory feelings about life.

The triumph of the first story of *Currents* was that he was at last writing imaginative fiction from his own inner experience. It is authentic, immediate, alive. The reader is captured as Namson writes of the world of Manhattan skyscrapers and boardrooms, of restaurants and theaters, of a sybaritic luxury he knew intimately. Through this world dances his hero, a businessman-poet with "a dream looped so carefully about my neck." The story is funny-bitter. The hero is reflective and removed, even as he openly loves it all; and lurking behind his celebration is a fundamental criticism of it and a wish to leave it behind. It is a remarkable self-portrait, a description of himself and the life he was leading. "Just tell the waiter, quietly, you want *more,*" he wrote.

As Namson turned 34, the adoption agency told them that their request for another child would be granted. Soon after this came a big surprise: Sarah was pregnant. They canceled the second adoption and eagerly awaited the birth. This was the start of a momentous year. The first story in *Currents* was published in a little magazine—a climactic event in his writing career, their little girl was born and he became a millionaire. It looked as if his compromises had worked out, as if he could have it all. Perhaps he would really be able to combine writing, business, family and social life into a cohesive life structure.

By 35, however, this life had become oppressive. What had seemed to be a great integration soured. "On the surface I was successful. In my gut I wasn't." He was so plagued by "tremendous stomach tension" that he drank and smoked marijuana more heavily in an attempt to relieve his distress. Moreover, his need to realize the Dream had grown.

Namson desperately wanted to leave Asch and Company and write full time. He longed for the autonomy he could have as a writer but would never get as long as he worked for Cyril.

> Sometime by the end of the '50s or the early '60s I was absolutely certain I wanted to leave. Certain because I had finally made up my mind that what I really wanted to do with my life was to write, and certain because I had made all the money I needed.

He had needed to make his mark in business, to make himself a millionaire. Having done this, Namson felt more free to leave the business and more able to put writing at the center of his life. He was committed to writing in a new way, a feeling buttressed by his new recognition as a writer. With the publication of his story in 1961, "I received some notice of me as a writer." A serious critic, doing a survey of literary magazines, singled out his story as "one of the sizeable nuggets . . . a softly sizzling portrait."

At the same time, he knew that his commitment to becoming a writer was beyond the understanding of his parents and uncles. His leaving business to write would be viewed by Cyril and the others as a betrayal—a betrayal of them personally and of their values. His departure from Asch and Company would not be amicable. In Cyril's mind, writing was something Paul could do in his spare time. He wanted Paul at his side, a trusted nephew and "crown prince," who would maintain and inherit the family business. "Cyril can read Proust and appreciate him, but he cannot understand how a young man in his own family could leave the world to spend his time writing novels."

In his anguish over this "gnawing conflict" Paul found help in an unexpected quarter. He was invited to Boston where Timothy Leary was studying hallucinogenic drugs. Paul volunteered as a subject. To his surprise the experience was quite helpful. It gave him a detached view of his struggles. He could see more clearly, he thought, the fundamental conflict between his values and Cyril's. At 35, he resolved to face Asch:

> I made the speech in 1962. I had thought about it from the day I started. But in those months before, I would get up and stalk around and say to

Sarah, "I am going to discuss this with Cyril. I will complete whatever obligations I have, and then we—I—will leave and we will go to some other life."

He told Cyril that he would complete all his present obligations, but "Cyril kept adding obligations." These kept Namson at Asch and Company for nearly two more years. "I was never more alert or efficient in all the years there." But he was taking drugs regularly, and his sleeplessness took on the proportions of insomnia. His guilt over turning away from Cyril, knowing how important he was to him, was almost more than he could manage.

His distress was reflected in his writing, where, as always, he struggled to come to grips with the turmoil inside himself. He began a novel about his darker, despairing feelings regarding the business world. This novel, *The Bridge Game*, was his "first serious attempt" to write a long work at his highest level. The bridge game symbolizes the high-finance "games" of big business which the hero, like Namson, respects as games but has no respect for as a life. The hero is a professional bridge player who lives in a never-never land of high-powered bridge tournaments, drug experiences and parties. He lives an empty, cynical life, and dies in a senseless accident at 29.

From age 34 to 36 Paul worked steadily on *Currents* and *The Bridge Game*. The one reflected mainly his love of the business world, the other his despair of it. This writing grew out of his ambivalent relationship with this world and, ultimately, helped him to leave it.

Just before his 37th birthday, Paul gathered himself together and made the final break with Cyril. It was the "hardest thing I've ever done."

> When we finally had it out it was a complete rejection of Cyril's values. It was like walking out on the family. He felt that in the course of the last twelve years I had become committed to a way of life and a set of values that was their way of life and their set of values. And for a while I did. I don't think he realized what a serious involvement writing had become.

They parted in a cloud of guilt and acrimony. When Cyril realized that he couldn't stop Paul from going, he turned away in fury. They have had almost no contact since.

Namson left Asch and Company in June 1963. The Namsons began with a summer on Cape Cod. Sheridan was six and Lucy was two. He wanted to complete *The Bridge Game*, the novel he had been working on for the previous two years. This book reflected his disenchantment with business, with drugs and with himself, and led back to Sheridan Fisher. It contained Fisher's experience of bitter weariness at the end of

his life, as Namson understood it, together with Paul's experience of
bitter weariness in his last few years with Cyril. In the novel the hero
uses drugs to sustain his pursuit of prizes despite his weariness and despair. He can't leave the competitive world and yet he finds it unbearable to remain. Paul completed the book that summer. "I did half of it
in a period of two years, the last half in three months."

When they returned to New York that September, *The Bridge Game*
was accepted for publication and Namson began work on another novel,
*Markers*, which was to trace the history of his life in business. Everything
looked good at that time. Leaving Asch and Company brought an end
to his "stomach tension." He experienced a gratifying burst of energy
resulting in three hundred pages of new manuscript. It seemed he would
be able to establish himself as a writer without great difficulty.

That fall, however, he began to realize that the transition would take
more time and effort than he had imagined. He learned, for example,
that the termination of his involvement in the business world could not
be accomplished easily or quickly. Although Namson was no longer working at Asch and Company, he was still involved in business affairs. "I
set up trusts for the children and gave quite a bit of money away. That
takes time. I had so many other things that most writers don't have,
such as property, and there were banks and stockbrokers who called." His
fortune of about $5 million did not free him as much as he had expected;
it kept him in the world of high finance and philanthropy. He gave money
to various institutions, including the Gordon Archives, where he became
a trustee.

During the first few years of trying to be a full-time writer, the structure of his life both changed and remained the same. Namson did succeed in putting writing more at the center of his life. He hired a secretary to relieve him of business concerns. "I took over Sarah's dressing
room and turned that into a secretary's office. I found that without a
secretary I couldn't get anything done because of the demands on me
and on my time." Such efforts helped him keep his financial activities
more limited, but they did little to reduce the demands of the "high
life" he and Sarah lived.

He was trying to graft writing onto their old life together, a life he
remained attached to. But the old conflicts between writing, business and
the "high life" remained, in altered form. Moreover, he was struggling
with the pain of losing his place in the business world, and with the difficulty of making a place for himself in the writer's world.

It was a profound shock as well as a profound change. The profound
change was that I was spending my morning energies, my best energies,

doing exactly as I wanted. The biggest shock was the realization that what I was doing was not useful from the point of view of society. What I had done before, even with the ambivalence of being in the investment business, was very well regarded. I had been in a position where my days were a parade of people wanting things from me, which I had the power to give. I was in a position of great power and great reward.

Now suddenly I was working harder, although that is debatable from the world's point of view. But four hours a morning of concentrated writing is much harder than eight hours in a business day. You are dragging stuff out of yourself and it's a very intense kind of activity, and with no help from the outside. I mean, nothing comes to you through the mail or through the phone—it is all coming out of your past and unconscious and so forth.

Writing was "a much more solitary kind of achievement," and he wanted to prove to himself that he could "do it all alone." He missed the sense of achievement and the affirmation he had received in the business world. He wanted a similar experience as a writer. He waited for the news to come in, telling him that he was a writer.

Here I am, working away at these books. Suddenly I realize that this is not an activity the world recognizes, not a multi-million-dollar conglomerate. As defined by American society it was useless and there was no reward for it. The sense of uselessness was much more profound than at the level of money. Suddenly my activities just don't matter in the world. Suddenly I no longer exist. I lived in a kind of void until the book was published.

But there was yet another struggle, which occurred after publication. He would be validated only if the world read the book and found it a worthy effort. Then the product would exist, he would exist, and the "solitary achievement" would have been made. And if it did not?

*The Bridge Game* came out in the fall of 1964, just after Paul turned 38. It was at the time he most needed affirmation. The affirmation was at best modest. It came in a muted voice, out of his past: "*The Bridge Game* was reviewed in the *Saturday Review of Literature* and *The New York Times*. But the best review was written by my old teacher Austin Garrison and published in his small magazine." Indeed, the reviews were bitterly disappointing.

His second published novel, and his most ambitious effort to date, thus gave him very little. He was left with the awful sense of uselessness, of not existing. What he began in June 1963 with such high hopes and serious intentions was not working well eighteen months later. At this point he had been hard at work on *Markers* for a year, and the writing was going well. He was able to sustain the hope that he would succeed with *Markers*, despite the lack of success of *The Bridge Game*. He was disappointed but not defeated.

Namson began searching for an undertaking that would give him a sense of usefulness and at the same time facilitate the writing of *Markers*. He decided to leave New York. Leaving the "high life" might enable him to write more productively.

> There was a mounting sense of pressure in New York, and distraction. It sprang up in the years when I was most involved with writing art criticism, which was an easy thing for me while I was in business. There had been a buildup over these years of art reviewing, of a really hectic, art-social life in New York, and it just seemed to me we were spending too much energy on parties. I mean the fact is that if you go out every night and you're drinking heavily and so forth, it isn't that easy to write in the morning. You can go through a business day hungover, but you can't really write.

He thought of teaching as a possibility. It would get him away from New York while involving him in what seemed eminently useful work. His job explorations led him back to Brown and Austin Garrison, who offered him a one-year appointment as an assistant professor in the Creative Writing Department.

> It seemed exactly what we wanted. There was something appealing, a nostalgic value. I had a very definite idea of what I thought might be useful to students of creative writing. I felt I had a few things to show the academy.

Paul began his search for a teaching position in January 1965 in the wake of the publication of *The Bridge Game*. He began teaching at Brown in the fall of 1966, a year and a half later. During the interim he continued his work on *Markers*. This was his "major effort"—an attempt to write a book beyond anything he had yet done, and a demonstration to himself and the world that his previous failure could be overcome. He completed it in the spring of 1966, a few months before turning 40.

> *Markers* was accepted immediately by the publisher. But they offered me an advance that I felt was insulting. I had gotten $2500 as an advance for *The Bridge Game* and it seemed to me this book was a step forward and more ambitious. It was also the most autobiographical book I'd done. I felt in some way I was being asked to sell myself too cheap. I felt they were buying me in that sense, and I just couldn't let it go for that.

His publisher had let him down. He had wanted to be treated by them as a serious writer. They did not refuse him encouragement, but they offered it in small measure. For Paul, who desperately needed affirmation, it was not enough. He felt "outraged and disgusted." "I asked my agent to withdraw it, and I never have submitted that novel again."

This was his second major defeat, and in our view the "culminating event" of his early adulthood. He went that summer to the Cape. At the time of his fortieth birthday, he felt discouraged and in need of isolation. He had made his major effort to establish himself as a writer of serious fiction, and he had not been affirmed. Indeed, the whole writing enterprise was in serious question just three years after he had broken out of the executive world to pursue his Dream.

Namson's life structure during the first five years of the Settling Down period, from age 32 until 37, was relatively stable. Writing was a small component, an appendage to his life as a cultured Manhattan businessman. As we have seen, however, this structure was shot through with irreconcilable conflicts. He realized that he must break away from Cyril and the business world. It was imperative to build his life about his own values and not the family's; to pursue his Dream and not the dream Cyril had for him; to speak out clearly and in his own voice.

At 37, he broke with the man who had been a combined uncle, father, mentor and boss, and plunged into writing full time. He tried to move business to the periphery of his life structure and writing to the center. In taking this step he was betting that he could become a writer, that the world would affirm his writing work as it had his business work. He was trying to become his own man.

By his fortieth birthday he had completed two novels. Neither brought him the affirmation and the sense of usefulness that were so important to him. In this sense his gamble had failed. What could he reasonably expect of himself now? What modification of his Dream would make it more consonant with his talent?

To keep faith with the Dream, Namson would have to create a life structure giving stronger support to the writing. He addressed this problem in planning the Brown year. His present life structure gave too much space to business concerns and the "high life"; it could not provide adequate space for his writing. A radical change would have to be made.

At the same time, Namson was beginning to realize that the business world had served valuable functions for him. He needed to keep some parts of it, or to have something equivalent in his life. He missed many things that had excited him there. Some involvement in the world outside his writing room was necessary to nourish and sustain his writing. Although he needed a "bare room" in which to write, he also needed a "fussy room" to provide the experiences out of which he crafted his fiction. Earlier, business had seemed an overwhelming distraction. Now he could see that it had also been an essential source of nourishment for his art. It was the nexus from which he had created *The Bridge Game* and *Markers*. Having completed them, "I felt I had done as much subjective fantasy as I could." Where would his material come from now? His beginning awareness of this problem influenced his decision to seek an academic position. If the academic world stimulated him as business had, it might provide new material for his fiction.

At 40, therefore, Paul Namson entered a new period of his life. He was faced with the task of reappraising and modifying his life structure, and of moving from early to middle adulthood. In Chapter 18, we shall follow his life through the Mid-life Transition and its aftermath. First, however, we must have a look at the character of the Mid-life Transition as a developmental period.

# IV The Mid-life Transition and Entering Middle Adulthood

# 13 The Mid-life Transition

The late thirties mark the culmination of early adulthood. At around forty a man can make some judgment regarding his relative success or failure in meeting the goals he set himself in the enterprise of Becoming One's Own Man. Success here means that the enterprise has flourished: he has achieved the desired position on his "ladder"; he has been affirmed within his occupational and social world; he is becoming a senior member of that world with all the rewards and responsibilities seniority brings.

Often a man looks forward to a key event that in his mind carries the ultimate message of his affirmation by society. This "culminating event" takes on a magical quality in his private fantasy. If it goes the right way, he will know that he has truly succeeded and is assured of a happy future. A poor outcome, on the other hand, will mean that he has failed in a profound sense, that not only his work but he as a person has been found wanting and without value.

When a man experiences a developmental crisis in the late thirties, it stems from the overwhelming feeling that he cannot accomplish the tasks of Becoming One's Own Man: he cannot advance sufficiently on his chosen ladder; cannot gain the affirmation, independence and seniority he wants; cannot be his own man in the terms defined by his current life structure. Whatever the degree of his success or failure—no matter whether he is advancing brilliantly or in the depths of crisis—as long as a man is concerned primarily with these questions he has not yet emerged from the period of Becoming One's Own Man.

At around 40, a new period gets under way. The Mid-life Transition ordinarily has its onset at age 40 or 41 and lasts about five years. For the fifteen men in our sample who completed this period, the average age at termination was 45.5, the range 44 to 47. We doubt that a true Mid-life Transition can begin before age 38 or after 43.

The Mid-life Transition is a bridge between early adulthood and middle adulthood. As in all transitions, a man must come to terms with the past and prepare for the future. Three major tasks must be worked on.

• One task is to terminate the era of early adulthood. He has to review his life in this era and reappraise what he has done with it.

• A second task is to take his first steps toward the initiation of middle adulthood. Although he is not yet ready to start building a new life structure, he can begin to modify the negative elements of the present structure and to test new choices.

• A third task is to deal with the polarities that are sources of deep division in his life. Let us consider the three tasks in turn.

## Reappraising the Past

The initial focus in the Mid-life Transition is on the past. The major task is to reappraise the life structure of the Settling Down period, within the broader perspective of early adulthood as a whole and even of pre-adulthood. A man's review of the past goes on in the shadow of the future. His need to reconsider the past arises in part from a heightened awareness of his mortality and a desire to use the remaining time more wisely. Past and future coexist in the present, but he suffers from the corrosive doubt that they can be joined.

Now the life structure itself comes into question and cannot be taken for granted. It becomes important to ask: What have I done with my life? What do I really get from and give to my wife, children, friends, work, community—and self? What is it I truly want for myself and others? What are my central values and how are they reflected in my life? What are my greatest talents and how am I using (or wasting) them? What have I done with my early Dream and what do I want with it now? Can I live in a way that combines my current desires, values and talents? How satisfactory is my present life structure—how suitable for the self, how viable in the world—and how shall I change it to provide a better basis for the future?

As he attempts to reappraise his life, a man discovers how much it has been based on illusions, and he is faced with the task of *de-illusion-ment*. By this expression I mean a reduction of illusions, a recognition that long-held assumptions and beliefs about self and world are not true. This process merits special attention because illusions play so vital a role in our lives throughout the life cycle.

The profound human ambivalence toward illusion is reflected in our everyday language. On the one hand, illusion has a negative connotation. It is associated with magic, sleight of hand, enchantment, errors of perception and belief. In a culture highly committed to science, technology and rationality, illusion is generally regarded as inappropriate or even dangerous. The word itself derives from the Latin *ludere*, to play. While playful illusions can be accepted as part of the imaginative world of child-hood, an adult is expected to be more realistic, practical, down to earth. The loss of illusions is thus a desirable and normal result of maturity.

On the other hand, our culture recognizes that illusions have their value even in adult life and that giving them up is often painful. We enjoy magic as a game of illusion. We use the term "disillusionment" to refer to a painful process through which a person is stripped of his most cherished beliefs and values. To be disillusioned is not merely to have lost one's illusions; it is to become cynical, estranged, "unable to believe in anything." This is one possible outcome of the loss of illusions, but not the only one.

To identify the broader process which is so important in the Mid-life Transition, I use the term "de-illusionment." The process of losing or reducing illusions involves diverse feelings—disappointment, joy, relief, bitterness, grief, wonder, freedom—and has diverse outcomes. A man may feel bereft and have the experience of suffering an irreparable loss. He may also feel liberated, free to develop more flexible values and to admire others in a more genuine, less idealizing way.

Illusions can be tremendously harmful; but they can also inspire works of great nobility and accomplishment. They play a crucial, helpful and hurtful part in the lives of most persons during early adulthood. Some reduction in illusions is now appropriate and beneficial, but it is neither possible nor desirable to overcome all illusions in the Mid-life Transition or even by the end of middle adulthood. Illusion continues to have its place—a mixed blessing, or a mixed curse—all through the life cycle. The best way to avoid illusions is not to want anything very much. And that is hardly a prescription for a full life.

Early adulthood provides a fertile ground for illusions. Individual capabilities and drives are at their peak. A man must "believe in" himself—even in the face of reality, if need be—and in significant persons, groups and ideologies, so that he can shape a course toward a better life for himself and others, according to his lights. "Good enough" development in early adulthood means that he has aspirations, makes commitments to persons and enterprises, and strives with some enthusiasm and discipline toward valued goals.

## Modifying the Life Structure

As the Mid-life Transition proceeds, the emphasis gradually shifts from past to future. A man must make choices that will modify the existing life structure and provide the central elements for a new one. He must begin planning for the next phase. As he makes a commitment to these choices and embarks upon a new pattern of existence, the transition is over and a new period—Entering Middle Adulthood—begins.

Some men make significant changes in the *external* aspects of the life structure during the Mid-life Transition. The more drastic changes involve divorce, remarriage, major shifts in occupation and life style, marked decline in level of functioning, notable progress in creativity or in upward social mobility.

Other men make fewer and less visible external changes. They tend to "stay put" during the Mid-life Transition, remaining in the same marriage and family, the same surroundings, occupation and even work place. If we look more closely, however, we find that important though less obvious changes have occurred. A man's marital relationship is different, for better or worse. His children are growing up and family life is taking new forms. His parents have died or have become more dependent, and this has considerable impact upon his role as son and family member. Even if he is in the same work place, the character of his work has been altered as a result of changes in technology, in organizational structure or in him. Seemingly small promotions or demotions have greatly affected his work activities, his position in the work world, and the personal meaning of work for him. Finally, he has been influenced by changes in the nation and the world, such as war, depression and social movements of all kinds. These changes affect everyone in some way, but the effects are mediated by a man's age and period of development.

The Mid-life Transition also brings significant changes in the *internal* aspects of a man's life structure. He works on various developmental issues that have special urgency at mid-life. He may change appreciably in social outlook, in personal values, in what he wants to give the world, in what he wants to be for himself. The inner changes may be highly conscious and openly expressed, or subtle and hidden. They may come out in dramatic external changes. Even if the changes merely color the fabric of his life without grossly altering it, they give it a substantially different meaning.

A primary task of the Mid-life Transition is to modify the life structure of the thirties and to create the basis for a new structure appropriate to middle adulthood. The final test of the developmental work done here, as in all transition periods, is the satisfactoriness of the life structure emerging from it. Whatever the nature of the developmental work done, and however modest or profound the structural changes wrought, the individual's life in the mid-forties will differ in crucial respects from that in the late thirties. In Chapter 16 we shall examine more closely the changes occurring in various elements of the life structure.

## The Individuation Process

Throughout the life cycle, but especially in the key transition periods such as infancy, pubescence and the Mid-life Transition, the developmental process of *individuation* is going on. This term refers to the changes in a person's relationship to himself and to the external world. The infant, leaving his mother's womb, must gain some idea of his separate existence. He must decide where he stops and where the world begins. He must separate himself from his mother, yet maintain a tie to her. He must form a sense of "reality" that allows him to accept his surroundings as having an independent existence not necessarily subject to his control. The child's world gradually expands to include his family, neighborhood and friends; and his self becomes more complex through his relationships with other persons and institutions.

These changes are part of the individuation process. In successive periods of development, as this process goes on, the person forms a clearer boundary between self and world. He forms a stronger sense of who he is and what he wants, and a more realistic, sophisticated view of the world: what it is like, what it offers him and demands from him. Greater individuation allows him to be more separate from the world, to be more independent and self-generating. But it also gives him the confidence and understanding to have more intense attachments in the world and to feel more fully a part of it.

Every developmental transition, as I have said, involves termination and initiation: the termination of an existing life structure and the initiation of a new one. In order to accomplish this, a person must reappraise and modify the existing life structure. This is a challenging and difficult job; it would perhaps be impossible if individuation were not simultaneously playing a role. In a transition period, individuation is the underlying process that links termination and initiation. It prepares the inner ground, laying an internal basis on which the past can be partially given up and the future begun.

In the Early Adult Transition, a boy-man begins his novitiate in the adult world and takes an important step in the individuation process. He must loosen his ties to the pre-adult world and the pre-adult self. Depending in large part on how well individuation goes at this time, he forms a valued adult identity and becomes capable of living with a greater degree of autonomy. He has more responsibility for himself and others and gains competence in his various social roles.

At best, however, a man in his mid-twenties is but a step beyond adolescence. His pre-adult self, with its ties to parents and the pre-adult world, operates with great force throughout early adulthood. Although some developmental gains may be made in the Age Thirty Transition, he will not be much more individuated in the late thirties than he was at 25. After the Early Adult Transition, the next great opportunity for developmental work on individuation is the Mid-life Transition. In this period, a man must modify the early adult self (including, as it does, the baggage of unresolved problems from childhood and adolescence) and the life structure of the late thirties. Greater individuation is needed if he is to form a life structure more appropriate for middle adulthood.

What are the most significant changes to be made in mid-life individuation? Most investigators emphasize a single facet of the process. Erikson gives primary emphasis to Generativity vs. Stagnation as a stage of ego development in the middle years. According to Jaques, the central issue at mid-life is coming to terms with one's own mortality: a man must learn now, more deeply than was possible before, that his own death is inevitable and that he and others are capable of great destructiveness. In her biographical study of Goya, Martha Wolfenstein proposes that the reworking of destructiveness was the basic process in his transformation, during his forties, from an excellent court painter to an artist able to deal with the universals of human tragedy. Bernice Neugarten identifies the basic mid-life change as a growing "interiority": turning inward to the self, decreasing the emphasis on assertiveness and mastery of the environment, enjoying the process of living more than the attainment of specific goals.

Jung first proposed the distinction between the first and the second half of life, with the years around forty as the meridian. He showed that a new effort at individuation begins at mid-life and continues through the remaining years. Unlike many later writers who adopted his term but not his complex understanding of its meaning, he distinguished many facets of the individuation process.

Steering a course somewhere between the single-factor emphasis of some investigators and the tremendously complex approach of Jung, we shall discuss four tasks of mid-life individuation. For a given individual some of these may be more problematic or more conspicuous than others, but all of them are present and all must be considered in a general understanding of adult development. Each task requires a man to confront and reintegrate a polarity—that is, a pair of tendencies or states that are usually experienced as polar opposites, as if a person must be one or the other and cannot be both. As he becomes more individuated in middle adulthood, a man partially overcomes the divisions and integrates the polarities.

## Four Tasks of Mid-life Individuation

The four polarities whose resolution is the principal task of mid-life individuation are: (1) Young/Old; (2) Destruction/Creation; (3) Masculine/Feminine; and (4) Attachment/Separateness.

Each of these pairs forms a polarity in the sense that the two terms represent opposing tendencies or conditions. Superficially, it would appear that a person has to be one or the other and cannot be both. In actuality, however, the paired tendencies are not mutually exclusive. Both sides of each polarity coexist within every self. At mid-life a man feels young in many respects, but he also has a sense of being old. He feels older than the youth, but not ready to join the generation defined as "middle-aged." He feels alternately young, old and "in-between." His developmental task is to make sense of this condition of in-between and to become Young/Old in a new way, different from that of early adulthood.

The Destruction/Creation polarity presents similar problems of conflict and reintegration. The Mid-life Transition activates a man's concerns with death and destruction. He experiences more fully his own mortality and the actual or impending death of others. He becomes more aware of the many ways in which other persons, even his loved ones, have acted destructively toward him (with malice or, often, with good intentions). What is perhaps worse, he realizes that he has done irrevocably hurtful things to his parents, lovers, wife, children, friends, rivals (again, with what may have been the worst or the best of intentions). At the same time, he has a strong desire to become more creative: to create products that have value for himself and others, to participate in collective enterprises that advance human welfare, to contribute more fully to the coming generations in society. In middle adulthood a man can come to know, more than ever before, that powerful forces of destructiveness and of creativity coexist in the human soul—in my soul!—and can integrate them in new ways.

Likewise, every man at mid-life must come more fully to terms with the coexistence of masculine and feminine parts of the self. And he must integrate his powerful need for attachment to others with his antithetical but equally important need for separateness.

All of these polarities exist during the entire life cycle. They can never be fully resolved or transcended, though some utopian thinkers have held out this promise and some great religious prophets have been seen by others (though rarely by themselves) as having done so. They are not specific to the Mid-life Transition, but they operate here with special force.

Every developmental transition presents the opportunity and the necessity of moving toward a new integration of each polarity. To the extent that a man does this, he creates a firmer basis for his life in the ensuing phase. To the extent that he fails, he forms inner contradictions that will be reflected in the flaws of his next life structure. It is human both to succeed and to fail in these tasks: even as we resolve old conflicts and reach new integrations, we also create the contradictions that will in time stimulate further change and development.

The individuation process and the integration of polarities are ultimately internal and must be carried out within the person. I want to emphasize, however, that a polarity is not solely an inner matter. It is part of a man's life. The opposing tendencies exist both within the self and in the external world. As individuation progresses, a person not only becomes internally more differentiated and complex; he also develops more effective boundaries that link him to the external world and enable him to transact with it more fully. Moreover, the factors that influence how he deals with a polarity are external as well as internal. The splitting of young and old or of masculine and feminine occurs in our culture and social institutions as well as in each individual personality. We can understand a man's struggles to reintegrate a polarity only if we place these struggles within the context of his life and take account of both self and world. Developmental work on the four polarities will be discussed further in Chapters 14 and 15.

# The Mid-life Transition as Developmental Crisis

Some men do very little questioning or searching during the Mid-life Transition. Their lives in this period show a good deal of stability and continuity. They are apparently untroubled by difficult questions regarding the meaning, value and direction of their lives. They may be working on such questions unconsciously, with results that will become evident in later periods. If not, they will pay the price in a later developmental crisis or in a progressive withering of the self and a life structure minimally connected to the self.

Other men in their early forties are aware of going through important changes, and know that the character of their lives will be appreciably different. They attempt to understand the nature of these changes, to come to terms with the griefs and losses, and to make use of the possibilities for growing and enriching their lives. For them, however, the process is not a highly painful one. They are in a manageable transition rather than in a crisis.

But for the great majority of men—about 80 percent of our subjects— this period evokes tumultuous struggles within the self and with the external world. Their Mid-life Transition is a time of moderate or severe crisis. Every aspect of their lives comes into question, and they are horrified by much that is revealed. They are full of recriminations against themselves and others. They cannot go on as before, but need time to choose a new path or modify the old one.

Because a man in this crisis is often somewhat irrational, others may regard him as "upset" or "sick." In most cases, he is not. The man himself and those who care about him should recognize that he is in a normal developmental period and is working on normal mid-life tasks. The desire to question and modify his life stems from the most healthy part of the self. The doubting and searching are appropriate to this period; the real question is how best to make use of them. The problem is compounded by the fact that the process of reappraisal activates unconscious conflicts— the unconscious baggage carried forward from hard times in the past which hinders the effort to change. The pathology is not in the desire to improve one's life but in the obstacles to pursuing this aim. It is the pathological anxiety and guilt, the dependencies, animosities and vanities of earlier years, that keep a man from examining the real issues at mid-life. They make it difficult for him to modify an oppressive life structure.

A profound reappraisal of this kind cannot be a cool, intellectual process. It must involve emotional turmoil, despair, the sense of not knowing where to turn or of being stagnant and unable to move at all. A man in this state often makes false starts. He tentatively tests a variety of new choices, not only out of confusion or impulsiveness but, equally, out of a need to explore, to see what is possible, to find out how its feels to engage in a particular love relationship, occupation or solitary pursuit. Every genuine reappraisal must be agonizing, because it challenges the illusions and vested interests on which the existing structure is based.

The life structure of the thirties was initiated and stabilized by powerful forces in the person and his environment. These forces continue to make their claim for preserving the status quo. A man who attempts a radical critique of his life at 40 will be up against the parts of himself that have a strong investment in the present structure. He will often be opposed by other persons and institutions—his wife, children, boss, parents, colleagues, the occupational system in which he works, the implicit web of social conformity—that seek to maintain order and prevent change. With luck, he will also receive support from himself and from others for the effort to examine and improve his life.

Why do we go through this painful process? Why should a crisis so often be our lot at mid-life? In Chapter 2 I noted several sources of difficulty stemming from the era shift between early and middle adulthood. Moreover, we need developmental transitions in adulthood partly because no life structure can permit the living out of all aspects of the self. To create a life structure I must make choices and set priorities. In making a choice I select one option and reject many others. Committing myself to a structure, I try over a span of time to enhance my life within it, to realize its potential, to bear the responsibilities and tolerate the costs it entails.

Every life structure necessarily gives high priority to certain aspects of the self and neglects or minimizes other aspects. This is as true of the Settling Down structure of the thirties as of all others. In the Mid-life Transition these neglected parts of the self urgently seek expression. A man experiences them as "other voices in other rooms" (in Truman Capote's evocative phrase). Internal voices that have been muted for years now clamor to be heard. At times they are heard as a vague whispering, the content unclear but the tone indicating grief over lost opportunities, outrage over betrayal by others, or guilt over betrayal by oneself. At other times they come through as a thunderous roar, the content all too clear, stating names and times and places and demanding that something be done to right the balance. A man hears the voice of an identity prematurely rejected; of a love lost or not pursued; of a valued interest or relationship given up in acquiescence to parental or other authority; of an internal figure who wants to be an athlete or nomad or artist, to marry for love or remain a bachelor, to get rich or enter the clergy or live a sensual carefree life—possibilities set aside earlier to become what he now is. During the Mid-life Transition he must learn to listen more attentively to these voices and decide consciously what part he will give them in his life.

## Sequences Through the Mid-life Transition

In Chapter 10 we distinguished several sequences through the Settling Down period: (A) Advancement within a stable life structure; (B) Serious failure or decline within a stable life structure; (C) Breaking out:

trying for a new life structure; (D) Advancement which itself produces a change in life structure; (E) Unstable life structure. A man's sequence through the Settling Down period influences the way in which he embarks upon the Mid-life Transition and works on its tasks. To get an overview of the various forms of the life course, let us briefly look at the ways men in each of the five sequences moved from Settling Down through the Mid-life Transition.

## Sequence A. Advancement Within a Stable Life Structure

The twenty-two men exemplifying this sequence had achieved moderate or notable success by the end of Settling Down, according to the terms of their particular enterprises (see the table on page 152). They had "come a long way" during their thirties and had moved from junior to senior positions in their worlds. Still, as the phase of Becoming One's Own Man draws to a close the struggle is often acute. A man is awaiting a culminating event that will mark the outcome of his efforts in the Settling Down period.

The culminating event is a marker for the end of Becoming One's Own Man and the start of the Mid-life Transition. To understand its significance, however, we must place it within the ongoing developmental process. In some cases this event served to precipitate the Mid-life Transition with great force, as it did with the biologist John Barnes, whose Mid-life Transition is described in Chapter 17. In other cases, such as Jim Tracy (see Chapter 19), this event occurred after the Mid-life Transition had begun to take shape. A man's reaction to the culminating event is heavily influenced by when it occurs in the transitional process.

Occasionally the culminating event is a great success both externally and in the man's private experience. This was rare in our sample. The great majority of men experienced this event as a failure or a flawed success. The outcome was usually good enough so that it could not be considered a total disaster, and in the eyes of others it was often quite favorable. But in certain crucial respects it was blemished, it did not sustain all the special hopes he had had in mind.

We can better elucidate the main themes and variations on this mode of entry into the Mid-life Transition by considering the four occupational groups in turn.

• THE NOVELISTS. A man who has won a place for himself during his thirties as a serious novelist is no longer content merely to write another novel. As he comes to the end of Becoming One's Own Man, he wants the next novel to be special: to win the Pulitzer Prize, to be acclaimed by the critics or general public, to mark him as the best contemporary writer of his genre (classical novel, mystery, comedy or whatever) and a fitting successor to the earlier giants. It rarely works out this way. The outcome is usually well below the man's fondest hopes. Even if this novel is well received, he is regarded as "good" but not "great," as not yet having fulfilled his early promise. He may take his place within the ranks of the established writers, but he is hardly unique.

A qualified success at this time is subjectively not much better than a gross failure. It is likely to evoke a man's worst fears: that he will never realize his potential, or—the most terrifying thought of all—that the potential was never really there. All right, he has proven himself as a competent writer of books that do well in the commercial or critical arena. That is not enough. His original Dream was to be much more. What will he leave for posterity? What place will he have in the history of the novel? Whereas earlier his main aim was to establish himself as a novelist, he now has a more formed identity and is concerned with the value of his "body of work" as a whole.

• THE EXECUTIVES. Like the novelist, the executive in Sequence A advances during his thirties toward a marker event of special significance—a key promotion, a better job in a new company or some other change indicating that he has "made it." To the extent that this culminating event works out favorably, the executive completes his Settling Down ladder and is launched into a new occupational and social world.

For a few executives this event had a highly favorable outcome, but for most it was a failure or a flawed success. For every executive at about 40 who gains the prize and the affirmation he has been seeking, there are perhaps twenty who get little or nothing. (The failure results partly from individual incompetence, partly from organizational power struggles and mainly from the pyramidal structure of management.)

If a man succeeds, he must deal with the bittersweet consequences of success; the world he enters is likely to differ enormously from anything he had anticipated and to raise fundamental questions about himself and his life. If he fails in certain crucial respects, he must come to terms with the implications of the failure. A man who is stopped or slowed down at this point has little hope for further advancement. Nagging questions present themselves: To what extent have I failed? What does the failure mean—what does it say about me as a person and about the occupational-social world I have been so involved in? What alternative options interest me and how feasible are they?

Many executives remain stuck for several years in a painful work situation—feeling humiliated, knowing they have no future there, doing work of no importance to themselves or the company—until finally, through some combination of inner readiness and external pressure, they are able to leave. This was the case with Jim Tracy (see Chapter 19). Those who leave more quickly will spend several years exploring various possibilities, and working on the developmental tasks of the Mid-life Transition, before they can start building a new structure and restabilizing their lives in the next period.

• THE BIOLOGISTS. Those we studied had faculty positions in first-rate universities and had been identified by their early thirties as promising young scientists. Five of the ten continued their career advance and exemplify Sequence A. By 40, they had achieved some degree of national recognition as scholars and were members of the scientific establishment in their special fields. Yet for all five the entry into the Mid-life Transition, at age 39 to 41, was marked not only by a well-deserved sense of success but also by severe disappointment and in some cases despair.

They had indeed reached the top rung of the Settling Down ladder. Now the question was: Where do I go from here? It was no longer a matter of climbing a well-marked ladder by performing in well-defined ways. The rules had become more complex and the stakes had grown. A man now had to demonstrate his real creativity and develop significant ideas at the forefront of his field. And he had to do this at a time of stock taking, just when he could see more clearly than ever before the limitations of his previous work, and when he was most afraid that the well of creativity was running dry. All of these men continued to work productively for the next several years, but all devoted a good deal of time and effort to the developmental tasks of the Mid-life Transition. And, as this period came to an end, their careers and lives had changed in important ways. The biologist John Barnes is a classic example of external success and inner despair, as we shall see in Chapter 17.

• THE WORKERS. Only the most limited possibilities of continuing occupational advancement are available to the worker after 40. The general shape of his occupation in the company is well established by his mid-thirties. After that he may gain in seniority or in small advantages, but he has almost no prospects for major advance or for creative fulfillment in the job. At the same time, we found more diversity in work history and in life course than most images of the industrial worker suggest.

Of the ten workers we studied, five showed some degree of advancement within a stable life structure over the course of Settling Down. Two men were doing quite well by their own lights as the Mid-life Transition started. Nick D'Amico had moved from mechanic to freelance draftsman to Designer I (the top level for hourly workers). He had a new house under construction in the suburbs and the possibility of promotion onto the bottom rung of management. Ralph Ochs had worked in the company's plumbing department since age 18 and sought no further promotion. He enriched his work life in the forties by being a shop steward, an active union member and a senior figure in relation to the younger workers; and he found important satisfactions in the family.

Three other workers had shown some advances, but their lives were more in question. Vincent Minelli at 40 had security but no satisfaction as an unskilled White worker in the supply department of a company with an increasingly Black labor force. His satisfactions came chiefly from his moonlighting work, his children and his senior position in the extended ethnic family. He had fantasies of moving to Australia. Larry Strode, a skilled Black worker with fifteen years' seniority, a shop steward and occasional foreman, felt increasingly oppressed by the factory situation. He started his own barber shop (a culminating event after years of moonlighting as a barber) and completed high school. At 41, he planned to leave the factory in a few years and get into an occupation of greater value to himself and the community. At 45 he did become a mental health worker (see Chapter 18).

## Sequence B. Serious Failure or Decline Within a Stable Life Structure

The seven men in this group include two workers, three executives and two biologists (see the table on page 152). Before the end of the Settling Down period, they knew that they were doing badly and their prospects were limited. Only with the start of the Mid-life Transition, however, did they honestly face the bleak reality and begin to consider alternative possibilities. One might suppose that, once a man acknowledged the gravity of his situation, he would arrive at a new adjustment within a few weeks or months. Actually, we find that the process of accommodation ordinarily requires several years. During the course of the Mid-life Transition, he has an opportunity to assimilate the fact that his earlier goals are beyond him, and he can come to terms with the blows to his self-esteem. It is not until this period approaches its end, however, that a man can make firm choices on which to build a new life.

At the start of the Mid-life Transition, a man in Sequence A has gained a senior position in his chosen world and is trying for something beyond that, something very special to him. A man in Sequence B, on the other hand, does not achieve senior membership in the enterprise of his dreams. As the Mid-life Transition begins, he must decide what to do with his life now that he knows he cannot be a foreman, a great novelist, a corporate executive, a scientist of a certain standing, a respected member of his local community. Some men never recover from the crushing defeats they suffer in Becoming One's Own Man. They enter a decline from which no escape is possible, for internal as well as external reasons. An example is Luke Doby, the Black worker described in Chapter 10. At age 47 he was divorced, alone, unemployed, increasingly disabled and approaching death. Another example is Mike Gallagher, an executive: over the course of the Settling Down period he became alcoholic, was divorced, and moved laterally in the company to a "non-position." At 39, when we interviewed him, he had nowhere to go; at 40 he died of cancer.

In some cases, a man whose efforts at Becoming One's Own Man went badly uses the Mid-life Transition to form the basis for a new life. His failure is in some respects a boon. It shakes him out of a rut. He is able during the Mid-life Transition to free himself from the tyrannical hold of the Settling Down commitments, which often were unrealistic. He finds new goals, new satisfactions, new aspects of the self to be developed and enjoyed. Without giving up entirely his interest in advancement, he defines the ladder more broadly. External success and failure become less important as criteria for inner well-being. The quality of his total life acquires greater significance than the quantity of his success on any single dimension.

An example is Leo Heinz (see Chapter 5), a middle manager who at 39 was defined as a failure and was shifted to a non-position. He spent five miserable years stewing in this job, until at 44 he left the company and became a business consultant. He then used his technical skills but avoided the stresses of managerial authority and rivalry. Another example is William Paulsen, the worker whose life through the novice phase we examined in Chapter 8. We shall trace his steps through the subsequent periods in Chapter 18.

## Sequence C. Breaking Out: Trying for a New Life Structure

In this sequence, a man establishes a life structure in early Settling Down, lives within it for three or four years, and then early in Becoming One's Own Man (say at age 36 or 37) finds it unbearable and "breaks out." The breaking out includes a distinctive marker event such as leaving his wife, quitting his job or moving to another region. For the next few years he makes a concerted effort to build a new structure more in accord with his values and aspirations. Unfortunately, it is extremely difficult to make a radical change at this time in life. The new structure is likely to be a compromise. By 40, he may have made important changes in his situation, but he is still involved in relationships he had seemingly given up when he took the decisive step, and is not able to devote himself sufficiently to his new activities and choices.

At the start of the Mid-life Transition, this man finds himself in a bind. On the one hand, he is still trying to achieve the goals to which he recently committed himself; he is still actively engaged in the effort of Becoming One's Own Man. On the other hand, he is beginning to question the new pattern of living and to see the illusions and contradictions in it. In the Mid-life Transition he has to ask again what it is that he really wants. Having made a big move only three or four years earlier, he is now faced with the possibility that this new course may not be viable in the world or suitable for the self. He is entering a transition longer and more profound than that in Becoming One's Own Man.

We find that a man whose life takes this sequence goes through a series of painful changes over a span of twelve to fifteen years or more: he forms a flawed Settling Down life structure at 33, breaks out of it at 37, discovers at 41 that the current structure has crucial flaws, and uses the Mid-life Transition to modify it. At 46, if he has done enough developmental work, he will start forming a more satisfactory structure in the period of Entering Middle Adulthood.

The outcome of the Mid-life Transition is rather disappointing for some of these men, while for others the years of struggle finally yield a better life—a life richer than they had before and than is attained by many others who have struggled less to improve their lot. Two of our biographees exemplify the latter sequence. One is the novelist Paul Namson. In Chapter 12 we followed his life through the Settling Down period; we shall complete the story in Chapter 18. The other is James Tracy, the executive; his Mid-life Transition and its aftermath will be described in Chapter 19.

## Sequence D. Advancement Which Itself Produces a Change in Life Structure

In this sequence, advancement during the late thirties brings about a modification in the Settling Down life structure. A man takes an upward step that is not just another advance within the same structure. It produces a qualitative change in the character of his life. He gets more than he bargained for. This change has major consequences for the onset and course of the Mid-life Transition. Three of our men are in this category (see the table on page 152).

An example is the executive Roger Mohn (see Chapter 10). In his early thirties he was an hourly worker with considerable responsibility in a job he loved. At 37 he became manager of the purchasing department in his plant. This advance changed his occupational world and led him to a new neighborhood and life style. At 40 came the culminating event: he was promoted to be head of manufacturing, with a budget of $9 million and an enterprise of 400 people. His great success was also his downfall. The years from 41 to 44 were the low point of his life, in contrast to the high point from 33 to 36 when he ran a shop. During the Mid-life Transition he had a serious illness of uncertain prognosis, which intensified his concern with death and with the meaning of his life. He got through this period largely through his attachment to his family and the strength of his increasingly independent wife. When he was 44 a company reorganization led to the departure of many colleagues and to his lateral shift into a less responsible position. He was in the throes of the Mid-life Transition, trying to decide whether to stay put in a secure but humiliating position in the only company he had ever worked for, or to try for something better. (For the next step, see Chapter 18.)

## Sequence E.  Unstable Life Structure

Only three of our men—a worker, a biologist and a novelist—are in this category. They did not reach 40 during the time we studied them. None was able to stabilize a life structure in the Settling Down period. Their lives in the late thirties seemed to be built on quicksand. It was hard to see how any of them could attain a genuine sense of seniority or resolve the contradictions in his adult life.

The worker, Hank McCloud, had not yet formed an occupation at 37, and seemed unable to hold a job. His main source of strength was his recent marriage and family. In his late thirties, Curt Ruger was moving from biological research to teaching and administration. At 39, he was not quite an academic biologist and not quite an educational administrator. He felt that he had made a series of compromise choices in work, marriage and other aspects of life. Now he had a meager basis on which to build for the future. At 36, Darryl Osborn lived a chaotic life—occasionally writing novels, doing a few movie scripts in Hollywood, bouncing around the country on and off of drugs, unmarried and without stable relationships. He had no structure within which to work at Becoming One's Own Man.

At the end of the Settling Down period, the men in Sequences C, D and E have not formed a stable, integrated life structure containing an adequate place for the Dream or for other important aspirations. Those in Sequence E have lived within an unstable structure throughout this period, and the costs of the instability become increasingly heavy. Those in Sequences C and D formed an integrated structure at the start of Settling Down and then tried to change it (via breaking out or via advancement) in the late thirties. Unfortunately, it is very difficult to create a new structure at this time. Despite a man's good intentions and heroic efforts, the structure he tries to create in Becoming One's Own Man contains serious flaws: it is a compromise between the oppressive earlier structure and the ardently desired new one, containing elements of both in uneasy coexistence. He cannot quickly eliminate the negative elements from the past, no matter how intolerable they may seem. Similarly, he cannot quickly incorporate new elements or give formerly minor elements a central place in the structure.

A man in Sequence C, D or E thus begins the Mid-life Transition with a life structure that is quite fragile and beset by the contradictions which led him to seek to change it during the Settling Down period. He must also begin the Mid-life Transition without having reached the top of his ladder. During the Mid-life Transition, strong forces impel him both to pursue and to question the goals of Becoming One's Own Man. The outcome of the process started in the late thirties will be discernible only as the transition comes to an end in the mid-forties.

Thus, at 38, James Tracy divorced his first wife and remarried, but not until 46 was he able to include both families in his life structure and to stabilize his relationship with his second wife (see Chapter 19). Paul Namson quit his executive position in the family firm at 37, eager to become a full-time novelist, but he could not give novel writing a central place in his life structure until age 46 (see Chapter 18). In his mid-thirties, William Paulsen started trying to get out of his working-class occupation—a mixture of advancement and breaking out—and only in his mid-forties did he begin coming to terms with the failure of this effort (see Chapter 18).

# 14 Mid-life Individuation: Young/Old, the Major Polarity

As I mentioned in the previous chapter, individuation is a process in all developmental transitions. In the Mid-life Transition, individuation creates a link between the ending of early adulthood and the start of middle adulthood. It provides a basis upon which the life structure of the Settling Down period is modified and a new life structure is created. In Chapter 16 I shall discuss some of the specific changes made in the life structure during the Mid-life Transition. In this chapter and the next, I want to focus upon the more underlying process of individuation.

We have identified four primary tasks in the individuation process. Each task involves the reintegration of a fundamental polarity in the character of living. The polarity has sources within the self and in society. The four polarities, already briefly described, are Young/Old, Destruction/ Creation, Masculine/Feminine and Attachment/Separateness. The one that is most central to all developmental change is the Young/Old polarity. This chapter will deal with it, the next with the remaining three polarities.

In common parlance, children are young, the elderly are old, and the rest of us are in between. But our language is ambiguous. The term "old" sometimes refers to an age category: those who are elderly or aged. At other times it refers to a process of aging or decline, as when a man of forty says, "I am getting too old for this sort of thing," and is told, "You're only as old as you feel."

In their fullest meaning, the terms "young" and "old" are not tied to specific age levels. They are symbols that refer to basic psychological, biological and social qualities of human life at every age. We are both young and old at every age. We start becoming old at birth, just as we remain young in certain respects during old age.

Ultimately, "young" is an archetypal symbol with many meanings. It represents birth, growth, possibility, initiation, openness, energy, potential. It colors the meaning we give to many concrete images: the infant, sunrise, the New Year, the seed, the blossoms and rites of spring, the newcomer, the promise, the vision of things to come. We are young at any age to the extent that these associations color our psychological, biological and social functioning.

Conversely, "old" is a symbol representing termination, fruition, stability, structure, completion, death. Its images include Father Time, the Grim Reaper, the Rock of Ages, the Wise Old Man, the dotard, winter, midnight. The immovable object of age confronts the irresistible force of youth. I use the terms "young" and "old" in this symbolic sense, and I use other terms in referring to a particular age level or the process of aging.

Being Young, like being Old, has advantages and disadvantages, strengths and limitations. Each state can be given positive as well as negative meanings. To be Young is to be lively, growing, heroic, full of possibilities; but it is also to be fragile, imperfectly developed, impulsive, lacking in experience and solidity. Similarly, the Old person (whatever his age) may be seen as wise, powerful, accomplished, "able to hear the dictates of heaven" (Confucius)—but also as senile, tyrannical, impotent, unconnected to the life around him.

The Young/Old polarity—the splitting of Young and Old, and the effort to reintegrate them—is the polarity of human development. It is the basic polarity to be worked on in every developmental transition. The symbolization of being both Old and Young—of death and rebirth, destructuring and restructuring, mortality and immortality—is inherent in the very nature of a developmental transition. We feel Old in that a phase in our lives is coming to an end and must be permitted to pass. Yet we also feel Young, since the potential for a new period carries with it the qualities of rejuvenation and growth.

A major developmental task of the Mid-life Transition is to confront the Young and the Old within oneself and seek new ways of being Young/Old. A man must give up certain of his former youthful qualities—some with regret, some with relief or satisfaction—while retaining and transforming other qualities that he can integrate into his new life. And he must find positive meanings of being "older."

For Jung, an archetype is an elemental image that has been established over thousands of generations in human evolution. It has come to exist in every human mind. To understand its function, consider how we employ psychic or instinctual energy. We are born with a pool of such energy that is transformed, over the course of development, into a variety of more specific drives and impulses relating to aggression, sexuality, dependence, power, creativeness. The *potential* for complex motives and feelings is there from the start. How it develops, and what forms it takes in the individual life, depends on specific circumstances and experiences.

Similarly, an archetype is a *potential* for further development. It evolves in the individual psyche from an initial, undifferentiated image into an increasingly complex "internal figure." It becomes a person in one's head, a being with whom one has an ongoing relationship—loving, fighting, admiring, depreciating—much as one does with a person in the external world. We have archetypes for the bad self and the good self, the mother (not just my particular mother, but a maternal figure who helps and threatens me in numerous ways), God, devil, authority, healer, muse. The archetypes exist within us as organizing factors that shape and are shaped by our experience over the life course. In each person, some develop to a high degree, others remain dormant.

In Jungian theory, the *Puer* is the archetype of being Young—a child, a youth, a person of any age who is at the start of a developmental process. In childhood, this archetype evolves as the child experiences its own growth, brings plans and possibilities into realization, and observes the growth of animals, flowers, projects, relationships. With "good enough" development (in Winnicott's sense), the child forms an internal figure of himself as Puer: a budding person with remarkable potentials in a world full of opportunities and dangers.

The *Senex* in Jungian theory is the archetype of being Old—elderly, senescent, a person of any age who is at the end of a developmental process. Starting in childhood, we form a sense of what it means to be aging, declining, suffering a loss of our former powers, dying. Many experiences contribute to this process. People around the child get sick, infirm, conspicuously old; they die. So do pets, plants and other living things. Toys and other objects are destroyed and exist no more. The child may get sick or hurt in some way that arouses his own and others' anxiety. Not yet understanding the nature of aging and death, he develops primitive fantasies that give meaning to these symbols. He tries to grasp the distinction between "living" and "dead" beings, and between animate beings and inanimate objects.

Just as the experience of being Young can, under favorable conditions, continue through old age, so does the experience of getting Old begin in childhood. The child's experience of his own and others' aging contributes to the formation of an internal figure of himself as Senex: a person in decline, no longer full of promise but having to relinquish the powers so essential to the Puer.

In every transitional period, throughout the life cycle, the internal figures of Young and Old—what Jung called Puer and Senex—are modified and placed in a new balance. The end of the preceding period stimulates Old thoughts and feelings about being in a rut, rotting, coming to the brink of death. The start of the new period stimulates Young thoughts and feelings about being reborn, making a fresh start, discovering fresh possibilities in the self and new vistas in the world. The task in every transition is to create a new Young/Old integration appropriate to that time of life. Especially with the change in eras, there is normally an increase in the Old qualities of maturity, judgment, self-awareness, magnanimity, integrated structure, breadth of perspective. But these qualities are of value only if they continue to be vitalized by the Young's energy, imagination, wonderment, capacity for foolishness and fancy. The Young/Old connection must be sustained.

It is not easy to maintain the balance. A person of any age may become prematurely Old and lacking in youthful qualities. A child of six may have been so deprived that he loses all sense of excitement, play, anticipation of the future. He is emotionally a withered old man, fighting a futile battle against emptiness and decline. An adolescent may be so weighted down by a morally constraining family, or by having prematurely to take on heavy adult responsibilities, that his youthful passions are stifled and he cannot sustain the dreams on which early adulthood is built. A man of 40 or 50 may be so in the grip of the Old that he is stagnant, dry, hardly connected to the world around him or to anything he can value in himself, having little to give others or to receive from them. It is as though the Young had been totally extinguished.

At the other extreme, a man may become so anxious about aging and dying that he denies these concerns altogether and attempts to remain the perpetual Young. We see this in the man of twenty-five who remains tied to the family or who leads a transient life without serious attachments and responsibilities. He is, as it were, poised between boyhood and early adulthood, unable to complete the Early Adult Transition and make the commitments on which a first adult life structure can be formed. He is terrified at the thought of becoming an adult, yet he can no longer remain a child. Living in a kind of limbo, he acts very "adolescent" but feels lost and unattached.

We also see this clinging to the Young in the man of 40 to 50 who insists on remaining youthful in the early adult sense, trying to have now the good times that he earlier missed. His problem is not that he wishes to be youthful, but that he remains stuck in an early adult conception of Young and Old. His developmental task is to become older than he was— that is, middle-aged. To do this, he has to make more use of the Old qualities than before, while finding age-appropriate forms through which to express his youthful qualities as well.

Throughout the life cycle, the archetypal Young and Old coexist within

us. The internal Young has great energy and capacity for further development in many directions. The internal Old has attained a high degree of
structure, has gone as far as he can in realizing his potential, and can now
develop no further. Every era has its characteristic Young/Old balance. In
pre-adulthood the Young is normally predominant, the Old just taking
shape. In early adulthood, the balance is more even but the Young is normally stronger. Middle adulthood should be the time of optimal Young/Old
balance: a man can have a firmer structure with which to use his considerable energy, imagination and capacity for change. Middle adulthood is,
in this sense, the center of the life cycle. In late adulthood the structure
becomes heavier and the internal resources more limited, though the possibilities for vital action and development continue.


## The Sense of Mortality and Wish for Immortality

In the Mid-life Transition the Young/Old polarity is experienced with
special force. As early adulthood comes to an end, a man is assailed by new
fears of the "loss of youth." He feels that the Young—variously represented
as the child, the adolescent and the youthful adult in himself—is dying.
The imagery of old age and death hangs over him like a pall.

A number of changes commonly occurring at around 40 intensify the
sense of aging. A man experiences some of these changes as minor and
takes them in stride, but others strike with great impact, arousing his
anxieties about getting old and confronting him with his own mortality.

One important change, as we have seen, is the decline in bodily and
psychological powers. In his late thirties and early forties a man falls well
below his earlier peak levels of functioning. He cannot run as fast, lift as
much, do with as little sleep as before. His vision and hearing are less acute,
he remembers less well and finds it harder to learn masses of specific information. He is more prone to aches and pains and may undergo a serious
illness that threatens him with permanent impairment or even death. These
changes vary widely in their severity and their effects on a man's life. Reduced strength and agility may be less distressing to an accountant than to
a professional athlete (or a fierce competitor at tennis who cannot bear to
lose his standing on the local ladder).

The decline is normally quite moderate and leaves a man with ample
capacities for living in middle age. But it is often experienced as catastrophic. A man fears that he will soon lose all the youthful qualities that
make life worthwhile. When youth is totally lost, all that is left is to be

totally old. At an archetypal level, Young is immortal, Old is the brink of death.

Reminders of mortality are also given by the more frequent illness, death and loss of others. A man may suffer distressing losses at any age. The meaning they have for him will depend partly on the developmental period he is in at the time. In his late thirties and early forties, the probability of such losses goes up considerably. His parents, now ordinarily in their sixties or seventies, are more likely to die or to be faced with problems of retirement, illness and dependency. A lot more people, it seems, are dying or getting seriously ill. There are more accidents and heart attacks, more divorces, depressions, alcoholism, job failures, troubles with children or parents, suffering of all kinds.

A man's sensitivity to the increase in others' misfortune and suffering is accentuated by his own entry into the Mid-life Transition. He notices these problems more in others, and resonates to them with greater feeling, partly because he is starting to come to terms with his own mortality.

The sense of aging and mortality is accentuated by the change in generational status at around 40. In the terms of Ortega y Gasset (see Chapter 2), a man is part of the "initiation" generation from about 30 to 45. He is establishing his niche in society and pursuing his youthful aspirations. During the Mid-life Transition, from about 40 to 45, he starts taking his place in the "dominant" generation. By the middle forties, he is clearly in a generation senior to that of the thirties. The question is not whether he will enter a new generation but on what terms—with what degree of satisfaction, respect, competence, status.

Finally, the culmination of the Settling Down enterprise intensifies his sense of mortality. At around 40 a man reaches a turning point. He must now form an enterprise qualitatively different from those of early adulthood. No matter how well or poorly he has done with the ambitions of his thirties, he is likely to experience a letdown in the Mid-life Transition. Even if he has accomplished a great deal and is on the path to greater attainment, his basic orientation toward success and failure normally begins to change. It is no longer crucial to climb another rung on the ladder—to write another book, get another promotion, earn more of the rewards that meant so much in the past.

Giving up the intense concern with success is especially difficult if a man has not attained his earlier goals. He has to deal first with his bitterness toward others, his contempt toward himself, and his illusion that life would now be marvelous if only he had been able to seize the gold ring. A man may be more free to question the real value of success, once he has tasted it. But the man who manages to reach his youthful goals often gets caught up in the excitement of success. He may need a few years to discover how little meaning it has for him.

Every man in the Mid-life Transition starts to see that the hero of the fairy tale does not enter a life of eternal, simple happiness. He sees, indeed, that the hero is a youth who must die or be transformed as early adulthood comes to an end. A man must begin to grieve and accept the symbolic death of the youthful hero within himself. He will gradually discover which of the heroic qualities he can keep, which new qualities he can discover and develop in himself, and how he might be a hero of a different kind in the context of middle adulthood. Humanity has as yet little wisdom for constructing the "portrait of the hero as a middle-aged man." That archetype is still poorly evolved.

For many reasons, then, at 40 a man knows more deeply than ever before that he is going to die. He feels it in his bones, in his dreams, in the marrow of his being. His death is not simply an abstract, hypothetical event. An unpredictable accident or illness could take his life tomorrow. Even another thirty years does not seem so long: more years now lie behind than ahead.

Why should the recognition of our mortality be so painful? Why can we not come to know it and accept it, once and for all, in childhood or adolescence? Why does it come up in every developmental transition, to be partially resolved and partially denied, only to confront us again in the next?

A primary reason, I believe, is the wish for immortality. This is one of the strongest and least malleable of human motives. It operates with great force during early adulthood as an aspect of the Young archetype. A young man has the desire to live forever, to play a part in some eternal drama, to be assured permanent tenure in heaven or in history. Like other elemental drives, this one is the source of many illusions and self-deceptions. But it is also a fundament for our love of life, our sense of self, our urge to create products of lasting value, our wish to be involved in the world and experience richly what it offers us. It is reflected in the trauma that accompanies every advance toward acknowledging our short-lived existence in this world. We never entirely give it up, though our awareness and understanding of it normally change as we become more individuated adults.

At mid-life, the growing recognition of mortality collides with the powerful wish for immortality and the many illusions that help to maintain it. A man's fear that he is not immortal is expressed in his preoccupation with bodily decline and his fantasies of imminent death. At the most elemental level, he feels that he is fighting for survival. He is terrified at the thought of being dead, of no longer existing as this particular person. In the words of the old song, "Everybody wants to go to heaven, but nobody wants to die."

Beyond the concern with personal survival, there is a concern with meaning. It is bad enough to feel that my life will soon be over. It is even worse to feel that my life has not had—and never will have—sufficient value for myself and the world. The wish for immortality plays a powerful part in a man's reappraisal of his life at 40. He often feels that his life until now has been wasted. Even if, in cooler moments, he finds some redeeming qualities, he is still likely to feel that his life has not enough accrued value. He has not fulfilled himself sufficiently and has not contributed enough to the world. What he has been and what he has produced are of little consequence. In the remaining years he wants to do more, to be more, to give his life a meaning that will live after his death.

A man at 40 may have been so beaten down by an oppressive environment, or so consumed in the struggle for survival, that he cannot make the developmental effort to give his life a new meaning. The inner flame is extinguished and no further potential can be brought into being. He exists without hope or sense of value. Such men often die in their forties or fifties. The immediate cause of death may be illness, accident or alcoholism. The basic cause is that neither he nor society can make a space for him to live, and he just withers away. There are too few available resources, external or internal, to sustain his life. Alternatively, he may live a long and trivial existence if he finds a protective environment and accepts a limited life.

A dramatic example of decline in middle adulthood is Howard Hughes. During this era he converted a small fortune into a fantastic empire. At the end, with all his power, he died of starvation, disease and emotional isolation. He could invest his money with great profit, but he could not invest his self in any enterprise or obtain psychic income from it. He finally suffocated within the cocoon he had built around himself.

Mid-life defeat has been portrayed in countless novels and plays. It is a recurrent theme in the work of Chekhov, Ibsen and Strindberg (especially the plays they wrote after age 40). In *The Iceman Cometh*, Eugene O'Neill depicts the small world of Harry Hope's saloon and boardinghouse. Most of its members are middle-aged men who maintain their youthful illusions but have lost all real hope. The central character, Hickey, a salesman of about 40, visits annually to nourish their dreams and to indulge himself in the role of savior and Santa Claus. At the end, Hickey gives up the illusory rescue of others and acknowledges his own illusions, his struggle with the archetypal figure of Death (symbolized as the Iceman), and his feelings in the aftermath of killing his wife. O'Neill wrote this play in the aftermath of his own debilitating mid-life crisis.

Lillian Hellman's play *The Autumn Garden* deals with similar themes in a more genteel, Southern world. In a later comment on this play, Hellman said: "I suppose the point I had in mind is this—you come to a place in your life when what you've been is going to form what you will be. If you've wasted what you have in you, it's too late to do much about it. If you've invested yourself in life, you're pretty certain to get a return. If you are inwardly a serious person, in the middle years it will pay off." During the Mid-life Transition, it is hard to know how much one has wasted oneself or invested in life, and what kind of further return one will have during the middle years. This was clearly a question for Hellman herself when she wrote the play, in her middle forties.

If his development has not already been too impaired, a man in the Mid-life Transition begins to accept his mortality and to give up his most grandiose illusions of immortality. This does not mean, however, that the wish for immortality disappears. On the contrary, with normal development this wish becomes more conscious, more subject to reflective thought, more modest and realistic in its aims. Making an effort to increase the actual value of his life, he strengthens his claim on the immortality for which he still deeply yearns. Whatever his religious views or his secular philosophy of life, he believes that this claim depends largely on his own self-fulfillment and social contribution. He wants to leave a trace, however small, on the course of humankind.

A man in the Mid-life Transition is troubled by his seemingly imminent death. He is beset even more by the anxiety that he will not be able to make his future better than his past. As he seeks to modify and enrich his life, he has self-doubts ranging in intensity from mild pessimism to utter panic: "Can I make my life more worthwhile in the remaining years? Am I now too old to make a fresh start? Have I become obsolete? What shall I try to do and be for myself, for my loved ones, for my tribe, for humanity?" The worst feeling of all is to contemplate long years of meaningless existence without youthful passions, creative effort or social contribution. The self-doubts are intensified by the Old, which evokes powerful feelings of disintegration, despair and death. It is his voice within that says, "There is no more time—the end is here."

During and after the Mid-life Transition a man tries to transform the Young/Old of youth and create a middle-aged self, wiser and more mature than before yet still connected to the youthful sources of energy, imagination and daring. He comes to grasp more clearly the flow of generations and the continuity of the human species. His personal immortality, whatever its form, lies within that larger human continuity. He feels more responsibility for the generations that will follow his own. Acquiring a greater individuality, a firmer sense of who he is and what matters most to him, he also understands more deeply that he is a drop in the vast river of human history. Slowly the omnipotent Young hero recedes, and in his place emerges a middle-aged man with more knowledge of his limitations as well as greater real power and authority.

In a poem written when he was about 50, the American poet Theodore Roethke portrays his experience of mortality. This poem, entitled "The Dying Man," is dedicated to Yeats. It reflects Roethke's struggles, in the flower of middle adulthood, to accept the actuality of death while his own vitality and desire for immortality are at their height:

> . . . he dares to live
> Who stops being a bird, yet beats his wings
> Against the immense immeasurable emptiness of things.

Although a major effort toward the recognition of mortality begins in the Mid-life Transition, a more profound spiritual acceptance of it is not likely to occur until late adulthood. Yeats's poem "Vacillation" published when he was 67, depicts this process. The title suggests that, despite the fierce pride with which Yeats wishes to approach death, his spirit is still clouded with uncertainty.

> No longer in Lethean foliage caught
> Begin the preparation for your death
> And from the fortieth winter by that thought
> Test every work of intellect or faith,
> And everything that your own hands have wrought,
> And call those works extravagance of breath
> That are not suited for such men as come
> Proud, open-eyed and laughing to the tomb.

It may have taken Yeats some years longer to imagine entering the tomb neither "open-eyed and laughing" nor in sadness and fear, but with quiet acceptance of the unknowable losses and gains to come.

## The Legacy

Imagery of the legacy tends to flourish during the Mid-life Transition, as part of the work on the Young/Old polarity. A man's legacy is what he passes on to future generations: material possessions, creative products, enterprises, influence on others. Men differ enormously in their views about what constitutes a legacy. Although the real value of a man's legacy is impossible to measure, in his mind it defines to a large degree the ultimate value of his life—and his claim on immortality.

In estimating the merit of their legacy, some men place the highest value on raising children and maintaining familial-tribal continuity. They want their children to grow up and live as adults in accord with family traditions. During early adulthood a man may take special pleasure in begetting children and seeing them develop in variations of his own image. During middle adulthood, however, the satisfaction is of a somewhat different order. His offspring take their place in the adult world. He experiences their self-development and attainments as the fruits of his early adult labors. Their lives, their personal satisfactions, accomplishments and contributions are an essential part of his legacy. He will live on partly through them.

The joys and despondencies parents feel in middle age often seem excessive. The parents' preoccupations with "how the children are doing" make more sense when seen in the context of the legacy: they reflect basic parental feelings about the value of one's contribution to posterity and one's claim on immortality. No man who truly cares about his fatherhood can be without these feelings. In moderation, they enrich life. In excess, they become an albatross around the neck of both parent and offspring.

A man's legacy may include the material possessions he hands down to his family and others. At mid-life he often becomes increasingly concerned with the value and security of his estate. He gets more interested in making charitable contributions and helping worthy causes. He cares more about the well-being of his community, religious organization, college, union, professional society. It is important to him that they merit his support. He needs to believe that an institution is of enduring value; only then will bequeathing something to it add to his own enduring value. The altruism is, in part, a vehicle of the search for immortality.

For many men at mid-life, work is the most significant component of the life structure and the major source of the legacy. The artist (scientist, craftsman, builder), who creates his own unique products, wants his work to constitute a treasure that can live forever—in his name. The idea of winning the Nobel Prize, the Pulitzer Prize, or the "Man of the Year" award in his local society is suffused with this meaning. A man who develops and manages institutions—a political leader, educational administrator, owner of his own small shop or farm—would like his institution to be his monument, an edifice that he helped to create and that will be part of his legacy. The man in a health, education or welfare occupation hopes that his work as healer, teacher or reliever of suffering will create a legacy of better lives in future generations.

During the Mid-life Transition he must move toward a more realistic view of his occupational legacy. If he is very successful at 40, he may have a rather inflated view of his past achievements and his future prospects. In the Mid-life Transition he comes to the depressing realization that his previous successes are not so grand as he had imagined. At best, they form a prelude to the main work, a basis on which a more substantial project can be constructed. But the important achievements remain for the future. His initial success is like a promissory note: an assurance but by no means a guarantee of better work to come. It is still more deflating to realize that, even if he is very effective in his new work, the result will not be as monumental as the omnipotent Young man might have wished, nor will it give him the expected happiness. To the extent that he heals the wounds produced by this ego deflation, he can get on with the serious work and form a "good enough" legacy. Indeed, as the work itself becomes more interesting to him, he may become more genuinely productive than ever before, as we shall see in the cases of Tracy, Barnes and Namson.

Often, a man who has worked hard during his thirties comes to recognize in the Mid-life Transition that his cumulated achievements and skills do not provide a basis for further advancement. He cannot become a writer, educator, political leader or violin maker of the caliber he imagined. He will never rise to the level he sought in the military, the corporation or the church. He will fall far short of his early Dream. This is a crucial turning point. He may decide to continue in his present job, doing work that is increasingly routine and humiliating. He may change to another job, or another occupation, that offers more challenge and satisfaction. Or he may reduce his interest in work, performing well enough to keep employed but investing himself more in other aspects of life such as family or leisure.

The withdrawal of involvement in the job is a well-known phenomenon among low-status workers in many organizations who have "nowhere to go" occupationally after a certain age. It also occurs among business executives, professionals and others who complete a first career at mid-life. While remaining nominally in their defined occupation, they spend much of their time in a variety of philanthropic, civic and other serious activities through which they hope to generate a legacy.

Several executives told us with quiet eagerness of their intention to retire from business early, perhaps at 50 or 55. They would then devote themselves not to making a profit or achieving production objectives, but to working on improving the quality of life for others. This is, so to say, the "Hyde-Jekyll" complex. In Stevenson's novel the virtuous Dr. Jekyll was transformed at times into the villainous Mr. Hyde. Reversing the sequence, an executive regards himself as a mercenary, exploitive Hyde who will someday (before it is too late) transform himself into a socially valuable Jekyll. He cannot yet allow himself the luxury of living the good life, but he hears Jekyll's voice urging him to save his soul and create a legacy for immortality.

A man's legacy involves family, work or other valued contributions that ensure his immortality. Immortality may mean that his eternal soul exists in an eternal heaven, or that he has a place, small or large, in human history. The desire for an immortalizing legacy is a powerful, "normal" human urge. It stems from the wish for omnipotence and the archetypes of the Young and the Self as eternal figures. This desire can have destructive consequences if it grows, unchecked, into overly elaborate, magical forms, as in the Faust legend. On the other hand, if it is nipped in the bud by early failure and disappointment, it may lead to a loss of belief in the self and a denial that anything in the world is worth bequeathing a legacy to.

With "good enough" development, the wish to create a valued legacy enriches a man's life in middle adulthood. The developmental work of the Mid-life Transition modulates the tyranny of his Dream and the urgent demands of ambition and competitive rivalry. He has more inner freedom to be himself and is less driven to meet tribal requirements. This does not mean, however, that it is time at 40 or 50 to withdraw from involvement and responsibility in society. He has major contributions to offer as father, grandfather, son, brother, husband, lover, friend, mentor, healer, leader, mediator, authority, author, creator and appreciator of the human heritage. These contributions constitute his legacy.

In every era, a man normally has the need and the capability to generate a legacy. But in the Mid-life Transition the meaning of legacy deepens and the task of building a legacy acquires its greatest developmental significance. As we learn better how to foster development in adulthood, "creating a legacy" will become an increasingly important part of middle adulthood. This will add both to the personal fulfillment of individual adults and to the quality of life for succeeding generations.

# 15 Mid-life Individuation: The Other Polarities

We turn now to the three other polarities that figure so centrally in the Mid-life Transition. All of these polarities come up for reworking in every transitional period, and they are never fully resolved. Still, the progress made during the Mid-life Transition provides a groundwork for reappraising and modifying one's past life and for building a new life structure in Entering Middle Adulthood.

## The Destruction/Creation Polarity

In the Mid-life Transition, as a man reviews his life and considers how to give it greater meaning, he must come to terms in a new way with destruction and creation as fundamental aspects of life. His growing recognition of his own mortality makes him more aware of destruction as a universal process. Knowing that his own death is not far off, he is eager to affirm life for himself and for the generations to come. He wants to be more creative. The creative impulse is not merely to "make" something. It is to bring something into being, to give birth, to generate life. A song, a painting, even a spoon or toy, if made in a spirit of creation, takes on an independent existence. In the mind of its creator, it has a being of its own and will enrich the lives of those who are engaged with it.

Thus, both sides of the Destruction/Creation polarity are intensified at mid-life. The acute sense of his own ultimate destruction intensifies a man's wish for creation. His growing wish to be creative is accompanied by a greater awareness of the destructive forces in nature, in human life generally, and in himself.

For the man who is ready to look, death and destruction are everywhere. In nature, each species eats certain others and is eaten by still others. The geological evolution of the earth involves a process of destruction and transformation. To construct anything, something else must be destructured and restructured. In human reproduction, an ovum and a sperm are joined to create a new being; but many others are left to die. In every species (with the possible exception of man in the next evolutionary phase), far more offspring are created than will live through adulthood. The vast initial supply meets the food requirements of other species, allows for the ravages of a harsh environment, and yields a sufficient number of adults to ensure the survival of the species. The "balance of nature" is a mixture of destruction and creation. Both are essential to the overall harmony and evolution of the world.

A snowstorm does not wish to hurt the trees that fall in its wake. A bird is interested not in destroying a worm or damaging a bush, but in obtaining food and building a nest. The human being, however, often acts out of hatred, malice and vindictiveness, with the specific desire to cause pain and destruction. Homo sapiens is one of the very few species that preys on itself, engages in collective torture and individual sadism, and creates social structures in which large segments of the population are systematically deprived, oppressed, destroyed in body and soul.

Yet ours is also the only species that seeks to transcend its "animal nature" and to attain new heights of moral, intellectual and esthetic development. The evolution of human society is a testament to these visionary dreams, but our progress is pitifully slow. In working toward a higher Good, we also produce its antithesis—the conception and the actuality of Evil. The answer is not to give up our creative aspirations, but to learn how to live better with the Destruction/Creation polarity.

No man can get to age 40 without some experience of human destructiveness. Other persons, including those closest to him, have in some ways damaged his self-esteem, hindered his development, kept him from seeking and finding what he wanted most. Likewise, he himself has at times caused great hurt to others, including his loved ones.

In reappraising his life during the Mid-life Transition, a man must come to a new understanding of his grievances against others for the real or imagined damage they have done him. For a time he may be utterly immobilized by the helpless rage he feels toward parents, wife, mentors, friends and loved ones who, as he now sees it, have hurt him badly. And, what is even more difficult, he must come to terms with his guilts—his grievances against himself—for the destructive effects he has had on others and himself. He has to ask himself: "How have I failed my adult responsibilities for loved ones and for enterprises that affect many persons? How have I failed myself and destroyed my own possibilities? How can I live with the guilt and remorse?"

His developmental task is to understand more deeply the place of destructiveness in his own life and in human affairs generally. Much of the work on this task is unconscious. What is involved, above all, is the reworking of painful feelings and experiences. Some men articulate their new awareness in words, others in the esthetic terms of music, painting or poetry. Most men simply live it out in their daily lives. In any case, a man must come to terms with his grievances and guilts—his view of himself as victim and as villain in the continuing tale of man's inhumanity to man. If he is burdened excessively by his grievances or guilts, he will be unable to surmount them. If he is forced to maintain the illusion that destructiveness does not exist, he will also be impaired in his capacity for creating, loving and affirming life.

It is necessary that a man recognize and take responsibility for his own destructive capabilities. Even without hostile intentions, he will at times act in ways that have damaging consequences for others. As a father, he may discipline his children for the best of reasons and to the worst of effects. In a love relationship, his feelings cool unexpectedly and he withdraws from the relationship; it makes no sense to marry, yet the other person feels abandoned and betrayed. As a boss, he must demote someone who is worthy but incompetent, damaging that person's self-esteem and future prospects. No act can be totally benign in its consequences. To have the power to do great good, we must bear the burden of knowing that we will cause some harm—and in the end, perhaps, more harm than good.

It is hard enough to acknowledge that we can be unwittingly destructive. It is most painful of all to accept that we have destructive wishes toward others, even loved ones. There are times when a man feels hatred and revulsion, when he would like to leave or assault his loved ones, when he finds them intolerably cruel, disparaging, petty, controlling. He often feels an intense range or bitterness without knowing what brought it on or toward whom it is directed. Finally, he has actually done hurtful things to loved ones on purpose—with the worst of intentions, and in some cases with the worst of consequences.

Men at 40 differ widely in their readiness to acknowledge and take responsibility for their own destructiveness. Some have no awareness that they have done harm to others or might wish to do so. Others are so guilty about the real or imagined damage they have inflicted that they are not free to consider the problems of destructiveness more dispassionately and place it in broader perspective. Still others have some understanding that a person may feel both love and hate toward the same person, and some awareness of the ambivalence in their own valued relationships. In each case, the developmental task is to take a further step toward greater self-knowledge and self-responsibility.

Even the most mature or knowledgeable man has a great deal to learn at mid-life about workings of destructiveness in himself and in society. He has to learn about the heritage of anger, against others and against himself, that he has carried within himself from childhood. He has to learn, also, about the angers he has accumulated over the course of adulthood, building on and amplifying the childhood sources. And he has to place these internal destructive forces within the wider context of his ongoing adult life, setting them against the creative, life-affirming forces and finding new ways to integrate them in middle adulthood.

The learning I have just referred to is not purely conscious or intellectual. It cannot be acquired simply by reading a few books, taking a few courses, or even having some psychotherapy, though all of these may contribute to a long-term developmental process. The main learning goes on within the fabric of one's life. During the Mid-life Transition, we often learn by going through intense periods of suffering, confusion, rage against others and ourselves, grief over lost opportunities and lost parts of the self.

The Destruction/Creation polarity surely played as fundamental a part in the middle adulthood of the poet John Milton as in any man who ever existed. Living in mid-seventeenth-century England during a period of cataclysmic social change, blinded at 42, suffering severe misfortunes in his personal life, dedicated to a lawful social order, believing in a just God and enraged at the injustices perpetrated in God's world, he was a respected statesman and scholar and one of the great poets of Western civilization. In the following lines from *Paradise Lost*, he gives us a glimpse into his (and our) experience of the mid-life struggle:

> *Which way shall I fly*
> *Infinite wrath and infinite despair?*
> *Which way I fly is hell; myself am hell;*
> *And in the lowest deep a lower deep,*
> *Still threat'ning to devour me, opens wide,*
> *To which the hell I suffer seems a heaven.*

One possible fruit of a man's labors on this polarity is the "tragic sense of life." The tragic sense derives from the realization that great misfortunes and failures are not merely imposed upon us from without, but are largely the result of our own tragic flaws. A tragic story is not merely a sad story. In a sad story the hero dies or fails in his enterprise or is rejected by his special love; the unfortunate outcome is brought on by enemies, poor conditions, bad luck, or some unexpected deficiency in the hero.

The tragic story has a different character. Its hero is engaged with extraordinary virtue and skill in a noble quest. He is defeated in this quest.

The defeat is due in part to formidable external difficulties, but it stems above all from an internal flaw, a quality of character that is an intrinsic part of the heroic striving. The flaw usually involves hubris (arrogance, ego inflation, omnipotence) and destructiveness. The nobility and the defect are two sides of the same heroic coin. But genuine tragedy does not end simply in defeat. Although the hero does not attain his initial aspirations, he is ultimately victorious: he confronts his profound inner faults, accepts them as part of himself and of humanity, and is to some degree transformed into a nobler person. The personal transformation outweighs the worldly defeat and suffering.

Shakespeare's *King Lear* is one of the great tragic stories in our literature. King Lear voluntarily gives up the throne: he seeks to relinquish his monarchical and paternal power, hand on his legacy to the next generation, and begin a new life. The quest fails. Lear's failure and his final transformation have a common source in his tragic flaws. He wants to give up power—and to keep it. He is unable to bestow his legacy and blessing upon his daughters because his paternal love is too tarnished by pride and narcissistic self-indulgence.

His two older daughters, like him, are less interested in love than in power. They flatter him and receive the royal inheritance. His youngest daughter, Cordelia, will say only that she loves him—and he gives her nothing. After the succession, the ascending forces of destruction lead to civil war and invasion. Caught in the chaos, Lear goes mad, and in the process becomes sane as never before. He is reconciled with the loving Cordelia and is at last ready to be a parent and person in the most life-affirming sense.

The engulfing power of human destructiveness is stated in the following lines:

> *If that the heavens do not their visible spirits*
> *Send quickly down to tame these vile offences,*
> *It will come,*
> *Humanity must perforce prey on itself,*
> *Like monsters of the deep.*

The "heavenly spirits" are not metaphysical. They are the creative forces within every psyche which, if developed sufficiently, can transform the inner "monsters of the deep." They are represented in the play by Cordelia. She is the spirit of imagination, the feminine principle, the source of love and forgiveness. But these qualities exist not solely in her, or in women. Lear's early rejection of her is a crucial expression of his tragic flaw, and his reconciliation with her is the basis for his ultimate victory. His victory is the discovery of this spirit within himself. As he becomes able to recognize and integrate the Cordelia in his own psyche, he can moderate his destructive, power-seeking, narrowly masculine desires.

At the end, Lear welcomes the prospect of imprisonment with Cordelia:

> Come, let's away to prison;
> We two alone will sing like birds i' the cage.
> When thou dost ask me blessing, I'll kneel down
> And ask of thee forgiveness. So we'll live,
> And pray, and sing, and tell old tales, and laugh
> At gilded butterflies. . . .
> And take upon 's the mystery of things,
> As if we were God's spies: and we'll wear out,
> In a wall'd prison, packs and sects of great ones
> That ebb and flow by th' moon.

The "packs and sects of great ones/That ebb and flow by the moon" are the groups that split humanity into warring sects. They represent the forces in collective life that make for destructive antagonisms, and the forces in the self that propel each of us toward these ends. They are counterbalanced by the forces of love, play, reconciliation. The balancing of these opposing forces can advance significantly in middle adulthood, though it cannot be fully realized there—or ever.

The reworking of destructiveness at mid-life is exemplified by Shakespeare himself. Plays such as *King Lear* and *The Tempest*, written in his early and middle forties, represent the highest flowering of his genius. Even as he wrote of King Lear's voluntary retirement from the throne, and of Prospero's retirement from his rule of the magic isle, Shakespeare was contemplating his own voluntary retirement from the magic world of writing and from the power struggles of the commercial theater. He gave up writing in his late forties and died at 52.

It is almost too painful to contemplate what further flowering Shakespeare might have come to, had he been able to continue writing in his fifties and beyond. He wrote *King Lear* and *The Tempest* during his Midlife Transition, in the heat of his own conflicts between destruction and creation. At this point power and love seemed totally antithetical to him. To seek and wield power was destructive, vain, illusory. To be loving, especially with daughters, was to be joyous, blessed, forgiven, engaged in "the mystery of things." In his plays, as in his personal life, he sought to resolve the conflict by renouncing power entirely and entering a quiet world of love. This is not really a solution. Lear dies before he can test his newfound wisdom, and *The Tempest* conveniently ends as Prospero begins the sea journey that will lead to his new life.

Unfortunately, Shakespeare himself was not far enough into middle adulthood to have made much progress in resolving this conflict. The great developmental task of this era is not to retire early from worldly responsibilities, or to try vainly to free oneself from all passion and destructiveness, but to seek a new balance of power and love. It is critically important, both to society and to the individual in middle adulthood, that he accept the burdens and the pleasure of responsibility, that he learn to exercise authority with some wisdom and compassion, and that he tolerate the guilt and pain that are the price of the self-conscious use of power.

Examining the lives of several hundred artists in many countries and historical epochs, Jaques concludes that all artists go through a mid-life crisis. They become more aware of their mortality and must face their destructiveness more directly. Some men terminate their artistic careers during this time. Those who continue their artistic work in middle adulthood, perhaps after a fallow period of several years, undergo a change from what Jaques calls "precipitate" to "sculpted" creativity. The latter work, while not necessarily better in all respects, is more profound and universal. It reflects the developmental changes that begin with the Mid-life Transition.

If artists exhibit creativity in its most dramatic forms, men with other talents demonstrate their individual modes of creativity as they begin to resolve the great polarities of mid-life development. The result does not have to be a remarkable painting, symphony or novel. Creation takes myriad forms—products of all kinds, relationships, imaginative acts, social enterprises. Whatever its form, a man's new creativity in middle adulthood comes in part from his new relationship to his own destructiveness, and from an intensification of the loving, life-affirming aspects of the self.

## The Masculine/Feminine Polarity

The distinctions between male and female, masculine and feminine, are "obvious" and yet often unclear. Let me briefly state their meanings as I will use them. The terms "male" and "female" refer to biological genders. A male is a boy in pre-adulthood, a man in adulthood. A female is a girl and then a woman. With few exceptions, every human being starts life with the biological potential to be a male or a female, but not both. A male fetus will develop a reproductive system, musculature, and other biological features that distinguish men from women.

The terms "masculine" and "feminine" refer to the *meanings of gender*. They go beyond the purely biological to the social and psychological differences between male and female. In the course of our lives, all of us receive powerful messages regarding the fundamental differences between boys and girls, men and women. Images of the masculine and the feminine are contained in all religions, political ideologies, family patterns and social institutions. The imagery exists in every society, though its specific content varies.

Every male selectively draws upon and adopts the gender images of his culture. Gender plays an important part in his relationships with mother and father, brothers and sisters, male and female friends, teachers, lovers, and other figures who exist in reality or in his imagination. Through the experience with his mother, for example, a boy develops powerful feelings, fantasies and conceptions regarding the feminine: the nurturing, good mother; the depriving, destructive mother; the erotic, seductive mother. Likewise for father, siblings and others. Out of these relationships he generates an internal cast of characters who represent the forms of masculinity and femininity that have significance for him. He develops attitudes, wishes and fantasies about the masculine and feminine in himself and about his relationships with other men and women. Feelings about masculinity and femininity enter into a man's gender identity—his sense of who he is as a man, who he wants to be, and who he is terrified of being.

In most societies, there has been a splitting along gender lines: men are masculine, women are feminine, and no one can be both. The integration of masculinity and femininity has been advocated as a spiritual goal by certain religions and philosophies, such as Buddhism, but with rare success. (Even here, the integration was seen as achievable only by a small elite, chiefly upper-class or monastic males, and only after years of struggle.) In the lives of most persons, and in the social institutions of almost all societies, the splitting of masculine and feminine has prevailed. Two antithetical principles—variously identified as masculine and feminine, light and dark, Yang and Yin—distinguish male from female.

During the last several hundred years, there has been a slow reduction in the ancient gender distinctions. There is a greater recognition that women are not categorically different from men, that they have much the same desires as men and can develop much the same skills. Women are now allowed to be more "masculine" and to engage in certain traditionally masculine pursuits, while men are permitted to be more "feminine." Nonetheless, a considerable splitting between masculine and feminine still exists in our social institutions and our individual lives. Scientists have not yet clearly established the degree to which the various social-psychological meanings of gender coincide with basic biological differences between males and females.

The Masculine/Feminine polarity was of great importance to all the men in our study, though the specific content and conflicts varied enormously. Every man has his own gender identity. It is plain from their lives that the effort to attain one's manhood is at its peak in early adulthood. As a young man starts making his way in the adult world, he wants to live in accord with the images, motives and values that are most central to his sense of masculinity, and he tends to neglect or repress the feminine aspects of his self. Any part of the self that he regards as feminine is experienced as dangerous. A young man struggling to sustain his manliness is frightened by feelings and interests that seem womanly. One result of this anxiety is that much of the self cannot be lived out or even experienced in early adulthood.

What does it mean to be masculine or feminine? What personal qualities are included within the Masculine/Feminine polarity?

• One meaning of femininity in a man is *homosexuality*—the desire for a sexual relationship with another man. This is the form of femininity that elicits the most anxiety and moral outrage. Indeed, one of the main reasons that other forms are so tabooed is that they are considered "signs" of unconscious or unadmitted homosexuality. Actually, femininity and homosexuality are far from identical. Many homosexuals have strong masculine identifications and personal qualities, and many men who are strongly heterosexual in their love lives have intense interests, traits and feelings deriving from feminine aspects of the self.

Five of our forty men—two biologists and three novelists—discussed their homosexual activities or concerns. It seems likely that a few others had had homosexual experiences or interests but were not ready to talk about them, and still others had homosexual feelings at a more unconscious level. One biologist had had a period of extensive homosexual activity in his youth. When he was in graduate school the homosexuality was discovered by the university authorities. They allowed him to continue his career only after he agreed to give it up and enter psychotherapy. Over the next ten years he had several heterosexual love affairs and was married for a year at age 29 to 30. When we last saw him, at 39, he had not remarried and his love life was still problematic. Another biologist entered a gay world in his twenties, through his interest in art and theater. During a severe age thirty crisis, he decided on his own to obtain psychotherapy and work on his relationships with men and women, his fears of his own creativity and his commitment to biology as an occupation. By his late thirties he had formed a satisfying marriage, started a family, and entered a highly creative phase in his work.

• Another set of qualities often associated with manliness is *bodily prow-*

ess and toughness—the stamina to undertake long, grueling work and endure severe bodily stress without "quitting." As opposed to this meaning of masculinity, the feminine is conceived of as frail, weak, vulnerable to attack, not having the bodily resources needed to sustain a persistent effort toward valued goals. Masculinity in this sense is often symbolized by the marine, the wrestler and the surgeon; we found many other forms in the various occupations. As we have seen, this image of masculinity was of great importance to Jim Tracy as athletic boy, youthful military officer and rising young executive. The biologist John Barnes (see Chapter 17) was expressing a similar imagery in his involvement in hockey, skiing and sailing, and in his sense of himself as the indefatigable scientist who could spend endless hours in the laboratory without complaining or giving up.

The novelists were more aware of the sides of themselves they considered feminine, but they could draw upon it only with considerable conflict. They were by no means free of the "machismo" masculinity usually attributed to other occupations. Six of our ten novelists had a strong concern with bodily endurance and prowess. Some of these had served in the military, trying desperately to prove themselves as men in combat and having to overcome fears which they regarded as cowardly, shameful—and feminine. Many had a lifelong interest, as participants and spectators, in competitive sports such as football, basketball and boxing. It was hard to say whether they were more attracted by the competitive aspect or by the bodily skill, endurance and power.

• A related meaning of masculinity involves achievement and ambition. It is portrayed by the heroic man on a quest for a treasure, be it the Holy Grail, the Nobel Prize, the Great American Novel or the Executive Suite. This theme is related to the traditional division of labor in the family. The woman has been primarily responsible for raising the children, managing the household and other work that keeps her within the domestic orbit. The man, on the other hand, has been the primary link between family and community. He has had the ultimate authority. His primary responsibility, carried out through his occupation, is to provide for the family's material well-being and community standing. In the last few centuries, with the increasing separation of family and occupation, a man's work has become steadily more important as the basis for his contribution to the family and for his self-esteem as husband, father and person.

The division of labor between husband and wife intensifies another aspect of the Masculine/Feminine polarity. The qualities regarded as masculine involve success in work, getting ahead, earning one's fortune for the sake of self and family. The qualities regarded as feminine involve building the nest and ministering to the multiple needs of husband and children. The feminine woman is the devoted wife who tries to further her husband's advancement. If she has a job, it is as an unmarried woman seeking a husband, or in an occupation such as teaching or nursing where she is appropriately maternal, subordinate and non-competitive with men. To the extent that a man has these "feminine" qualities or engages in these kinds of work, he must deal with his own and others' feelings that something is missing in him as a man.

This conflict played an important part in the life of Paul Namson (see Chapters 12 and 18). It was hard for him to give up his career as business executive, partly because this work was a vehicle for his masculine strivings. Similarly, his difficulty in giving himself to writing novels stemmed partly from its feminine meanings as a creative, esthetic activity: writing yielded no immediately useful product, it came out of his own painful feelings, and it was considered "queer" in several respects within his family and business world. We find another version of this polarity in Bill Paulsen (see Chapters 8 and 18), the worker who sought desperately to enter the managerial ranks of industry. Becoming a manager represented in part a validation of his manliness. His self-deceptive "puffery" was a way of handling the anxiety that he did not quite measure up, that he was doomed forever to remain with the "girls" on the shop floor rather than joining the men who run the show.

• The concern with *power and weakness* is yet another facet of the Masculine/Feminine polarity. For many men, the essence of masculinity is power: exercising control over others, being (and being recognized as) a person of strong will, a leader who "gets things done." The opposite pole, symbolized as feminine, is to be weak, submissive, unassertive, subject to victimization by others who have more power and are ready to use it exploitively. This version of the masculine and feminine is the analogue, in terms of social relationships, of the concern with bodily toughness-frailty noted above.

When the splitting of power and weakness takes an extreme form, a man regards any sign of weakness in himself as intolerably feminine and dangerous. He goes to great lengths to deny its existence. His anxiety is heightened by every sign of biological and social decline at mid-life. Perhaps the most marked form of splitting, with excessive overvaluation of the masculine and anxiety about the feminine, is the authoritarian personality. Variations on this theme are to be found, however, in all men.

• Finally, the Masculine/Feminine polarity is often reflected in the distinction between *thinking and feeling*. It is often assumed that men are by nature more logical and "reasonable" than women—more analytical and intellectual, cooler, more interested in how things work. Women in turn are supposed to be more emotional and intuitive, more likely to make decisions on the basis of feelings rather than careful analysis. This definition of masculine and feminine is part of the broader pattern that ties masculinity to skilled work in a specialized occupational structure, femininity to motherhood and caring for the emotional needs of children and husband.

In its extreme form, this polarization requires a man to be a kind of thinking machine. To be truly masculine, he must devote himself to his occupation in a highly impersonal way. He can allow himself a narrow range of "manly" feelings relating to assertiveness, rivalry and task attainment. But he is not permitted feelings that involve dependency, intimacy, grief, sensuality, vulnerability. Such feelings are associated with childishness and femininity.

Within our study, the men who specialized most highly in thinking at the expense of feeling were the biologists. For the most part, they were not involved in the power-seeking, "macho" forms of masculinity. They did not compete for political power or financial success or sexual conquest. But, despite their often gentle manner, they competed fiercely in the realm of the intellect. Trying to establish themselves in the "first rank" of biological science, they showed no mercy to their rivals and felt contempt for everyone, including themselves, who might fail to make it. James Watson, winner of the Nobel Prize for his part in discovering the structure of the DNA molecule, has vividly described the competition in his book *The Double Helix*. The philosopher Bertrand Russell wrote of his own efforts to get out of this pattern (see Chapter 2). John Barnes is but one of the biologists in our study whose one-sided commitment to the battle for intellectual supremacy was accompanied by an alienation from feeling and all other aspects of the self that he experienced as feminine. In Chapter 17 we shall witness the strength of this polarization in his early adulthood, and the efforts he made to reduce it in the Mid-life Transition.

If we look at the entire set of qualities just described, we discover a multifaceted pattern of masculinity in opposition to a complementary pattern of femininity. A unifying theme in the masculine pattern is a concern with *doing, making, having*. A man is supposed to get out there and do something: perform, accomplish, produce, bring home the bacon. If his body is a vehicle for demonstrating his masculinity, he tries to acquire special strength, endurance, sexual virility, athletic prowess. If his mind is the preferred vehicle, he uses thought as a weapon in the struggle to win, to outmuscle his rivals, be it in science, art or chess. Whatever the arena, he wants to establish his place in the world of work and of men. He wants to become a productive, independent, responsible, authoritative man who has the mental and bodily capacities needed to attain his goals.

The feminine is at the opposite pole. To be feminine is to lack bodily strength and stamina, to be more concerned with feeling than with thought. A woman may be clever in a feminine way, but she can't be expected to be consistently logical, to stay with a difficult work task, or to analyze a problem without letting her feelings get in the way. In this view, it is the feminine in a man that leads him to be soft and dependent, to accept second best rather than fight for the top. It is feminine of him to experience great depth of feeling, to be "sensitive," submissive, esthetic.

Perhaps the ultimate difference is in the ways of creating. In this imagery, the masculine form of creation is to produce something by making it according to one's own design: planning, molding, erecting, transforming raw materials into a new product. The specifically masculine form of creation is to build a bridge, invent a mousetrap, improve the design of a car. The feminine form is represented by conceiving and raising children. In a sense, a woman creates an embryo, an infant and an adult. But she does not "make" the child grow. Rather, she *enables* it to grow, and she does this best when she accommodates to the inner laws of growth that govern its evolution.

Artistic creation is strongly feminine in this respect. The painter, composer or writer often has the experience of starting with a rudimentary image or idea. It is like being pregnant: he has within himself a seed that must be nurtured, given birth to, brought into being. The muses are female. When a youthful artist cannot accept the creative-feminine as part of himself, he may imagine it as a muse inspiring his creative efforts. In middle adulthood he may become more accepting of the feminine, and allow the muse to be an intrinsic part of himself. This is a task of the Mid-life Transition.

As I have said, young men differ widely in the relative predominance of the masculine over the feminine and in the degree to which the feminine must be inhibited or split off from the conscious ego. A man may be almost entirely cut off from the aspects of himself that he considers feminine. He allows himself no intimacy, no awareness of his own weakness or dependency, no deviation from his masculine strivings. He may become a fearless adventurer, a military hero, an ambitious seeker of power or of intellectual accomplishment. No matter what vehicle he fashions, it will be narrowly in accord with his masculine imagery and values, and it will exclude all feminine qualities except those that are expressed unconsciously.

A man who is afflicted with this exaggerated masculinity may be a responsible father, but his children will experience him as unloving, distant and demanding. He will regard women as either maternal or sexual; not both. To him the former are devoted mothers and wives but are sexually unexciting. The latter are good for sexual conquest and fun, but horrifying as mother, wife, sister or daughter. It is not possible for this man to have an intimate, mutual relationship with a woman. He puts very little of himself into any relationship. He is contemptuous of the sexual woman and he puts the virtuous woman on a pedestal, but he is emotionally close to neither. He cannot have a friendship with a woman. He does not wish to know any woman well because he is afraid to know himself well—especially the less masculine aspects of himself.

Of course, the splitting is usually not so severe. A man and his wife or lover often work out a psychological "division of labor" in their relationship. The man is primarily responsible for certain interests and feelings, the woman for others. They establish a modus operandi in which the strengths of one complement the weaknesses of the other. Usually, his special functions involve the qualities considered masculine, hers, feminine. There may also be interesting reversals, as when he has an interest in cooking or the sharing of feelings, or when she is more involved than he in occupation.

A complementarity of this kind is a source of both strength and weakness. While each partner is lacking in some respects, between them they cover a wide range of skills, feelings and modes of living. Together, they form a whole person. A man may thus derive from his wife many of the feminine qualities he cannot nourish in himself. With time, and a good relationship, he may come to accept and develop these qualities. As long as he relies on her to supply them, however, he remains incomplete and one-sided. The same is true for her.

Although there are variations in degree, the gender distinctions operate with great force in contemporary society. The great majority of men in early adulthood form an identity suffused with "masculine" images, desires and values. No matter how much a young man wants to grow beyond the traditionally narrow view of masculinity, the idea of manliness is still of great importance to him. He strives to take his place in the world as a male adult. In doing so, he must feel some anxiety about the feminine and must control or repress it to some degree. He must give greater priority to the masculine as he understands it. He can make room for the feminine, but he cannot fully integrate the two.

The difficulty in integrating the masculine and feminine in early adulthood has many sources. It stems partly from cultural traditions, partly from personal immaturity. A young man in his twenties is just barely out of adolescence; he is not developmentally ready to resolve all his preadult conflicts and achieve a highly integrated personality. He has to "go with what he's got," which means building a first adult life structure that reflects and sustains his inner conflicts. The difficulty in integration stems also from the magnitude of his evolving life tasks. In the twenties and thirties his energies are devoted to forming an occupation and a family. Ordinarily he must meet heavy financial demands, pursue his goals, and face the stresses of day-to-day living. There are also biological reasons for the usual predominance of the masculine over the feminine among men in early adulthood.

In short, a man normally works out a partial integration of the masculine and feminine in the late teens and early twenties, at the start of early adulthood. He may resolve the conflicts further during the Age Thirty Transition. During the phase of Becoming One's Own Man, in his late thirties, there is a surge of masculine strivings, an intense effort to achieve a more senior, "manly" position in the world and to reduce the strength of the "little boy" in the self. Most men get to the late thirties with roughly the same balance of masculine and feminine they had in the early twenties. The Mid-life Transition is the next major developmental opportunity to reintegrate the Masculine/Feminine polarity.

## Developmental Gains in Middle Adulthood

In the Mid-life Transition the balance may finally be improved. This is not simply a matter of a quantitative drop in the strength of the masculine emphasis, and an increase in the feminine. What is required is a qualitatively new integration of the two. The developmental task is to come to terms in new ways with the basic meanings of masculinity and femininity. A man must form a new relationship to the various archetypal figures in his head that represent maleness and femaleness. He must modify the existing life structure and work toward a new one. In this new structure, the feminine will have a larger and freer part. The masculine may be reduced in some ways, but it may also gain fuller expression when one is less constrained by the need to inhibit the feminine. Finally, when masculine and feminine are less rigidly divided within the self, a man can combine them more creatively in work, in personal relationships, in solitude and in his personal experience of living.

This change may involve a man's *relationship to his mother*, especially to the figure of mother within his psyche. In early adulthood he normally carries within himself a little boy and a mother who are engaged in a complex relationship. The mother may be symbolized as a powerful source of care and protection; as a powerful enemy who can deprive, smother and destroy him; as a weak figure who may abandon him or leave him open to assault from a vengeful father; and so on and on. In the Mid-life Transition a man can partially free himself from these images and anxieties. He is then less afraid of a woman's power to withhold, devour and seduce. He can give more of himself, receive more from her, and accept her greater independence. He is more ready to work collaboratively with a woman or to work as a subordinate under her without feeling emasculated. Similar processes are involved in his efforts to free himself from the tyranny of internal fathers who make it difficult for him to become more manly and to utilize the feminine.

Likewise, the Mid-life Transition opens the possibility for change in the character of a man's *love relationships with peer women*. In early adulthood, a man wants a special woman to provide things he needs but to a large extent lacks within himself. This pattern, with numerous variations, has been the traditional basis for stable family life in early adulthood. In middle adulthood, however, this division of labor is neither necessary nor desirable. A man can now reclaim the qualities he formerly denied in himself and projected onto women. He can begin to recognize that various archetypal figures—the inspiring muse, the tender lover, the one who nurtures the young—are in actuality parts of himself. These internal figures are capable of further growth and use if he will acknowledge them, love them, and integrate them within his life. He will then be more able to love a woman for herself, rather than for providing what he cannot accept in himself.

The further integration of the Masculine/Feminine polarity at midlife also makes it easier and more rewarding to *become a mentor*. A man can serve various mentor functions in early adulthood, but it is hard to become a mentor in a fuller sense until the forties. A novice or junior adult has some of the dependency and incompleteness of a child, but he also has the independence, inner resources and developmental capabilities of an adult. A "good enough" mentor must take account of both. If he regards his protégé primarily as a child, he will be overly giving or controlling and will make the relationship too unequal. On the other hand, if he regards him as a fully developed adult, he will be of help in certain specific respects (such as providing information or job opportunities) but he will not grasp and respond to the younger man's developmental needs.

With greater resolution of the Masculine/Feminine polarity, a man is better able to combine the multiple aspects of the mentoring role. He can be more caring for a younger man without getting anxious about the homosexual meanings that are actually involved or that may be attributed to him by others. Not having to maintain a rigid division between work (thinking, performing, achieving) and personal relationships (loving, caring, fostering development), he can combine work and friendship in various admixtures. He can be more critical and task-oriented in personal relationships, more compassionate and judicious in the exercise of authority. As his needs for power and success are modulated, he can give of himself with less competitive rivalry, envy and fear of being surpassed. As his sense of his own development is strengthened, he can better understand and support the development of other adults.

The work on this polarity also enables a man to have more developed *mentoring relationships with women*. Very few men in early adulthood have female protégées. In the work world, a woman is usually much lower in the social and occupational scale than the man she works for; advancement to his position may be entirely closed to her. Much more is involved, however, than social distance or lack of opportunity. The majority of men do not form serious friendships or non-romantic relationships with women. Being a woman's mentor is hardly imaginable to many men.

If a man in early adulthood does begin a mentoring relationship with a woman who is his student, subordinate or friend, he tends to shape it to suit his masculine orientation. Seeing her as a bright student or worker, he may emphasize her intellect and abilities to the exclusion of other personal qualities, including her femininity. Or he may paternalistically regard his female student as a charming little girl who does her lessons well but cannot hope ever to grow up and do a man's work. Daddy's smart girl traditionally grows up to be the intelligent, cultured wife of a successful man; she has no occupation of her own, but she works hard to raise their family and promote his advancement. If she enters a highly masculine work world (such as law, medicine or business), a woman may find herself becoming "one of the men," with all their masculine strengths and limitations. Exaggerated masculinity can distort the personal development of women as much as of men.

The male mentor may discover that his protégée is an attractive woman. He may then offer limited mentoring largely as justification for a sexual relationship; this kind of mentoring is fraudulent and not likely to facilitate her development. In some cases they form a complex relationship that has sexual, loving and mentoring aspects. The value of these loving-mentoring relationships varies greatly. The woman may gain a good deal in terms of her personal and occupational development, though she may also be badly hurt. It is hard to combine mentoring and romance for long. By its nature, mentoring almost invariably ends in separation or modest friendship after a few years, whereas the preferred outcome of a serious romance is an enduring, equal relationship in marriage. If the mentoring couple do marry, they have the advantage of considerable intimacy but they are faced with the problem of transforming the relationship to eliminate the mentoring. A husband cannot remain his wife's mentor. Like anyone in the recipient position, she must in time grow up and go out on her own, or her development will be impaired.

Fuller integration of the Masculine/Feminine polarity enables a man to mentor younger women with less hurtful intrusion of his masculine values and sexual needs. He can appreciate a woman's feminine qualities without having to deny or exploit them. As he seeks to develop his own feminine side, he can learn from her and have a more equal relationship. He is freer to enjoy the erotic aspects of their relationship without having to be directly sexual. His efforts at integration offer her a model and a source of moral support for her own efforts to be a person who is both feminine and achieving.

Mid-life struggles with the Masculine/Feminine polarity—and their frequently mixed success—are evident in the lives of all four men whose biographies we are presenting. In the following chapters we shall examine in some detail the lives of these men in the Mid-life Transition and its aftermath.

## The Attachment/Separateness Polarity

We use the term "attachment" in the broadest sense, in order to encompass all the forces that connect person and environment. To be attached is to be engaged, involved, needy, plugged in, seeking, rooted. Attachment in this sense is a general condition that has many sources and takes many forms. I am attached to the external world to the extent that I care about it, hate it, want to obtain what it offers, find it interesting or confusing or frightening. My inner readiness to be attached is strengthened by many feelings and motives—dependency, sexuality, aggression, ambition, affection, envy. The environment too may elicit my engagement by being exciting, challenging, hostile, depriving. I am attached when I am trying to adapt to, participate in or master the external world.

At the opposite pole is separateness. This is not the same thing as isolation or aloneness. A person who is alone, yet actively involved in planning a future activity or in feeling resentful over a past rejection, is nonetheless firmly attached to the external world. A person is separate when he is primarily involved in his inner world—a world of imagination, fantasy, play. His main interest is not in adapting to the "real" world outside, but in constructing and exploring an imagined world, the enclosed world of his inner self.

Separateness fosters individual growth and creative adaptation, though it can be harmful when carried to an extreme. The most pathological form of separateness is represented by the schizophrenic person whose world is totally private and who has only minimal relationships to people and objects in the environment. A more "healthy" form of extreme separateness is meditation and reverie, in which the person temporarily withdraws attention from the environment and is entirely occupied with inner experience. A less extreme example of separateness is the child absorbed in play. The play goes on, as Winnicott has told us, at the boundary between "reality" and "illusion." The child creates a setting, a cast of characters and a scenario depicting his imagined possibilities for living. The play is for the self: it allows the child to explore who he is and what he has in mind for the future. It is of no direct value in the world, although it may prepare him for later adaptation.

The professional novelist or composer at work is separate in that he is involved with his self, drawing upon his inner resources and trying to create a product that will be esthetically pleasing to himself. Since the writing of words or music is part of his occupation, he is also in a condition of attachment. He is trying to create a product that will be pleasing to a certain audience and that will provide him an income and reputation.

The creative artist thus works on the boundary between attachment and separateness. He sees himself as part of humanity, and he cares about the fate of his products in the future of humanity. Art is his occupation. Through it, he participates in society and is attached to society. To be creative, however, he must maintain some degree of separateness. His work must express and please himself, must be true to his own vision. Although his techniques and products are shaped by various external pressures, their ultimate source is within himself. If he cannot withdraw sufficiently from the engagement with others and draw upon his own creative resources, his work will become repetitive, dry and unconnected to the self.

Persons of all ages and occupations must deal with the Attachment/Separateness polarity. If we become too separate, our contact with the world is lost and our capacity for survival jeopardized. If we become too attached to the environment, we endanger our capacity for self-renewal, growth and creative effort. Although a balance of attachment and separateness must be found at every age, it will necessarily change from one era of the life cycle to the next.

In pre-adulthood the child is developing an ego capable of managing his powerful drives and using them for socially constructive purposes. The emotional forces of attachment must be harnessed in the service of adaptation. The child has to form stable relationships, acquire information and skills, and mature to the point where he can begin living as a relatively independent adult. With "good enough" conditions of development, he acquires the learning, values and character traits required for adaptation within his culture. Nonetheless, the forces of imagination and fantasy enable him to maintain some degree of separateness from the external world. The separateness allows him to nourish his creativity, sustain his individuality and develop his inner Dream. He must be attached enough to make a place for himself in society; but he must be separate enough to be able to strike out on his own, question the traditional forms, and make life better for himself and others.

In early adulthood the balance ordinarily shifts markedly toward attachment at the expense of separateness. During the twenties and thirties, a man is tremendously involved in entering the adult world and doing his work for the tribe. He forms a family and occupation, and accepts a series of increasing responsibilities (each step usually coming before he is quite ready to take it). He must cope with the stresses of financial hardship, changes in residence, illness, death, war, depression, natural disaster and "acts of God." It is difficult to find time for separateness—for solitude, play and quiet self-renewal. Separateness is made difficult partly by external urgencies: the rent must be paid, the children cared for, the work accomplished, the crises met. There are also the internal urgencies: he wants to establish his niche in society, attain his goals, become a hero. He tries to "make something of his life," and the tribe insists that he pay his dues. Between the internal push and the external pull, the Attachment/Separateness balance tilts strongly in the direction of attachment.

Middle adulthood requires a more equal weighting of attachment and separateness. During the Mid-life Transition, a man needs to reduce his heavy involvement in the external world. To do the work of reappraisal and de-illusionment, he must turn inward. He has to discover what his turmoil is about, and where he hurts. He wants to find and lick his wounds. Having been overly engaged in his worldly struggles, he needs to become more engaged with himself. In this period the archetypal Self takes on greater definition and vitality. It becomes a more active internal figure, someone that the conscious ego must learn to talk with and listen to. The Self is the "I" a man has in mind when he asks, "What do I really want? How do I feel about my life? How shall I live in the future?" He is feeling, in effect, that his present relationships, goals and style of living are in certain crucial respects not right for the Self. He needs to separate himself from the striving ego and the external pressures, so that he can better hear the voices from within.

To the extent that a man succeeds in this task during middle adulthood, the Self acquires an importance for him roughly equal to that of the external world. He can draw more upon his inner resources and is thus less dependent on external stimulation. He enjoys solitude more, since he has internal company when other persons are absent. He places less value on possessions, rewards and social approval. He lives more in the present and gains more satisfaction from the process of living—from being rather than doing and having. More in touch with his own feelings, he can be more esthetic, sensual, aware.

As a man becomes more individuated and more oriented to the Self, a process of "detribalization" occurs. He becomes more critical of the tribe—the particular groups, institutions and traditions that have the greatest significance for him, the social matrix to which he is most attached. He is less dependent upon tribal rewards, more questioning of tribal values, more able to look at life from a universalistic perspective. He can better appreciate his social origins without having to disparage other peoples and cultures. Having less need to idealize certain individuals and groups, he is less inclined to condemn others. If as a young man he broke away from his origins, he may now attempt some form of rapprochement. He may feel that he was cheated or done in by the tribe during early adulthood, and may go through a stormy period when, like Job, he rages against the tribal God. To the extent that he resolves these conflicts, he can move toward a broader, less dependent perspective. He forms a more universal view of good and evil, and a more tragic sense of their coexistence in himself and in all humanity. His spirituality may take the form of an explicit religious doctrine, but often he tries to free himself from formal doctrine in order to attain a personal understanding of what it means to be human.

The turning inward and the detribalization are part of the shift toward less attachment. The result of this shift is normally not a marked disengagement from the external world but a greater integration of attachment and separateness. A major developmental task of middle adulthood is *to find a better balance between the needs of the self and the needs of society.* A man who attends more to the self, who becomes less tyrannized by his ambitions, dependencies and passions, can be involved with other individuals and perform his social roles in a more responsible way than ever before. He can respond more to the developmental needs of his offspring and other young adults if he is more in touch with his own self and responding to its needs. He can develop greater wisdom if he is less focused upon the acquisition of specific skills, knowledge and rewards.

In order to care more deeply for others, he must come to care more deeply for himself. Caring means that he is mainly concerned not with material comfort and success, but with self-development and integrity. It means that he will exercise authority with greater imagination and compassion. It means that, while he enjoys the power and the tangible rewards of leadership, he gains even greater satisfaction from creating a legacy, enjoying the intrinsic pleasures of work and having more individualized, loving relationships.

A man in early adulthood is full of intense desires: to win, to be right, to achieve the noble Dream, to be highly regarded by those who matter (or, perhaps without admitting it, by everyone). With further development in middle adulthood, some of these desires fade away. Those that remain have a less urgent quality. They can also be realized more fully. He can be more loving, sensual, authoritative, intimate, solitary—more attached and more separate.

# Conclusion

If he is to make significant mid-life changes in love relationships, occupation, leisure and other important aspects of his life, a man must become more individuated. He must confront the great polarities that are basic divisions in the individual and in society. In successive developmental periods from infancy through old age, especially the major transitions, a man has an opportunity to reduce the internal splitting. Though he can never entirely overcome the divisions, he finds new ways of being Young/Old, Masculine/Feminine, Destructive/Creative and Attached/Separate, according to his place in the life cycle.

Some men have suffered such irreparable defeats in pre-adulthood or early adulthood, and have been able to work so little on the tasks of the Mid-life Transition, that they lack the inner and outer resources for creating a minimally adequate life structure in middle adulthood. They face a middle age of constriction and decline. Other men form a life structure that is reasonably viable in the world but poorly connected to the self. They perform their social roles and do their bit for themselves and others, but their lives are lacking in inner excitement.

Still other men make a start in the Mid-life Transition toward a middle adulthood that will have its own special satisfactions and burdens. For them, middle adulthood may be the most loving and creative season in the life cycle. They are less tyrannized by the ambitions, instinctual drives and illusions of youth. They are more deeply attached to others and yet more separate, more centered in the self. For them, the season passes in its proper rhythm.

The Mid-life Transition is not the last opportunity for change and growth. Work on our developmental tasks can continue through middle adulthood and beyond, and there are later transitional periods to facilitate the process. As long as life continues, no period marks the end of the opportunities and the burdens of further development.

# 16 Modifying the Life Structure During the Mid-life Transition

At the deepest level, a man's tasks in the Mid-life Transition are to work on the polarities that animate and divide him. This inner reintegration enables him to modify the life structure of the Settling Down period. In Chapter 13 we considered changes occurring in the domain of work: the meaning of success and failure and the place of a man's occupation in his life structure. I want now to discuss changes in three additional components of the life structure: the Dream, mentoring and fathering young adults, and marriage. In Chapter 18 we shall see how these various modifications contribute to the formation of a new life structure in the ensuing period, Entering Middle Adulthood.

## Modifying the Dream

As a man attempts in the Mid-life Transition to reappraise his life during early adulthood, he tries to understand and evaluate the place of the Dream in it. In what ways has the Dream been lived out, compromised or left out? If there has been a "culminating event" at the end of Becoming One's Own Man, what consequences does it have for the Dream?

Most of the men in our study had a discernible Dream. There were great variations, however, in the changing place of the Dream in the evolving life structure. The Dream may be modest or heroic, vaguely defined or crystal clear, a burning passion or a quiet guiding force, a source of inspiration, strength and corrosive conflict. Some men make the pursuit of the Dream the central element in the life structure and build everything else around it. For other men, the pursuit of the Dream is in continuing conflict with another occupation or way of living. This conflict is a dominant motif in their lives. Still other men never form an articulated Dream.

The Dream grows out of a primordial sense of self-in-world. It lends excitement and vitality to one's life. It is associated with the "I am" feeling: the experience that "I exist," that self and world are properly matched, that I can *be* myself and can *act* in accordance with the self. My life is enriched to the extent that I have a Dream and give it an appropriate place in my life—a place that is legitimate and viable for both my self and my world. If I have no Dream or can find no way to live it out, my life lacks genuine purpose or meaning.

Like most profoundly good things, the Dream is a mixed blessing. Certain aspects of the Dream are conscious and tied to reality. But other aspects are less conscious, less rational and more illusory. The central illusion is this: "If I attain the Dream—if I become a great novelist or scientist, if I make a special contribution to humanity or to my clan, if I gain great power—then life will be good and everything really important will come to me."

For example, a young biologist wants to work in a particular kind of university, to do research in genetics, and in time to become a senior investigator and professor. Beyond this, however, he has other, more private fantasies and aspirations. He imagines that success in achieving the specific goals will bring all sorts of other rewards. He will be not merely a senior but a *distinguished* investigator, a Nobel laureate, a figure of historic importance in his field. Or he will achieve distinction at a more local level, through his contributions to the university or the community. Whatever the specific goals, reaching them is—in John Barth's apt phrase —"the key to the treasure," the basis for the good life. The corollary is that if he fails to attain these goals his life will be a total failure and have no value.

The Dream thus contains an imagined self having a variety of goals, aspirations and values, conscious as well as unconscious, and pursuing his quest within a certain kind of world. A man's Dream is his personal *myth*, an imagined drama in which he is the central character, a would-be hero engaged in a noble quest. It portrays a complex world: a natural landscape, a varied cast of characters, social institutions and conflicting groups. The plot involves elemental struggles between good and evil, truth and error, beauty and ugliness, and the outcome has portentous consequences for that entire world. The "hero of the Dream" is but one of many figures in the man's self. To the extent that this figure plays a predominant part in the evolution of the life structure during early adulthood, other internal figures and parts of the self tend to be neglected.

The youthful Dream is a prime example of the ground in which illusions develop. It is a vision of the adult self living the good life. While creating a soil in which joyful hopes can flower, it also nourishes illusory beliefs: that I am capable of accomplishing everything the Dream envisages, that certain others will unequivocally support my efforts, that fulfilling the Dream will bring me true happiness.

The Dream derives in part from the normal omnipotence fantasies of early childhood, when the distinction between wish and reality is poorly established. Some degree of "normal omnipotence" is required to strengthen one's courage in early adulthood when the possibility of realizing the Dream often seems slight. The hero can use a touch of arrogance, though in the end it may be his downfall. As Goethe said, "For a man to achieve all that is demanded of him, he must regard himself as greater than he is." One function of the mentor, and the wife, is to sustain the young man's Dream without questioning it too much or making excessive demands that he attain it.

A young man's Dream becomes increasingly rational and reality-based as he works to build it into his life. He gains admission to the appropriate institutions, develops the needed skills and qualities of character, makes concrete plans and strives to reach his goals. Yet he is not simply pursuing his career within a particular social matrix. A myth always has some basis in reality, and we must take account of the reality in seeking to understand its workings. But when we say that a man is enacting his myth, or pursuing his Dream, we are making plain that his activity has a far more profound meaning. A myth is a construction; it serves human needs and it reflects meanings stemming from deeper, often unconscious sources in the personality and in the culture.

The more illusory aspects of the Dream become evident during the course of the Mid-life Transition. I have already mentioned one of the most pervasive illusions: if the hero is successful he will live happily ever after. Discovering that this is not so, and dealing with the consequences, is often a mind-boggling process for highly successful men in the Mid-life Transition. Most men whose lives are imbued with a Dream have to deal with the consequences of failure, or of flawed success.

There is also the illusion of omnipotence: as long as the hero is true to the Dream he is invincible; he may suffer momentary defeats and at times all may appear lost, but if he perseveres he will triumph. Beliefs of this kind tend to be strongest in the Early Adult Transition, when the Dream is taking shape and has less grounding in reality, and in Becoming One's Own Man, when one has the "now or never" urge to realize the aspirations of early adulthood. Jung speaks of "ego inflation," when a man experiences his internal hero figure as all-powerful. The inflation is followed, says Jung, by a period of "deflation" in which the hero is badly wounded. Painful as it is, deflation is a necessary step in overcoming the internal dominance of the hero and forming a more integrated self during the Mid-life Transition.

The tendency to minimize those parts of the self that don't fit into the Dream leads to various illusions about the self. It is hard for a man to acknowledge that he wants things that have nothing to do with the Dream or are actually antithetical to it. He may also have the illusion that others in his life exist solely to play their part—as allies, enemies, foils, background players—in the myth-drama. A man's wife is often a major beneficiary and victim of this process: he loves and rewards her if she performs well in her appointed role, which is generally maternal and caring and makes things easier for him. But he has difficulty regarding her as a whole person and considering her independent talents and aspirations.

Finally, there is the illusion that the ultimate outcome of the heroic enterprise must be total success or total failure. The only success that matters is total success. To succeed partially is to fail. The hero can have no flaws. The Dream must be perfectly realized.

The illusions, the sense of omnipotence and the excitement of heroic drama give the Dream its intensity and its inspirational qualities. But they contribute also to the *tyranny of the Dream*. Reducing this tyranny is a major task of the Mid-life Transition, whenever the Dream has had an important place in a man's life and he is in the grip of its myth. The task is not to get rid of the Dream altogether, but to reduce its excessive power: to make its demands less absolute; to make success less essential and failure less disastrous; to diminish the magical-illusory qualities. Later, a man may continue to seek excellence, but he gains more intrinsic enjoyment from the process and product of his efforts and he is less concerned with recognition and power. The men who have written most eloquently about the corrupting effects of ambition, and about the importance of "being" and "self-actualization," generally came to their insights in middle adulthood after a Mid-life Transition in which they began slowly and painfully to reduce the tyranny of a powerful Dream.

In reworking the Dream, a man also modifies the meaning of the *ladder*. As we have seen, the image of the ladder plays a central part in the definition of the Settling Down enterprise. At around 40, when he reaches the top rung of his early adult ladder, a man has to reappraise the ladder itself. It is not just a matter of evaluating how well he has done within the current definitions of success and failure. He has to question the basic meanings of success and failure, and the value of the ladder.

If a man has largely attained his goals, he asks: "What good are they? Of what value are my accomplishments to others, to society, and especially to myself? What have been the costs? Where do I go from here?" If he has failed in significant respects, he asks: "Is the failure irrevocable or can I still achieve what I wanted? Can I accept the failure and live without the things success might have brought? What are the alternatives—can I find a better way of living for the coming years?"

It is time in the Mid-life Transition for a man to modulate the powerful imagery of the ladder. Without losing all desire for accomplishment, power and excellence, he comes to be less driven by ambition and more aware of the magical qualities he formerly attributed to reaching the top of the ladder. It is no longer *essential* to succeed, no longer *catastrophic* to fail. He evaluates his success and failure in more complex terms, giving more emphasis to the quality of experience, to the intrinsic value of his work and products, and their meaning to himself and others.

The imagery of the ladder is widespread in literature and mythology. The youthful hero (warrior, artist, noble contributor to humanity) is engaged in a quest that is often symbolized in terms of upward movement. The Faust story is a classic portrayal of the man at mid-life making a last desperate effort to achieve omnipotence by selling his soul to the Devil. In his case, the goal was power through knowledge—the hubris of the scientist. Yeats, who wrote his greatest poetry after mid-life, often depicted his experience of major developmental transitions. His poem "The Circus Animals' Desertion" contains these lines:

> . . . Now that my ladder's gone,
> I must lie down where all ladders start,
> In the foul rag-and-bone shop of the heart.

The relationship between Jung and Freud began when Jung was 31. Freud was 19 years older. It ended when Jung, then 38, stormily withdrew both from the friend-mentor ties and from his position of leadership in the psychoanalytic movement. The separation occurred when Jung was in the developmental period of Becoming One's Own Man. After a severe mid-life crisis, he went his own way, did his most creative work and established his own school of depth psychology. In his late adulthood Jung was pressed to authorize publication of the correspondence between Freud and himself conducted during his thirties. Acknowledging his reluctance to publish "that accursed correspondence," he wrote a friend:

> For me it is an unfortunately unexpungeable reminder of the incredible folly that filled the days of my youth [NB: age 31–38, DJL]. The journey from cloud-cuckoo-land back to reality lasted a long time. In my case Pilgrim's Progress consisted in my having to climb down a thousand ladders until I could reach out my hand to the little clod of earth that I am.

Men who have pursued the Dream in early adulthood must reduce its hold in the Mid-life Transition. Other men have betrayed the Dream, and must deal with this. Elia Kazan's novel *The Arrangement* is about a man who at 40 began a valiant struggle to regain his lost Dream or to kill himself. He had become an advertising executive rather than the novelist of his early Dream. Having succeeded in climbing the wrong ladder, he was now trapped in a fraudulent, empty life. His marriage was based on a relationship between his wife and the executive (but not the novelist) in him. They had been living for some years in an arrangement that was destructive to both of them. He was withholding the most valued parts of himself from the world and could not really love, work or play. He had lost touch with his Greek ethnicity and with the parents and extended family who represented it. During his early forties, he sought to confront the realities of his life, to overcome the illusions, to get off the ladder and to understand what he really wanted. Alternately clear-headed and "out of his mind," he had to sink to rock bottom before finding a basis for change. It took several years before he could commit himself to the choices around which a new life structure might be built.

Reviewing Kazan's novel when he was himself in his early forties, the novelist James Baldwin poignantly stated the issue:

> Though we would like to live without regrets, and sometimes proudly insist that we have none, this is not really possible, if only because we are mortal. When more time stretches behind than stretches before one, some assessments, however reluctantly and incompletely, begin to be made. Between what one wishes to become and what one *has* become there is a momentous gap, which will now never be closed. And this gap seems to operate as one's final margin, one's last opportunity, for creation. And between the self as it is and the self as one sees it, there is also a distance, even harder to gauge. Some of us are compelled, around the middle of our lives, to make a study of this baffling geography, less in the hope of conquering these distances than in the determination that the distance shall not become any greater.

Baldwin's own early adulthood was very different from that of Kazan's hero. He found far greater obstacles on the path to the writing career, though perhaps fewer seductions to lure him away from it. Still, Baldwin remained true to the Dream. By age 40 he was a distinguished writer and probably the foremost Black American writer of his generation. Yet he too had to acknowledge the distance "between the self as it is and the self as one sees it." In this book review, he links himself to the rest of us who "are compelled, around the middle of our lives, to make a study of this baffling geography." The geographical study, if I may extend the metaphor, is a mapping expedition in a territory often experienced as a desert, with long stretches of sand enlivened by occasional oases. The traveler discovers that some of the perceived water holes are mirages, others real, and that the territory contains far more resources than he has been able to see. Slowly he learns how to look below the surface and to make use of the treasures he finds there.

A person like Baldwin, who has lived his early adulthood more fully and with greater fidelity to the Dream than Kazan's hero, can draw more heavily on his earlier life in creating a new structure for Entering Middle Adulthood. Yet he too goes through a mid-life crisis. He experiences the disparities between early Dream and present reality, between the life he had hoped for and the life he has forged. Despite his success—and, because of his success—he has the sense of "a gap which will now never be closed." Acknowledging this gap is, as Baldwin claims, "one's last opportunity for creation."

Middle adulthood can be a creative era if, and only if, a man comes to terms with the gaps and contradictions and illusions that are so central in even the most creative early adulthood. When a man no longer feels that he must be a remarkable writer, craftsman or leader, he is more free to be himself and to work according to his own wishes and talents. The chances are that he will contribute more to society when his life contributes more to and expresses more of his self.

# Relationship with Young Adults: Mentoring and Fathering

There are, as we saw earlier, parallels between a man's relationship with a mentor and that with a special woman. The termination of an intense mentor relationship is in many ways like the ending of a love affair or a time of marital crisis. The younger man—and usually the older as well —goes through a process of de-illusionment. The younger man realizes, with some mixture of insight and distortion, that the relationship is not as beneficent as he had imagined; the mentor is less admirable, less devoted to him, more concerned with his own needs and interests—in short, more human—than he had previously recognized. If he can come to appreciate and tolerate the mentor's human frailties, and if the two of them can find a mutual basis for being friends or colleagues, they may find a way to form a new relationship. Usually, they do not.

Again, a key issue for the man in the Mid-life Transition is whether he can confront his illusions. He must come to terms with the little boy in himself who urgently needs a mentor figure to sustain him as he struggles to become the hero. As a man must give up the ladder and the Dream in their early adult forms, so must he give up the mentor. After the early forties it is almost impossible to be a protégé, though one can always use good counsel and friendship. It is time to become more of a mentor oneself.

If a man has had good enough mentoring, and if he can resolve some of the basic polarities of the Mid-life Transition, he will gladly take on greater responsibility for furthering the development of young adults. A young man in his thirties may do an excellent job of teaching, supervising and guiding younger persons. To be a mentor in a deeper sense, however, he must first have done the work of the Mid-life Transition.

The process of becoming a mentor in the Mid-life Transition is related in part to the change in generations. A man of 35 is fully adult, but he is still closely tied to people in their twenties. He is a half-generation older than they, and more in the position of older brother than father. As he passes 40, however, the difference is increased to a full generation. Young people regard him more as boss or "dad" than peer, and feel more separated from him by the barriers of age, authority and social network.

Initially he may feel great disappointment and loss at being ejected from the youthful generation. But gradually he finds that he too is changing. He is entering a world of work, family and community life in which his most immediate relationships are with people in their forties and fifties. He is becoming more distant from (and dominant over) the world of early adulthood. He is becoming a "senior" adult, something quite different from the "junior" adulthood of the thirties and the "novice" adulthood of the twenties.

The movement toward a more senior position is clearest when it involves a tangible advance in status: promotion to a higher level in the work organization; recognition as a more established writer, physician, skilled worker; entry into the senior level of the extended family, with responsibilities for the older and younger generations; gaining a more respected, senior position in religious, civic and other organizations. There are many forms of seniority and many levels of achievement, but some advancement is neeeded so that a man can make a place for himself in the middle adult generation.

At mid-life a man may have much contact with persons in their twenties and thirties, but he cannot participate as a full peer in their world. Even when the relationships are equal in many respects, he must offer them something distinctive that reflects his greater maturity, his membership in the generation of middle adulthood. As he forms a social base in his own generation, he can more readily reach across the generational boundaries and establish relationships of mutual benefit. He can keep what is youthful in himself, get in touch with both the Young and the Old in others, and use his middle age to enrich his relationships with the younger and older generations. If he remains too tied to young adults, he will be isolated from his own generation and split off from the Old in himself, and he may then lose all generational ties. At the other extreme, his ties with younger people may atrophy; but this is likely to mean that he is alienated from the Young in himself and has become prematurely Old.

Being a mentor with young adults is one of the most significant relationships available to a man in middle adulthood. The distinctive satisfaction of the mentor lies in furthering the development of young men and women—facilitating their efforts to form and live out their Dreams, to lead better lives according to their own values and abilities. Nurturing the development of children and adolescents is a major, age-appropriate function in early adulthood. It is the more elemental form of the parental impulse. During middle adulthood, a man can take a further step and nurture the development of young adults. Mentoring utilizes the parental impulse, but it is more complex and requires some degree of mid-life individuation. As he gains a stronger sense of self, and of his own continuing development in middle adulthood, a man is more able to foster the development of other adults.

There is a measure of altruism in mentoring—a sense of meeting an obligation, of doing something for another being. But much more than altruism is involved: the mentor is doing something for himself. He is making productive use of his own knowledge and skill in middle age. He is learning in ways not otherwise possible. He is maintaining his connection with the forces of youthful energy in the world and in himself. He needs the recipient of mentoring as much as the recipient needs him. It is time that this simple truth become more widely known.

The self-rejuvenation and creative work of both mentor and subject are furthered in "good enough" mentoring. But there are numerous hazards, and no relationship can be entirely free of them. The mentor is tempted to play the omnipotent Pygmalion, who, like Professor Higgins in Shaw's play and My Fair Lady, egocentrically tries to make his Eliza Doolittle (female or male) into an image of his own choosing. In the end Eliza must rebel in order to pursue her/his own development.

Another hazard is that the mentor is continually tempted to exploit the relationship, guiding the subject's work toward his own ends and using it for his own fame or fortune. Or, fearful that his protégé may outshine him, the mentor may engage in destructive forms of discipline and control. At the other extreme, the mentor may devote himself with excessive altruism to the student's needs, creating an imbalance that is ultimately destructive for both. Of course, both parties make their contribution to the nature and outcome of every relationship.

Mentoring is part of a developmental process that Erikson has called "generativity." Through this process, a man in middle adulthood forms a growing awareness of the continuity of human life and the flow of generations. He feels a concern for the upcoming generation of young adults, who must in time be ready for the responsibilities of middle age. It leads him to accept other burdens of his generation—exercising authority, providing leadership, making decisions that will have significant consequences for a widening circle of others. The basic process is similar for the farmer in his village, the worker in his factory or union, the executive in his firm, the political leader at a local, national or international level.

In his biography of Gandhi, Erikson has vividly portrayed the years from 40 to 60. At the start of middle adulthood, Gandhi returned to India from South Africa and embarked upon his political career. At 50, he led the Ahmedabad strike that became a testing ground for militant non-violence and established him as Mahatma, the leader of the entire nation against colonial rule. As he formed new relationships with his followers and with the generation of young adults, Gandhi was also working to be a good father to his young adult sons. The coexistence of his political success and his paternal failure, and the intensity of his investment in both, illustrate the complexities and paradoxes of adult development.

We have discussed in Chapter 15 the ways in which a man's mid-life work on the Masculine/Feminine polarity can affect his capability for mentoring, especially for being a mentor to women. This is potentially one of the most significant gains of the Mid-life Transition.

Good mentoring is one of the special contributions that persons in middle adulthood can make to society. Given the value that mentoring has for the mentor, the recipient and society at large, it is tragic that so little of it actually occurs. We are held back by limitations in our individual development and in our institutional structures. These limitations serve to intensify intergenerational conflict and undermine relationships between the youthful and middle-aged generations.

The process of becoming a mentor has parallels to the process of becoming a *father* in new ways to offspring who are entering early adulthood. As a man passes 40, his older children are likely to be in or near adolescence. Both father and offspring must give meaning to the fact that they are approaching early adulthood while he is leaving it behind. No longer a youthful father raising small children, he is a father entering middle age and seeking new ways of relating to his adolescent and young adult off-spring. As their generational status changes, he faces new responsibilities and new opportunities. At best, they can form mutually satisfactory relationships that include some degree of loving, teaching, learning, supporting, working and playing together. But this is not easy, and it is more the exception than the rule. If he continues to treat them as if they were small children, they may submit and fail to develop their own autonomy, or they may move away in defiance and contempt.

The difficulties between parents and their youthful offspring have been examined almost entirely from the viewpoint of the offspring. Much has been written about the damage done to the youth by their variously doting, controlling, rejecting, moralistic, seductive and withholding parents. If we also consider these relationships from the vantage point of the parents, we are less prone to make one generation the villain and the other the victim of the struggles that are so inherent in cross-generational relationships. Each side is necessarily part of the problem; with greater understanding it may also be part of the solution. Looking at the youth from a developmental perspective, we can more readily appreciate how their adolescent growing pains are reflected in their conflicts with parents. Well, parents too have growing pains; and they too need to be understood from a developmental perspective. I shall speak here of fathers. The same basic problems hold for mothers as well, though the specific issues may be different.

At around 40 a man is deeply involved in the Young/Old polarity. This developmental process has a powerful effect upon his relationships with his offspring and with young adults generally. When his own aging weighs heavily upon him, their exuberant vitality is more likely to arouse his envy and resentment than his delight and forbearance. He may be preoccupied with grievances against his own parents for the damage, real or imagined, that they have inflicted upon him at different ages. These preoccupations make him less appreciative of the (often similar) grievances his offspring direct toward him.

If he feels he has lost or betrayed his own early Dream, he may find it hard to give his wholehearted support and blessing to the Dreams of young adults. When his offspring show signs of failure or confusion in pursuing their adult goals, he is afraid that their lives will turn out as badly as his own. Yet, when they do well, he may resent their success. Anxiety and guilt may undermine his efforts to be helpful and lead him instead to be nagging and vindictive.

Feeling acutely the failure or emptiness of his life, he may resolve that they will have it better, that their success will make up for his disappointments. The genuine desire that his children be happy, according to their lights, is one of the great gifts a parent has to offer. When a father desperately wants his children to have the specific things he himself has missed, however, the paternal interest too easily becomes a tyrannical demand from which they must in time free themselves.

As he resolves the mid-life polarities within himself, a father can respond with more genuine care and wisdom to the needs of his offspring. He can value their youthful hopes, accept their youthful awkwardness, and offer his gifts with respect for their individuality.

## Modifying the Marriage

Many men are able to consider seriously in their late thirties and early forties marital problems that they previously ignored or only dimly acknowledged. A man may come to recognize that the marriage was flawed from the start. Without being strongly in love, he married for reasons such as family pressure, convention, rebellion, social mobility or guilt. It was thus difficult for the couple to create a satisfactory marital relationship. Over time things got worse rather than better. He remained in the marriage mainly out of attachment to family life, children and tradition. Now a great fog of illusion has been lifted. Suddenly he feels free for the first time to see his wife as a person and to understand the nature of their relationship. He is assailed by new realizations, each with its own admixture of insight, distortion and self-justification: there is no excitement between them; he cannot share his main interests and concerns with her; she regards him more as one of the children than as a friend and lover; she is disappointed over his failure to accomplish their early goals; she is resentful over his successes that have involved him in a world she cannot enjoy or share.

A man may discover at any age or period that his marriage is very different from what it seemed. But the process of change is different from one period to the next. During the late thirties, he may become acutely dissatisfied with his marriage. Struggling to become more a man and to be affirmed more by society, he comes to feel that his wife regards him as a little boy. He experiences her as overly controlling or smothering in some respects, depriving and humiliating in others. He may find another woman who is more understanding, sharing and sensually evocative, and with whom he feels more of a person. This may lead to a "breaking out"—divorce and perhaps remarriage—or to a life structure that includes both the wife and the "other woman."

When a man becomes dissatisfied with his marriage during the period of Becoming One's Own Man, he tends to attribute the problems more to his wife than to himself. He may overcome certain illusions about her and about the marital relationship, but he finds it difficult to examine his illusions about himself. His developmental thrust is more toward mastering the external world than toward exploring the self.

In the Mid-life Transition a man is more able to look at himself and deal with illusions about himself. He is more ready to ask: "How did I contribute to the marital difficulties? Did I want my wife to be a certain kind of maternal figure? What led me to enter the marriage, to stay in it for so long, and then to question it?"

Working on these questions is never easy, and the man himself is often only dimly aware of his changing thoughts and feelings. At the height of the difficulty he may be unable to talk clearly about it or to sort out the issues in his own mind: he feels trapped and without clear direction, pulled in opposite ways from the outside, full of conflict and despair inside.

Sometimes it is the wife who takes the initiative in reappraising the marriage. Being more free of familial responsibilities in her late thirties or early forties, she seeks to expand her own horizons and start new enterprises outside the home. She becomes the voice of development and change. Through the "division of labor" that often occurs in a marriage, the husband may then become the voice of the status quo. Moreover, a man who feels that his own youthfulness is in jeopardy may be more threatened than pleased by his wife's invitation to modify their lives. If he can accept her liberation from a primarily domestic role, the partners can work together toward a new and more intimate relationship, sharing well what they have in common and pursuing their separate interests on a more autonomous basis.

In some families, the wife's growing assertiveness and freedom are accompanied by the husband's severe decline. He has less authority and involvement in family life and feels increasingly obsolescent at work. When this occurs, it is a serious problem for the entire family.

Often it is the husband who makes the first steps toward change. In the period of Becoming One's Own Man or Mid-life Transition, he feels a strong need to modify their life. He tries—usually in an awkward or confused way—to convey this to his wife. Though sympathetic to his plight, she is afraid of rocking the boat. She regards his disappointment and malaise as an indirect assault upon her—an accusation that his troubles are basically her fault. She fears that his dissatisfactions, if faced by both of them, would lead to the recognition of more serious problems in their marriage and life structure. In this case he is the initiator of change, though often muddled in his initial efforts to clarify the problems and find a new direction, while she is the voice of stability and self-restriction.

The marital difficulties that surface in the Mid-life Transition may lead to various changes, from separation and divorce to reworking and improvement of the marriage. In some cases the grievances remain and increasingly divide the couple. They may divorce later (often, at around 50) or continue for years in a state of war or cold peace.

A developmental perspective is useful in understanding the marital difficulties. It often becomes obvious, after some years of marriage, that the husband and wife have developed at different rates and in different directions. The flaws that were present in the marriage at the start, plus other problems that entered over the course of time, become unbearable to one of the partners. The other partner, while actually having many grievances, denies them and clings to the status quo. The marital strains usually come to a head during a transitional period—especially the Age Thirty Transition or the Mid-life Transition—or during a crisis in Becoming One's Own Man. The conflict may be contained for several years, until a new transitional period or a marked change in circumstances upsets the equilibrium. The relationship will improve only if both partners are ready to work conjointly on it and are able to synchronize their developmental efforts more fully.

A man at this age may enter a serious love relationship with a younger woman. The spouse who "flies the coop"—it is usually the husband, but increasingly the wife—is typically the object of moral judgment rather than critical understanding by others. Those who place great value on the stability of the family often make an automatic negative judgment: men who do such things are seen as morally corrupt or temporarily unhinged. Or they see him as suffering from "middlescence," a term that carries a fine mixture of sympathy and depreciation. Ardent advocates of liberation, on the other hand, are often equally stereotyped in finding a man praiseworthy for getting out of his rut and doing his own thing.

If we are to understand it better, we have to look at the extramarital relationship from a developmental perspective. It reflects a man's struggles with the Young/Old polarity: he is asserting his youthful vitality at a time when he fears that the Young in him is being crushed by the dry, dying Old. If he is seeking merely to recapture his adolescence, or to keep it fixed immutably, the search will be in vain. On the other hand, the exploration of new relationships with women of various ages may enable him to get more in touch with the feminine in himself and others and to resolve the Masculine/Feminine polarity. He may then be able to utilize his youthful energies in a form appropriate to middle adulthood.

As the Mid-life Transition nears its end in the mid-forties, a man has to make new choices or recommit himself on different terms to old choices. If he is to improve his current marriage, or to enter a new one that will be an improvement on the old, he must become less illusioned about himself. He has to accept some responsibility for those aspects of his own motivation and character that keep him from forming more adult relationships with women. He will have to work for several years to develop a new kind of relationship with a wife or lover who is ready to join him in this mutual effort. Otherwise he will remain in a stagnant marriage destructive to both partners, or he will embark upon a new marriage (or a new set of relationships with women) that repeats the old hurtful themes with new variations.

The biographies to be presented in the following chapters will illuminate many of the changes I have just discussed regarding marriage, fatherhood, mentoring and the Dream. In Chapter 18, we shall see how the efforts made to reappraise and modify the life structure during the Mid-life Transition lead to the formation of a new structure in the next period, Entering Middle Adulthood.

# 17 The Life of John Barnes, Biologist

John Barnes was born in 1925 and grew up in a well-to-do, conservative, upper-class New England family with strong Puritan traditions. Integrity, Victorian sexual mores, strict control over emotion, avoidance of self-display, high intellectual achievement and public service were emphasized in his pre-adult world and exemplified by his father, a minister's son and successful Wall Street lawyer. John was the youngest child of middle-aged parents, a replacement for their one previous son who had recently died and been greatly mourned. He was cared for by servants and sent to boarding school at age 13.

As a child, he felt closest to the caretaker of his parents' summer estate, who taught him cabinetmaking and "was almost a foster father" to him. His family lacked intimacy and the free flow of affection. He was attached to his parents, especially his reserved father, with whom he shared a love of the sea and sailing. His mother preferred her oldest daughter and toward John was often critical and controlling.

> I have always suffered, I choose to believe, from a feeling of being low man on the totem pole in our family. To some extent, this was related to the parents being so much older. But in a very major way it was related to having two older sisters who, in the days when it made any difference— when the crunch came, they were right and I was wrong, no matter what the problem was. And the result of this is that I had a very severe "youngest member complex," which I still have to a very major extent, I'm afraid.

His early experiences of being a "mere replacement" and "low man on the totem pole" in the family, and far from first in his mother's affections, are the beginnings of a recurrent life theme: the desperate desire and striving to be first, yet ending up second, after all.

In a series of elite private boys' schools, he was a highly successful student and athlete. Falling short was always distressing to him. Though not very gregarious, he always had one or two close friends. When he was 8, his oldest sister began graduate school in biochemistry. Both brothers-in-law, one of whom John especially admired, were biological scientists as well. By age 12, he had formed the specific Dream of becoming a biochemist who would make great discoveries. Family encouragement, school success in science and hours in his home chemistry lab nourished his Dream and built his confidence.

John was attracted to several girls during his high school summers but was shy, afraid of intense involvement, constrained by family taboos and afraid of "being beaten out" by more forward fellows. Looking back, he feels he retreated to the security of his lab: "I didn't have to be concerned about these other things, I could always imagine that they weren't that terribly important."

## The Novice Phase

John Barnes went through his *Early Adult Transition* (age 18 to 23) as an undergraduate at Harvard College and in military service. For many young men, this is a time of discontinuity and experimentation. In John's case, there were few changes during these years. His school life, his relationships with parents and others, his Dream and life goals underwent no major revisions. Though secretly worried about the impersonal quality of his dealings with the few girls he managed to date, he found no way to change this.

In service, from age 19 to 21, in environments very different from those of his pre-adult world, he felt freer to open himself to new experience. He became fascinated with the construction machines his outfit employed and imagined himself running a construction company. This rival Dream reappears in his fantasy to this day. He also recalls with some excitement his first sexual experiences. Though these were neither full-fledged love affairs nor intimate friendships, he could now approach women sexually and felt more like a man.

At 21, he returned to college and pushed aside the interests that had started to blossom in the army. He soon began an affair with Ellen, an attractive Vassar student: "We got right into the sex routine here, fairly rapidly and, from my point of view, enjoyably. I guess I was carried away. It was my first experience along those lines. Carried away in the sense that we eventually got married."

He and Ellen were married right after graduation from college, largely he believes because this was "the right thing to do." She tried to back out at the last minute but he persuaded her to go through with the wedding. At 23, neither of them was able to face the problems in their relationship. He was unaware that Ellen did not enjoy their lovemaking but could not discuss it with him. Also, her interest turned from science to art, which held no interest for him. Neither could get involved in the other's Dream. Their relationship was not intimate, but he was not aware then that anything was missing. "It was not quite like an 'arranged marriage' in the foreign sense, but it might just as well have been."

In the period of *Entering the Adult World*, from age 23 to 28, John was an enthusiastic and successful graduate student at Yale. He earned his Ph.D. in biochemistry and stayed on for a year as a postdoctoral fellow. During these years, he did research under a prominent woman scientist he admired. She was clearly his mentor in the sense of being teacher, adviser and sponsor, but the relationship did not become very personal. He was completely dominated by his Dream: "Science, my work, the lab occupied me all my waking hours. It would never have occurred to me to be openly concerned—other than a lunchtime conversation or something like that—about national policy or anything else in those days. Grand times in the lab and that is all one did, really."

Barnes recognizes that his exclusive concern with mastery of his discipline, with hardly a thought about the wider scientific or social implications, was typical of the apprenticeship years in the physical sciences. But he also feels that his narrowness reflected naïveté about himself and the world around him. He connects it with his extraordinarily strong commitment to the Dream and with his omnipotent feeling that "I could do anything I would turn my hand to, simply by deciding I wanted to do it."

He was not able to invest much of himself in his marriage during these years. The sexual relationship was suspended for long periods. Ellen complained of his absence and his unresponsiveness to her feelings. They had their first child when he was 26, the second two years later, but parenthood failed to improve the marriage.

The *Age Thirty Transition*, from age 28 to 34, was a time of important changes in every area of Barnes's life. His career was marked by rapid growth and advancement. At 28, he was a relatively unformed novice, working in his mentor's laboratory. By 30, after a fellowship abroad, he found an exciting problem of his own on the frontier of his field and accepted an assistant professorship at Columbia University. He felt at home in this major institution in the Eastern intellectual establishment. It was the school to which his father and many generations of his family had gone. In joining the Columbia faculty, he strengthened his ties with family tradition.

Two years of painstaking, solitary experimentation led to an important discovery at 32, clearly a high point in his life. He spoke of the joys of his work and of "The Time of the Big Excitement":

I mean it's absolutely *consuming* . . . but you can only maintain this kind of excitement for relatively short periods of time. The drudgery of actually doing it took a couple of years. The high levels of excitement don't last for very long. In this sense they are quite equivalent to, say, sporting events, the other thing I get a big kick out of. As soon as we made the one crucial test, it showed a whole field opening up . . . and this was instantaneously obvious—just like opening a door. And *that* is the exciting part!

The most dramatic time in my scientific career came that December. I'd have to look it up in my lab book, but it's all written out in big capital letters. We were sitting in the lab one night in front of the spectrophotometer, just carefully mixing carefully prepared solutions, and we got a spectacular result for which I am now famous. I mean, there is no magic to it. We just went through some perfectly straightforward operations and came up with what was at the time a very unexpected result. You don't think twice about it today. But that was very exciting. And in the course of about a week we produced more fundamental information than in the entire rest of my scientific career, either before or since. I've actually done fairly well since then. It's worth a lot of dull drudgery to have such periods of real excitement. They wouldn't excite anyone else obviously. It's a very personal thing.

With the publication of his discovery, he "became recognized . . . as a promising young biochemist!" Early promotion (at 33) to a tenured position was a powerful affirmation. He felt that he had proven his worth in the scientific elite.

Many scientists are engaged in a modern form of the ancient heroic quest, complete with the vanquishing of rivals for the supreme (Nobel) prize. (More than half of our scientists also experienced themselves, in their first marriages, as rescuers of a damsel in distress.) In fantasy, John Barnes was now the young hero, charging ahead toward a future of ever more fundamental discoveries and the acclaim of his world.

The change in his marital life was initially painful, yet ultimately an improvement. A few months after their move to Columbia, Ellen asked for a divorce. She was in love with someone else and wanted to remarry. An attempt at reconciliation was followed by a "civilized" divorce. Despite Barnes's relief at this solution to a mutually hurtful situation, the breakup of his marriage initiated a crisis:

Well, it was a big shock to a number of things. One, to be so totally unaware, initially, that the situation was getting as bad as it obviously was. I was perfectly aware that it wasn't very good, but it didn't occur to me as anything extreme. And there was a very personal insult in that Ellen had been carrying on with a young man without my knowing about it for some time, a fellow I knew perfectly well. The insult was not that she was doing this, but that I didn't recognize it. And *that* really shook me up. Obviously

I was not tuned in to the local environment and that message came through very strongly.

From the moment of the initial break, through the next few years of trauma, the development of awareness of what people were thinking, with or without their saying it, took place. I'm no expert at it now, but I'm a damn sight better than I was. I time it from that point, because never before had my lack of concern with this kind of thing been brought so forcefully to my attention. It had been stated often enough by other people, but I used to write it off. It finally came home at that point—a little late, I must say, but still. My wife tried to explain what she missed in our relationship by referring to "understanding" and "feelings." But I simply did not understand what these words meant to her. They didn't mean much to me at the time. And discussions along these lines, including a family therapy session, are what catalyzed the change, among other things. I think she was probably right, even though I didn't really know what she was talking about at the time. It's made a lot sense since.

During the next three years as a bachelor, Barnes deliberately made more room in his life for personal relationships. He got closer to one of his sisters and her family than ever before, and had several affairs. At 33 he felt ready to marry again. His courtship of Ann, though somewhat deliberate and awkward, provided a good basis for a relationship that became increasingly intimate over the years.

Ann was single, his own age, and an extremely competent research associate in a different area of biology. She blamed herself for her failure to get the Ph.D. degree and for her limited professional advancement, and she found much satisfaction in her work for admired senior scientists. Her background, formative experiences and interests were so similar to John's that the two seemed to be "cut from the same cloth." Their relationship, though not very romantic or passionate, grew from congeniality into a deep bond of affection and mutual understanding neither had ever experienced before. They were well suited to play complementary rather than competing roles, in the social as well as the psychological sense. She admired his work and understood his struggles in the competitive academic system. He, in turn, respected her as a scientific, intellectual and sports companion and supported her career aspirations. They married at 34, after a year of courtship.

## Settling Down and Becoming One's Own Man

Barnes's stable life structure of the Settling Down period, from age 34 to 41, was built upon the choices and developmental changes of the Age

Thirty Transition. He defined his tasks as a new member of the senior faculty and worked very hard for advancement. At the same time, he and his wife developed their relationship, built a life together and became parents. They bought a modest house in a lovely small town with a yacht harbor. Avoiding formal social life whenever possible, they led an active life, often just the two of them, enjoying each other while working together in house and garden, hiking and skiing, but above all on their beloved boat away from it all.

Ann Barnes, too, strictly controls her emotions, but she is more perceptive and more strongly involved with others. Through their deepening relationship, he gradually learned to sense her moods, to understand her as a person and to share his personal concerns. Ann often drew his attention to relationships and emotional issues that he had ignored. He, in turn, was supportive to her through three difficult years of psychoanalysis during her (and his) late thirties.

Occupationally, the Settling Down period began in the aftermath of his big discovery and early promotion. It was a time of high hopes and great self-confidence. A year later, at 35: "There began to be some question about whether what I was doing professionally was, in fact, going to save the world; 'saving the world' is always couched in the terms that the world will recognize that they have been saved and give you due adulation." He realized, with a shock, that he had been working for the last three years on the spin-off from the original discovery. If he wanted a distinguished research career, it was high time to define a fundamental new problem and to organize a large research enterprise. His uncertainty about what was the most promising direction for his research grew into a minor crisis. For the first time, he had serious doubts about his creative talent. His Dream of running a construction company now reappeared in full force. He had fantasies of running bulldozers and of leaving science altogether. The crisis was short-lived, as he embarked on an ambitious new project.

But young Professor Barnes found himself increasingly involved in the governing structure of his department. He became known as an articulate speaker and leader. Teaching and administration began to take up much of his time, while his research project moved at a snail's pace. He felt increasingly constrained under an autocratic chairman.

At 37, Barnes became director of his own lab, refused several job offers, and received an early promotion to full professor. His project had been funded, but progress was slow and the chances for success uncertain. At this point, an old friend in the university administration put pressure on him to take on the chairmanship of a related department that was in decline. As his friend was well aware, this special mission appealed to John Barnes's ambition to become number one as well as to his aristocratic sense of noblesse oblige—all the more important because of his strong family tie to Columbia. On the other hand, Barnes knew that the chairmanship would interfere with his research, and he had the scientist's low opinion of administration as a form of work. Despite serious misgivings, he began the chairmanship at 38.

Barnes's striving to become his own man proceeded along two lines: his attempt to become a scientist of the first rank through pioneering research; and his advancement to leadership positions in the laboratory and the university. Between 33 and 37 he became a "senior member" in his institution. Yet, as he told us several years later, he still felt very "junior," much as he had in relation to his family in childhood. His inner autonomy, too, was still very limited. The largely unrecognized "little boy" in him still needed to become number one and constantly sought recognition from his colleagues. This made him vulnerable to the pressures of the university and deflected him from the pursuit of his Dream.

Predictably, John Barnes took his administrative mission seriously and succeeded in strengthening the department during his three-year term. He looks back on this as a job well done. But the chairmanship brought major changes in his professional life, in his view of society, and in his relationship to himself. He gave much less time and energy to research, delegating most of it to others. He experienced this change with a profound sense of loss: he was separated not only from "the lab," the symbolic cradle of science, but from the creative part of his Self. At the same time, he became increasingly involved in policy issues affecting his department, his university and his discipline at the national and international levels. He became chairman in 1963, and his social involvement received great impetus from the crisis in the nation's life during the 1960s. He wanted to contribute not only to basic science but also to the solution of social problems.

When John and Ann were married, they tried to have children but did not succeed. Ann then reconciled herself to this and invested more in her career. She was in psychoanalysis during her late thirties. At 40 "the bombshell dropped": she was pregnant. Terrified that parenthood would destroy her career, her marriage and the degree of inner equilibrium she had achieved through psychoanalysis, she was angry with her husband for making her pregnant. John was pleased with the prospect of another child, but accepted her decision to get a legal abortion on the grounds of age. Legal permission for abortion was not granted. As she later realized, she was secretly delighted to become a mother.

At 41, Ann delivered a healthy boy they named Henry after John's father. Despite ample means for paid help, Ann decided to become a full-time mother for a while. The first two years of her "retirement" were extremely difficult. She missed her work keenly and struggled with feelings of resentment, depression and anxiety about motherhood. This stressful period began just when her husband was moving into his own mid-life crisis.

Barnes's Dream assumed greater urgency as he approached 40. He believed that most creative work in science is done before then. A conversation with his father's lifelong friend around this time made a lasting impression on him. The older man confided that he had by now accepted his failure to become a "legal star" and was content to be a competent and respected tax lawyer. He had decided that stardom is not synonymous with the good life; it was "perfectly all right to be second best." At the time, however, Barnes was not ready to scale down his own ambition. Instead, he decided to give up the chairmanship and devote himself fully to his research.

He stepped down from the chairmanship as he approached 41, and his project moved into its final phase. This was a crucial time for him, the culmination of years of striving. For several months, one distraction after another claimed his attention and heightened the suspense. He became the father of a little boy, and that same week was offered a prestigious chair at Yale. Flattered and excited, he felt that this was his "last chance for a big offer." But in the end Barnes said no. He found that he could not make a change at this stage of his work. Also, their ties to family and friends, and their love of place, were now of much greater importance to him and Ann. She said: "The kudos almost got him, but now we are both glad we stayed."

## The Mid-life Transition

A few months after refusing the Yale offer, Barnes completed his research project and solved the problem. To his great disappointment, a team at another university had found the solution two weeks sooner. Neither Barnes nor his rivals were nominated for the Nobel Prize. Although his was an achievement of great importance and brought him international recognition, Barnes had a feeling of deep failure. At 41, he had completed a line of research begun twelve years before. The frontiers of biology were now shifting and there was no chance that the body of his work built throughout early adulthood would merit the prize in the future. He had not become a scientist of the first rank and there seemed little chance he would ever do so. Completion of the project was the culminating event of his early adulthood and the beginning of his Mid-life Transition.

The year immediately following the end of the project, from age 41 to 42, had the character of a moratorium, a breathing spell when he avoided making new commitments but did a lot of inner work. In his mind, he was a failure and his life lacked direction. During the interviews two years later, memories of this time were still so painful that he could hardly discuss them. His wife was more able to identify what had happened:

> I often have wondered what would have happened had the problem been finished when he was 25 or 35 rather than 41. He finished it at the same time that this feeling of "I-don't-know-ism" comes on—at least judging by all our friends. Oh, my brother had it terribly. He was just awful. But it seems to get over by the time you're 45 or so. So that, combined with a sabbatical, finishing his problem, Henry suddenly forcing John to think about kids again . . . he was just thinking: Oh, my other kids are just about old enough now! And the messy department situation, which was obvious at the time. All of these together made it miserable for him for two or three years. And added to the fact that I was not very helpful there for a while. While I was retiring, so to speak, I found it very hard.

The Barnes family spent half of that first year in Europe, supported by a Guggenheim fellowship. Barnes had a post as a visiting professor at the British university where his friend Dennis was a leading scientist. Everywhere, Barnes was recognized as a pioneer in his field. These six months were professionally very fruitful, and were of even greater value personally. He discovered that several of his European counterparts, even those more successful than he, were plagued by feelings of disappointment and uncertainty much like his own. He had long and intimate talks with Dennis:

> One of my very good friends happens to be an Englishman who is in almost precisely the same situation. He is a little further advanced professionally than I am, but we are almost identical in terms of age, marital problems, business problems, if you will, and approach to life. It's very amusing. We both have very strong professional drives which we discuss considerably and aren't sure they're a very good thing. And we both have the tendency to lone-wolf it.
>
> We discussed all aspects of our family problems and the intimate details of our professional lives and our feelings about where the future is going. We're both suffering from the same problem, you know: we've done what we set out to do ten or fifteen years ago—now what? He's a fellow of the Royal Society, a big wheel scientifically. You'd think this would be all solved. But it isn't for him and it isn't for me. We worry and talk about this a great deal.

Although they preferred to consider these problems in terms of external options and rational choices, Barnes and his friend came to confide what each could barely admit to himself: acute disappointment at not winning the Nobel Prize, a feeling of failure in the face of considerable achievement. They agreed that they had an inordinate desire for recognition, that their lives were far too dominated by ambition. They were self-contained, removed from others. In some way, not clear to them, they were not as good husbands or human beings as they wished to be.

Little Henry was then only a year old and Ann was having a difficult time with new motherhood and the interruption of her career. Both Ann and John felt they were receiving less from the other than they had before the child was born. She was resentful toward him for the pregnancy. He resented her decision to care for the youngster in their comfortable English house rather than accompany him on a trip to the Middle East. Only the warm friendship with Dennis and his family kept them from feeling utterly miserable.

During the year following their return to Columbia, the family life improved greatly. Ann made friends with mothers of children Henry's age and learned that her difficulties were no worse than the others'. She became involved in community activities. Henry, a healthy and active but "pretty easy" 3-year-old, was a great pleasure. They enjoyed taking him on hiking and camping trips. He kept them from long-distance sailing but otherwise didn't interfere with their middle-aged lives as much as they had feared. They bought a choice piece of land and made plans to build a new and bigger home. This expressed Ann's growing sense of herself as a wife and mother and of her place within the community. She was much more content with her life and was not suffering from the old depressions. One remaining problem was Ann's reluctance to have sexual relations because of her fear of another accidental pregnancy. Despite this, John—who turned 43 this year—felt very committed to his marriage and spoke warmly of their increasing closeness.

Barnes's professional life too was in a state of transition. It took almost three years to complete his full monograph on the major project. He obtained grants to continue research in this area, and many students and junior faculty were employed in his lab. But his own interest in it was limited. He began a small project in a new area but was not ready to make a big personal investment in it.

Just as he began the new work, the university administration urged him to take the chairmanship of his original department, which was in desperate straits. He was the unanimous choice for this mission and reluctantly accepted it for a three-year term.

Now 44, Barnes started the chairmanship and began to rebuild the department. He also became an associate dean of the medical school and informed himself about the school's organizational structure, politics and personalities. He invested enormous time and energy in these tasks. The challenge excited him and he was clearly a fine administrator. Yet he did not see this as a valued or enjoyable part of his professional life. He denied any interest in leadership or power, and was frustrated because administration kept him away from research. He strongly maintained that he accepted this burden only out of a sense of obligation to the university. At the same time, he understood that this temporary assignment offered him a way to keep busy and feel useful while he did the inner work that would enable him to take a new step.

Barnes felt that he had reached an impasse in his life. For some time now, he had been unable to make the critical decisions that faced him. Worse, he could not find a basis on which to make them. His Dream of becoming a scientist of the first rank had formerly given meaning to his life and provided clear goals. The enterprise of the first half of his life was now completed, but his Dream was unrealized and, as it seemed, unrealizable. Suddenly there was nothing to strive for. Life had no meaning.

In interviews just before and after his 44th birthday, Barnes expressed an urgent need for a worthwhile enterprise to which he could devote his life. But how could he define what was worthwhile? He seriously considered giving up his profession. Perhaps it was a mistake to continue on a path chosen when he was 12 years old. He wanted to make a social contribution but could not think of a suitable role. The ten interviews ranged over all aspects of his life. Again and again, he returned to the same question: should he recommit himself to research? Each time he approached the problem from a different angle, bringing out another conflict. It became clear that he was working on a number of mid-life issues and attempting to manage the painful feelings associated with them. This was especially hard because of his rationalistic approach.

One problem was the discrepancy between his youthful Dream and his actual accomplishment. Asked whether he had come to terms with his failure to win the Nobel Prize, he frankly admitted: "Well, I don't know about coming to terms with it, but clear recognition of it, certainly. So is anything (in research) worth doing if the prize is still not around the corner?"

Despite his justified pride in many past accomplishments, he regarded himself as not "in the first rank." To a man of his aspirations, this was a bitter blow.

> I think I can place myself fairly accurately in the scientific spectrum at the moment as being, well, toward the top of the second class. There

are the real luminaries at the top—regardless of how they got there. And then there's the rest of us, arrayed in various rings below. In the second class, I would stand fairly well, I think, in terms of reputation in my own field.

I think the status level at the moment is just about what it deserves. You know, good, solid, well-recognized but not brilliant. And that's probably the way it is. I'd like to think of it differently, but obviously something's going to have to happen to change my mind as well as everybody else's. And it's a little hard to see that happening at the moment. So, I don't know, it's a very . . . it's a very tough business.

Concern about aging increased his pessimism about his prospects as a researcher. He was in excellent health and participated actively in several sports. Though he often felt fatigued, he thought "much of it would go away" if he reduced his work pressures and got more exercise. But he was very much afraid of a decline in his mental powers and creativity: "One does atrophy," and "I haven't had a really good idea in years." At times he is eager to begin work on a big problem in the new area, to feel creative and experience again the excitement of discovery. But he fears it may be too late for him:

The only problem that interests me is the one which is going to topple the field, or not topple it, but, well—shake its foundations. We really have to begin at the fundamental level. To work out one more detail on some otherwise well-understood system is to me just not interesting. But, I mean, it's also impossible to do, for most of us. But going right along parallel with that feeling is also the feeling that: Jesus, you know, you're getting on and . . . It's characteristic of the field, as we all know, it's not historically well documented, but by the time you're 40 you've blown it.

. . . the decision about what to do is an agonizing one because *it's a little late.* If you make a mistake now, it isn't as though you can run back in the lab and, you know, use up a few months of your time. If you decide to do anything, by and large it means cranking out a tremendous machine, to get money, to hire some people, to get the job going and the lab set up, and it takes a long time. If you're going to do it, and you make a mistake, you've lost not a few months but a few years. And that's too long. So you have to choose wisely. Well, goddamnit, there's a lot of smart fellas around now and, uh, how are you going to make sure that you choose something that's a little more intelligent than what they do? And the answer is generally that you do not. So it's a very agonizing problem. And since the young fellows coming along are very good, and have got a little more time to worry about it than you do, there's the tendency to think that, well, maybe this lab work really isn't so important, you know. Maybe we can make our contribution in some other area.

We might say that John Barnes was in the process of giving up the image of himself as the youthful hero. He had become aware of several illusions about himself. One was the sense of omnipotence. "Until very recently," he said, "I really felt that I could do *anything* I would put my hands to. That is slowly going now, I think. But this was a very strong component of the whole thing."

Another trait about which he felt great shame and embarrassment was the wish for kudos—for great recognition and acclaim:

> What I keep thinking I would like to do is get off in a corner where I could do my own work, and just see. Now why isn't that totally satisfying and why don't we just head in that direction? Well, I don't know what the answer is, but my impression is that the answer is very unpleasant. And here's where I simply can't get away from the thing that really does trouble me, which is an intense desire for kudos. Now that means being recognized. There are various levels within that. By all odds the most intense and most important is one's professional colleagues; most, of course, are not at the institution where you work. The only way in which you maintain kudos there is to carry out research which is significant in quality and, if it is highly significant, the larger the amount the more the kudos obviously. You have a team that is producing the maximum amount, which is always much more than you can do with your own hands. It's a big organization. So you sit behind a desk and you don't do anything, really, you become a research administrator, willy nilly. . . . You realize very quickly, even with the graduate students, that there's a thing that counts. Sure, it's getting something accomplished, but why does it count? It counts because you get kudos for it from your peers, scientifically. . . . I realized this as a graduate student, I suppose. But it didn't really take the kind of grip that it has at the moment.

He would like to overcome this childish wish to be "first":

> Why do you want kudos anyway? What difference does it make? It doesn't. It seems to me there must be something missing from one's inner man if you need to be supported by having the adulatory comments of the external world in whatever form they come.

Barnes's relationships with students and colleagues provide a beautiful example of a man in the middle of a generational transition. He can no longer accept a more senior person as mentor. The idea of becoming a mentor himself is attractive, but he is just starting to move in that direction. The issue of mentoring came up in his response to a picture in the Thematic Apperception Test showing a young man and a middle-aged man. Barnes told a story about two actual scientists: the youthful Perutz working with his mentor, Sir Lawrence Bragg. In the story, they are talking

about a problem Bragg "gave" to Perutz, for which the protégé won the
Nobel Prize some twenty years later. Later, Barnes and the interviewer
had the following exchange:

> DJL: In 1960, you were Perutz, right? (Barnes bursts into laughter.)
>
> B: And now we're Bragg (laughing).
>
> DJL: Which one are you now?
>
> B: My ideas are still better than anybody else's. I'm just not quite as
> confident about that as I used to be (laughter).
>
> DJL: Maybe you're the guy in between, somewhere in the middle . . . ?
>
> B: Somewhere in the middle is really an accurate description. I don't
> know how to put myself there. I still have a feeling that there's something
> left professionally, in the sense of thinking and doing myself. It's difficult
> to put myself in the Bragg situation. Not that he doesn't have a lot left,
> but still, we're not of that advanced scientific age. The other thing, I really
> have no one in the Perutz category. It's hard to have this kind of a situation.
> I have nobody that I'm fostering as an individual, much younger, because
> I think, "Boy, this is the greatest guy to come down the pike."

In this connection, he referred to his "youngest member complex":

> I'm amused that it has only become evident to me very recently that
> within our department I'm looked on as one of the older men [chuckles].
> Incredible! I'm just not used to that at all. When the students think about
> talking to younger faculty, they are not including me, and that's come as
> something of a shock, I must say. This has ramifications in all one's deal-
> ings. I always tended to think, until very recently, that the other fellow's
> ideas were probably better than mine, because in general he was a year or
> two older. That, I think, is dictated by my early experience as the young-
> est member in the family.

During his early forties the social value of his work and the meaning
of his life have assumed increasing importance for him. In his twenties and
thirties Barnes had enjoyed work "at the expense of other responsibilities,"
and had taken for granted that his work had social value. During the Mid-
life Transition he came to question this.

The questioning was stimulated partly by social changes occurring in
the late 1960s, changes that echoed Barnes's own inner depression and
self-devaluation. One was the dethroning of the scientist as culture hero.
Science and technology were no longer hailed as instruments of progress,
but attacked as agents of destruction and dehumanization. Instead of
research, the new movements demanded social change and greater "relevance" in the university. At the same time, the Nixon administration was
sharply curtailing funds for basic research and graduate education. For

Barnes, these were direct attacks on what he held most sacred. Yet he could not help but agree with the critics:

> The new element that's been injected—which is a very disturbing one, I must admit—is that in the early sixties research in molecular biology was very much "in," and today it's very much "out." The tenor of the public clearly is: "The hell with this goddamned research, let's get on with the delivery of something"—health care or pretzels or what it is they want. Which is a definite change. I think the real shocker to me was: "My God, isn't that tremendous, we got to the moon, now let's close up the program." . . . Yet I'm also inclined to be sympathetic with the feelings of the public. I think maybe we *do* have more than we need.

As a liberal in the late 1960s, Barnes had difficulty finding public goals worth pursuing or social movements worth joining, and this coincided with his personal sense of futility. While his own commitment to science was in question, he couldn't see his way to a new role, either as a teacher or an administrator. He felt guilty applying for research funds:

> I guess I have a hang-up on that. The only problem I can see that's of any significance is population control, in which I have no expertise at all. There isn't any other single problem which makes the slightest bit of difference. If you don't solve the population problem, you can forget the rest of it.

At 44, in his more optimistic moods, he was attracted by various humanitarian causes and social programs, perhaps most strongly by efforts to rebuild the inner cities. He was appalled at the contrast between his own luxurious life and the squalid housing in the city nearby. However, he had no special expertise in this field.

> Probably in this day and age it's almost impossible to consider making a positive contribution. So the other way to look at it is, you want to do something which is clearly not negative. . . . I'm very intrigued by organizations like the Peace Corps, which seems to be so totally altruistic. I would say the answer at the moment is very mixed. I'm not at all convinced that you can help people in that way. Sometimes you may help people most by hitting them over the head with a brick—at least a figurative one. It's very hard to know how to be altruistic. . . . It's very clear that you don't help people in the standard way we thought in the past about helping them.

Barnes had found no basis at 44 on which to make new life choices. The ultimate despair is that life may have no meaning at all:

> The thing that's distressing to me at the moment is the absence of a goal that I consider worthwhile. I have to couch it in the framework of

science, because that's the only thing I'm really trained to do. But I think the problem is perfectly general. I don't in all honesty see a goal that's worth having at the moment. . . . This is what really shakes me up. It worries me much more than what the hell I'm going to do in the next year or two in detail. Usually people say, well, you know, the preservation of the human race. Why? That's not a useful goal as far as I'm concerned, if that's all there is to it.

Barnes often asked himself whether it was really necessary to have a goal. His brother-in-law had retired early and enjoyed himself, but this did not seem satisfactory:

There are two things I enjoy—being in a lab and being on a boat. Both of these are just personal enjoyments. But neither one of them necessarily contributes a damn thing to anybody else. Now maybe that's all right; I mean, so what? I don't know, it's tough to really see it. About twice a month my wife and I decide we're going to toss in the sponge. We'll just resign and go off on the boat. The youngster's old enough, so that's no problem. That's marvelous. It certainly sticks your head in the sand, gets you away from everything and you don't have to bother about contributing to anything anymore. But it isn't enough.

Even the wish for symbolic immortality, for leaving a legacy, has come into question:

But the leaving behind thing is intimately related to the question of whether I think it makes a damn whether anybody leaves anything behind or not. That's a value judgment on society. If it really isn't worth saving, then whether you leave something behind or not really doesn't make any difference.

John Barnes's pessimism at 44 expressed yet another aspect of mid-life despair. The dark side of life—death and destructiveness, evil in the world and in himself—came home to him in a more immediate way than ever before. He wanted to be the hero who gains immortality by saving the world; and at the same time he wanted to destroy the world or run away and let it destroy itself. Along with his strong humanitarian concerns, he had doubts that society is worth saving: "My feelings about humanity are unprintable."

It was apparent from Barnes's description of his dreams, of his problems in dealing with anger, of his attitude toward the interviewing (he once half-jokingly reproached the interviewer for having "singularly failed" to redefine and solve his problems), that in this phase of his life feelings were beginning to mean much more to him. This reflected and intensified a change going on more generally in the course of his Mid-life Transition.

Barnes had always presented himself as a rational, tough-minded person, somewhat removed from others and rather unaware of his own feelings. Now he was becoming much more interested in understanding others and himself. Just a few years earlier, he was astonished when people told him how angry he had gotten at a meeting; now he began admitting to his wife how angry he got at meetings.

The change was also evident in his relationship with his father. Until his early forties, this relationship had been rather distant. He was not able to say much about his father's death when it occurred, but his grief and anger were indirectly expressed in the themes of death, violence and abandonment described in his dreams. At the end, he reminisced about his father for the first time, said how "very fond" he had been of him and how much he regretted that his father never permitted him truly to know him.

Gradually, John Barnes was losing the illusion of immortality. His growing sense of mortality was expressed in his comment on a picture in the Thematic Apperception Test. It was of a woman sitting with her face buried in her arms: "She is distraught," he said. "Maybe this is part of the trauma—there really isn't any future!"

When we talked with John Barnes again at age 46, his Mid-life Transition was ending. He was still struggling with some of the contradictions in his life and had not found any one thing to replace his Dream. But he had greatly clarified his problems and had begun to define a life structure for middle adulthood.

His family life was continuing along the lines established earlier. With his mother's death soon after his father's, John's entry into the oldest generation of the family was complete. He, Ann and Henry had moved into their new home by the sea, which gave them much pleasure. Satisfied that his mission as department chairman had been accomplished, he stepped down at 46 and began a large project in his new research field. He was elected to the National Academy of Science.

The most striking change between 44 and 46 was his greatly decreased concern for advancement and recognition, and his ability to gain intrinsic satisfaction from work and social contribution. He and his wife were considering how to use their wealth in a socially constructive way. They had recently made a loan to a Black university employee, enabling him to buy a home in the suburbs. Barnes belittled this as a mere "conscience-salving" effort, but it clearly meant a great deal to him. He was sensitive to the problems for the recipient in this relationship and concerned about members of the man's family in an individualized way.

A second change was the waning tyranny of the Dream and a lessened compulsion "to do the right thing," in favor of greater inner autonomy.

"And so I'm coming around to the point of view that it really isn't so much whether it's administration or straight research or teaching or whatever," he said. "The burning issue is that the collection of things you do should seem worthwhile, from your own point of view."

At 50 Barnes had shaped a relatively satisfactory life structure for middle adulthood. His marriage and family life continued to go well. His wife had found a satisfactory balance between involvement in family, part-time professional work and the ecology movement. His relationship with his nine-year-old son gave him great satisfaction. He had administrative duties as head of a large laboratory, but resisted pressures to take chair-manships and other leadership positions in the university. He was actively involved in the new research projects and discovered with relief that his creative powers were undiminished. His lab was sought out by a stream of graduate students and postdoctoral fellows, and he greatly enjoyed his mentor relationships with several talented young people.

He had given up the image of himself as a youthful hero going out to save the world, but had not yielded to the threatening specter of the dried-up, dying old man. He accepted himself as a middle-aged man of considerable achievement, experience and integrity—and of serious short-comings. He felt privileged to be able to do work he enjoys, and he was content to make a modest social contribution as parent, concerned citizen, scientist, teacher and mentor to the younger generation. He had a sense of well-being.

# 18 Entering Middle Adulthood

A man is in the Mid-life Transition as long as he is involved in terminating early adulthood and initiating middle adulthood—as long as he is, so to say, within the great divide that separates and connects the two eras. At around 45 (plus or minus two years), the developmental tasks change. He can no longer give so much energy to reappraising the past and reintegrating the polarities. It is time to begin a new period, Entering Middle Adulthood. The main tasks now are to make crucial choices, give these choices meaning and commitment, and build a life structure around them. Like Entering the Adult World in the twenties, this period follows a cross-era transition and is devoted to forming a life structure for the start of a new era.

Some men make satisfactory provisional choices during the Mid-life Transition and by 45 are ready to commit themselves to these choices and create a new structure. These men form an integrated structure early in Entering Middle Adulthood and use the remainder of this period to enrich their lives within this framework (see Ralph Ochs and Richard Taylor, below). This sequence is most likely to occur when the developmental work of the Mid-life Transition serves mainly to reaffirm and enhance the choices that a man made in a previous period, or that he made provisionally during the early forties.

For example, Richard Taylor decided at 40 to make novel writing his primary occupation. This was an important but provisional choice. If it had not worked, he would have been faced at 42 or 45 with the dreadful task of giving it up and forming another occupation. Fortunately, it did work, and by 45 the occupation of novelist had become a pillar for his emerging life structure. Similarly, at 40 he married the woman he had loved for several years; they hoped for a good and durable marriage but did not yet know what they could build together. Over the next few years this crucial but provisional choice, like that of occupation, became firmly established in his life.

In most cases, a man is not able to form a stable structure at the start of Entering Middle Adulthood. For various reasons, the life he has at 45 does not feel right to him or does not work well enough for others so that they will help sustain it. Although he wants to make major commitments and build a new structure, it is not easy to do so. He may need most of the period of Entering Middle Adulthood to establish the choices on which a new life structure can be built.

Many new steps must be taken, and their exact nature and phasing vary widely. A man may separate from his wife, quit his job, terminate a significant relationship with a friend, mentor or lover, move away from his present neighborhood or region, break out of his whole early adult world. These are, as it were, negative choices. They create a space within which he may succeed in improving his life, but he may find himself temporarily—and unhappily—suspended within this space until he can go on to make some positive choices and start the restructuring.

The rebuilding process, too, requires many steps. He must do some exploring to determine what options the world holds for him—and often there seem to be none. He has to make and test various preliminary choices. Some do not work; he has to overcome his disappointment and go on to others. He may enter a series of casual or serious love relationships before finding one that provides a mutually satisfactory basis for enduring choice; he may find that the answer is no such relationship at all; or he may find no answer. He may try several jobs, or several occupations, before settling for one that suits him well—or poorly. He may make several geographical moves before finding a place that he likes or that offers him a tolerable niche.

In short, an integrated structure may emerge early or late in Entering Middle Adulthood, or not at all. A man stays in this period, however, as long as his predominant developmental task is to create a satisfactory structure. The period ends when the task changes and he enters a new transition.

Let us look at some of the diverse ways in which men go about Entering Middle Adulthood. As I've mentioned, the men in our study ranged in age from 35 to 45 during the initial interviewing. Two years later we did follow-up interviews with most of them. The four men chosen for more intensive study (Barnes, Namson, Paulsen and Tracy) were again interviewed a few years later. We had minor contact after the regular interviewing with a few others. As a result, we have additional information on the lives, after age 45, of fifteen men who were aged 42 to 45 at the outset.

On the basis of these lives, we have constructed a picture of the changes that occur in Entering Middle Adulthood. Although this picture is more sketchy than those for the preceding periods, it does show some of the common themes and individual variations during this period. The average age at which it began was 45.5. The earliest was 44, and none of the men reached 47 without beginning this period. We doubt that it can start before 43 or after 48.

Taking each occupational group in turn, I shall describe the lives of several men in the period of Entering Middle Adulthood.

# Workers

The workers, like the other occupational groups, exhibit a wide range of variability in the nature and satisfactoriness of the life structures they form in Entering Middle Adulthood.

Perhaps the most stable, yet continually evolving life was that of Ralph Ochs. At 45, he is still working in the plumbing department of the factory where, at 18, he started as an apprentice to his father. A man of great integrity and modest aspirations, he enriched his life over the course of early adulthood by his active involvement in organizing and running a union, becoming a shop steward, and, as he passed 40, having increasingly mentorial relationships with other workers. His major investment is now in his family. He speaks with unusual perceptiveness and caring about his three adolescent children. He would like all three to go to college. His eldest son is graduating from high school and has no interest in college. Ochs recognizes that this is a source of tension between them, and he is trying with considerable tact and insight to be helpful but not overly controlling. He takes delight in the talents and projects of his youngest daughter, the brightest and most successful of the children. He enjoys and works at being an active father.

Larry Strode left a Black middle-class home in the South following military service in World War II. At 40, after fifteen years in the same factory, he was a skilled worker, shop steward and occasional foreman. He was oppressed by the realization that he could advance no further in industry and that his life was of little value. During his Mid-life Transition (age 40 to 45), he started his own barber shop, continued at the factory, completed high school, explored the work world for alternative occupations, and tried desperately to improve his failing marriage. The son of a minister, he had long wanted a career that would more directly benefit human minds and souls. At 45, Strode began to build a new life structure. He left the factory and became a mental health worker at a local hospital, while continuing to manage his barber shop. He separated from his wife, and divorced her a few years later. During the late forties he tried to develop a new occupation and family life (including the children of his former marriage, with whom he was strongly involved). At 49, when we last saw him, he was just beginning to succeed in making a life different from that of his early adulthood.

Perhaps the most devastating story is that of Luke Doby, an uneducated Southern Black worker. He moved north at 16, married at 18, became a construction worker and raised a family of eleven children. He recalls his 37th year as a season of funerals: "Every time you look around, somebody die." At 38 his spleen was removed and his wife had surgery to prevent further childbearing. These events marked the beginning of a precipitous decline. He could find no way to become his own man.

When I first saw him at 41, Doby was working as a janitor in a factory. He regarded this as the worst year of his life. His medical condition had forced him to leave construction work, which he symbolized as "outside," masculine and a source of pride. The only jobs he could find were janitorial, and this was "inside," feminine and demeaning. He was becoming obsolete in the family, which his wife was managing largely with welfare funds. Over the next several years he would drop by my office occasionally. At his request, I helped arrange for his brief hospitalization at 43, when he was drinking heavily and afraid to go "on the street." He was the repeated victim of bizarre accidents. Once he was picked up in a car by some men, robbed and dumped miles away with severe stab wounds in the chest and back. A year later he was struck by a motorcycle and lost an eye. A state mental hospital admitted him several times, and released him without adequate discharge plans. Twice he was in rehabilitation programs that gave brief on-the-job training but left him unemployable. At 46 he was divorced by his wife. When I saw him last, at 47, he was getting stabilized in the life of a permanently unemployed, disabled, isolated man, barely connected to his children (now aged 9 to 30) and having few ways to "pass the time."

Luke Doby made a profound impression on me and remains a curiously important figure in my mind. He reminds me of a story by Poe called "The Man of the Crowd" that I read more than thirty years ago. The narrator observes a man walking in the downtown crowd, with a manner so mysterious that he decides to follow him. The man wanders aimlessly for hours. In the end, Poe realizes that the man is not going anywhere; he is haunted by a past so painful that the story cannot be told, and he endures a present that has no meaning. He may live briefly or for some years, but all that awaits him is death. He can find no way to begin the next phase of his life.

## William Paulsen:
## Completing Early Adulthood and Entering Middle Adulthood

For Bill Paulsen, too, the Mid-life Transition was troubled. As we saw in Chapter 8, he began his Settling Down period around the age of 32, and built a life structure that remained stable for the next eight years. The central components of his life during the thirties were his job at Bowles & White in Florida, his family and his new home.

For the first time, Bill felt established in an occupation that provided an opportunity for advancement. He described himself as a "computer operator," which was his euphemism for a job as a clerical worker who did the routine tasks of processing data. He was paid by the hour and earned $75 a week. As data processing became more important to Bowles & White's operation, he assumed a more supervisory role. He taught new people how to operate computers and supervised their work.

> My computer operators would often read a procedure written by an experienced programmer and not understand what the man was trying to tell them. So the engineers would bring in some of their new procedures and say, "Here, Bill, would you read this? See if you can understand it and if those nuts that you got working for you can understand it. Let me know what we can do to get the information across to them." I went back and suggested, "Let's reword this or put an extra step in this procedure." Then I would go over it with my computer people. I'd say, "Okay, any questions?" And nobody would say a word, no questions at all. I'd say, "All right, you guys are on your own."

He saw himself as a link between workers and managers, helping each group understand the other. He was a "chaplain," mediator and "father confessor." Soon he aspired to become the supervisor of the entire data-processing section. A thread of self-deception ran through Paulsen's description of his life. He exaggerated his talent for mediating between workers and managers. Not wanting to think of his job as clerical, he was overly optimistic about his chances for advancement. So, as he established himself in the job, he was sowing the seeds of future problems.

His family was a key element in the Settling Down life structure. He continued to feel that he would be "completely lost" without Ruth. It was still difficult for them to talk openly, and all too easy to withdraw angrily from budding disputes. Whatever the problems, the marriage remained valuable to him. He accepted the difficulties as a part of being married.

Beneath the appearance of an unchanging marriage, however, their life was in fact going through major modifications. When Bill was 33, Ruth had become pregnant and given birth to their only child. Pete's birth radically altered the nature of their life. They were no longer a young couple out "whooping it up." Instead, they saw themselves as more mature, stable and devoted to home and family. Bill began to think more in terms of the future and the kind of life he wanted for the three of them. Ruth expressed the meaning of Pete's birth this way: "It gave us a purpose to go on or something to build toward. I think our lives were never complete before he came."

Paulsen drew a happy portrait of himself as father to Pete. He saw himself as a kind, interested and companionable father to his son, as his father had been to him. But he acknowledged that his feelings for Pete were mixed: "I can't live with him sometimes and I can't live without him." He exercised the responsibilities of fatherhood, but his relationship to Pete was marked by his persisting boyishness. He wanted to be both a father and a brother to Pete. Ruth understood this well:

> Pete, unfortunately, is spoiled. He feels that anything he wants he should get. He knows his father cannot say no to him. He tells me, "Daddy can't say no to me, but you can. . . ." If I leave the two of them alone, they'll fight. I go out for an hour and come back and there's been some sort of a fight. Pete's gone into his room and closed the door. I'll come in and say, "What's happened?" "He got upset. I said something the wrong way. He went off, stalked off into his room. He's mad at me." But within an hour, half hour, they're back loving one another.

An important part of the Settling Down structure was their home in Florida. It had always been important for the Paulsens to have a place of their own. During the first three years in Florida, they had a "small but beautiful place" while Bill established himself at Bowles & White. "Share-croppers" then moved into the area and "it began to look like a pig sty." Along with many of their friends, Bill and Ruth decided to move. They found just the house they wanted near Fort Lauderdale.

> It was a beautiful home. My wife and I often said when we came back here that it would give us nothing but pleasure if there was a way to lift that house off its foundation and fly it up to New York or Connecticut and put it down on a piece of property. It was a beautiful, comfortable home.

By age 35, Bill had established his family in the home they all wanted. He developed a strong love of fishing, and it became a very important leisure-time activity. "I love to fish," he said. "I'm the type of man—I learned this from my father—who could go out at six in the morning and fish until midnight. If I didn't catch one fish I'd still be happy because I had a chance to get out by myself or with a group of guys and just relax and have a little fun." This was a good time in his life. In every respect he was doing better than before. He had a gratifying occupation, a beautiful home and family, and enjoyable leisure activities. He had come a long way from the age thirty crisis. His greater self-confidence and assertiveness were reflected in another difficult encounter with his mother.

When Paulsen was 38, his mother joined them after a long family squabble. Although she lived in a nearby apartment, she made great demands and was enormously trying. Her presence again became a source of intense conflict between Bill and Ruth. Perhaps because of the tension, Ruth developed a duodenal ulcer and was hospitalized again. Finally, Bill realized that his mother's presence placed an intolerable burden on Ruth and their marriage. Six months after his mother's arrival, he sent her back to Virginia. Although it was a difficult decision, he chose to support Ruth against the demands of his mother and family. The family then agreed to place his mother in a nursing home.

In his late thirties, Paulsen came to feel that "my capabilities were far above those of anybody else and that I would probably become supervisor of the whole department. Without realizing it, I would walk around and give the impression that I was above everybody else." After receiving no encouragement for this view of himself, he began to wonder whether he was capable of handling a supervisory position: his qualifications were inadequate, he had no experience in management and no training to be a manager.

By 39, his dream of becoming a supervisor at Bowles & White had begun to sour. For more than a year Bill was in a state of intense conflict. He felt ready and eager for advancement. He thought he had performed well and earned the support and affirmation of the company. He wanted to be a more senior member, to become more his own man within the organization and to assume greater responsibility and authority. On the other hand, he had doubts about his managerial abilities and education.

It became clear that he was not going to be promoted. He had gone as far as he could at Bowles & White. Bill, Ruth and Pete were comfortably settled in Florida. He liked working for Bowles & White, but he wanted urgently to get promoted. What should he do? Should he settle for what he had or try to get what he wanted elsewhere?

At 40, Bill and Ruth decided to move back north, largely on his initiative. His reasons were complex. In our view, his sense of urgency reflected the need to become his own man. He knew what he wanted, but he had failed to get it. Bowles & White did not affirm his aspiring self. He left Florida full of self-doubt, yet driven to try again.

While trying to make this decision at 39, Paulsen had developed chest pains and had become convinced that he had heart disease. Extensive medical investigation had indicated that his pain was muscular and caused by his "nervousness." Though his anxiety had been relieved, he was aware of the toll taken by his defeat at Bowles & White and the great tension he was under. For the first time, moreover, he thought of himself as being older and as vulnerable to disease, disability and death. He began to take care of himself, cutting down on his drinking and trying to stop smoking.

The move began well. Paulsen got a good job at the Bing Company in New York, in the computer section of a plant that built aerospace simulators. He was paid more than at Bowles & White and, most important, his boss, a young engineer, liked him and took an interest in him. When his boss was transferred to another plant in Hampton, New York, he warmly invited Paulsen to join him. Pleased, he accepted the invitation even though it meant another move. In Hampton, he was "an administrator in charge of all their documentation for computer application," and procured the software for the computer operation. The computers were used with various aerospace simulators. During his first three months at Hampton, he was involved in developing the simulation for the Apollo spacecraft.

Paulsen then worked on the Lunar Excursion Module for the space program. He and his family spent eight months in Texas, where he worked as a "technical administrator" on the project. He next went to Cape Kennedy for the installation of a second LEM simulator. This was an exciting time for him. He felt he was doing a good job; his boss appreciated his efforts and valued his capabilities.

> I thought from all appearances that I was going to be going someplace after I finished up those aerospace installations. I was going someplace in the sense that I might go up to supervisor over a small group of people or even a manager. This was almost intimated to me by a couple of people up there.

This was in many ways the high point of Paulsen's work career. He liked his boss and his job, and felt his boss liked and supported him. He believed he had finally done well enough, at 42, to be promoted to a supervisory position. It looked as though his gamble would pay off, and that the goal he had first sought in Florida would at last be his at the Bing Company. It was reassuring that, for the first time, he had a boss who was interested in helping him.

His boss was then made managing director of a program to develop a simulator for the F-111 fighter plane. He asked Bill to join him. Bill

agreed. "I figured, this is it." After a few months on the F-111 project, however, Bill knew he had made a mistake. The program was "going steadily
down, down, down." Instead of being promoted to supervisor, he was
doing the same work as before. He became moody and argumentative.
The situation worsened. His boss, to whom he had tied his own future, left
the company. In serious corporate difficulty, Bing merged with the Western
Corporation.

Shortly after this a number of employees were laid off. Among them was
Bill Paulsen. Bill's gamble at 40—to give up the good life in Florida and
find a supervisory job in the East—had failed at 42. This was the culminating event of the Settling Down period and the start of the Mid-life
Transition.

The Settling Down period thus proved to be a time of sharp contrasts.
With the move to Florida at 32, he had created a stable and satisfying life
structure. He established himself in a promising and satisfying occupation.
He and Ruth had a home they loved. Fishing became a major avocation.
Then he reached for more than he could obtain. It was not unreasonable
to hope to become a supervisor in his unit, a higher hourly job. But supervising "the whole department," and moving up to a management position,
was a huge leap. It is seldom made, especially in the late thirties. Bill sought
more responsibility and more pay. Bowles & White denied him both.

Bill's need to become his own man was paramount at 40. It led him to
make substantial changes. The family gave up its home in Florida for an
apartment in New York, something none of them wanted. The stability
of the previous eight years was replaced by instability and uncertainty. It
was a gamble based on Bill's estimation of his capabilities—an estimation
that rested all too uneasily on his capacity for self-deception. Bill now
placed his work at the center of his life. He was less attentive to his family,
home and leisure pursuits. These aspects of his life structure, so centrally
important in Florida, were shifted to the periphery as he pursued his occupational Dream.

At age 42, the gamble lost, Paulsen was assailed with doubts, question-
ings and despair. This was the beginning of his Mid-life Transition, and it
was truly a time of crisis. Desperate, he finally found a job with the P-E
Company in Connecticut. The only job he could get had no supervisory
responsibility at all. After seven months, the company's government con-
tracts expired and Bill was laid off.

> I felt, "This can't go on." Fortunately a man—this Mr. Kippman who
> lives in my apartment complex—got hold of me one night and said, "I
> understand you're looking for a job." I said, "Sure, I'm always looking as
> long as the money is there." So he and I sat down and he wrote a résumé

for me so he could sell his company on me and get me in. If this ever gets back to the company we're killed, the two of us.

The ruse was successful. At 44, shortly before our interviews began, Paulsen got a job at United Electronics, with an income of $11,000 a year. The résumé gave the impression that he had had experience in quality control, and United Electronics hired him as a quality control engineer. In his desperation, Bill misrepresented himself and took work beyond his competence. The company was new and struggling to establish itself. It had no quality control program when Bill started, and he was "running around the plant like a madman." There was considerable conflict between workers and their bosses: "In time, the company will get itself straightened out. Until that time we just have to fight the battle of management and peons, so to speak. Right now I'm in the middle of that battle."

Once again, Bill pictured himself as the man in the middle, making peace between workers and managers. As in the past, he believed that his skills as a mediator would get him promoted. His boss was grooming him, as he thought, to be "manager of quality control."

> Joe thinks I'm fabulous. I'd say that I was the logical choice for the job, but I'm afraid there is something that may keep me from it—my own personal makeup, the way I talk to people. I think I give the impression to some people that maybe I'm above them because of my position. If I do this, and I was told this once before, it's not my intention.

Though he still dreamed of getting a management position, he could think more seriously about his limitations.

> I'm quite sure that I can do it, but it's a fact that I haven't had too much experience at it in the last five years. I tend to think and administer from the working man's class, the subordinate class, as opposed to orienting my-self to management's point of view. I tend more to go toward the lower people than I do toward the big ones. If you get put into that slot, you get more responsibility than you've had to cope with before. Naturally there will be some situations where I'll be completely lost, but I feel I've always got somebody to talk to, to get help from.

It was an old theme. He was afraid that he wouldn't be able to perform, and at the same time reassured himself that he could do the job. Increasingly, these reassurances seemed shallow and unconvincing, even to Bill. After two previous failures, he was scrambling to realize his Dream, only to find it more elusive than ever.

His marriage and family were bothering him, too. Ruth was able to talk more openly with our interviewer about their difficult time. She knew how much he wanted to build a better life for the three of them, and how rough it was. But she was beginning to feel that Bill would not be able to work things out. The turmoil of their entire life was eroding the marriage. "It's a slow process getting out from under. The strain is showing in many ways. Maybe the both of us are afraid what the results would be if we got into a really good argument."

She described an evening when Bill was 43. They were visiting friends and got into an argument. Bill got angry and stomped out of the house. "If he walked out," Ruth said, "I knew that would be the end of everything. But he came back ten minutes later. That's the closest we came to actually bringing everything out into the open." For Ruth, this incident demonstrated how close they were to breaking up their marriage.

Another problem was their home. They missed the home in Florida: "I don't like apartment living and neither does my wife. We want a house so bad we can taste it, but we just can't see our way clear right now." His low income and job instability forced them to live in apartments. The apartment was a symbol of their turmoil and rootlessness. Ruth no longer looked forward to going to work or coming home. She too fought feelings of despair. "At this stage I just accept it. I guess that's something you have to go through. I don't count on things anymore because perhaps I'd be too disappointed if they didn't work out."

Paulsen's health problems increased during these two tumultuous years, between his 42nd and 44th birthdays. His physician examined his lungs and said that he had to stop smoking because "things don't look very good down there." But, under the massive stress, he couldn't stop.

After working just a few months, Bill was laid off at United Electronics and again began the agonizing search for a job. Four months later, he found one and took it although it was sixty miles from home. Given the job market in 1970, he felt lucky to find work at all. It was a small plant and he was the only worker in quality control. There was tension on the job and the daily commute was arduous. He began drinking heavily for the first time since the difficult years after his father's death.

Just before Bill's 45th birthday, a dramatic event occurred. It had a major impact on the course of his life:

> I was going to work on a Monday and I woke up at 5:30. I sat up and got this burning sensation in the back of my head. I didn't think that was right. I'd never had anything like it before. I woke my wife up and told her to get me over to the hospital. She got me there and they called in this neurosurgeon. After a couple of angiograms they knew that I had had a brain hemorrhage, but they couldn't locate it. They kept me in the hospital for about a month, but still couldn't find anything, so the doctor sent me home. I was home for about a week when I collapsed on the livingroom rug and

went back into the hospital again. They performed another angiogram. This time the doctor found out what the trouble was. He operated and was able to patch up the ruptured blood vessel. I spent from the middle of March until June in the hospital. It was very serious. That's why I say I'm a walking miracle today. The neurosurgeon explained it to me about two weeks after I had been released from the hospital. He said I was very fortunate and that he thanked God that he was able to repair it. From the beginning of April when he did the job until the beginning of June I couldn't do a darn thing. He told me it would be until at least November before he would think of letting me go back to work.

Paulsen faced a multitude of problems. Although he had hospitalization insurance, he had to pay the $3,000 doctor's bill himself. He was ineligible for social security insurance or a veteran's pension. He couldn't get unemployment compensation because he was still employed by his company.

His supervisor promised to hold his job until he could return in a few months. But when he finally told the firm that he was ready to return, they said that they had replaced him and had no opening. Bill applied for unemployment compensation, but it didn't start until Christmas Eve. He started looking for work, with no success. More than a year later, he was still unemployed. He was painfully blunt in assessing his situation:

It's on my nerves that I haven't got a position yet. And it doesn't look as though there's going to be anything in the near future. I feel I'm not supporting my family the way I should be. I can't depend on my wife to work. Thank God she has been for the last year or so while I've been laid up like this. If it wasn't for her the family would have just gone to hell. We've had a real rough time. I got rid of one car last year because the damn thing was going to be sitting for six months or more. And there are expenses, quite a bit. We've been fortunate in being able to manage so far. It's been very tight. Very, very tight. But at least we've been paying a good portion of our debts and have been able to keep food on the table.

I feel that I'm not contributing to the welfare of the family. I have no income except unemployment and to me this is not a source of income. I just do not like being on it. But the employment situation in the state of Connecticut as far as I'm concerned is quite pathetic. Instead of getting better it's getting worse. Although local newspapers have a lot of jobs, these companies don't want to touch people like myself.

They won't take you on and you can't get a reason as to why. Well, there are three things I can think of: I don't have the background, I don't have the degree, or I'm too old. You tell them you had cerebral hemorrhages and enjoyed full recovery, but all they see is cerebral hemorrhage. Recovery is way to heck over here to the side, but they can't even see it. They don't want to take a chance. I don't know what the hell I'm going to do.

I'm running into a big blank wall. I feel that I'm useless, no good to anybody. I realize that that's wrong, but even so I get that feeling. I get into
these depressed moods. I don't talk to anybody. It's almost like I was a clam
and just closed up and the heck with anybody else who is around. This is
wrong, but it's exactly the way I feel because I can't find a decent job.
I'm absolutely useless because I can't support my family the way they should
be. This is foremost on my mind. The idea that I can't provide the necessi-
ties, that the money is not there and that we cannot get my son what he
needs, it makes me feel like a dope, like an asshole.

By this time, Bill was almost 47 and had been on unemployment insurance for more than a year. He had been job hunting energetically but
without success. His chances of getting what he wanted were slim. He
struggled to accept the idea of taking a lower-level job. An important shift
was taking place in his feelings about himself and his future.

I'm living for the present now. God willing, if a good job comes along
then it may be that I'm going to want to stay with it for the rest of my
life. I don't know. On the other hand, I may work there for a month or
so and then say this is not for me and go looking someplace else. But I
don't like that. I feel as though I'm a little too old right now to go from
one job to another in a short time. This has happened in the past three
or four years. I don't like that feeling because I'm not only upsetting myself but I'm fouling up the well-being and the harmony of family life. I'm
making my wife a nervous wreck by going from one job to another, by
moving to a different area, maybe two, three times a year. And my son, of
course, good Lord! His education right now is more important than a
lot of other things. If I keep moving him around, his education is going to
suffer, and I don't want that to happen. The only way I can work on something like that is to locate a good position someplace in a small company,
or even a large company for that matter, where I can function with no lying
about it, shall I say, no bluffing.

For the first time, he talked of settling for a small job that he knew he
could do, rather than overreaching himself. His major concern was not
advancing to a managerial position; that Dream was gone. He was ready
to settle for a good deal less—a job with a stable income that would give
his family a settled life.

Paulsen feared the consequences of unemployment. He was aware that
sitting at home doing nothing had some appeal for him. He felt guilty
about not providing for his family, but he also enjoyed being looked after.
It frightened him to think that he could settle into the life of an invalid,
and he was quick to insist that "I can't go this route."

The period from age 42 to 47 had been a transitional time, as he moved from the life structure of the Settling Down period through various changes to a new structure. He went through a series of jobs. The family lived in apartments in many locales. There were increasing tensions between Bill and Ruth. He nearly died, and he was an invalid for many months. He was out of touch with his old friends and unable to make new ones. He felt rootless, lonely, defeated. His feeling of desperation turned to despair.

At the same time, important developments were taking place. Paulsen was making a critical re-evaluation of himself and his capabilities. In his job at United Electronics, he had begun to come to terms with the fact that he would never be a manager, that he had lost the bet he made at age 40. Giving up this aspiration carried with it the hope that he might be able to settle for more limited goals and seek other satisfactions.

There is evidence that Bill Paulsen at 47 was planning for a modest future. It was as if his illness had both forced and enabled him to come to grips with the reality of his life. He seemed ready to make his peace with the world, to live with fewer illusions and to provide a stable life for his family. He was starting the period of Entering Middle Adulthood.

# Novelists

At 39 Kevin Tyrone was a novelist and a professor of English. (For his earlier life, see Chapter 6.) Although his novels were "difficult" for the average reader and not commercially successful, the critics considered him a writer of remarkable promise who might become one of the foremost novelists of his generation. Over the next six years, the struggles of Becoming One's Own Man and the Mid-life Transition led him into new explorations of self and world. Although he didn't complete a novel during this time, he wrote some unsuccessful plays, involved himself in the world of the theater, and participated in various educational projects. Several years were devoted to terminating the intense relationship with his long-term mentor. His marriage, which had been a vital support for his creative writing since his early twenties, came more deeply into question. During a severe mid-life crisis in his early forties, he searched for new relationships, new occupational options, and new ways to deal with his own aging, destructiveness, femininity and separateness.

At 45, Tyrone began to establish a life structure for Entering Middle Adulthood. Returning to his novels, he started on a major work in four volumes, which he completed over the next several years. He reaffirmed his commitment to the marriage, but on new terms and with a clearer understanding of its meaning and limitations. After the peregrinations of the early forties, his life after 45 was in many respects continuous with that of the thirties: he was a husband and father in the same family, still a novelist and professor. Yet there were significant changes in all aspects of living, and in the self that engaged in them.

Allen Perry, too, had been a "promising young novelist" (see Chapter 9). His first book, published when he was 25, was an immediate success with both the general public and the critics. In the ensuing years he formed a stable marriage and family, created a space within which he could work as full-time novelist, and published several more novels that strengthened his reputation as a serious writer. Despite some difficulties in his mid-thirties, when he suffered a bitter parting from his most important mentor and wrote a disappointing novel, life went reasonably well until his early forties.

The culminating event of his early adulthood came at 41, when the publication of a major novel brought great praise and established him in the senior generation of American novelists. During the next several years, his marriage got more complicated and his literary efforts came to an impasse. Perry started a tragic novel that would bring to more mature expression various themes from his earlier work. After achieving great success, the hero of the novel was to suffer a grievous defeat, stemming from his own tragic flaw. Perry struggled to write this book even as he dealt with parallel issues in his own life.

At 45, he felt acutely the need to contain his inner conflicts and get on with the novel, but it would not be created. In his late forties, while not entirely giving up on the partly-written novel, he gave more time to other activities—writing a play, writing for literary journals, and involving himself more in public affairs. At 49 he was still trying to form a satisfactory life structure for Entering Middle Adulthood: his career as a novelist lay fallow and his other serious interests did not comprise a sufficiently meaningful occupation. Many novelists return to their trade after a fallow period of five or ten or more years, but they return on a new basis and within a new life structure. Others leave it for a new kind of writing or a new occupation altogether. This is one of the choices Allen Perry will face in his Age Fifty Transition.

Richard Taylor, a Black novelist, went through these periods in a different way. (His life through the Age Thirty Transition was described in Chapter 5.) His thirties were devoted largely to the battle for survival. He took assorted jobs in fields such as journalism and public relations, and worked on his novels whenever he could make the time. His first few novels received limited notice and sales. For almost the entire decade he had a serious but on-again, off-again relationship with a special woman.

At 40, Taylor began a momentous effort to create a more integrated life structure and realize his youthful Dream. Marrying his loved woman, he decided to risk everything in order to write the great Black American novel that was burning within him. He and his wife spent a frugal year in a tropical country while he completed it. He put all of himself into this book, and its publication at age 41 was the culminating event of his early adulthood. The initial response from critics and the public was at best mixed. The book was not a total failure, but it was far from being the dramatic success he had anticipated. Its limited success was bitterly disappointing to him. The year of sacrifice and the effort to become his own man (with all the special meanings this has for a Black man in American society) had seemingly come to nothing. A man of less tenacity might have quit altogether. During the Mid-life Transition, from roughly age 41 to 45, he tried to heal his wounds and continue his efforts. During this time his major novel came to be more widely read and appreciated, especially among Black youth. He wrote two minor novels in order to sustain himself as a novelist, and did other forms of writing as well. For the first time he was earning his living entirely as a serious writer.

By 45 Richard Taylor had created the basis for a new life and was Entering Middle Adulthood. He and his wife had stabilized the marriage and started a family. He had established good adult relationships with the grown sons of his first marriage. Now a senior member of his writers' world, he was assuming various leadership and mentoring functions with the younger generation of Black writers. He could say, for the first time, "I am a writer." While less driven by ambition, he looked forward to a creative, responsible life in the future.

Of course, he still felt keenly the racism and social injustice of modern society, and he had the burden of knowing how little he could do about it. Though he was a senior writer, he still had his mark to make. He had major responsibilities as father to two generations of sons and daughters, as husband to a loving, autonomous wife, as son to aging parents, as brother to less fortunate siblings, as writer to society, as middle-aged Black man to his people—and as person to himself. His prospects were brighter than ever before, but the challenges and difficulties were greater.

## Paul Namson:
## The Decade of the Forties

For Paul Namson, the Mid-life Transition and Entering Middle Adulthood saw the culmination of the contradictions of his life, and in the end pointed toward a resolution of them. In Chapter 12 we described the evolution of his life through the Settling Down period. At his fortieth birthday, he had just withdrawn his novel *Markers* from his publisher and, feeling weary and defeated, gone to Cape Cod for the summer of 1966. He wrote and prepared for a year of teaching at Brown.

The prospect of this new job pleased Namson. It was "a sort of confirmation of my usefulness. I also felt flattered. I knew Austin admired my writing." He left for Brown with high hopes for a year of teaching and writing. He was eager to teach creative writing and felt he "had a few things to show the academy." He also planned to "take another look at *Markers*."

These hopes proved to be illusory. He taught two sections of a writing course and, although he enjoyed it, found that "teaching drew on the same energies as writing." He could not do both, and was not able to return to *Markers*. He did begin a new novel, *Gallery*, but made less progress than he would have liked. Brown got him away from the distractions of Manhattan, but it presented him with a whole new problem. Offered an associate professorship at the end of the year, he decided to turn it down. "It was clear that I could not write and teach at the same time."

Actually, Paul and Sarah were tempted to remain at Brown. Both were taken with the bucolic life they led there. For the first time Paul was an integral part of family life. It was a new experience for him to eat his meals with Sarah and the kids, to have cookouts and play catch with Sheridan in the backyard. He and Sarah found this "greater family closeness" appealing. She, particularly, wanted to stay, but for Paul it was clearly not a viable solution.

He returned to New York at 41 "meandering in a spirit of uncertainty." He resumed the work on *Currents*. During this time he became absorbed with a curious idea which became another of his "distractions": he and Sarah should find an island and consider moving there. Brown had been "sort of an island." If he could find a real one, they would have the advantages of Brown without the difficulties. He would be out of the art world and the "high life," and would center his life around writing and family. After some searching, he found an island in the Caribbean.

> Sarah and I flew down alone. When we got there I looked around, looking at it partly as a real estate investment—partly as this fantasy of a home on an island, but also partly as an investment. What we saw was old and undeveloped and owned in very large tracts of land. I saw that a killing could be made by buying up a big tract of land. A section owned by a very prominent Boston family was for sale. I found myself making an offer for $1.7 million. After much dickering and a couple of months and a couple of more trips I finally bought it.

Again the contradictions were operating. Trying to create an island for his work and his family, Namson got himself back into the investment business. "It was a full-time distraction for two years; I had no idea it would take as much time as it did." He purchased the property, sold part of it, and built a beautiful new home into the ruins of an old sugar mill. This required a great deal of his attention and a number of trips to the island. This was time away from his writing, but it was a great success financially. He made a large sum of money and gained a magnificent new "fantasy home" in the process. He might be uncertain of his standing as a writer, but there could be no question as to his business skills.

When Namson was 42 and in the midst of his belated real estate venture, a fortuitous event helped him to begin forging a new stance as a writer. The need for an island retreat disappeared as he gained a new sense of direction and purpose. As a result, Paul and Sarah decided against moving into the house. By 43, the whole venture seemed a "slight regression" to him.

> I give you my word that if I had to do it all over again I never would do it—playing this strange neurotic game of investment business on the side. When I was in the investment business, I was writing. And while I am writing, suddenly I am dabbling in the investment business again.

The unexpected event was this: In 1968 a mammoth publisher asked Paul to write a biography of Sheridan Fisher. They offered a fee of $12,000 and required that he begin immediately. The idea of doing a biography, especially one of Fisher, was very appealing to him. It would give his writing a new focus. The well of "subjective fantasy" seemed dry. A commissioned biography would enable him to publish a full-length book for the first time since *The Bridge Game* came out in 1964. He would feel productive. He would exist as a writer.

As it turned out, "after two chapters of the biography we began to have trouble. I wanted to do Fisher's life, and they wanted Fisher's world —a more sociological study. I put the thing aside and returned to *Currents*."

He wrote a new section of *Currents*, consisting of two long "stories." They were immediately bought and published in a serious magazine. Namson was getting back into writing again. His new approach was to combine fiction with biography. By 43 he felt less restless and less isolated in his writing room, and he was getting more connected to the world of writers and publishers.

Meanwhile, his father was dying. He had a stroke and became a complete invalid early in 1969. Paul spent a great deal of time during that winter and spring at his father's bedside. He suffered the painful experience of his father's dissolution and his own aging.

Namson was also made aware of the fragile structure of his immediate

family. His son, Sheridan, at 12, was in almost total rebellion. He rarely
went to school and was usually in his room listening to rock music. Sarah
and her son were at an impasse: both were yelling and screaming, slam-
ming doors and not communicating. Paul remained at the edge of this
maelstrom.

Two family battles were going on during the time of our interviews,
when Namson was 43. One was between Sarah and Sheridan, the other
between Sarah and Paul. As Paul became more intensely committed to
his writing, the feeling of greater "family closeness" that had characterized the Brown year faded.

> I'm generally impatient with her, and I would rather read than go out.
> I'm not saying the idea of breaking out of the marriage has never occurred
> to me, but it is more complicated. Because, well, there are those times when
> I guess I'm good company and all. I suppose they are not as frequent as
> she'd like. I don't do anything to explain. If, in relation to Sheridan, Sarah
> is getting almost no satisfaction, in relation to me I guess she thinks I have
> become colder, increasingly selfish and critical.

Sarah was being left out in the cold. When Paul began writing more
actively at 43, he refused to make room for their old "high life." This
added to the distance between them. Both felt acutely lonely.

> One thing I didn't know I might miss, later on, was a profound intel-
> lectual relationship. I don't think we've ever had that. I don't know really
> what I feel now. Romantic love isn't that important to me anymore. Oh, I
> have fantasies. Maybe it isn't as large a factor in my life. I feel more lonely
> than I did in the earlier years of my marriage. There is this feeling that
> maybe somewhere out there there's somebody who would share a more
> intellectual life with me. But anyhow, I haven't done anything about that.

It became increasingly important to Paul that Sarah take his writing
more seriously.

> I want it treated at least as respectfully as she used to treat my work at
> Asch. I'm sure Sarah would never have thought of walking into a confer-
> ence when I worked for Asch to tell me, "There is an auction of china," or
> something like that. Very often she really does not treat this work with the
> same respect as business.

When we first interviewed him at 43, he could see some light but was
still wandering in Dante's "dark wood." He was profoundly concerned
with issues of bodily death, symbolic immortality and legacy. He was
well along in forming an intellectual view of these issues, but the deeper
emotional currents continued to roil. He often had the terrifying feeling
that:

. . . life has no structure. You are just jelly. You are nothing. You are just something that oozes out under the door. I might have that kind of anxiety at night—or just thinking, you know, there is no structure.

Preoccupied with the actuality of death, he had to consider the question of immortality:

The only solace I can find is that some of these words may last. And not only written words, but the spoken word. The nearest I can come to any idea of immortality is some little bit of me rubbing off on a few people— my wife, my children, a few friends. But, ah! It is hard, very hard, to accept that nothing will be left.

He was faced, at the same moment, with the desire that his writing form an enduring, valuable legacy in his name, and with the acceptance of his limitations as a writer. What good is it to write when the value of the writing is uncertain but in any case not "supreme"?

In the end I think any artist must feel that all he can do is present himself. One has recognition of one's limitations. I have no illusions. There is that myth of A for effort and now I find there are none . . . What approval will satisfy me now? In the end the approval must come from me. There is nobody who can give me what I want anymore. I would like one day to be taken seriously as a writer, but now it is all up to me. I must satisfy myself when I write. I must honestly say, not only am I not satisfied, but I can't imagine ever being satisfied. I believe that the supreme work of literature of the very highest levels is beyond me. So I work against something that is impossible for me, and yet I also say I am doing it from choice, like Sisyphus, and it is worth the effort.

Namson's growing seriousness was reflected in his changing concern with "comfort." He had spent most of his energies during early adulthood in a search for financial rewards and material comforts. He tried to give up the striving for money and power at 37, when he left Cyril Asch, but it was not until his early forties that he began to reappraise the meaning of comfort:

I don't seek comfort as much now as I did twenty years ago. A lot of my life in the past twenty years has to do with the dream of comfort. And a lot has to do now with the disillusionment about just where comfort lies. I still seek comfort in material things, but I don't think that is where comfort will be. I think it would come from other people in terms of compassion, love and tenderness.

At 43, Namson returned to the Fisher biography on his own. At the same time, a serious art publisher commissioned him to write the biography of another artist. By the time of his 44th birthday, both of these biographies were ready for publication. His novel *Currents*, which he had completed the year before, was not yet published. "I hope that the Fisher book will bring enough interest in me, again, to get *Currents* published. I think *Currents* is the best thing I have ever written. I would like to see all my children into print."

At 44 his writing was going better. The family was coming back together again; the household was more at peace. Sheridan was in school and doing well enough. Paul had begun to face the strains in his marriage and hoped he and Sarah could work things out together. The old relationship had come to an end. It seemed clear that whatever they came to in the future would have to be built around Paul's writing life. He felt the marriage could change because of Sarah's strengths; she was, Paul felt, "adaptable in a way that I am not." At the same time, he was ready to assume more responsibility for the problems in the old relationship.

> It is oversimplifying things to say that Sarah loves parties and Paul doesn't, and all of that. I mean, a lot of people think that. I would typically like to leave earlier than she does, but I've been very interested in the social scene. The same with houses. At some level I must have wanted it too, and I went after it as she did. We both wanted to go to the chic parties and the interesting lofts.

He could also acknowledge how critically important it had been for him to be with Sarah:

> I've given a lot and also been a bastard at times. What Fitzgerald took from Zelda, or to put it more positively, what she gave Fitzgerald, is not all that different from the kind of relationship Sarah and I had. So there was that complexity and that kind of symbiotic relationship.

At this point, Paul had changed a good deal, Sarah less. Their growing differences created new problems:

> There's been a more radical change in me, a new degree of seriousness, commitment. There was another side of me when she married me, but it certainly wasn't my whole life. The fact is, I have made the other choice. Sarah has been consistent, I think. What she is now and has been consistently is less necessary to me, or useful to me, or helpful to me, or a lot of things, than it was when we got married. So undoubtedly that will present problems. . . . Now she complains I don't spend enough time with her. She feels she never sees me. But I go into my study, I just insist. It is now understood—no, she must not intrude when I am working.

By age 45, the turmoil of the Mid-life Transition was subsiding and a new life structure beginning to emerge. During this period, from age

40 to 45, Namson had wrought remarkable changes in his life and within himself.

At the end of the Settling Down period, as he turned 40, it seemed almost certain that the bet he had made in leaving Asch and Company at 37 had been lost. One novel had been published, with poor success. The second, which meant so much to him, was of so little interest to the publisher that he himself aborted its publication. As the Mid-life Transition began, he was faced in a new way with the most basic questions: "What kind of writing, if any, can I do well? Can I build a life that will contain and facilitate the writing? What are the contradictions and flaws, in myself and in my world, that must be overcome if I am to have a chance for a better life?"

At the start of the Mid-life Transition, Namson provided himself with a moratorium. He tried to create a space in which he could reappraise his life, develop a clearer sense of his possibilities and limitations, and search for a new way. For a year, at Brown, he moved business and the "high life" to the periphery and family to the center of his life structure. In the island real estate venture, it was as if he had to return briefly to business in order to say goodbye to it. In a similar vein, writing the biography of Sheridan Fisher was his way of saying farewell to the art world and of terminating more adequately his relationship with Fisher (while incorporating more of Fisher into himself). The two biographies gave him a respite from the more subjective work of novel writing. They also led to a creative integration of biography and fiction in his subsequent writing.

By age 45, Namson began the period of Entering Middle Adulthood —building a first structure for this season of the life cycle. Writing was, at last, a central component in his life structure, and most of the old "distractions" had been removed from it. He was developing a mode of writing that satisfied him more fully and gave him the hope of greater recognition from the world. He had a stronger sense of responsibility for his own life, for both his achievements and his defeats. His family was more securely established, though he and Sarah were just beginning to work out a new basis for their marriage.

We can take only a glimpse into his life during the late forties. His former mentor, Austin Garrison, re-entered the story briefly in a new way. Garrison started a new publishing firm, especially for writers who might not otherwise "see their children into print." He published *Currents* when Paul was 46. Two years later, Namson completed his novel *Gallery*, a long work growing out of his experiences at the Gordon Archives. He had found in that world another "fussy room" which nourished his writ-

ing. He also became intrigued with the life of Beatrice Gordon, a bene-
factor of the institution, and began work on her biography. Like him,
she had led a multifaceted life, combining a lively interest in business
with a productive career as a painter. Her life, too, provided nourishment
for his writing.

As he entered middle adulthood, Paul Namson was coming to accept
and value the feminine in himself and others. He was absorbed in the
biography of a woman with whom he identified. He was, finally, drawing
more freely upon the artistic, creative side of himself that had animated
and plagued him since boyhood. Then it had seemed that he could not
be both artistic and manly. Now he knew that to be fully a man he had
to utilize the feminine as well as the masculine aspects of himself. In this
and other ways, he was resolving the great mid-life polarities and entering a genuinely productive season of his life.

## Biologists

Each biologist's life course was heavily shaped by his career within an
elite university, where he sought to advance up the ladder of academic
rank and scientific reputation. His life course was also shaped by the
common sequence of developmental periods and by specific features of
individual personality, ability and external circumstance. Again we find
individual variations on common themes.

Almost from the start, Earl Northrop had a brilliant but flawed career. He became an assistant professor at 32, after doing some "very promising" research in a government agency. Over the next few years his research was solid but not outstanding. At 35 he was promoted to an intermediate rank largely on the grounds of his scholarly breadth, his success
in teaching an important course, and his contributions to the administration of his department. At 40 came the crucial promotion: he was made
professor with tenure, and thereby joined the senior ranks of his university and his scientific field. Again, however, the reward was blemished.
He had continued to be an excellent teacher, and had written several
comprehensive reviews of the work in his field, but it was becoming evident to him and others that he would probably never make a highly creative contribution through his own research. As he put it:

> I became aware of the conflict in me, the strain of the intellectual
> side. . . . I lack what is needed to be really original in some imaginative
> sense. . . . It's an impediment to being in the very first rank.

During his Mid-life Transition, Northrop started coming to terms with what it meant to be a senior, semi-distinguished man in a university where the "second rank" is not good enough—and where most of the senior faculty are in this painful condition. He did better than most in facing these issues without illusions or hypocritical self-justification.

When I interviewed him at 44, Northrop was at the height of his tormenting reappraisal. His marriage, like his work, was adequate but unexciting. The marital difficulties were severe enough to cause him some anguish, but not so bad that he would seriously consider therapy or divorce. He was a devoted father and family man. An intensely pacifistic, nature-oriented, introverted person, he was deeply disturbed by our part in the Vietnam war, the violence of urban life and the pollution of the environment. He had no close collaborators or friends and, despite his many students and acquaintances, felt utterly isolated at work: "If I retired or got sick, no one would come to see me—or even notice that I was gone." He would have loved to be a professor in another first-rank university, but the few offers came from lesser ones that his pride kept him from considering.

In our follow-up interview at age 46, the period of active questioning was over. For now he would stay put. He was finding small ways to enrich his family and work life, but there was little sense of reaffirmation in these choices. The structure was very provisional and open to change. Two years later Northrop took a chairmanship at a minor but growing English university—a further, but still tentative step toward building a satisfactory life structure in middle adulthood.

Four of the ten biologists left their current university during their late thirties or early forties, some because they were not continued, others in response to offers that attracted them elsewhere. Each of these men went through a change not merely in job but in the character of his work and of his life as a whole. All of them had to come to terms with the experience of exile, and of liberation, attending their departure from an elite university.

Five of the biologists remained at the same university into their forties and attained senior positions. (The outcome for one was uncertain.) For some of them the success was as tainted as it was for Earl Northrop. Others had a greater sense of personal satisfaction and accomplishment. Every biologist we interviewed during his early forties, regardless of his external success or failure, was going through a Mid-life Transition of moderate or severe crisis. A classic example of the successful man in crisis is John Barnes, whom we met in the previous chapter.

## Executives

Like the biologists, the executives live within a highly institutionalized world, and their sense of occupational progress is strongly influenced by their advancement through the organizational hierarchy. There are important similarities as well as differences in the stresses and the satisfactions available to men in these work worlds.

David Jaffe was an engineer by education and early work experience. At 31 he embarked upon a managerial career. Although he worked hard to get ahead, his main involvement was in family and community. At 38, his ambitions heightened and he made a big effort for advancement to the position of purchasing manager. He also decided to get a bigger and better home. This was partly in response to the growth of his family, but it was also the fulfillment of a Dream. His home was his castle, and having a lovely home of his own meant that he had arrived. Building a new home was his main project during the time of Becoming One's Own Man. Through his engineering and contracting skills, and his patience, he built a much more expensive home than he could have bought.

The twin culminating events of early adulthood came at 41: the Jaffe family moved into their new home, and he received his promotion. The home was a complete success. It gave them a more comfortable life and a more respected position in the community, where he was becoming a senior member. The promotion to purchasing manager was a total bust. The company had just been bought by a large corporation and purchasing policies were established from the top. He felt oppressed and humiliated. Despite the severe disappointment, he remained in this job for four years, refusing several attractive job offers in other states. He is one of the few men in our study who has lived his entire life, with the exception of a few years in military service, within an area no more than fifty miles across. If there is a traditional, tribal man—analogous to the traditional woman—he is it. The central elements of his life structure, in order of priority, were family, religio-ethnic community and occupation. He worked hard at his trade, but he left it behind at the end of the day and his most important satisfactions were elsewhere.

During the years from age 41 to 45, Jaffe stayed put and worked on various issues of the Mid-life Transition. At 45 he found his job unbearable. One day, in a fit of desperation, this cautious, deliberate man quit —impulsively, without knowing what he would do next. He still would not consider a big geographical move, but luckily found a job as purchasing manager at United Electronics, within commuting distance from home. I first interviewed him soon after he started this job at 45, and again two years later. The life structure he had begun at 45 was more secure and he was progressing well within it, but there were nagging questions. He was in top management, as Number 2 to the General Manager for Production. Though he had hopes of becoming a vice president, he knew about the instability of a "rapid growth" company and its leadership—and he counted on nothing. His familial nest was emptying, his aging mother-in-law was a heavy responsibility, and a new phase of life was in the offing.

Roger Mohn, also an engineer by education, has spent his entire work life within a single company. (For accounts of his life in earlier periods, see Chapters 10 and 13.) Happily employed as head of the metals shop, he was unexpectedly promoted into middle management at 37, just in time for Becoming One's Own Man. The three years as purchasing manager were difficult but exciting. At 40 the culminating event was a promotion to head of manufacturing. This rapid advance in authority and income took him far beyond his youthful aspirations and managerial skills.

The promotion marked his entry into the Mid-life Transition. Within a year Mohn had developed an ulcer. He felt isolated and lonely. He thought a good deal about his college years and the friends who had meant so much to him; they were in another world that he had left behind and could no longer reach. A loving father and family man, he felt out of touch with his wife and children. At 42 he became ill with a cancer of uncertain prognosis. In the years from 42 to 44 he hit rock bottom. He was preoccupied with concerns about his own death, about the welfare of his family, and about giving his life some meaning when present and future were so bleak. His family life sustained him through this otherwise unbearable period.

When he was 44, a company reorganization eliminated most of his peers and gave him a "lateral shift" to a position of equal salary but less responsibility. He experienced the reorganization as a "blood bath," an "absolute slaughter" of the others and a humiliating demotion for himself. After several months, although he had offers from other companies, he decided to stay put: "I feel more secure in the surroundings I know than in a new environment."

The wish for security was only part of his reason for staying, I believe. At a deeper level, Mohn was ready to begin Entering Middle Adulthood and had made the basic choices for the next life structure. He had given up all pretense of interest in the competitive rivalries of the corporate world and in further advancement up the executive ladder. His strongest feeling at this time was relief—relief that he could remain in a well-pay-

304 THE SEASONS OF A MAN'S LIFE

ing, unchallenging job, and relief that his cancer now seemed under control. He lived more in the shadow of death than most of us, but he had reaffirmed his ties to life. He was content with the two central components of his life: his family and his leisure interests. He was learning to spend time with his loved and loving daughters, who were teaching him the pleasures of hiking, fishing and nature. He was getting closer to his wife, and at the same time supporting her expansion from the home to new occupational and community involvements. As he acquired greater skill in the arts of intimacy and solitude, he was emerging into middle adulthood with a life fuller than ever before.

The third executive whose story we shall tell is James Tracy. In Chapter 11 we followed him through the Settling Down period. In the next chapter we learn about the unexpected changes wrought in the periods of the Mid-life Transition and Entering Middle Adulthood.

# 19 The Life of James Tracy (III)

In Chapter 11 we saw how in his late thirties Jim Tracy divorced his first wife, married Joan and started a second family while maintaining the relationship to his first children. This occurred in his Settling Down period. By 41, he and Joan had a baby boy and were building a new home. But the problems of living with two families, and of giving his new family a central place within a new life structure, were just beginning.

The year from age 40 to 41 had been a momentous one in Tracy's work life. When he was 40, his mentor, Don Bond, suddenly left Ajax. Walter Johnson was promoted into Bond's position as group vice president, and Jim Tracy advanced to become general manager of the division. This was the promotion he had long desired, but it came as a blemished success. His relationship with Johnson had never been close. Moreover, he initially held the new position on a probationary basis, and he had to prove himself in it. He went through a year of watching, waiting and doubting.

At 41, the probationary period came to an end. Tracy was officially endorsed in the new position. He was also given a fancier title and some additional fringe benefits. Yet once again he regarded the promotion as a blemished success. He was still under Johnson's questioning glance and controlling hand. It was time, he felt, for him to be a group vice president—to be in Johnson's position rather than under him. Tracy was not yet his own man:

> They made me a general manager and also a corporation vice president. There are fifteen corporation vice presidents, and the whole company is really a billion-dollar corporation. The scope of the job didn't change. I felt, although they never told me, as if they threw me a bone to keep me around.

Tracy was at 41 a vice president earning more than $100,000 a year and responsible for a multimillion-dollar enterprise employing thousands.

But this last promotion, which was the culminating event of his early adulthood, produced serious doubts about his occupational future and touched off his Mid-life Transition. The apparent promotion was in many respects a lateral move—the kiss of death. His chances for further promotion now seemed dim. He stayed on at Ajax, but he felt trapped. He was at the beginning of a crisis period in his work, his family and his life generally.

His attitudes about the arms business began to change in the next few years. He had helped to perpetuate the view that weapons themselves were not dangerous: "It's the person behind the gun that's the nut." But his opinions about guns and the weapons business were being modified by changes in society and by his own mid-life questioning. Dissent against the war in Vietnam was at its peak in 1969. His doubts were magnified by his feelings that he had gone as far as he could at Ajax. He was re-evaluating his own life and his place in society. He was also confused about his role when Black workers led a major strike against the company.

Tracy was depressed by the violence in our culture. His social concerns were intensified by his awareness of his own decline and limited control over his work and life. He no longer regarded himself as the omnipotent leader. This was complicated by ambivalence toward the Black strikers: he bravely led executives across the picket lines, but he also identified with the Blacks and wanted Ajax to be more humane in its policies. For the first time, he himself felt like an underdog.

In one of our last interviews as he turned 45, Jim spoke about his personal philosophy:

I have been honest, straightforward, and not underhanded. I said there has been a lot of luck in it; there were people who guided me for one reason or another. But, with all this, I can honestly say that I haven't trampled on anybody and haven't gone against principles to cut corners. People get what they deserve. If you are decent to people, ultimately you're going to get treated decently in return. My basic belief is that if you're honest and straightforward with your people, ultimately you get paid back. You don't have to be underhanded. You don't have to be a sharp dealer to get ahead. If you are any good, ultimately you are going to go to heaven. I guess that is my basic philosophy.

Jim worked to live up to his high standards. Both personally and professionally, he seemed to have increasing success. But he was questioning his entire life and seeking a new way. This is illustrated by a recurring dream of the early forties:

I'm flying in an airplane and for some reason, nobody really knows, we're flying very low over a road with telephone poles. I'm sitting there, afraid we're going to crash and the pilot is going to tear off a wing or something. He's going over bridges and we haven't crashed, yet.

Tracy felt that his former life was coming to an end. He didn't want to live as before. He wanted to be less up in the air, more firmly rooted to the ground. He was beginning to acknowledge that he could not retain control over every given situation in his life.

The acute fear of losing control is related to the dismantling of the earlier life structure. Giving up the aggressive, achieving stance raised the question: "What's left of me?" Perhaps the "bitch goddess" success would turn away from him.

> Every once in a while, I just think, my God, the whole goddamn roof is going to fall in. This is sort of what scares me at 45. I'm about halfway through and what is the second half going to be like, because the first half has been pretty good, business-wise. I sometimes think about what will the long downhill slope be like. Will I end up at 65 making $15,000 or $10,000 a year? I think one of these days the whole goddamn roof is going to fall in. I just can't keep going like this; that scares me a little bit every once in a while.

Tracy talked about the possibility of early retirement at 55, teaching at a university or occupying a top executive slot in a smaller company close to home. He was moving away from the early aspirations of power toward the role of mentor-teacher in a less imposing organization.

> I want a company that would pay me the same amount of money, or reasonably the same amount of money, that I'm making now. I want to live where I'm living now and have a job anywhere within an hour's drive. I've worked for a big company my whole business career. I think in a smaller company you've got more flexibility. I don't like to travel on business trips away from home. I detest it. I don't have any goal. Oh, sure, I'd like to succeed, take my boss's place as a group vice president, but I'm not as hard driving as I used to be. I think I'm probably as effective as ever, but I don't have the energy or driving ambition to succeed that I used to have. I don't have the great desire to be president of Ajax. I really don't.

Tracy's attitudes toward himself had also changed by his mid-forties. He could now recognize and value the softer and more caring aspects of his personality.

> I think I'm not hard driving enough. I have a guilt complex about being too easy on people, and not enough of a taskmaster. Instinctively, I'm soft and compassionate toward people, to a fault. The hardest thing in the world for me is to sit down face to face with somebody and tell them what they are doing wrong. I just find that terribly difficult to do. I am not a very

good disciplinarian. I don't really believe in it. I try to get people to do things by reason, logic or example. I wish I were tougher; life would be a lot easier. I had a boss who said the only real problem you have is you wear your heart on your sleeve. I get emotionally upset about people, that is what he told me. I am not really very rough.

The flaws in his second marriage also became more evident. Under pressure, Joan was not able to function as the desired helpmate and Jim was left alone to deal with an extremely painful series of events. It was a rock-bottom time.

When Jim was 42, his daughter Linda was in her first year of college. After becoming pregnant, she married Alex, 23, an unskilled laborer in a garage. Later that year Jim's oldest son, Robbie, at a private prep school, began experimenting with drugs. He developed paranoid notions about the faculty, had several severe outbursts and was asked to leave. Not long afterward, Robbie attempted suicide:

I was out of town. My former wife called Joan and said, like a complete jerk, "Robbie tried to commit suicide. What should I do?" Joan said, "Take him to the hospital." They took him to the local hospital and the doctors took one look at him and zipped him up to Franklin State Hospital. By the time I got home, he was in Franklin. If I had just been home . . . but I wasn't. That's what happened. His mother had him committed on a Thursday. I didn't know about it until I got home on Friday.

Jim was furious at Victoria for involving Joan, and at himself for being unavailable to help his son during a traumatic event. He felt stuck between wives one and two. He wanted to keep Victoria out and bring Joan in. He and Joan drove to the hospital and visited Robbie in a locked ward.

Neither Joan nor I had ever seen Franklin before. He was in one of those awful wards with bars all over the place, with wild, far-out people. Joan and I marched in, and we got locked into a visiting room right in the middle of all of it. It really shook her up. When she went with me subsequently, she'd sit in the parking lot with all of the car doors locked, and I'd visit him.

Joan withdrew from the situation. Locking herself in the car effectively symbolized her alienation from his children. It made Jim sharply aware that he could not bring together two important elements in his life: Joan and the children from his first marriage. Her withdrawal undermined his formerly idealized view of her.

Tracy got his son released from the hospital and into brief treatment with a private psychiatrist.

The private psychiatrist told us that Robbie had very strong violent tendencies. This sent Joan right up the wall, thinking about our two little boys. "We're going to have a madman in the house, what are we going to do?"

Robbie was then hospitalized at a private institution. The doctors there disagreed with the private psychiatrist's evaluation, but thought that there wasn't much hope for further education in school. Jim spent much of his time arranging for therapists and tutors. Joan tried to get involved, but her experience with the psychiatrists and the state hospital had badly frightened her. The incident reactivated her guilt about breaking up Jim's first marriage. She began to see a private psychiatrist, who recommended that she have little or nothing to do with Jim's family. So Jim was forced to deal with the problems from his first marriage on his own. Recognizing that he had not been involved enough in Robbie's early life, he tried to compensate by reaching out to his son under extremely trying circumstances.

During this same year, Jim's brother, George, also went through a rough time. His wife ran off with a much younger married man. All attempts at reconciliation failed. George soon married a much younger woman. The similar plights of the brothers pulled them together. Jim became aware that George had resented him during childhood: "I was always very fond of him, and it turned out he wasn't very fond of me at all. . . . There's a good feeling between us now. I know that if I ever want anything I can call him, and vice versa, with no questions asked."

At this time Tracy became more parental toward his mother and father, both in their seventies. And he continued getting closer to Linda and Robbie. Linda asked him to help her husband, Alex, get a job. He jumped at the chance, and got his son-in-law a modest job at Ajax. He also got Robbie summer jobs elsewhere. Giving became more important in his forties.

Tracy felt that he was cheating when he used company time and resources to help his family, and that this might endanger his future at Ajax. A conflict developed between work and fatherhood:

> I've never once involved our personal time, like weekends or evenings, to straighten out something with Linda or Rob. I've stolen it away from work time. I do the absolute minimum amount of outside activity, to the point where I should be doing a hell of a lot more if I were doing my job right. It's costing me in mental anguish. What it's costing me in my image at Ajax I honestly don't know. I feel guilty.

He was also upset about taking time away from his current family to work on problems in the first family. Joan added to the distress: "She thinks she has married a family rather than me. She feels that she has withdrawn from her family and all of her former friends, and now totally leads my kind of life."

Some of their troubles stemmed, however, from Joan's first marriage. Her son, Kevin, now ten years old, wanted his name changed from Corcoran to Tracy so the other children would not make fun of him, and he could feel more a part of his current family. Jim and Joan began adoption proceedings. This led to a long legal battle with Corcoran, "a somewhat alcoholic, withdrawn, graying man living in their former home fantasizing about Joan's return."

> I mean, without a doubt, Joan can't stand Corcoran. He uses Kevin as the only connecting link he's got between the two of them, and he isn't about to give it up. The only time he calls is when he's about three-quarters shot. He'll call Friday night from a bar and start talking to her and she gets all upset.

Corcoran's calls drained Joan, who took out her anger and frustration on Jim. Corcoran was a ghost who would not depart. While the conflict enraged Jim, it also made him more sensitive to Joan's problems and frailties. He was learning to accept her limitations.

He also spent more time with Kevin and Tommy than he had with his first children. He even became a scoutmaster:

> It's a pain in the neck some of the time, but I get rejuvenated once a month when I stand up in front of 50 kids and just have them hang on my every word. For an hour and a half every month, if you're helping these kids at all to grow up right, my God, it's worth it. Just looking at those faces, I get all charged up again.

Still, there was continuing conflict between his job and his new family. When they first married, he wanted Joan to stay at home and nurture their family. But the attractive, 28-year-old newlywed had within a few years retreated into a cocoon. She felt that he should give less time to his work and more to her and the family:

> Joan doesn't understand that there are certain things that I have to do in my job that I don't necessarily want to do, which take me away from home. She just gets a little depressed, and doesn't talk as she usually does. It's no great outward scene, she just withdraws for a while until she gets used to the idea and then it's all right. It isn't accepted as a normal course of our lives. I guess she is dependent on me and likes me to be there, but her whole life seems to orbit around me to a greater degree than it should.

The conflict made Jim more aware of Joan's dependency and self-restriction. It also evoked his concern about her growth as a person. He wanted to get her out of the "hausfrau" role and into the world, and he supported her psychotherapy.

Tracy began doing things her way, restricting his life to please her. He turned down invitations to be with other men and gave up activities that meant much to him. He sold his boat, built a swimming pool, worked in the garden and fixed up their house. He centered his leisure time around Joan and the family. To please Joan, he chose to restrict his vision and his existence. He tried, in his own way, to have as "peaceful" and "stable" a family life as possible. But the costs were great.

Jim's initial illusions about Joan and the new marriage were largely dissolved by these experiences. The "two families" crisis peaked between his forty-first and forty-fourth year, when he worked on the tensions between families, and between family and work. He became more supportive of Joan and his children, and more giving and intimate with others.

The first years of his Mid-life Transition, from age 41 to 44, were marked by severe problems and chaos. The later years, from 44 to 46, were characterized by greater reflectiveness, integration and planning. By 46, Tracy had decided to leave the world of the large corporation. He was putting his family in the center of his life. The crisis was abating. He was learning to deal with the complex issues facing both his families, and to understand Joan's strengths and limitations. They shared a growing interest in antiques, and she opened a shop in downtown Hartford. He was giving up the Dream of becoming a top corporation executive.

## Entering Middle Adulthood

The period of Entering Middle Adulthood led to major changes for Tracy. We have few details, but the main outlines of his new life are clear.

When he was 46, Joan developed allergies and her doctor suggested a drier climate. Within three weeks, he submitted his resignation to Ajax. The corporation offered him jobs in other parts of the country, but he refused. He had to begin afresh. They decided to move to Colorado.

Jim's feelings about his time at Ajax came out in a discussion of his legacy.

I think I am pretty well cast for what I have done. I don't feel cheated or that I haven't been able to do something that I should have been able to do. I think I've been phenomenally lucky in a lot of respects. I don't have any regrets. I'm proud I got where I am, and achieved what I achieved. . . . An ambition I always had in the marines was to be a general. I mean, I'm running a big business and I satisfied that ambition. You think of your job whether it is in the marines or business—there really isn't much difference between the two—in terms of getting people to do your work for you. I seem to be able to instill loyalty in them. I am pretty open and straightforward with people. I generally communicate pretty well, particularly to those that have worked for me. . . . Well, Joan, Kevin and Tommy will think I am a pretty good father, husband and provider. I think Linda will think the same thing. I don't know what Robbie will think. If I popped off tomorrow, I can't see anybody getting all upset about it, other than my immediate family. . . . I will just be erased from the Ajax blackboard. I will be missed by no one but my family. Managers are replaceable and don't really matter unless they are *the* driving force for the company.

Tracy was pleasantly surprised by the reactions to his departure. He received warm messages of support and affection, which were pleasing but difficult to accept.

Initially, his parents were upset with the move, but soon his mother wrote and said she understood. His brother supported the decision. Linda and her husband were now living with their three children in Tennessee, where Alex was a successful Ajax salesman. Robbie was "a lot better" and would graduate from high school shortly at the age of twenty. He was off drugs, involved in photography, had a girlfriend and was "as normal as 50 percent of the people around." In sum, his family was in pretty good shape and supported his new move.

In leaving Ajax, Tracy was not only giving up his leader-executive role in the weapons industry, but also moving permanently out of huge hierarchies. Although he did not know exactly what he would do in Colorado, he eagerly anticipated the change. He considered working in a small hardware business of his own, running an antique shop with Joan, teaching, or acting as consultant to corporations.

The move to Colorado was a move into middle adulthood. At 47, Tracy experienced less despair and generated more options. He had the sense that he could find his own way and live with it. Whatever he did in Colorado, it was apparent that he would relate to his work and family in a new manner.

In 1973, we received a letter from Jim Tracy. He was now general manager of an appliance distribution business in Denver:

Colorado is great! The family loves it, particularly the children. Joan is much better physically, and from that standpoint, it was certainly the right thing to do. The business end still has to prove itself out, but I am reasonably optimistic. This is a very fast-growing area, and if this connection doesn't work out, conceivably there will be other things to do.

He now had more time to talk.

# V Conclusions

# 20 Tasks and Possibilities of Adult Development

We began this investigation by asking: What do we mean by the human life cycle, and what are the seasons within it? Is there such a thing as adult development? Can we identify a sequence of developmental periods in adult life comparable to those in childhood and adolescence?

Our study has provided some initial answers to these questions. The answers are of necessity tentative. Further research is needed to test and extend our present understanding, but we now have a basis on which to proceed.

We identify four overlapping eras in the life cycle, each lasting some twenty-five years. The eras provide a view of the individual life as seen from a distance. Each era is distinguished by its overall character of living, which has biological, psychological and social aspects. The eras form the skeletal structure of the life cycle. Once we have understood the nature of an era from the perspective of the total life cycle, we can examine more specific processes and events as they unfold within it.

The developmental periods give a more detailed and interpretive view. They fall within, and are shaped by, the succession of eras. They are the means by which the developmental work of an era is carried out, and they provide the linkage between the eras. The cross-era transitions are perhaps the crucial turning points in the life cycle. In the Early Adult Transition, the Mid-life Transition and the Late Adult Transition, a man creates a basis for living in the era just getting under way. These transitional periods are the sources of renewal—or of stagnation—that shape the character of the developmental sequence. The combined perspective of eras and periods is a means of exploring the total life and the process of development at specific times in its course.

The foundation of our theory of developmental periods is the concept of the individual life structure. The life structure evolves through a sequence of alternating periods. A relatively stable, structure-building period is followed by a transitional, structure-changing period. The major developmental tasks of a structure-building period are to make crucial choices, to create a structure around them, to enrich the structure and pursue one's goals within it. These periods ordinarily last six to eight years. In a transitional period the major tasks are to reappraise the existing structure, explore new possibilities in self and world, and work toward choices that provide a basis for a new structure. In the course of a transitional period a man may choose to involve himself in new persons and places, or he may retain his marriage, job and social network but establish different relationships and live out different aspects of the self. The transitional periods generally last four or five years.

## Eras and Periods in the Life Cycle

When we began this work, nothing in the literature of psychology and social science suggested that we would find a sequence of eras and periods unfolding in orderly progression. That idea was not the starting point for our research. Quite the contrary. It was only after we had traced in detail the intricate design and course of many individual lives, each one unique in its patterning, that we could begin to grasp the underlying order. The idea of individual life structure emerged from our efforts to see the shape of a man's total life at a given time, and to understand how this shape evolved over the years.

• AGE LINKAGES. One of our greatest surprises was the relatively low variability in the age at which every period begins and ends. It was not a prediction we made in advance, nor a predisposition in our thinking. This finding violates the long-held and cherished idea that individual adults develop at very different paces. The traditional idea has a basis in fact: those who study development in terms of a single aspect, such as biological aging, psychological maturity or occupational career, find considerable variability in the ages at which particular changes occur. There seem to be no regular periods in the development of these single aspects. Similarly, specific events such as marriage, starting a family, death of loved ones, and retirement may occur at very different ages. Only when we look at development in terms of the evolution of life structure do the periods follow an age-linked sequence.

For every period we can give a typical age of onset. This is the age at which the period most frequently began among the men in our study. There is a range of two or three years on either side of the average age. This range may seem very small to those who expected no order at all, but it is enough to have great significance. The variability in the time-table for adult development is slightly higher than that for child development. It means that we cannot use chronological age as a simple criterion of the developmental period a particular man is in. One man at 39 is starting the Mid-life Transition, another is still at the height of Becoming One's Own Man. The developmental periods are age-linked, but they are not a simple derivative of age. The timing of a period, and the kind of developmental work done within it, vary with the biological, psychological and social conditions of a man's life.

• SEQUENCE. We find that the periods occur in a fixed sequence. As long as a man continues to develop, he will traverse the periods in the order given. He cannot go from period three to five without going through four. For a man in period three, the path to further development must cross four and five—there are no shortcuts or alternative routes. He can navigate a period in myriad ways, but he cannot avoid it. In the present, if he is to find some satisfaction and create a basis for life in the next period, he must deal with the current developmental tasks.

Developmental impairments and defeats from the past may prevent a man from beginning a new period and working on its tasks. He is then in a state of decline. He is stuck. Developmental blocking of this kind can occur in adulthood, as in childhood, as a result of overwhelming biological, psychological or social insult. Thus, a large percentage of men in some groups may have such difficulty with the tasks of the Mid-life Transition and Entering Middle Adulthood that they cannot create the basis for even a moderately satisfactory life in middle age.

• HIERARCHICAL STAGES AND SEQUENTIAL PERIODS. Some theories describe developmental stages that follow an ascending or hierarchical order: a person advances from one level to the next, each stage representing a higher capability. The stage theories of Lawrence Kohlberg, Jean Piaget and Jane Loevinger are of this kind, and they have contributed to our understanding of human development.

Other theories, such as Erikson's and ours, posit a sequence that is not hierarchical. One period is not higher or better than the preceding ones. Again, the imagery of the seasons is useful. Spring is not intrinsically a better season than winter, nor is summer better than spring. Each season plays its essential part in the unfolding of the life cycle, and the sequence follows a prescribed course. Winter is a fallow, quiet time in which the previous growth comes to an end and the possibility of new growth is created. It is the ultimate transitional period. Unless the creative work of winter is done and the seeds take root, nothing further can grow. Spring is a time of blossoming, when the fruits of the winter's labor begin to be realized. The blossoms will not appear unless the seeds have been nourished, and the blossoms in turn make way for the blooming, fully grown flowers.

So too with our developmental periods. The Early Adult Transition provides the cross-era shift into early adulthood. The next three periods—Entering the Adult World, the Age Thirty Transition, Settling Down—permit a man to build a first adult life structure, to modify it, and then to create another through which he attains the culmination of early adulthood. At about forty he enters the Mid-life Transition. Now he must terminate the early adult era and plant the seeds for middle adulthood, when he will go through a similar sequence of building, modifying and rebuilding the life structure. The tasks of one period are not better or more advanced than those of another, except in the general sense that each period builds upon the work of the earlier ones and represents a later phase in the cycle. There are losses as well as gains in the shift from every period or era to the next.

• EVALUATION. A more judgmental approach is needed when we consider how a man has fared during a given period. We must ask how well he has met his developmental tasks. How satisfactory is the life structure he forms in a structure-building period? How well has he managed, in a transitional period, to reappraise the past and create a basis for the future?

In extreme cases, we can readily say that a man has done especially well or poorly. This man was clearly unable to reappraise and modify his life in a transitional period and now cannot create an adequate new structure. That man, after a painful transition, has formed a new structure in which his life is exciting, productive, valuable to himself and others. In most cases, however, the picture is more mixed and evaluation difficult. What we are evaluating is not simply how well a person has succeeded in carrying out a specific chore or in adapting to a single, concrete situation. We are asking: How well has he met his basic life tasks? What has he done with his life?

These questions take the scientist, the clinician and the educator into strange territory. We are legitimately interested in understanding and fostering the quality of life, but we need great wisdom lest we evaluate too superficially. Very little is known about the tasks of adult development and the problems of building and modifying a life. We must learn how to explore this territory in greater depth, with greater regard for the powerful shaping forces in the individual and in society. We need to examine lives, to attempt individual and institutional innovation, and to seek new directions. But our work will lack intrinsic value and public credibility if we make premature evaluations and promote easy but ineffective methods.

• OVERLAPPING AND CONNECTING PERIODS. We have tried to identify each period in its own right, to indicate when it occurs and how it contributes to the evolution of the life course. In the actual process of development, however, each period is "interpenetrated" with the others. The current period is predominant, but the others are present in it. It is not the case that a period begins, runs its independent course, and ends, to be followed by another period that has its own totally separate character. The successive periods are not like links in a chain, each tied to the others but intrinsically independent of them.

The life cycle is an organic whole and each period contains all the others. The developing individual is like a long-distance traveler: from time to time he changes vehicles, fellow passengers and baggage of all kinds, but the past does not simply disappear. He is now engaged not only with his current locale but with the various worlds he has lived in and the worlds he is moving toward. The past and future are in the present.

The coexistence and interpenetration of periods is beautifully captured by that master of (his own) biography, Marcel Proust, in *Remembrance of Things Past*:

> For man is a creature without any fixed age, who has the faculty of becoming, in a few seconds, many years younger, and who, surrounded by the walls of the time through which he has lived, floats within them but as though in a basin the surface level of which is constantly changing, so as to bring him into the range now of one epoch, now of another.

The paradox Proust identifies here is that man is "a creature without any fixed age" and yet is governed by time and by the "epochs" in his life. Only after we understand the profound significance of the epochs in our lives, as he did, can we understand the ways in which one is, at a single time, a child, a youth, a middle-aged and an elderly person. We are never ageless. As we gain a greater sense of our own biographies, however, we can begin to exist at multiple ages. In the process, we do not fragment ourselves; rather, we become more integrated and whole.

During the current period, a man works chiefly on the developmental tasks of this period. But he also does some work on the tasks of other periods. Tasks that will become primary in later periods may be activated early. The tasks of preceding periods are not completed and cast aside when those periods come to an end. If they are worked out reasonably well at the appropriate time, they continue to support further development in subsequent periods. Gains of the past form the ground on which current developmental efforts are built. Conversely, if previous periods produce enduring conflicts and limitations, a man's development in the current period may be seriously hindered or, in the extreme case, prevented altogether.

Entry into a new period often reactivates the unresolved problems and deficits of previous periods. These problems form a "baggage from the past" that makes it harder to deal with current tasks. The carryover of past conflicts and hurts may weigh so heavily that present tasks are overshadowed. When a person is having serious difficulties, it is important to examine first the life structure, tasks and concerns of the ongoing period. Continuing problems from earlier periods of childhood and adulthood then may be examined within this context, and we can see how they are hampering the current developmental work.

• UNIVERSALITY OF THE ERAS AND PERIODS. This conception of the life cycle is based largely on a study of men in the contemporary United States. Does it hold for American men generally at this moment in history? Does it have relevance in other societies and historical epochs? The first thing to be said is: we don't know. None of the insights and generalizations offered here are fully demonstrated truths. Each of them is a hypothesis that requires further testing. My previous work on "culture and personality" has taught me to be very cautious in positing universal features of human life; the history of social science is cluttered with disproved claims regarding such universals.

But, with these caveats, we energetically offer the following hypothesis: This sequence of eras and periods exists in all societies, throughout the human species, at the present stage in human evolution. The eras and periods are grounded in the nature of man as a biological, psychological and social organism, and in the nature of society as a complex enterprise extending over many generations. They represent the life cycle of the species. Individuals go through the periods in infinitely varied ways, but the periods themselves are universal. These eras and periods have governed human development for the past five or ten thousand years—since the beginning of more complex, stable societies.

In positing a combined biological, psychological and social basis for this developmental sequence, we are saying that none of these bases is sufficient in itself. No evidence now exists that the eras and periods stem simply from an unfolding of a biological, genetic program in the individual. Nor do they follow directly from a timetable established universally by social institutions or cultures. If this developmental sequence does hold to some degree for the species, its origins must be found in the interaction of all these influences as they operate during a particular phase in man's evolution.

Erikson has come to a similar view of the life cycle on the basis of his clinical, anthropological, historical and biographical inquiries. His ego stage of Identity vs. Identity Confusion reaches its culmination during the period we identify as the Early Adult Transition. His stage of Intimacy vs. Aloneness starts in the early twenties and runs through early adulthood. His next stage, Generativity vs. Stagnation, starts around forty and characterizes middle adulthood, while Integrity vs. Despair is the ego stage of late adulthood. He documents this view in his biographies of Luther, Gandhi, Freud, Hitler, George Bernard Shaw and William James—men whose lives span several centuries and continents.*

Jung's conception of adult development rests upon his analysis of individuals and of mythologies, religious systems, dreams and customs in numerous cultures and times. Others, such as Joseph Campbell and Mircea Eliade, have extended the anthropological basis of Jung's ideas. Jaques found evidence of a mid-life crisis in the lives of 300 artists in many countries over the last 500 years. Ortega y Gasset, taking a broad historical-philosophical view of human life over the last 2500 years, has identified a sequence of generations in society and in the individual life cycle. This sequence corresponds well to the eras and periods described here (see Chapter 2). In

---

* A word about the similarities and differences between our periods and Erikson's stages may be useful. We regard adult development as the evolution of the life structure; our developmental periods are successive phases in the process of building, modifying and rebuilding that structure. Erikson's mode of analysis, too, is concerned with the interconnectedness of self and world. He regards development, however, as a series of stages in ego development.

Each of Erikson's eight stages is governed by a crucial, problematic issue for the self in relation to the external world. The issue is stated as a polarity or contradiction between opposites. The developmental tasks of each stage derive from the central polarity. Thus, in the stage of Generativity-Stagnation the tasks include arriving at a "favorable balance" of generativity over stagnation; coming to terms with the actualities of stagnation and death; drawing more fully upon one's internal resources for generative purposes; accepting with less ambivalence one's responsibilities and obligations toward society in general and the next generation of adults in particular; acquiring the virtue of "caring" in new ways for individuals and institutions.

Erikson's ego stages have to do with the self as it is engaged with the world, but their primary focus is *within the person*. Each stage is defined in terms of attributes of a person: the capacity for commitment, the virtue of caring, the sense of trust. These personal qualities connect the self to the sociocultural world, and Erikson more than any other investigator has depicted the subtle but vast influence of the sociocultural world upon ego development. His biographical studies of Luther and Gandhi are unmatched in their sensitive portrayal of the ways in which historical, cultural and institutional forces enter into the shape and substance of an individual life.

Our approach makes use of Erikson's, but it shifts the focus somewhat. The concept of life structure is centered more directly on *the boundary between self and world*. It gives equal consideration to self and world as aspects of the lived life. We find a larger number of developmental periods, and we trace the developmental process in somewhat more detail. Still, there are many areas of convergence. Our view of the self includes Erikson's concept of the ego. Our view of the sociocultural world as an aspect of life structure is consistent with his way of thinking about society. His ego stages of adulthood fit well within the timetable of our eras and periods. Our view builds on and adds to his, and is not antithetical to it.

*The Coming of Age*, Simone de Beauvoir documents the transition from middle to late adulthood, and the nature of life in old age, in societies around the world. David Gutmann, studying the fantasies of men in several contrasting societies, has obtained findings consistent with ours.

In exploring the question of universality, it would help if we had more data on the *life cycle in earlier cultures*. We do have available, however, three documents going back some 2500 years (see the table on page 325). These documents reflect the wisdom of the ancient Hebrew, Chinese and Greek civilizations. The Talmud contains a section called "The Sayings of the Fathers" (Pirke Aboth), which outlines the "ages of man." Confucius, writing in China about 500 B.C.E., identifies six steps in the life cycle. Solon, a Greek poet and lawmaker in the 7th century B.C.E., divided the life cycle into ten stages, each lasting seven years.

These sources differ widely in cultural context and religion. Yet, despite the diversity of imagery and content, the three views of the life cycle are basically similar to each other and to the one presented here. (Unfortunately, all of them refer only to males; the neglect of the female life cycle has a long history.) If we place the timetable of our eras and periods over each of the ancient accounts, like a template, they show a remarkably close fit.

a. The pre-adult era occupies roughly the first 15 to 20 years.

b. Early adulthood extends from 15 or 20 until about 40. It contains an initial formative period of some 15 years (like our "novice phase") in which a young man enters the adult world, gets married and pursues an occupation. Only at 30 does he attain full strength (Talmud, Solon) and "plant his feet firm upon the ground" (Confucius). From 30 to 40 a man has his greatest strength and energy, but he has not yet attained his most mature capabilities. Early adulthood is thus a time of flowering, as well as a preparation for the next era.

c. Middle adulthood lasts from roughly 40 to 60. From 42 to 56, says Solon, "the tongue and the mind . . . are now at their best." In the next stage (56-63), "is he able, but never so nimble in speech and in wit as he was in the days of his prime." According to the Talmud, 40 is the age for "understanding" and 50 for "giving counsel." Confucius differs only slightly in idiom: "At 40, I no longer suffered from perplexities," and "At 50, I knew what were the biddings of heaven" (although it was not until 60 that he heard them with docile ear!). All agree, then, that the years from about 40 to 60 permit the greatest actualization of one's capabilities and virtues and the greatest contribution to society, despite some decline in youthful strength and energy.

d. For all three sources, late adulthood starts at around 60. Solon regards old age as a period of decline: at 70, man "has come to the time to depart on the ebb-tide of Death." The Talmud and Confucius offer a more developmental view of this era. According to the Talmud, the full wisdom and dignity of being an elder start at 60. At this age, says Confucius, I enter into a new relation to heaven—that is, to life and death, to the ultimate source of personal values, to the self—and through it gain a new kind of spiritual freedom transcending the old antitheses between desire and morality, between society and self.

e. The Talmud adds a final phase, which corresponds to our late late adulthood. At 80, a man attains a new strength (Gevurah) of advanced age. After 90, he lives on the far edge of the boundary between life and death.

One may also note, in addition to the ancient concepts of the "ages of man," the curious but suggestive outline presented in 1851 by the German philosopher Arthur Schopenhauer in *Parerga and Paralipomena: Short Philosophical Essays* (published in English translation by the Clarendon Press in 1974). He agrees with the Upanishad of the Veda that "the natural duration of human life" (barring accidents or illness) is 100 years, and then (slightly tongue-in-cheek) identifies a sequence of decades with appropriate planetary influences. At 30, for example, "Mars reigns, and a man is now impetuous, strong, bold and warlike." At 50 "Jupiter holds sway." Finally, "Uranus comes and then, as they say, we go to heaven. . . ."

THREE VERSIONS OF "THE AGES OF MAN"

*"The Sayings of the Fathers" (from the Talmud)*

    5 years is the age for reading (Scripture);
    10 for Misnah (the laws);
    13 for the Commandments (Bar Mitzvah, moral responsibility);
    15 for Gemara (Talmudic discussions; abstract reasoning);
    18 for Hupa (wedding canopy);
    20 for seeking a livelihood (pursuing an occupation);
    30 for attaining full strength ("Koah");
    40 for understanding;
    50 for giving counsel;
    60 for becoming an elder (wisdom, old age);
    70 for white hair;
    80 for Gevurah (new, special strength of age);
    90 for being bent under the weight of the years;
    100 for being as if already dead and passed away from the world.

*Confucius*

The Master said, At 15 I set my heart upon learning.
At 30, I had planted my feet firm upon the ground.
At 40, I no longer suffered from perplexities.
At 50, I knew what were the biddings of heaven.
At 60, I heard them with docile ear.
At 70, I could follow the dictates of my own heart; for what
      I desired no longer overstepped the boundaries of right.

*Solon*

  0–7 A boy at first is the man; unripe; then he casts his teeth;
      milk-teeth befitting the child he sheds in his seventh year.
 7–14 Then to his seven years God adding another seven,
      signs of approaching manhood show in the bud.
14–21 Still, in the third of the sevens his limbs are growing; his chin
      touched with a fleecy down, the bloom of the cheek gone.
21–28 Now, in the fourth of the sevens ripen to greatest completeness
      the powers of the man, and his worth becomes plain to see.
28–35 In the fifth he bethinks him that this is the season for courting,
      bethinks him that sons will preserve and continue his line.
35–42 Now in the sixth his mind, ever open to virtue,
      broadens, and never inspires him to profitless deeds;
42–56 Seven times seven, and eight; the tongue and the mind
      for fourteen years together are now at their best.
56–63 Still in the ninth is he able, but never so nimble
      in speech and in wit as he was in the days of his prime.
63–70 Who to the tenth has attained, and has lived to complete it,
      has come to the time to depart on the ebb-tide of Death.

# An Evolutionary Perspective

In a more speculative vein, I want to place this view of the life cycle in the perspective of human evolution. In 1932, the biologist G. P. Bidder published an evocative article in which he attempted to explain biological senescence—that is, the normal process of bodily decline. Senescence is not built into the life cycle of some organisms as an inexorable sequence leading to death. However, senescence occurs in all the land vertebrates, including man. Why, asks Bidder, is this?

The key factor, in his opinion, is that the members of every species of land vertebrate must reach and maintain a standard body size which is optimal for mobility and survival. The growth sequence proceeds as follows. First, the organism goes through a process of *positive growth* until it reaches an optimal size. A regulating mechanism is needed to limit growth when the optimal size is reached. This regulator produces a phase of *non-growth* that maintains the optimal state for a while, and then a phase of increasing *negative growth* for which death is a normal outcome. Bidder's reasoning is this:

> Adequate efficiency could be obtained only by the evolution of some mechanism to stop natural growth so soon as specific size is reached. This mechanism may be called the regulator. . . .
>
> I have suggested that senescence is the result of the continued action of the regulator after growth is stopped. The regulator does efficiently all that concerns the welfare of the species. Man is within 2 cm. of the same height between 18 and 60; he gently rises 2 cm. between 20 and 27, and still more gently loses 1 cm. by 40 or thereabouts.
>
> If primitive man at 18 begat a son, the species had no more need of him by 37, when his son could hunt for food for the grandchildren. Therefore, the dwindling of cartilage, muscle and nerve cell, which *we call senescence, did not affect the survival of the species; the checking of growth had secured that by ensuring a perfect physique between 20 and 40.*
>
> Effects of continued negative growth after 37 were of indifference to the race; *probably no man ever reached 60 years old until language attained such importance in the equipment of the species that long experience became valuable in a man who could neither fight nor hunt.*
>
> This negative growth is not the manifestation of a weakness inherent in protoplasm or characteristic of nucleated cells; it is the unimportant by-product of a regulating mechanism necessary to the survival of swiftly moving land animals, a mechanism evolved by selection and survival as have been evolved the jointing of mammalian limbs, and with similar perfection.

Though his main purpose is to identify the biological mechanism of senescence, Bidder here almost incidentally describes universal phases in the human life cycle and suggests how they have been affected in the course of evolution. His first phase, positive growth, corresponds to the era we call pre-adulthood. It extends from birth to about 20, when the individual attains full biological growth. Bidder's second phase, corresponding to early adulthood, lasts roughly from 20 to 40. During this time the individual's capacity for adaptation and mastery is at its height and he makes his primary contribution to the survival of the species. His third phase, from 40 to 60, is like our middle adulthood: the effects of the regulator begin to produce a slight biological decline but there is also a possibility for greater psychological development and social contribution under facilitating social conditions. In the fourth phase, from 60 on, increasing senescence culminates in death.

For our present purposes, Bidder is making two important points about the human life cycle. First, he draws a clear distinction between early and middle adulthood, with age 40 as an approximate turning point. Second, he maintains that, until very recently in human evolution, there was little experience of middle adulthood. By age 40 primitive man had completed his main reproductive, parental and occupational contributions to the tribe. With the decline of his social usefulness and adaptive capacities, his chances for survival beyond 40 were quite small. It was only with the recent emergence of language and more complex cultural forms that the tribe placed much value on sustaining individual life after 40.

The current evidence supports Bidder's viewpoint. The human species has existed for at least half a million years and perhaps more than three million years. Until five or ten thousand years ago man led a precarious, unsettled life in small societies that lived primarily by hunting, fishing and gathering food. The character of human life was transformed by the development of agriculture, the formation of more stable societies, the invention of more effective technologies, and the emergence of writing and other means of transmitting culture from one generation to the next.

In primitive hunting-gathering societies, only half the population reached age 20, and not more than 10 percent survived beyond 40. The high mortality rate in early adulthood was not due to earlier senescence, since 70 to 80 years has probably been man's normal life span for many thousands of years. It was caused by the ravages of illness, accident, warfare and inadequate food supply. Life after 40—the eras of middle adulthood and beyond—has been a significant part of man's collective experience for but a moment in our history.

Primitive man had little biological or tribal reason to continue living after 40. By that age the children were grown, the best years of productive labor ended, the contribution to the tribe fulfilled. By 40 a man was obsolete. The tribe needed only a small cluster of men in middle adulthood to contribute their ripening wisdom in positions of leadership and responsibility. A large number would have strained the tribe's resources.

United Nations data on the age composition of contemporary nations offers interesting comparisons. In Pakistan, where human fertility is high and living conditions among the worst, only 17 percent of the population is over 40. The figures are even lower in Ethiopia and Bangladesh. At the other extreme, 35 percent of the Japanese are over 40 years old, 36 percent in the U.S.A., and 42 percent in West Germany. Current predictions are that the percentages will rise in the industrialized countries over the coming decades.

The rapidly lengthening life span in modern society has stimulated widespread concern with the era of late adulthood. We are beginning to seek ways of improving the quality of life for the elderly, and of managing the economic burdens involved. Much less attention has been given to a problem of equal or greater significance: What about the rapidly growing percentage of the population in middle adulthood? Unless the quality of life in this generation is improved, the middle-aged will be under tremendous strain and society will continue to be short of creative leadership. More elaborate social structures have been developed in every aspect of society— agriculture, industry, government, religion, education, health care, science, art, even recreation. Occupational roles have become more specialized. We need more people who can contribute as leaders, managers, mentors, sources of traditional wisdom as well as vision and imagination. Modern society requires a vital, developing contingent in middle age.

The required work of middle adulthood is different from that of youth. It involves greater responsibility, perspective and judgment. A person in this era must be able to care for younger and older adults, to exercise authority creatively, to transcend the youthful extremes of shallow conformity and impulsive rebelliousness. The moderate mid-life decrease in biological capacity must be counterbalanced by an increased psychosocial capacity. In countless intellectual, emotional, moral, esthetic, managerial and reparative ways, the middle-aged must help in maintaining and developing the culture.

It is not that modern society has created middle adulthood as an era. The capability for living productively beyond 40 has been part of the human potential from the start. But only recently has society become better able to ensure that its members live out their full life span, rather than just half of it. Society is now doing better at keeping people healthy after 40. The more difficult problem is to foster psychological well-being and provide the conditions for a satisfying, productive life in middle adulthood. Nations vary somewhat, but the problem is universal. Its basic roots are in human evolution rather than in the nature of a particular society. The rapid development of powerful technology and of cumbersome institutional structures has created a need for greater numbers of productive middle-aged individuals. But the need has far outstripped our cumulative understanding of middle adulthood and our ability to foster life in it.

The large-scale extension of the average life expectancy beyond 40 is one of the great achievements in human evolution. It is a step in the "ascent of man." But the termination of early adulthood continues to be frightening and painful. This is partly because middle adulthood is such a recent acquisition in human evolution. Our profound anxiety at passing 40 reflects the ancient experience of the species: we still fear that life ends at 40. It is still profoundly threatening to move from early to middle adulthood. The threat is based on the equating of youth with strength and vitality, and of age—even middle age—with weakness, vulnerability and death.

A few thousand years is not enough to learn what to do with middle adulthood and with the institutions that shape its course. We are still feeling our way in the dark. As I make the shift from early to middle adulthood, the tribe offers little instruction, support or cultural wisdom. What I am losing is much more evident than what I may gain. I know that a new season is coming, that my life will be crucially changed. But what are the options that await me? I get many explicit messages and vague vibrations about mortality, loss, restriction; feelings that time is running out and that I may soon die or, worse, have a life without meaning for myself or others. But I get few positive images of the middle-aged hero— the lover, friend or mentor, the person of dignity, wisdom, authority, creativeness. Where is the contemporary parallel to Abraham, Buddha or Odysseus on his mid-life journey?

# The Developmental Work of Early and Middle Adulthood

My purpose here is not to add a new myth of heroic adulthood or to offer a sure path to salvation, joy and optimal development. It is, rather, to illuminate the dark a little and give a clearer view of the terrain. What is the nature of development in early and middle adulthood? What kinds of developmental work must be done?

The conception of eras provides a contour map, as it were, within which to examine the terrain of early and middle adulthood and to specify the developmental tasks that must be met. Within this framework, we have identified three sets of tasks. The three sets are closely interrelated, and all of them are essential to an understanding of adulthood. I shall review them briefly.

## Building and Modifying the Life Structure

One set of tasks has to do with the developmental periods and the evolution of the life structure. I have given special emphasis to the periods because, within the broader patterning of the eras, they provide the primary source of order and sequential progression. In a stable period the major tasks are to build a life structure and enhance one's life within it. In a transitional period one must terminate the existing structure, explore possibilities (in self and world) out of which new choices can be formed and make the initial choices that provide the basis for a new structure. The cross-era transitions require one to terminate the outgoing era and to initiate the next. In addition, every period has distinctive tasks that reflect its specific place in the life cycle.

## Working on Single Components of the Life Structure

A second set of tasks has to do with forming and modifying single components of the life structure. We have identified several components, such as occupation, family and mentoring relationships, which are often of central importance in a man's life. Developmental work is required if a man is to make a place in his life for a given component. The continuing work on these tasks contributes to the stability of adult life. At the same time this work changes from period to period and contributes to the evolution of the life structure. As I have said, psychologists and social scientists often focus on a single component without placing it in the context of the life structure. Our understanding of changes within a single component will, I believe, be increased when we examine it from a developmental perspective. Let me emphasize again: the individual life structure evolves through a series of age-linked periods; the more concrete changes within a single component are much more variable in their sequence and timing.

Of the many components that may have great significance in a man's life, five seemed of special importance in our study.

• FORMING AND MODIFYING A DREAM. In early adulthood a man has to form a Dream, create an initial structure in which the Dream can be lived out, and attain goals through which it is in some measure fulfilled. In middle adulthood his task is to modify or give up the Dream. He may recognize that he will not be able even partially to fulfill it. He then has to free himself from its excessive hold and to determine which other aspects of the self he will try to live out. If he has attained the Dream sufficiently, and finds it worthwhile (even though it does not provide the magical qualities he had hoped for), he may continue in the general direction it prescribes. But he is now less tyrannized by ambition, more concerned with the intrinsic value of his efforts, and more able to enjoy diverse aspects of living. The Dream may die stillborn or may flourish for many years. Even when it continues to play a part, its meaning and place in his life necessarily evolve over the sequence of periods. Each man finds his own balance of stability and change.

• FORMING AND MODIFYING AN OCCUPATION. The process of forming an occupation is never brief or simple. It occupies the entire novice phase of early adulthood, from roughly age 17 to 33. Some men stay in a single occupation during this time, but the majority make a few or many changes. Even if a man continues within one broadly defined occupation (such as plumber, novelist or manager), he will go through many qualitative changes in work place, status, identity, meaning and mode of work.

In the early thirties, with the start of the Settling Down period, he tries to define a work enterprise and ladder that will carry him to the culmination of his youthful strivings. He starts on the bottom rung of the ladder, as a junior member of his adult world. By about 40, and the end of the Becoming One's Own Man period, he has advanced as far as he can up the early adult ladder. A vital task of the Mid-life Transition is to make a place for himself in the middle adult generation and become "senior" within that world. Men differ enormously in the nature and personal importance of their early adult ladder, in how far they climb, in the meaning their ultimate success-failure has for them, and in the new work they undertake in middle adulthood.

• LOVE-MARRIAGE-FAMILY. Several tasks are included here, but they are so interrelated that it seems best to consider them together. What a man seeks in a love relationship, and what kinds of love relationships he is able to form, are continuing issues in adult life. If he is to have intimate love relationships with women, he must achieve some degree of sexual freedom and some integration of sexuality and affection. If he is to form an enduring, mutually valued marriage, he must become capable of fidelity and commitment. If he is to join his wife in creating a stable family life that serves the needs of parents as well as children, he must become ready to accept familial responsibilities and to derive the satisfactions offered by marriage and fatherhood.

No one can be far advanced in these tasks at the start of early adulthood. During the novice phase, a man is as much an apprentice with regard to living, husbanding and fathering as in other aspects of life. His loving is often characterized by impersonal pleasure seeking, macho power seeking or inhibition of passion and sensuality. If he seeks a serious relationship with a woman, his ideal is the "special woman" who will be his lover, friend and helper in search of the Dream. Yet he may marry a woman who does not appreciate and support his Dream, and in time they will have to deal with the consequences of this refusal. Sometimes his wife helps greatly in his heroic struggles and their relationship is idyllic at the start. It will have to be modified over time as both of them change in different directions. If she has a Dream other than that of becoming a wife and mother, the two of them will have to create an evolving life structure that can encompass their joint family and their separate occupations. There are endless variations in the patterning of familial relationships and their vicissitudes over time. All that is certain is that the patterning will change and will require continuing developmental work in the successive periods.

In early adulthood most men give work a higher priority than family, though the relative balance of the two is quite variable. A man's engagement in family life is often limited by his anxiety regarding the feminine in himself. For example, he may sharply separate the maternal and paternal functions, leaving the former to his wife. His heavy involvement in outside activities, and his avoidance of many caring-feeling functions when at home, sometimes obscure the strength of a man's investment in his family.

Fatherhood was tremendously important for most of the men in our study. They were gratified when things went well at home, and they experienced great anxiety and guilt when family life was too limited or full of conflict. Often, a man's sense of family and attachment to the children were strong enough to keep him in an otherwise stultifying marriage. Jim Tracy is but one of many examples. He also exemplifies a change that frequently occurs in the late thirties and early forties: he modulated his involvement in work and gave the family a more central place in his life structure. The developmental work of the Mid-life Transition contributes to this process. Through it, a man gets more in touch with the feminine in himself and others. He becomes more interested in being a mentorial father to his youthful offspring and in supporting his wife's need to expand outside the home.

• FORMING MENTORING RELATIONSHIPS. Initiating, modifying and terminating relationships with mentors is an important yet difficult task of early adulthood. Young men differ widely in their capability for evoking and sustaining these relationships. There are also great variations in the availability of mentoring opportunities in different social worlds.

A good mentor is an admixture of good father and good friend. (A bad mentor, of which there are many, combines the worst features of father and friend.) A "good enough" mentor is a transitional figure who invites and welcomes a young man into the adult world. He serves as guide, teacher and sponsor. He represents skill, knowledge, virtue, accomplishment—the superior qualities a young man hopes someday to acquire. He gives his blessing to the novice and his Dream. And yet, with all this supe-riority, he conveys the promise that in time they will be peers. The protégé has the hope that soon he will be able to join or even surpass his mentor in the work they both value.

A mentor can be of great practical help to a young man as he seeks to find his way and gain new skills. But a good mentor is helpful in a more basic, developmental sense. This relationship enables the recipient to identify with a person who exemplifies many of the qualities he seeks. It enables him to form an *internal* figure who offers love, admiration and encouragement in his struggles. He acquires a sense of belonging to the generation of promising young men. He reaps the varied benefits to be gained from a serious, mutual, non-sexual loving relationship with a some-what older man or woman. (There are other elements, which bring various advantages and disadvantages, when the relationship is sexual and when the mentor is much older, or the same age.)

Like all love relationships, the course of a mentor relationship is rarely smooth and its ending is often painful. Such relationships have favorable developmental functions, but they have negative aspects as well. There is plenty of room for exploitation, undercutting, envy, smothering and op-pressive control on the part of the mentor, and for greedy demanding, clinging admiration, self-denying gratitude and arrogant ingratitude on the part of the recipient. It is not always clear who is doing what for whom. After the relationship has been terminated, both parties are susceptible to the most intense feelings of admiration and contempt, appreciation and resentment, grief, rage, bitterness and relief—just as in the wake of any significant love relationship.

Many adults give and receive very little mentoring. Despite the frequent emphasis on teamwork and loyalty in business organizations, mentoring relationships are more the exception than the rule for both workers and managers. Our system of higher education, though officially committed to fostering the intellectual and personal development of students, provides mentoring that is generally limited in quantity and poor in quality. Educa-tional institutions and work organizations can do much more to assist the development of students and young adult workers. To do this, they will also have to support the development of teachers, managers and other workers in the generations over age 30. Until middle adulthood is a better time of life, most of those who are in it will be unable to contribute the mentoring urgently needed by younger generations. Many middle-aged men never experience the satisfactions and tribulations of mentorhood. This is a waste of talent, a loss to the individuals involved, and an impedi-ment to constructive social change.

• FORMING MUTUAL FRIENDSHIPS. In our interviews, friendship was largely noticeable by its absence. As a tentative generalization we would say that close friendship with a man or woman is rarely experienced by American men. This is not something that can be adequately determined by a questionnaire or mass survey. The distinction between friend and acquaintance is often blurred. A man may have a wide social network in which he has amicable, "friendly" relationships with many men and perhaps a few women. In general, however, most men do not have an intimate male friend of the kind that they recall fondly from boyhood or youth. Many men have had casual dating relationships with women, and perhaps a few complex love-sex relationships, but most men have not had an intimate, non-sexual friendship with a woman. We need to understand why friendship is so rare, and what consequences this deprivation has for adult life.

## Becoming More Individuated

The third and final set of tasks has to do with adult individuation. These tasks involve the basic polarities of Young/Old, Destruction/Creation, Masculine/Feminine and Attachment/Separateness. In transitional periods, a man has the task of reintegrating each polarity in a form appropriate to his new place in the life cycle.

These polarities have been of interest chiefly to psychologists, who have regarded them as aspects of the personality. In our opinion they must be considered from the conjoint perspective of person and society, for they exist as divisions within both. Each polarity exists within the self and is worked on by the self over time. It also exists within society and is modified by society in the course of its history. Consider the Young/Old polarity. An American man's sense of what it means to be young or old is shaped by cultural symbols and images, by the schools and occupations, by the realities and meanings of Medicare, retirement, social security, Florida condominiums, death and dying—and by the movies, television, rock music, professional sports and mod life styles. It is hard to integrate the Young/Old polarity in the self when the external world draws such a hard line between young and old and makes it so frightening to be other than young.

When more is done to foster development in pre-adulthood, young men will enter early adulthood with a relatively better integration of the polarities and a greater readiness to engage in developmental work on these and other tasks. Nonetheless, it is unlikely that more than a limited integration can be achieved by the end of the Early Adult Transition. Some degree of splitting and one-sidedness seems to be a built-in, normal feature of the self and the life structure in early adulthood.

Thus, a man in his twenties and thirties is normally full of youthful energies and aspirations. He is tilted, as it were, toward the Young pole of the Young/Old polarity. He has a strong need to accentuate his archetypally Young qualities and a corresponding need to minimize or repress his archetypally Old qualities. It is developmentally appropriate for him to maintain the unconscious wish and assumption that he is indeed immortal. He needs—and can have—more time before he confronts his own mortality and begins coming to terms with his own eventual death and the actual or eventual death of his loved ones. The Mid-life Transition is a developmentally given period for working on this process. He can then become more mentorial, create a legacy, and have the other satisfactions that stem from integrating the Young/Old polarity in a way appropriate for middle adulthood.

So too for the other polarities. Although the Masculine/Feminine imbalance can be much less marked than it usually is in our highly gender-split society, a man in early adulthood must give some priority to the masculine. His adult identity is colored by images of manliness, and he cannot fully utilize the qualities he regards as feminine. Greater integration is possible in middle adulthood: he now has greater *internal* freedom to enjoy the feminine in himself and others; and, in a "good enough" society, he is given greater *external* freedom as well.

A young man cannot be expected to integrate the Destruction/Creation polarity. He may have a good deal of knowledge and personal experience regarding certain kinds of destruction, such as war, crime, poverty or natural disasters. But as a youth he is not ready to experience fully the destructive forces in self, society and nature, and to give them a more profound meaning. In middle adulthood he may achieve a fuller integration of the Destruction/Creation polarity and become creative in ways not possible earlier.

In early adulthood, the powerful forces of attachment to the external world are reflected in a man's search for involvement, mastery, control, and material and emotional income. The Attachment/Separateness balance normally shifts in middle adulthood. He can now strengthen the forces of separateness. He can develop a stronger sense of self and a centering in the self, while maintaining his ties and responsibilities in the world.

## Fostering Adult Development

Clearly, a great deal must be done to support individual development in adulthood. Where a person's development has been severely hampered in the past, or is being thwarted in the present, new therapeutic approaches must be created, approaches that take account of the normal developmental processes involved as well as the more neurotic, pathological aspects. Individual and group counseling and educational efforts can help troubled individuals place their specific problems within a broader, developmental perspective.

But such approaches, though helpful, do not go to the heart of the problem. If we are to support adult development on a wider scale, we will have to modify the social institutions that shape our lives. Industry and other work organizations, government, higher education, religion and family—all of these must take account of the changing needs of adults in different eras and developmental periods. What is helpful in one era may not be in another.

In early adulthood, a man is faced with tremendous burdens as he attempts to form an occupation, start a marriage and family, meet heavy financial demands, modify his ties to the pre-adult self and world, and integrate his life as an adult. The Age Thirty Transition is frequently a time of crisis. At the end of the twenties, just when his life is getting more settled, many of his relationships, goals and values come into question. In the early thirties, as the Age Thirty Transition ends and Settling Down begins, he must make choices that have crucial consequences for his entire future. Some men have a crisis relating to Becoming One's Own Man in the late thirties; they find their life structure intolerable just when they are reaching the culmination of early adulthood.

The twenties and thirties are perhaps the most abundant and the most stressful decades in the life cycle. Given the tremendously difficult tasks of adaptation and development a young man must deal with, this era cannot be made easy or simple to traverse. Still, much can be done to reduce the excessive stress and to facilitate work on the developmental tasks.

If a man's early adulthood is dominated by poverty, recurrent unemployment and the lack of a reasonably satisfactory niche in society, his adult development will be undermined. His energies will go to simple survival rather than the pursuit of a Dream or the creation of a life structure that has value for himself and others. If he lives in a disorganized, fragmented, polluted, crime-ridden world, how can he keep the worst features of collective life from becoming part of his individual development?

But it is not simply a matter of gross poverty and social disorganization. Even when a man's circumstances are more comfortable—when he lives in a pleasant neighborhood and has a secure job or profession—many aspects of work, family and community life combine to produce heavy external pressure and inner conflicts. Starting a family and embarking upon an occupational career, when one's income is at its lowest point and one's adult status is still marginal, imposes terrible burdens on both husband and wife. If the extent and consequences of this problem were taken more seriously, much could be done to alleviate the stress.

For large numbers of men, the conditions of work in early adulthood are oppressive, alienating and inimical to development. Most people work in corporations, small companies, local or federal government agencies, schools, churches, hospitals—institutional structures of all kinds. This is a recent historical development. We are still learning how to create organizations that work productively, humanely and in ways that support the adult development of their employees and clients. The aims of productivity and profit making have had top priority in the industrial age that is now passing. As we move into an age in which production and power might be less overriding concerns, we have a chance to reorder our priorities. It remains to be seen whether we shall give higher priority to enhancing the meaning of work and to creating work organizations that foster development as well as productive efficiency.

At a more specific, personal level, we can try to improve the quantity and quality of mentoring in the work world. Most young men receive little mentoring, and good mentor relationships are rare indeed. Poor mentoring in early adulthood is the equivalent of poor parenting in childhood: without adequate mentoring a young man's entry into the adult world is greatly hampered. Some degree of emotional support, guidance and sponsorship is needed to smooth the way and make the journey worthwhile.

When the work world is hypermasculine—when women are absent or highly subordinated, and many qualities in men are devalued as "feminine"—a man will find it harder to integrate the Masculine/Feminine polarity. The freer participation of women in the work world is an important step toward the liberation of men from their one-sided masculinity and their anxiety about the feminine. Men need women as colleagues, bosses and mentors. These relationships enable them to form richer identities, to live out more aspects of the self, and to reduce the burdens created by the excessive masculinization of work. Changes of this kind will also free women from the constraints imposed by the excessive feminization of parenting and by the discrimination that restricts their participation in most of our institutions.

Further institutional changes are needed to permit better living and development in middle adulthood. Our institutions now are geared mainly to early adulthood. Whatever their limitations for young men, they are even more faulty for men in middle age. For example, the family in our society and in all others since the origin of the species is above all an institution for young adults. The family is for most of us a powerful symbol of tradition and personal immortality. It is a social arrangement through which youthful parents strive to rear their pre-adult offspring and to establish their own place in the world. The functions of the family change drastically as the offspring begin to leave the nest and the parents enter middle adulthood.

We are just beginning to ask the fundamental questions about the role of the family in the lives of its middle-aged members. The relationships of parents to their adult offspring (and to the succeeding generations) have a continuing importance in middle and late adulthood. In middle adulthood, if the family is intact, a man and woman must restructure their relationships with each other, with their offspring and grandchildren, with their parents and perhaps grandparents. What are the proper functions of the family, and what should be its structure and guiding values, under the new living conditions of middle adulthood? What kinds of supports are needed so that the middle-aged can better manage their developmental tasks and cope with the strains of family life? The problem is compounded when a person has more than one family, or no family, in the middle years.

Similarly, most occupations are defined and understood from the perspective of early adulthood. When we discuss or study an occupation, we usually focus on the process of entry and the kinds of work it requires during the initial five or ten or twenty years. But the nature of a man's work changes appreciably in middle adulthood. Much less thought, and certainly much less public discussion, have been given to the meaning of work in these years. How should jobs and careers evolve during middle adulthood? What new kinds of work are desirable from the viewpoint of the individual and of society? What can be done to provide for greater learning and rejuvenation within the same occupation, for shifting to a "second career," or for early retirement and change to new forms of work in middle adulthood?

As we move into the epoch of "postindustrial" society, major changes will be required in every aspect of social life. We must increase the possibilities for creative work and play. New archetypal Dreams will have to be generated and sustained in all segments of the population. Participation in mentor relationships must become a more widespread and valued part of adult living. There are important political and economic aspects to all of this, but no existing political viewpoint offers clear answers.

Issues such as these are beginning to be discussed, but the surface has only been scratched. There is strong individual and institutional reluctance to look more deeply. The questions are new. They evoke great anxiety and run counter to traditional ways of thinking. It is hard to explore their full complexity, let alone find rational answers. The paradox is that we must devote ourselves to the search for new solutions even though we know that we are as yet not up to the task and that it will take generations more of "muddling through" before significant advances can be made.

These problems are certainly not limited to our society. To different degrees, they hold for the entire human species during its present stage of evolution. Countless variations on the universal themes are produced by differences in culture and institutions, as well as in individual heredity and circumstances. Humankind is still learning how to meet the developmental tasks of the present eras and periods, and thereby to improve the value of life over its entire course. It is too much to expect that middle adulthood will be managed well by most persons in any society within the forseeable future.

I am not saying that the life cycle in its present form is immutable. The basic nature and timing of the eras will no doubt be modified in the future, but fundamental change of this kind is evolutionary. It requires hundreds of generations, not merely a few decades or centuries. In the longer run, our further progress in fostering adult development may be part of a transformation of human society and personality, and thus contribute to a new epoch in human evolution.

That chapter in history is still far off. For now, we have all we can do to understand the nature of the current life cycle and to work toward constructive change within it. If we cannot do so, the next chapter may never be written. Despite the difficulty of the problem, our only reasonable choice is to get on with the work.

Notes

xi  *Ray C. Walker*  As part of his work on the project, Walker completed
a senior thesis at Yale University Medical School: "Individuation and the
Mid-Life Decade in Men," Yale University School of Medicine, April
1970.

xiii  *Willy Brandt*  Barbara L. Kellerman, "Willy Brandt: Portrait of the
Leader as Young Politician," doctoral dissertation, Department of Political
Science, Yale University, 1975.

xiii  *development of women*  Wendy A. Stewart, "The Formation of the Early
Adult Life Structure in Women," doctoral dissertation in clinical psychology, Teachers College, Columbia University, 1976.

CHAPTER 1

4  *In academic psychology*  For examples of important early work in the
social sciences, see Karl Mannheim's seminal essay, "The Problem of
Generations," first published in 1928, reprinted in his *Essays on the
Sociology of Knowledge* (Oxford University Press, 1952), pp. 276–320,
and Arnold van Gennep, *The Rites of Passage* (University of Chicago,
1960 [original, 1908]). Our conception of "transition" owes much to
van Gennep's view of "passage."

Recent summaries of the social science literature are in the following
source works: Leonard D. Cain, "Life Course and Social Structure," in
R. E. L. Faris, ed., *Handbook of Modern Sociology* (Rand McNally,
1964); Orville G. Brim, Jr., and Stanton Wheeler, *Socialization After
Childhood* (Wiley, 1966); Orville G. Brim, Jr., "Theories of the Male
Mid-life Crisis," *The Counseling Psychologist*, 6 (1976), 2–9; Glen H.
Elder, "Age Differentiation and the Life Course," in *Annual Review of
Sociology*, Vol. I (Annual Reviews, 1975); and Matilda W. Riley, et al.,
*Aging and Society*, 3 vols. (Russell Sage, 1968 and 1972) (in Vol. III,
see especially John Clausen's chapter, "The Life Course of Individuals").

Within academic psychology the earliest relevant research on adult
development was that of Charlotte Buhler and her associates. See Charlotte Buhler, "The Curve of Life as Studied in Biographies," *Journal of
Applied Psychology*, 19 (1955), 405–9; Charlotte Buhler, "The Course
of Human Life as a Psychological Problem," *Human Development*,

11 (1968), 184–200; and Charlotte Buhler and Fred Massarik, eds., *The Course of Human Life* (Springer, 1968). See also the account by Buhler's collaborator, Else Frenkel: "Studies in Biographical Psychology," *Character and Personality*, 5 (1936), 1–34.

One of the first systematic efforts in academic psychology to create a combined biological, psychological and social view of development was made by my old friend and colleague Robert W. White. See *Lives in Progress* (Dryden Press, 1952) and *The Enterprise of Living* (Holt, Rinehart and Winston, 1972).

A broad and representative collection of studies, most of them done prior to 1960, has been assembled by Bernice L. Neugarten in *Middle Age and Aging: A Reader in Social Psychology* (University of Chicago, 1968).

5   *Jung used the term*   Jung's thinking about adult development and individuation evolved over many years, starting in his forties. There is no single article or book in which he gave a succinct statement of his views on this topic. The following works are relevant: *Man and His Symbols* (Doubleday, 1964); *Memories, Dreams, Reflections* (Pantheon, 1963); and *The Archetypes and the Collective Unconscious*, Collected Works, Vol. IX, Part 1 (2nd ed.) (Bollingen, 1968). See also Joseph Campbell, ed., *The Portable Jung* (Viking, 1971).

5   *Erikson is primarily*   Erikson's view of the life cycle is described in the following: *Childhood and Society* (Norton, 1950) and "Identity and the Life Cycle," *Psychological Issues*, 1 (1959), 1–171.

5   *This tradition includes*   Ernest Becker's last two books were *The Denial of Death* (Free Press, 1973) and *Escape from Evil* (Macmillan, 1976). Although Becker does not deal primarily with the life cycle and the problem of adult development, his ideas about adulthood lend themselves to a developmental approach.

The investigator whose work most closely resembles ours is Roger L. Gould. He independently arrived at a similar sequence of periods in adult development. His findings are based chiefly on his clinical experience with groups and with couples, and his emphasis is primarily on personality development. See his article "The Phases of Adult Life: A Study in Developmental Psychology," *American Journal of Psychiatry*, 129 (1972), 521–31. A fuller account is given in his book, tentatively titled *Transformations* (Simon & Schuster, 1978, in press).

Another important study paralleling ours is George E. Vaillant's *Adaptation to Life* (Little, Brown, 1977). This study deals primarily with the quality of a man's overall adjustment in adulthood, in a sample of Harvard men. Adjustment is shown to be heavily influenced by personality mechanisms of defense and coping. Although his main emphasis is on personality and adjustment, rather than on adult development, Vaillant gives evidence of significant change from about age 20 to 50.

Robert Lifton has in the past taken an Eriksonian approach in the broad field of "psychohistory." In his most recent book, however, Lifton begins to articulate his own view of adult development, drawing on various sources. See *The Life of the Self: Toward a New Psychology* (Simon & Schuster, 1976).

Theodore Lidz has written a comprehensive textbook on the life cycle, attempting to combine evidence from psychoanalysis and the social sciences: *The Person: His Development Throughout the Life Cycle* (Basic Books, 1968).

7 *"It's a long, long while . . ."* From the musical *Knickerbocker Holiday* by Maxwell Anderson and Kurt Weill (Anderson House, 1938), pp. 55–56. *"Do not go gentle . . ."* From Dylan Thomas, *Collected Poems* (New Directions, 1957).

8 *occupational or familial career* Some illustrative work on stages in family development and occupational development: Jesse Bernard. *The Future of Marriage* (World, 1972); Michael P. Fogarty, Rhona Rapoport and Robert N. Rapoport, *Sex, Career and Family* (Allen & Unwin, 1971); Marjorie Fiske Lowenthal, Magda Thurnher and David Chiriboga, *Four Stages of Life: A Comparative Study of Women and Men Facing Transitions* (Jossey-Bass, 1975); Cyril Sofer, *Men in Mid Career: A Study of British Managers and Technical Specialists* (Cambridge University Press, 1970); Harold Wilensky, "Life Cycle, Work Situation and Participation in Formal Associations," in R. Kleemeier, ed., *Aging and Leisure* (Oxford University Press, 1961); Donald E. Super, *Career Development: Self-Concept Theory* (College Entrance Examination Board, Research Monograph No. 4, 1963).

8 *option too restricted* My earlier research on career development includes the following collaborative studies: Myron R. Sharaf and Daniel J. Levinson, "The Quest for Omnipotence in Professional Training: The Case of the Psychiatric Resident," *Psychiatry*, 27 (1964), 135–49; Richard C. Hodgson, Daniel J. Levinson and Abraham Zaleznik, *The Executive Role Constellation: An Analysis of Personality and Role Relations in Management* (Harvard Business School 1965); Daniel J. Levinson and Eugene B. Gallagher, *Patienthood in the Mental Hospital: Role, Personality and Social Structure* (Houghton Mifflin, 1964); Daniel J. Levinson and Gerald L. Klerman, "The Clinician-Executive: Some Problematic Issues for the Psychiatrist in Mental Health Organizations," *Psychiatry*, 30 (1967), 3–15; Gerald L. Klerman and Daniel J. Levinson, "Becoming the Director: Promotion as a Phase in Personal-Professional Development," *Psychiatry*, 32 (1969), 411–27.

9 *A first step* Wendy A. Stewart, "The Formation of the Early Adult Life Structure in Women," doctoral dissertation in clinical psychology, Teachers College, Columbia University, 1976.

11 *the writer's world* Many persons helped us gain a fuller understanding of the writer's world. I would like especially to thank Bernard Malamud and Toni Morrison, with whom I discussed many aspects of the writer's work and career, with rich examples from their own and others' lives.

CHAPTER 2

22 *Biologists often* The use of age 30 as a reference point for deriving age curves of biological decline is discussed by Robert R. Kohn in *Principles of Mammalian Aging* (Prentice Hall, 1971).

25 *professional athlete* An account of the subsequent careers of professional

baseball players is given by Roger Kahn: *Boys of Summer* (New American Library, 1973). In his late thirties Jackie Robinson ended his baseball career and entered the world of business and politics: *I Never Had It Made* (Putnam, 1972).

26  *Great artists*    Elliott Jaques, "Death and the Mid-Life Crisis," *International Journal of Psychoanalysis*, 46 (1965), 502–14, reprinted in Elliott Jaques, *Work, Creativity and Social Justice* (International Universities Press, 1970).

28  *Spanish philosopher*    José Ortega y Gasset, *Man and Crisis* (Norton, 1958).

28  *ego stages*    Erik H. Erikson, *Childhood and Society* (Norton, 1950) and "Identity and the Life Cycle," *Psychological Issues*, 1 (1959), 1–171. In these and other writings, Erikson is somewhat elusive about the age linkages of the adult stages. The ages I give are, I believe, consistent with his general usage. For example, in his major biography dealing with middle adulthood, *Gandhi's Truth*, he identifies Generativity vs. Stagnation as the issue worked on in the forties and fifties.

31  *autobiography*    The quote is from page 1 of *The Autobiography of Bertrand Russell*, Vol. II, 1914–1944 (Little, Brown, 1968).

33  *C. G. Jung*    Jung's theory of mid-life individuation is not systematically described in any single work. One has to get a feeling for it from various sources. See page 344, note beginning *Jung used the term*.

33  *Jung was the first*    Among the early depth psychologists, Rank too placed great emphasis on separation and individuation in adulthood. See the volume *Will Therapy and Truth and Reality* (Knopf, 1945), containing several papers going back to 1926.

36  *facilitating environments*    Donald W. Winnicott has developed the idea of the "facilitating environment" for child development. See *The Maturational Processes and the Facilitating Environment: Studies in the Theory of Emotional Development* (Hogarth, 1965). The same basic idea needs to be applied to the facilitation of adult development.

37  *Examples abound*    A spirited defense of creativity in later life is given by the German poet Gottfried Benn in his article "Artists and Old Age," *Partisan Review*, 22 (Summer 1955), 297–319.

37  *Ernest Jones*    Jones's three-volume biography is entitled *The Life and Works of Sigmund Freud* (Basic Books, 1953, 1955, 1957).

38  *late late adulthood*    Research on the biological potential for increasing the average life span well beyond the eighties is reviewed by Albert Rosenfeld in *Prolongevity* (Knopf, 1976). Rosenfeld and most of the research biologists have little to say, however, about the psychological and social aspects of old age.

CHAPTER 3

47  *The fish is in the water*    The excerpt is from page 39 of an essay by Arthur Miller: "The Shadow of the Gods," *Harper's Magazine*, August 1958, pp. 35–43.

47  *"Oedipus"*    This excerpt is from the same essay by Arthur Miller, page 43.

59 *Jean-Paul Sartre* Sartre's concept of the "project" is discussed in his book *Existential Psychoanalysis* (Philosophical Library, 1953; paperback: Regnery, 1962).

CHAPTER 5

72 *The average age of onset* For each subject we determined the age at which every period began and ended. In some cases the determinations were made by the staff member writing the biography, and then discussed and modified in our staff meeting. The final determination thus represented a staff consensus. This procedure was commonly followed in the early stages, when we were working out our conception of the periods. The age ratings made later in the study were usually done jointly by two persons—the one writing the biography and myself. At this point we can say that two experienced researchers will ordinarily come within a year of each other in estimating the age at which a period begins or ends in a given case. We have not yet fully codified the criteria by which these determinations should be made. Such codification is an important next step.

We have ratings for every period on all our subjects. These quantitative findings are of interest in establishing a preliminary picture of the timetable of the periods, but it is important to emphasize that they, like other quantitative data in our study, are suggestive rather than conclusive. Much work remains to be done—by way of measuring more rigorously, clarifying the theoretical issues, studying other populations, sorting out the many factors involved—before firm generalizations on age linkages can be made.

CHAPTER 6

91 *"In Dreams Begin Responsibilities"* Appeared in Schwartz's book *The World Is a Wedding* (New Directions, 1948).

92 *early childhood* Winnicott's ideas about "transitional phenomena" in childhood are discussed in *Playing and Reality* (Basic Books, 1971). See also his earlier book, *The Maturational Processes and the Facilitating Environment: Studies in the Theory of Emotional Development* (Hogarth Press, 1965).

98 *my own experience* One of my important mentors as a graduate student was Else Frenkel-Brunswik. Many years later—indeed, just as I was beginning this study of adult development—I was invited to give a brief account of her life and work. This account contains, in muted form, my personal appreciation of her as psychologist, teacher and friend. See "Else Frenkel-Brunswik," *International Encyclopedia of the Social Sciences* (Macmillan and Free Press, 1968), V, 559–62.

100 *young novelist* The critic Harold Bloom maintains that young poets usually have such a symbolic figure, a great writer from the past whom they struggle to emulate and supersede. See his book *The Anxiety of Influence* (Oxford University Press, 1973).

101 *The internalization* The psychoanalyst Hans Loewald, in one of the

few papers on the ways in which psychoanalytic treatment contributes to adult development (and not solely to the resolution of pre-adult conflicts), proposes that the patient's internalization of the psychoanalyst is a major aspect of this process. See his article "On the Therapeutic Action of Psychoanalysis," *International Journal of Psychoanalysis*, 41 (1960), 16–33.

CHAPTER 10

155  *dying*  This process of decline in middle adulthood has been described by Stanley Rosenberg and Michael Farrell: "Changes in Life Course at Midlife: A Pattern of Psychosocial Decline," presentation at the annual meeting of the American Sociological Association, San Francisco, August 26, 1975 (available from authors, Dartmouth University Medical School).

CHAPTER 13

196  *Erikson*  Erikson's theory of Generativity vs. Stagnation is presented in "Identity and the Life Cycle," *Psychological Issues*, 1 (1959), 1–171. His fullest biographical example of this stage is *Gandhi's Truth* (Norton, 1969).

196  *destructiveness*  See Elliott Jaques, "Death and the Mid-Life Crisis," *International Journal of Psychoanalysis*, 46 (1965), 502–14, reprinted in Elliott Jaques, *Work, Creativity and Social Justice* (International Universities Press, 1970).

196  *Goya*  Martha Wolfenstein, "Goya's Dining Room," *Psychoanalytic Quarterly*, 35 (1966), 1, 47–83.

196  *"interiority"*  Bernice L. Neugarten, "A Developmental View of Adult Personality," in James E. Birren, ed., *Relations of Development and Aging* (Charles C. Thomas, 1965).

CHAPTER 14

211  *Puer*  For Jungian theory regarding Puer and Senex, see Carl G. Jung, *Man and His Symbols* (Doubleday, 1964); Marie-Louise von Franz, *The Problem of the Puer Aeternas* (Spring, 1970); James Hillman, "Puer and Senex," *Eranos Jahrbuch*, 36 (Zurich, 1968), 301–59; and James Hillman, "On Senex Consciousness," *Spring: Annual of Archetypal Psychology and Jungian Thought*, 1970.

212  *youthful qualities*  In an archetypal sense, the Young is characterized by energy and drive, the Old by structure and stability. The same distinction is found, in a highly sophisticated form, in modern theories of biology, psychology and social science. Energy and structure are two fundamental properties of all living systems—cell, biological organism, individual person, social institution and society. Every living system must have some form of energy, and it must have a structure through which its energy is contained and directed. Structure without energy is an inert form incapable of action or change. Energy without structure is

chaos. A system needs both in order to perform various functions and to evolve over time.

At the start of a developmental process, an organism has abundant energy and potential but a relatively limited structure. Its behavioral repertory is narrow, its adaptive capabilities restricted, and a great deal of energy is used for its internal development. In the course of development, the structure grows and differentiates into more numerous components capable of specific functions. The components are in turn integrated within a more complex structure. The structure gains more stability, functions for a while at its maximal level and gradually declines, ultimately to dissolve or to be transformed into a new structure.

Thus, during the early phases of development a system has maximal energy and an incipient, vulnerable structure. During the middle phases the system attains its optimal balance of energy and structure. In the final phases there is a decline in energy and an increasingly brittle structure, which finally breaks under external stress or runs out of internal resources. This process is repeated during every developmental period and over the life cycle as a whole.

215   ". . . hero as a middle-aged man."   In his novel Chimera (Random House, 1972), John Barth offers various portrayals of the youthful hero entering middle age.

215   wish for immortality   The importance of the wish for immortality, and the struggle to come to terms with one's own mortality, have been discussed from various psychological and philosophical viewpoints. In Freudian theory the wish for omnipotence and the assumption of one's own immortality are posited as part of the child's basic psychological functioning. Although Freud did not deal systematically with the kinds of change that occur in the course of adult development, he did take note of the persistence into adulthood of these childhood qualities. See, for example, his Religion: The Future of an Illusion (Norton, 1975). Jungian theory deals with these qualities in part through the concept of the "Puer" (see page 348, note beginning Puer). These are discussed, from a combined psychological-philosophical point of view, by the great Spanish philosopher Miguel de Unamuno in The Tragic Sense of Life (Dover, 1954; first English translation 1921). The anthropologist Ernest Becker has made a notable attempt at synthesis of anthropological and depth psychological views of the wish for immortality in his book Denial of Death (Free Press, 1973). This has been a theme in the writings of Robert Lifton; his most recent formulation is given in The Life of the Self: Toward a New Psychology (Simon & Schuster, 1976). Elliott Jaques draws upon the ideas of Freud and Melanie Klein in his essay "Death and the Mid-Life Crisis," International Journal of Psychoanalysis, 46 (1965), 502–14. Although these authors use diverse theoretical approaches, there is a growing convergence in our understanding of the immortality–mortality conflict as an issue in adult development.

217   in her middle forties   The quote by Hellman is from page 226 of the biography by Richard Moody, Lillian Hellman: Playwright (Bobbs-Merrill, 1972).

218   ". . . he dares to live"   The full title of the Roethke poem is "The Dying Man: In Memoriam: W. B. Yeats," in *Words for the Wind* (Indiana University Press, 1961), p. 190.

218   "No longer in Lethean"   Yeats's poem "Vacillation" is reprinted in M. L. Rosenthal, ed., *Selected Poems and Two Plays of William Butler Yeats* (Collier Books, 1966), p. 134.

CHAPTER 15

225   John Milton   The quote from *Paradise Lost* is in Book IV, line 73.

225   "tragic sense of life"   The concept of the "tragic sense" is developed by Miguel de Unamuno in his book *The Tragic Sense of Life* (Dover, 1954). For a discussion of tragedy in literature, see Richard B. Sewall, *The Vision of Tragedy* (Yale University Press, 1959).

226   Shakespeare's   My discussion of *King Lear* is heavily indebted to Harold C. Goddard, *The Meaning of Shakespeare* (University of Chicago Press, 1951).

228   all artists   Elliott Jaques, "Death and the Mid-Life Crisis," *International Journal of Psychoanalysis*, 46 (1965), 502–14.

232   authoritarian personality   Theodor W. Adorno, Else Frenkel-Brunswik, Daniel J. Levinson and R. Nevitt Sanford, *The Authoritarian Personality* (Harper, 1950; paperback editions by Wiley and Norton).

233   DNA   James Watson, *The Double Helix* (Atheneum, 1968).

239   grow up and go out   For a discussion of the role of mentoring in the career development of occupationally successful women, see Margaret Henning and Anne Jardim, *Women and Management* (Doubleday, 1977).

CHAPTER 16

246   the key   John Barth, *Chimera* (Random House, 1972).

247   Faust   Johann Wolfgang von Goethe, *Faust* (New Directions, 1941).

249   ". . . Now that my ladder's gone"   Appears on page 184 of M. L. Rosenthal, ed., *Selected Poems and Two Plays of William Butler Yeats* (Collier Books, 1966).

249   separation   Jung's account of his separation from Freud is described in his autobiography, *Memories, Dreams, Reflections* (Pantheon, 1963). See also Joseph Campbell's introduction to his selections from Jung's writings, *The Portable Jung* (Viking, 1971).

249   reluctance to publish   Jung's reference to his correspondence with Freud is contained in the introduction (pages xxx–xxxi) to William McGuire, ed., *The Freud/Jung Letters* (Princeton University Press, Bollingen Series XCIV, 1974). The letter was written on April 9, 1959, when Jung was 84; the memory was still vivid!

250   Reviewing Kazan's   See James Baldwin's review of Elia Kazan's *The Arrangement*, in *New York Review of Books*, March 23, 1967, p. 17.

254   Gandhi   Erik H. Erikson, *Gandhi's Truth* (Norton, 1969), pp. 314–21.

257 *husband's severe decline* Stanley Rosenberg and Michael Farrell, "Changes in Life Course at Midlife: A Pattern of Psychosocial Decline," presentation at the annual meeting of the American Sociological Association, San Francisco, August 26, 1975 (available from authors, Dartmouth University Medical School).

CHAPTER 20

319 *human development* The work of Kohlberg, Piaget and Loevinger is described in the following sources: Lawrence Kohlberg, "Stage and Sequence: The Cognitive-Developmental Approach to Socialization," in D. A. Goslin, ed., *Handbook of Socialization Theory and Research* (Rand McNally, 1969); Lawrence Kohlberg, "Continuities in Childhood and Adult Moral Development Revisited," in P. B. Baltes and K. W. Schaie, eds., *Life Span Developmental Psychology: Personality and Socialization* (Academic Press, 1973); Jane Loevinger, *Ego Development: Conceptions and Theories* (Jossey-Bass, 1976); Jean Piaget, *The Child and Reality: Problems of Genetic Psychology* (Penguin, 1976); Jean Piaget, *Moral Judgement of the Child* (Free Press, 1932); and Jean Piaget and Barbel Inhelder, *The Child's Conception of Space* (Humanities, 1963).

321 *"For man is"* Marcel Proust, *Remembrance of Things Past* (Random House, 1932). The quote is from *Sweet Cheat Gone* (translation by C. K. Scott Moncreiff).

322 *universals* For a discussion of the problems of determining universals in personality across many cultures, see Alex Inkeles and Daniel J. Levinson, "National Character: The Study of Modal Personality and Sociocultural Systems," in G. Lindzey and E. Aronson, eds., *Handbook of Social Psychology* (Addison-Wesley, 1968).

323 *anthropological basis* A Jungian approach to the study of myths is reflected in Joseph Campbell, *The Masks of God*, 4 vols. (Viking, 1959–68); Mircea Eliade, *Patterns in Comparative Religion* (Meridian, 1958); and Mircea Eliade, *The Myth of the Eternal Return* (Harper & Row, 1965).

   For Jung's own view of myth, see Carl G. Jung and K. Kerenyi, *Essays on a Science of Mythology* (Princeton University Press, 1949). See also the book by the American anthropologist Paul Radin (with commentaries by Jung and Kerenyi), *The Trickster: A Study in American Indian Mythology* (Schocken, 1972 [rev. ed.]).

324 *societies around the world* Simone de Beauvoir, *The Coming of Age* (Putnam, 1972).

324 *contrasting societies* David L. Gutmann, "Women and the Parental Imperative," *Commentary*, December 1973; "Individual Adaptation in the Middle Years: Developmental Issues in the Masculine Mid-Life Crisis," *Journal of Geriatric Psychiatry*, 9 (1976), 41–59; and "Mayan Aging: A Comparative TAT Study," *Psychiatry*, 29 (1966), 246–59.

324 *The Talmud* Philip Blackman, ed., "The Sayings of the Fathers," Order Nezikin, Tractate Avoth, 21st Mishna (Judaica Press, 1963 [2nd rev. ed.]).

324    *six steps*   The Analects of Confucius, translated and annotated by Arthur Waley (Vintage Books, 1938), Book II, p. 88.

324    *Solon*   Solon's account of the life stages is quoted by A. L. Vischer in *Old Age: Its Compensation and Rewards* (Macmillan, 1947), p.121.

327    *"Adequate efficiency"*   Bidder's original article is "Senescence," *British Medical Journal*, 2 (1932), 5831. The article is quoted and discussed by Alex Comfort in *Ageing: The Biology of Senescence* (Routledge & Kegan Paul, 1964).

328    *hunting-gathering*   For a review of data on the life span in hunting-gathering societies, see J. S. Weiner, *The Natural History of Man* (Universe Books, 1971).

339    *Issues such as these*   John Schaar has written a brilliant, evocative paper ("Legitimacy in the Modern State," in *Power and Community: Dissenting Essays in Political Science*, Philip Green and Sanford Levinson, eds. [Vintage Books, 1970]) that deals with some of these questions. He examines the evolving crisis in the legitimation of authority in all modern societies. Although he does not deal explicitly with adult development, his analysis applies most directly to people in middle adulthood, who carry the main burdens of authority in families and in society. To be a wise authority, in Schaar's terms, one must have made considerable progress in resolving the issues of the Mid-life Transition.

Grateful acknowledgment is made to the following for permission to reprint previously published material:

James Baldwin: excerpt from James Baldwin's review of "The Arrangement" by Elia Kazan, *The New York Review of Books*, Volume 8, March 23, 1967.

*The British Medical Journal*: excerpt from "Senescence" by Bidder, published in *The British Medical Journal*, ii, 1932.

J. M. Dent & Sons, Ltd., and New Directions: excerpt from "Do Not Go Gentle into That Good Night" by Dylan Thomas, Copyright 1952 by Dylan Thomas. By permission of New Directions and J. M. Dent Ltd., and the trustees for the Copyright of the late Dylan Thomas.

Doubleday & Company, Inc., and Faber & Faber, Ltd.: lines of poetry from "They Sing, They Sing," Copyright © 1956 by Theodore Roethke. From the book *The Collected Poems of Theodore Roethke*. By permission of the publishers.

International Creative Management: excerpts from *The Shadows of the Gods* by Arthur Miller, published in *Harper's* magazine, August 1958. Copyright © 1958 by Arthur Miller.

Little, Brown and Company in association with the Atlantic Monthly Press: excerpt from *The Autobiography of Bertrand Russell, 1914–1944*, Volume II.

Macmillan Co., Inc.: excerpts from *The Collected Poems of William Butler Yeats*: from "Vacillation," Copyright 1933 by Macmillan Co., Inc., renewed 1961 by Bertha Georgie Yeats; and from "The Circus Animal's Desertion," Copyright 1940 by Georgie Yeats, renewed 1968 by Bertha Georgie Yeats, Michael Butler Yeats, and Anne Yeats.

Richard Moody: excerpt from *Lillian Hellman, Playwright* by Richard Moody, Bobbs-Merrill Co., Inc., © 1972.

Princeton University Press and Routledge & Kegan Paul: excerpt from C. G. Jung: *Letters*, Volume 1: 1906–1950, edited by Gerhard Adler and Aniela Jaffe, translated by R. F. C. Hull. Bollingen Series XCV. Copyright © 1971, 1973 by Princeton University Press, p. 19. Reprinted by permission.

Random House, Inc.: excerpt from *Rememberance of Things Past* by Marcel Proust, translated by C. K. Scott Moncrieff.

The Richmond Organization: lyrics appearing on page 7 from "September Song" from the musical play *Knickerbocker Holiday*. Words by Maxwell Anderson, music by Kurt Weil. Copyright 1938 and renewed 1966 by Hampshire House Publishing Corp. and DeSylva, Brown, & Henderson, Inc., New York, N. Y. Used by permission.

# Index

A NOTE ABOUT THE AUTHORS

Daniel J. Levinson, the principal author of this book, is Professor of Psychology in the Department of Psychiatry of the Yale University School of Medicine, Director of Psychology of the Connecticut Mental Health Center and Director of the Research Unit for Social Psychology and Psychiatry. Before coming to Yale in 1966, he taught at Case Western Reserve and Harvard. Levinson is co-author of several books, including *The Authoritarian Personality* and *The Executive Role Constellation.*

During the course of the research upon which this book is based, the co-authors of *The Seasons of a Man's Life* were members of the faculty of the Yale Department of Psychiatry. Charlotte N. Darrow was Lecturer in Sociology. Edward B. Klein was Associate Professor of Psychology; he is now Professor of Psychology and Director of Graduate Training in Clinical Psychology at the University of Cincinnati. Maria H. Levinson was and continues to be Lecturer in Psychology. Braxton McKee is Clinical Associate Professor of Psychiatry, and conducts his own private psychiatric practice in New Haven.

A NOTE ON THE TYPE

The text of this book was set in Electra, a type face designed by William Addison Dwiggins for the Mergenthaler Linotype Company and first made available in 1935. Electra cannot be classified as either "modern" or "old-style."

It is not based on any historical model, and hence does not echo any particular period or style of type design. It avoids the extreme contrast between thick and thin elements that marks most modern faces, and is without eccentricities that catch the eye and interfere with reading. In general, Electra is a simple, readable typeface that attempts to give a feeling of fluidity, power and speed.

W. A. Dwiggins (1880–1956) began an association with the Mergenthaler Linotype Company in 1929 and over the next twenty-seven years designed a number of book types which include the Metro series, Electra, Caledonia, Eldorado and Falcon.

Composed, printed and bound by American Book-Stratford Press, Inc., Saddle Brook, New Jersey. Typography and binding designed by Camilla Filancia.